D0214519

Connections

Connections

An Introduction to the Economics of Networks

Sanjeev Goyal

Princeton University Press

Princeton and Oxford

Published by Princeton University Press,
41 William Street, Princeton, New Jersey 08540

In the United Kingdom: Princeton University Press,
3 Market Place, Woodstock, Oxfordshire OX20 1SY

ISBN 13: 978-0-691-12650-0 (alk. paper)
ISBN 10: 0-691-12650-X (alk. paper)

Library of Congress Control Number: 2007927826

A catalogue record for this book is available from the British Library

This book has been composed in Times and typeset by T&T Productions Ltd, London

Printed on acid-free paper ∞

press.princeton.edu

Printed in the United States of America

10 9 8 7 6 5 4 3 2 1

à Pauline

Contents

Acknowledgements

The idea of writing a book on networks first took shape in my mind while I was on a visit to Alicante, in 2004. I thought about the main themes that should figure in such a book and drew up a tentative list of chapters. In the clear Mediterranean light the project appeared both exciting and feasible. But on my return to Essex, lecturing and supervision work absorbed me, and it was only later, when we were in a new year, that I was able to put together an outline for a book.

When I started working on this book it seemed to me that networks was a young subject. As I searched for related work and got deeper into the material, I slowly began to realize that there exist rich literatures on networks and that some of them go back a long way. Fortunately, this growing knowledge has been accompanied by a realization that the disparate ideas, scattered across different subjects, constitute a general argument. In writing the book, I have tried to bring out this general argument, and the particular perspective that economics brings to the study of networks.

I first started to think about the role of social connections in the context of issues relating to learning when I was a graduate student at Cornell University. The conversations that Venkatesh Bala and I had at Cornell, and our joint research work since, have shaped my thinking on the subject in important ways.

I have also gained enormously from research collaborations with Yann Bra-moullé, Marcel Fafchamps, Andrea Galeotti, Christian Ghiglino, Matthew Jackson, Maarten Janssen, Sumit Joshi, Jurjen Kamphorst, Alexander Konovalov, Marco van der Leij, Dunia Lopez-Pintado, Jose Luis Moraga-Gonzales, Daniel Siedmann, Fernando Vega-Redondo, and Leeat Yariv. I have been particularly fortunate in having excellent doctoral students work with me on different aspects of networks. Ana Babus, Andrea Galeotti, Willemein Kets, and Marco van der Leij have freely shared their ideas as well as their enthusiasm for networks and they have also made detailed comments on the manuscript. I am grateful to Klaas Staal for sharing LaTeX files which have helped me in preparing the book for publication. I thank V. Bhaskar, Francis Bloch, Partha Dasgupta, Bhaskar Dutta, David Easley, Daniel Hojman, Alan Kirman, Rachel Kranton, Markus Mobius, Abhinay Muthoo, and Yves Zenou for encouragement and helpful comments. I am indebted to Jurjen Kamphorst, Hagey Levin, Arnold Polanski, Joon Song, Bastian Westbrock, and Ben Zissimos for comments on an earlier draft of the book.

Klaus Ritzberger invited me to lecture on networks at the Institute of Advanced Studies, in Vienna. I am grateful to him and to the students there, especially Fabian Berr and Philipp Servatius, who raised many questions and also gave me comments on an early draft of the book. Vincent Buskens and Werner Raub invited me to present an early draft of the book to an interdisciplinary audience consisting of sociologists and economists at the University of Utrecht. The lectures led to lively discussions and I would like to thank them, as well as Jeroen Wessie and the other members of the audience, for their thoughtful probing of the general approach as well as for their detailed comments on particular chapters. I also thank Hugh Ward for the invitation to present an outline of the book in the Political Economy Workshop at Essex.

I have been especially privileged in the support I have received from the Department of Economics at the University of Essex. They allowed me research leave to work on the book in the spring of 2006, and, after I joined the University of Cambridge, they generously allowed me the use of an office and all the usual facilities at Essex. I am also obliged to the Faculty of Economics at Cambridge for giving me leave for a term, which helped in completing the book.

Richard Baggaley at Princeton University Press has been a supporter of the book since the very beginning. It is a great pleasure to thank him for all his help in bringing the project to fruition. I am also grateful to four anonymous referees who offered encouraging and very helpful comments on an earlier draft of the manuscript. Finally, I would like to thank Jon Wainwright at T&T Productions Ltd for his careful copyediting of the manuscript and also for several suggestions which have improved the presentation.

The writing of a book finally takes place in the solitude afforded by our personal life. I thank my parents, my parents-in-law, and my sister and brother-in-law for their support. My wife has helped me organize my ideas and made suggestions on different chapters of the book. She has also successfully juggled the demands made by her professional life and by our children, and this has allowed me the peace of mind needed to write a book.

Connections

1

Introduction

1.1 Themes

I buy a new computer every few years. A computer is a sophisticated product and there are a number of different options open to me. To make an informed choice, I personally gather information on the different brands and models available—by going on the World Wide Web, visiting computer shops, and reading computer magazines—and I talk to my colleagues and friends to get tips about the different brands available. The time and effort I personally spend in collecting information depend very much on how well-informed my friends and colleagues are: if they are well-informed, then I rely upon their information and do not spend much time in collecting information myself.

My friends and colleagues face a similar situation, and their own efforts at collecting information in turn depend on how much information their acquaintances (including me) collect personally. Thus my efforts at collecting information personally will depend on the efforts of those whom I know, and the efforts of these individuals will in turn depend on the efforts of their friends, and so on. This suggests that individual choices concerning the gathering of information are shaped by the pattern of connections between persons in a society.

Indeed, it may well be worth my while to form connections with someone who is well-informed rather than carrying out the search myself. Moreover, I should compare the costs in terms of time and effort involved in forming such a connection with the potential benefits of obtaining valuable information. This line of reasoning leads us to the idea that the pattern of connections that obtain in a society will themselves reflect rational decision making of individuals.

This story helps us in framing two primary questions:

(i) What are the economic effects of the pattern of connections that obtain in a society?

(ii) What is the architecture of connections that emerges when individual entities form links with each other based on considerations of personal costs and benefits?

The study of these questions constitutes the subject matter of this book.

Relationships among individuals have a number of different dimensions. The first task is therefore to find a conceptual framework within which they can be described and then measured in a meaningful manner. We also need a language within which variations in relationships can be naturally expressed. The concept of a *network* addresses these requirements nicely: a network describes a collection of *nodes* and the *links* between them. The notion of nodes is fairly general: they may be individuals or firms or countries, or even collections of such entities. A link between two nodes signifies a direct relation between them; for instance, in a social context a link could be a friendship tie, while in the context of countries a link may be a free trade agreement or a mutual defense pact. Networks have been studied extensively in mathematics in the theory of graphs, and they have also been applied in a number of different subjects such as sociology, computer science, and statistical physics. Chapter 2 draws on these literatures to present the principal network concepts and notation which are used throughout the book. This chapter also identifies a number of common features in empirical networks. This discussion directs our attention to specific networks in our theoretical investigations of the subsequent chapters.

The first substantive part of the book, comprising chapters 3–6, studies the effects of network structures on individual behavior. Chapters 3 and 4 present and analyze games on networks, while chapters 5 and 6 study the generation and diffusion of information in networks.

A game on a network refers to strategic interaction in which players are located at distinct nodes of a network, and the effects of a player's actions on other players are mediated by the structure of the network. The key idea here is that the effect of player i on player j depends on where i is located in the network vis-à-vis j. Networks allow for a natural way of modeling differential influences across players. The idea of local social influence is a well-known instance of this idea. Smoking by a friend is likely to have a much greater effect on a teenager's decision on whether or not to smoke compared with the choices of the people whom she does not know personally. Similarly, a child usually learns the language spoken by her parents and neighbors. In the context of research by firms, similarly, the efforts of research partners have more spillovers on a firm's technological capabilities compared with research of other firms.

There is the issue of whether or not the actions of others increase an individual player's payoffs and her incentives to choose particular actions. Chapter 3 presents simple classifications of strategic effects in terms of positive and negative externalities and strategic substitutes and complements to bring out the range of possible strategic effects.

Over the last two decades, a number of important social and economic phenomena have been studied as arising out of network effects. Some examples of such phenomena are variations in crime, proliferation of research partnerships among firms, the prominence of mavens and opinion leaders, and differences in trust and social cooperation. This body of work has led to a rich set of models, which are taken up in chapters 3 and 4. The aim here is to show how the different models constitute special cases of the framework developed in chapter 3 and how they can be studied by using a set of common techniques. This presentation also highlights a number of interesting open problems.

Imperfect information is a key feature of economic environments. The next two chapters, 5 and 6, study the role that social networks play in the generation as well as the diffusion of valuable information. Chapter 5 considers situations where individual rewards depend only on personal actions, but the payoffs from different actions are not known. In such a situation the experience of friends, colleagues, and acquaintances, namely, the *neighbors*, is useful since it yields valuable information on alternative actions. The behavior of these neighbors is in turn affected by the choices and experience of their "neighbors" and so on. The chapter develops a theoretical framework to study the effects of network structure on individual choice and learning, over time. The aim is to characterize the properties of social networks that facilitate the diffusion of information about the payoffs from different actions.

Chapter 6 studies the role of social networks in labor market networks. The matching between workers and their employers is characterized by significant imperfections in information. Two types of information are especially prominent in labor markets: the information on job vacancies and the information on the ability of workers. This chapter develops models in which social networks convey information across individual workers and between employers and workers. The aim is to study the different ways in which social networks influence the employment status of individuals and shape the income inequality in a society.

One of the main insights of the first part of the book is that individuals can exploit their network position to their own advantage. Moreover, these advantages are related systematically to aspects of the network structure. In many contexts, the connections that define a network arise out of investments in relationships made by the individual entities themselves. Connections take on different forms and so the nature of investments will vary. In the computer purchase story, for example, the crucial resource is time. I will ask myself whether I should spend time on a personal search or if it would be more worthwhile to spend the time talking to others who may have collected information either personally or through their friends and colleagues. In the context of firms which are deciding on whether to carry out research in-house or to collaborate with other firms, the resources include personnel and financial capital.

These examples suggest two key ideas: one, individuals will trade off the costs and benefits from investments in connections, and, two, an individual's benefits from a connection may actually depend on the connections formed by others. Thus individual decisions on forming connections take place in a context characterized by *externalities*: if, for example, my friends invest in social connections which enable them to share information with others, then this may make it more attractive for me to invest in connections with them in turn. Similarly, if firms in an industry form connections, then this may alter the gains to a new firm from investing in alliances. So we are led to a study of strategic factors in the formation of networks.

The second part of the book, comprising chapters 7–10, is devoted to the theory of network formation. A game of network formation specifies a set of players, the link formation actions available to each player, and the payoffs to each player from the networks that arise out of individual linking decisions.

The above discussion highlights the possibility that a connection formed between players 1 and 2 may affect the payoffs to other players. This raises the important general issue about who has the power to decide on whether a connection is formed? One of the great attractions of networks is that they are amenable to subtle and quick transformations via local, and small-scale, linking and de-linking activity. This consideration leads us to develop a model in which link formation and dissolution take place at a single-person or at a two-person level and the process is dynamic. A network is said to be strategically stable (or in equilibrium) if there are no incentives for individual players, either acting alone or in groups, to form or delete links and thereby alter the network. Chapter 7 presents this general model and also develops a number of ways of solving games of network formation, which correspond to different levels of individual foresight as well as decision-making power.

The last decade has witnessed a number of exciting developments in the theory of strategic network formation. There have also been a number of attempts to model network formation in specific social and economic contexts. Examples of this work include the formation of information-sharing networks, research collaboration networks among firms, coauthorship networks, labor market networks, buyer–seller networks, and free trade agreements among countries. This body of work addresses three general concerns: (i) What is the architecture of networks that arise in equilibrium? (ii) What is the relation between equilibrium and socially desirable networks? (iii) What are the implications of strategic networking for the distribution of individual earnings? Chapters 8–10 discuss this work and also point out a number of open research questions.

1.2   Networks in Economics

Traditionally, economists have studied social and economic phenomena by using a framework in which interaction is centralized and anonymous. Moreover, prices have been the principal device of coordination among individual actions. The theory of general equilibrium and the theory of oligopoly reflect this approach. In recent years, a growing body of empirical work has argued that this approach is inadequate for an understanding of a number of phenomena such as the diffusion of innovations, variations in crime, differences in trust and cooperativeness, peer effects in academic performance, the proliferation of research alliances among firms, and the extensive use of personal contacts by both employers and workers in labor markets.[1] I now discuss empirical patterns in the diffusion of innovation to bring out the central role of the pattern of interaction.

Technological change is central to economic growth and social development. The process of technological change is complicated and involves many steps starting from basic research and going on to wide-scale adoption. But it is generally agreed that wide diffusion is important for the full gains of a new technology to be realized. This rate of diffusion, however, seems to vary greatly. Consider the following examples:

- It took a millennium for the water mill to be widely adopted in Europe; it is felt that the main reason for this slow pace of diffusion was the absence of significant mobility during pre-medieval and medieval times.

- The spread of new hybrid seeds has been central to the increase in agricultural productivity over the past century. The classical work of Ryan and Gross (1943) documents that hybrid corn seeds were adopted over a period of several years in the early twentieth century, in the United States. Moreover, diffusion of these seeds displayed clear spatial patterns: initially, a small group of farmers adopted the seed, followed by their neighbors adopting it, and this was followed by the neighbors of the neighbors adopting it, and so on.

- The period before the first prescription of a new medicine by doctors within the same city can vary widely. For instance, Coleman, Katz, and Mentzel (1966) found that this period ranged from six months to three years within a Midwestern town in the United States and also observed that a significant part of this variation is explained by the differences in social connections across doctors.

- The facsimile technology was available in 1843 and AT&T introduced a wire photo service in 1925. However, fax machines remained a niche product until the middle of the 1980s. Since then there has been an explosion in the use of fax machines.

The research on the determinants of diffusion suggests that the critical factor in the diffusion of a new technology is the uncertainty about its profitability. Information from governments and firms will alleviate this uncertainty. However,

---

[1] There is a large body of work on these subjects; see Ryan and Gross (1943), Coleman, Katz, and Mentzel (1966), Griliches (1957), and Conley and Udry (2005) for diffusion of innovations, Dasgupta and Serageldin (1999) for the role of trust and social capital, Glaeser, Sacerdote, and Scheinkman (1996) for patterns of crime, and Granovetter (1994a) for the use of social contacts in labor markets. For a pioneering discussion on the role of networks in economics, see Kirman (1997).

if the technology in question is complicated and involves substantial resources, such as adoption of crops or prescription of medicines, then it is clear that an individual is likely to place much greater faith in information from close friends, colleagues, and neighbors, and others in a similar decision situation. Moreover, in some instances, such as with fax machines, an individual's payoffs from adopting the product depend on whether others with whom she interacts frequently adopt the same product. Thus the patterns of interaction between individuals are likely to play a key role in shaping individual choice and therefore shaping innovation at an aggregate level as well.

This example allows us to draw out two important theoretical points. The first point is about the descriptive appeal of social interaction: in many economic contexts, social interaction between individual entities is clearly present. The second point is about the functional aspect of social interaction: such interaction facilitates the transmission of valuable information. This suggests that the structure of interaction may be viewed as an instance of informal institutions that supplement formal markets in the presence of imperfect or asymmetric information. To the extent that information imperfections are pervasive, this suggests a potentially major role for patterns of connections in shaping economic activity.

These considerations suggest an ambitious research program which combines aspects of markets (e.g., prices and competition) along with explicit patterns of connections between individual entities to explain economic phenomena. In the last decade considerable progress has been made in this research program. The present book provides an overview of this work.

The research on networks reported in this book is related to, but distinct from, two other strands of research in economics: the study of network industries (such as airlines, telecommunications, electricity, software industries) and the empirical work on social interactions. It is important at the very outset to clarify this distinction. In the literature on network industries, profit-maximizing firms own and control the functioning of their network;[2] by contrast, a large part of this book is concerned with social and economic networks where there is no single entity who owns the network. The focus is in developing a framework where individual entities create their own links with others and this shapes the structure of economic and social interaction.[3]

An influential body of empirical work in economics argues that individual behavior is shaped by the patterns of social interaction. This work makes the following important point: a significant part of the variation in behavior across individuals arises due to these individuals being members of *different groups.*[4]

---

[2] For surveys of the research on network industries, see Shy (2001) and Newberry (2002).

[3] This general framework is discussed in chapter 7.

[4] For example, Glaeser, Sacerdote, and Scheinkman (1996) argue that social interaction effects within a geographical neighborhood help explain variations in criminal activity, Bertrand, Luttmer, and Mullainathan (2000) show that ethnicity is important in understanding differences in participation in welfare

By contrast, the theoretical research on network effects (which is presented in chapters 3–6) is motivated by the idea that, *within the same group*, individuals will have different connections and that this difference in connections will have a bearing on their behavior.[5]

1.3 The Economic Approach and Other Subjects

The study of networks has become very popular in economics in the last decade. However, networks have been studied in sociology and mathematics for much longer and in recent years networks have also been extensively studied in statistical physics, computer science, business strategy, geography, and organization theory.[6] It is therefore important to clarify what an economic approach brings to the study of networks. I will argue that the distinctiveness of the economic approach lies in the different methodology that is used. This methodology in turn raises substantive questions which have received little attention in other disciplines.

The study of networks has been concerned with network effects as well as network formation in all the different disciplines mentioned above. However, within this broad similarity of themes there are important differences. The similarity as well as the differences will be discussed in specific contexts throughout the book. Here, I discuss the differences at a general level. Social efficiency is another central concern for economists, but plays a relatively minor role in the other disciplines. Related to this is a central concern of economics: the relationship between socially desirable outcomes and the outcomes that actually arise out of the purposeful activity of individuals. This relationship has received relatively little attention in the other subjects. These differences can be traced to a substantive methodological premise in economics: social and economic phenomena must ultimately be explained in terms of the choices made by rational agents.

To make the content of this methodological premise more concrete, and to see its scope, consider the computer purchase example again. In that context,

---

programs, Banerjee and Munshi (2004) argue that membership of a community influences rates of capital investment, while Duflo and Saez (2003) argue that social interaction affects the choice of pensions policy. See Glaeser and Scheinkman (2002) for a survey of some of this work.

[5] The identification of such network effects is only just beginning; see, for example, Bandiera, Barankay, and Rasul (2006), Bramoullé, Djebbari, and Fortin (2006), Conley and Udry (2005), Calvó-Armengol, Patacchini, and Zenou (2006), and Fafchamps, Goyal, and van der Leij (2006).

[6] There are a number of excellent books which summarize research in these subjects; see, for example, Bollobás (1998) and Harary (1969) in graph theory and mathematics, Burt (1994), Coleman (1994), Granovetter (1994a), Smelser and Swedberg (1994), and Wasserman and Faust (1994) in sociology, Barabasi (2002), Dorogovtsev and Mendes (2002), and Watts (1999) in statistical physics, Bailey (1975) in mathematical biology, Castells (1999) in geography, and Roughgarden (2005) in computer science. For a recent presentation of the theory of complex networks, see Vega-Redondo (2007); for an interesting collection of articles on economic activity in complex networks, see Kirman and Zimmermann (2001).

economists are particularly concerned with the incentives of individuals to gather information. Information is valuable as it influences choices of individuals and this in turn determines their purchase decisions. A simple way to study network effects is to examine the effects of adding links to a network. At first sight, it seems that adding links should benefit everyone, as more information sharing is made possible through additional links. However, an economic analysis of this issue proceeds via an examination of the effects of adding links on the incentives of individuals to collect information. If more information is freely available from social contacts, then there is a lower incentive to collect information personally. If private collection of information is costly, then the overall effect of adding links may well be a fall in the total information collected. The study of individual incentives and rational behavior thus yields an important insight into the potential negative effect of adding links.

This insight has important practical implications. To see this, consider the options available to a government which would like individuals to make more informed choices with regard to information technology. The government sends out information to individuals, who also collect information privately. In addition, people share information with their friends and colleagues. In a situation where new links are being formed and social networks are becoming denser, should the government increase or reduce its advertising? A simple-minded view is that denser networks will lead to better-informed individuals (due to greater sharing of information). If sending out information is costly, this suggests that governments can therefore invest less in sending out information. However, in a world where individuals respond optimally to the addition of social connections, this line of reasoning may be incorrect: new connections may actually lower the overall information available to individuals and the optimal response of the government should be an increase in investment.

These observations illustrate the key role of individual incentives in an economic approach to the study of networks. They also show how these incentives play a key role in the design of suitable public policies.

1.4   A Note on Style

The study of networks is thriving in economics as well as in a number of other subjects. I have therefore tried to provide an account of the economic approach which is broadly accessible as well as rigorous. The style of the book reflects these aims: the principal themes are motivated via simple examples and the main insights of the theory are discussed in nontechnical language. To complete the exposition, mathematical proofs of all the results are presented in appendices which accompany the chapters.

2

Networks: Concepts and Empirics

2.1 Introduction

The first aim of this chapter is to present the principal concepts relating to networks which will be used in this book. This presentation in section 2.2 will draw upon work carried out in the theory of graphs, in mathematical sociology, and in statistical physics. The study of networks has a rich and distinguished tradition in each of these subjects and there are a number of excellent books available. The exposition below borrows heavily from Harary (1969), Bollobás (1998), and Wasserman and Faust (1994).

The second aim of this chapter is to discuss these concepts in relation to empirically observed networks. This discussion is presented in section 2.3. The empirical study of networks has been a very active field of study in the last decade. The discussion highlights some of the key features that have been identified by this research. In doing so, it directs our attention to specific networks which are then taken up in the theoretical investigations of the subsequent chapters.

2.2 Concepts

There is a set of nodes, $N = \{1, 2, 3, \ldots, n\}$, where n is a finite number. Relationships between nodes are conceptualized in terms of binary variables, so that a relationship either exists or does not exist. Denote by $g_{ij} \in \{0, 1\}$ a relationship between two nodes i and j. The variable g_{ij} takes on a value of 1 if there exists a link between i and j and 0 otherwise.[1] The set of nodes taken along with the links between them defines the network; this network is denoted by g and the collection of all possible networks on n nodes is denoted by $\mathcal{G}$.

Given a network g, $g + g_{ij}$ and $g - g_{ij}$ have the natural interpretation. When $g_{ij} = 0$ in g, $g + g_{ij}$ adds the link $g_{ij} = 1$, while if $g_{ij} = 1$ in g, then $g + g_{ij} = g$.

---

[1] In this chapter, we consider links which are undirected, i.e., $g_{ij} = g_{ji}$. In some parts of the book (chapters 5, 7, and 8), we will study networks of directed links; most of the concepts defined here can be adopted in a natural way to cover directed links. See chapters 5 and 7 for definitions and additional notation relating to directed networks.

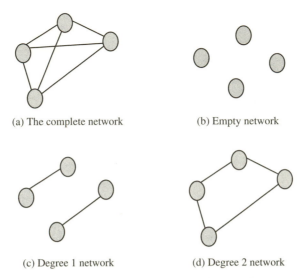

(a) The complete network   (b) Empty network

(c) Degree 1 network   (d) Degree 2 network

Figure 2.1.   Regular networks for $n = 4$.

Similarly, if $g_{ij} = 1$ in g, $g - g_{ij}$ deletes the link g_{ij}, while if $g_{ij} = 0$ in g, then $g - g_{ij} = g$.

Neighbors and degrees.   Let $N_i(g) = \{j \in N \mid g_{ij} = 1\}$ denote the nodes with which node i has a link; this set will be referred to as the *neighbors* of i. Let $\eta_i(g) = |N_i(g)|$ denote the number of neighbors of node i in network g. Moreover, for any integer $d \geq 1$, let $\mathcal{N}_i^d(g)$ be the *d-neighborhood* of i in g: this is defined inductively,

$$\mathcal{N}_i^1(g) = N_i(g) \quad \text{and} \quad \mathcal{N}_i^k(g) = \mathcal{N}_i^{k-1}(g) \cup \left(\bigcup_{j \in \mathcal{N}_i^{k-1}} N_j(g) \right).$$

Let $N_1(g), N_2(g), \ldots, N_{n-1}(g)$ be a division of nodes into distinct groups, where nodes belong to the same group if and only if they have the same number of links, i.e., $i, j \in N_k(g)$, $k = 1, 2, \ldots, n - 1$, if and only if $\eta_i(g) = \eta_j(g)$. With this notation in hand we can now describe a number of well-known networks.

A network is said to be *regular* if every node has the same number of links, i.e., $\eta_i(g) = \eta$, $\forall i \in N$ (and so all nodes belong to one group in the above partition).[2] The *complete* network, g^c, is a regular network in which $\eta = n - 1$, while the *empty* network, g^e, is a regular network in which $\eta = 0$. Figure 2.1 presents regular networks for $n = 4$.

---

[2] If the number of nodes is even, then a regular graph of every degree is possible; this is not true when the number of nodes is odd. For instance, in a network with $n = 5$, there exist no networks in which every node has degree 1 or in which every node has degree 3. In some parts of the book, interest will center on how the degree of a regular network matters and then it will be (implicitly) assumed that the number of nodes is even.

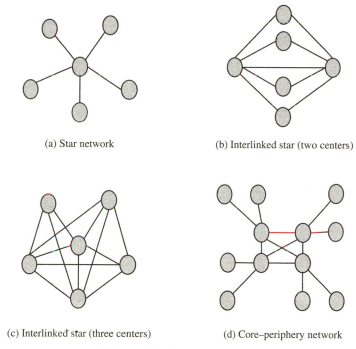

(a) Star network   (b) Interlinked star (two centers)

(c) Interlinked star (three centers)   (d) Core–periphery network

Figure 2.2.   Star and variants.

A *core–periphery* network structure describes the following situation. There are two groups of nodes, $N_1(g)$ and $N_k(g)$, with $k > |N_k(g)|$. Nodes in $N_1(g)$ constitute the periphery and have a single link each and this link is with a node in $N_k(g)$; nodes in the set $N_k(g)$ constitute the core and are fully linked with each other and with a subset of nodes in $N_1(g)$. The star network is a special case of such an architecture in which the core contains a single node. Figure 2.2 presents a core–periphery network.

An *interlinked stars* network consists of two groups $N_k(g)$ and $N_{n-1}(g)$ which satisfy the following condition: $N_i(g) = N_{n-1}(g)$ for $i \in N_k(g)$. The star network is again a special case of such an architecture with $|N_{n-1}(g)| = 1$ and $|N_1(g)| = n - 1$. In an interlinked star network, nodes which have $n - 1$ links are referred to as central nodes or as hubs, while the complementary set of nodes are referred to as peripheral nodes or as spokes. Figure 2.2 presents interlinked stars with two and three central players.

An *exclusive groups* network consists of $m + 1$ groups, a group of isolated nodes $D_1(g)$, and $m \geq 1$ distinct groups of completely linked nodes, $D_2(g), \ldots,$ $D_{m+1}(g)$. Thus $\eta_i(g) = 0$ for $i \in D_1(g)$, while $\eta_j(g) = |D_x(g)| - 1$ for $j \in D_x(g)$, $x \in \{2, 3, \ldots, m + 1\}$. A special case of this architecture is the *dominant group* network in which there is one complete component with $1 < k < n$ nodes while $n - k > 0$ nodes are isolated. Figure 2.3 illustrates exclusive group networks.

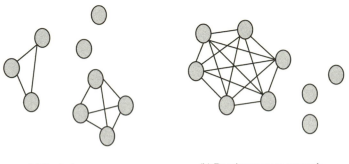

(a) Exclusive groups   (b) Dominant group network

Figure 2.3.   Exclusive group networks.

Figure 2.4.   Line network.

A *line* network consists of two groups of nodes, $N_1(g)$ and $N_2(g)$, with $|N_1(g)| = 2$ and $|N_2(g)| = n - 2$. As the name suggests, the network has the form of a line; the two nodes with one link each are at the two ends of the line, while the nodes with two links are in between. Figure 2.4 presents a line network with $n = 6$ nodes.

These figures give us a first impression of how different networks can look! The examples all contain relatively few nodes; in some economic and social contexts of interest, such as the diffusion of information or the evolution of social coordination and cooperation it is more natural to consider networks with a large number of nodes. When analyzing large networks it is more convenient to work with distributions of links.

The *degree* of node i is the number of i's direct connections; so $\eta_i(g) = |N_i(g)|$ denotes the degree of node i in network g. The degree distribution in a network is a vector P, where $P(k) = |N_k(g)|/n$ is the frequency/fraction of nodes with degree k; thus $P(k) \geqslant 0$ for each k, and $\sum_{k=0}^{n-1} P(k) = 1$. This degree distribution has support on $\mathcal{D} = \{0, 1, 2, \ldots, n - 1\}$. The *average* degree in network g is defined as

$$\hat{\eta}(g) = \sum_{k=0}^{n-1} P(k)k = \sum_{i \in N} \frac{\eta_i(g)}{n}. \tag{2.1}$$

In a star network the degree distribution has support on degrees 1 and $n - 1$, with $n - 1$ nodes having degree 1, and 1 node having degree $n - 1$. The average degree in a star is $2 - 2/n$.

An important concern in the study of networks is the variation in the degrees. This variation is interesting in its own right but it also has an important instrumental aspect: degree may be related to node behavior and well-being. Indeed, one of the primary motivations for the study of networks in economics is the issue of how nodes extract advantages on account of their connections. There are a number of different ways of measuring variations in degrees. Let us start with two standard measures: the variance and the range.[3] The *variance* in the degree distribution is defined as

$$\text{var}(g) = \sum_{k=0}^{n-1} P(k)[\hat{\eta}(g) - k]^2. \tag{2.2}$$

The degree variance in a star grows with n, while the variance in any regular network is 0 for all n. The *range* of degrees in network g is

$$R(g) = \max_{i \in N} \eta_i(g) - \min_{j \in N} \eta_j(g). \tag{2.3}$$

The range has a maximum value of $n - 2$ and a minimum value of 0. The range in a star is $n - 2$, while the range in any regular network is 0.

The description of a network in terms of a degree distribution allows for an elegant way to study the addition and the redistribution of links. The idea of adding links is captured in the relation of first-order stochastic domination; similarly, the idea of redistributing links is captured in the relation of mean-preserving spreads and second-order stochastic domination. Given a degree distribution P, let the cumulative distribution function be denoted by $\mathcal{P} : \{0, 1, 2, \ldots, n - 1\} \to [0, 1]$, where

$$\mathcal{P}(\eta) = \sum_{x=0}^{\eta} P(x). \tag{2.4}$$

Let P and P' be two degree distributions defined on $\{0, 1, 2, \ldots, n - 1\}$ and $\mathcal{P}$ and $\mathcal{P}'$ the two corresponding cumulative distribution functions, respectively.

Definition 2.1. P first-order stochastically dominates (FOSD) P' if and only if $\mathcal{P}(k) \leqslant \mathcal{P}'(k)$ for every $k \in \{0, 1, 2, \ldots, n - 1\}$.

Definition 2.2. P second-order stochastically dominates P' if and only if

$$\sum_{k=1}^{x} \mathcal{P}(k) \leqslant \sum_{k=1}^{x} \mathcal{P}'(k)$$

for every $x \in \{0, 1, 2, \ldots, n - 1\}$.

Definition 2.3. P' is a mean-preserving spread of P if and only if P and P' have the same mean and P second-order stochastically dominates P'.

A simple example of first-order shift in degree distribution arises when we move from a regular network with degree k to a regular network with degree

---

[3] For an introduction to the measurement of inequality, see Sen (1997).

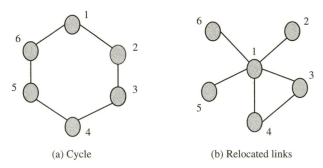

(a) Cycle   (b) Relocated links

Figure 2.5.   Mean-preserving spread in degree distributions.

$k + 1$. A simple example of a second-order shift arises when we move from a cycle with $n = 6$ nodes to a network in which node 1 is linked to all nodes, nodes 2, 3, and 4 have just this one link with node 1, while nodes 5 and 6 have two links each, a link with node 1 and a link with each other. Figure 2.5 illustrates such a mean-preserving spread transformation of the degree distribution.

In particular, note that if P first-order stochastically dominates P', then the mean degree under P is higher than that under P', but the converse is not true. Similarly, if P' is a mean-preserving spread of P, then the variance under P' is higher than that under P, but the converse is not true.

Walks, paths, and distances.   A major concern throughout the book will be the ways in which a node can be reached from another node in the network. The first step in understanding this issue is the notion of *walk*: a *walk* is a sequence of nodes in which two nodes have a link between them in the network (they are neighbors). Note that a node or a link may appear more than once in a walk. So a walk is the most general sequence of nodes and links possible in a network, subject to the restriction that any two consecutive nodes must have a link in the network. The length of a walk is simply the number of links it crosses; this is simply equal to the number of nodes involved minus one.

A walk in which all links are distinct is called a *trail*. A trail in which there are three or more nodes and the initial and the end node are the same is called a *cycle*. A trail in which every node is distinct is called a *path*. Formally, there is a *path* between two distinct nodes i and j either if $g_{ij} = 1$ or if there is a set of distinct intermediate nodes $j_1, j_2, \ldots, j_n$ such that $g_{ij_1} = g_{j_1 j_2} = \cdots = g_{j_n j} = 1$.

Figure 2.6 represents a network with $n = 5$. A possible walk in this network is 2, 3, 4, 3, 2. This walk contains the links g_{23} and g_{34} twice and the nodes 2 and 3 also appear twice each. This walk is therefore not a trail. A possible trail in the network is 3, 4, 5, 3. Next note that this trail does have three nodes and the initial node and the terminal node are the same, so this trail is a cycle. However, since node 3 appears twice this trail is not a path. A possible path in this network is 2, 3, 4, 5.

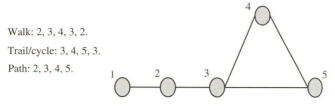

Walk: 2, 3, 4, 3, 2.

Trail/cycle: 3, 4, 5, 3.

Path: 2, 3, 4, 5.

Figure 2.6. Walks, trails, cycles, and paths.

Two nodes belong to the same *component* if and only if there exists a path between them. A network is *connected* if there exists a path between any pair of nodes $i, j \in N$. It follows that there exists only one component in a connected network. In the case of an unconnected network, the components can be ordered in terms of their size, and the network has a *giant component* if, informally speaking, the largest component covers a relatively large fraction of the nodes while all other components are small.[4]

The notion of *minimality* will play an important role in this book. Intuitively speaking, minimality of a network reflects the idea that no link is "superfluous." A component is said to be *minimal* if the deletion of any single link in the component breaks the component into two components. A network is said to be *minimal* if the deletion of any single link in the network increases the number of components by 1.

The *geodesic distance* between two nodes i and j in network G is the length of the shortest path between them, and will be denoted by $d(i, j; g)$. Throughout this book distance in a network will refer to geodesic distance. We will define $N_i^d(g)$ as the set of nodes which are exactly a distance d from node i in network g and let $\eta_i^d(g) = |N_i^d(g)|$ be the number of nodes which are a distance d from node i in network g. If there is no path between i and j in network g, then by convention set $d(i, j; g) = \infty$. In other words, for any node i in network g, $\sum_{d=1}^{d=\infty} \eta_i^d(g) = n - 1$.

When g is connected, the average distance between nodes of a network g is

$$d(g) = \frac{\sum_{i \in N} \sum_{j \in N} d(i, j; g)}{n(n-1)}. \tag{2.5}$$

The average distance in a star network is $2 - 2/n$, which is bounded above by 2 (irrespective of n), while the average distance in a line is bounded below by $n/4$ (approximately).

If the network is not connected, then the average distance in the network is by convention set equal to the average distance of the giant component. Clearly, in a situation where the network is fragmented, and no giant component exists,

---

[4]The existence of giant components is an asymptotic property of graphs; for a formal treatment of this subject, see Bollobás (1998).

the average distances can be calculated for each of the components via a natural modification of the above formula.

Centrality.   We turn next to the concept of *centrality*. The centrality of a node in a network captures a number of ideas relating to the prominence of a node in a network.[5] Here, we will present three measures of centrality which illustrate some of the main ideas. It is useful to start with the notion of degree centrality as it is the simplest. Degree centrality captures the relative prominence of a node vis-à-vis other nodes in terms of the degree. The (standardized) *degree centrality* of a node i in network g is simply the degree of this node divided by the maximum possible degree:

$$C_d(i;g) = \frac{\eta_i(g)}{n-1}. \tag{2.6}$$

This notion of centrality can be extended to study centralization of the entire network. Let i^* be the node that attains the highest degree centrality in g and let $C_d(i^*;g)$ be this centrality. The *degree centralization* of a network g is defined relative to the maximum attainable centralization and is

$$C_d(g) = \frac{\sum_{i=1}^{n}[C_d(i^*;g) - C_d(i;g)]}{\max_{g' \in \mathcal{G}}[\sum_{i=1}^{n}[C_d(i^*;g') - C_d(i;g')]]}. \tag{2.7}$$

In any component the minimum degree is 1, while the maximum possible degree is $n-1$, so the maximum possible (standardized) centrality is $(n-2)(n-1)/(n-1)$. So the definition can be restated as

$$C_d(g) = \frac{\sum_{i=1}^{n}[C_d(i^*;g) - C_d(i;g)]}{n-2}. \tag{2.8}$$

The star has a degree centralization measure of 1; by contrast, the degree centrality of any regular network is 0.

We now turn to a measure of centrality which is based on proximity. The total distance from node i to all other nodes in the network g is $\sum_{j \neq i} d(i,j;g)$. This distance will be related to the number of nodes in a network and to facilitate comparison across networks of different size, it is useful to normalize the measure by multiplying with the minimum possible total distance, which is $n-1$. The *closeness centrality* of node i in network g is defined as

$$C_c(i;g) = \frac{n-1}{\sum_{j \neq i} d(i,j;g)}. \tag{2.9}$$

This measure of centrality has a natural analogue at the aggregate network level. As in the case of the group degree centrality measure, this measure is built upon differences across nodes in a network and is normalized to account for maximum attainable differences. Let i^* be the node that attains the highest

---

[5] For an excellent overview of different notions of centrality, see Freeman (1979).

closeness centrality across all nodes and let $C_c(i^*; g)$ be this centrality. The closeness centrality measure for network g is[6]

$$C_c(g) = \frac{\sum_{i=1}^{n}[C_c(i^*; g) - C_c(i; g)]}{(n-2)(n-1)/(2n-3)}.$$ (2.10)

It is easy to verify that the closeness centrality of a star is 1, while that of a cycle is 0.

The computations suggest that degree centrality and closeness centrality are equal for networks such as the star and the cycle, respectively. However, this is not true for other networks. Consider, for example, a line network with $n = 7$. The degree centrality is 0.05 while the closeness centrality is 0.277; this suggests that the measures do capture rather different aspects of centrality.

The measure of closeness centrality is based solely on the length of the shortest paths between nodes in a network. In some contexts it is quite possible that links are not perfectly reliable and so the number of paths of different lengths may all matter. More generally, it is possible that actions of a person may have implications for the actions of her neighbors, which may in turn feedback on the initial individual, and so on. These considerations motivate the study of a notion of centrality which allows for a richer range of direct and indirect influences in a network. Bonacich (1972) developed such a measure of centrality and we now turn to it.

Consider the adjacency matrix G of network g; in this matrix an entry in a square corresponding to a pair $\{i, j\}$ signifies the presence or absence of a link. Let G^k be the kth power of the matrix. The 0 power matrix $G^0 = I$, the $n \times n$ identity matrix. In G^k, an entry g_{ij}^k measures the "number" of walks of length k that exist between players i and j in network g. The following example illustrates this idea.

Example 2.1. Consider a network with three players, 1, 2, and 3. Suppose links take on values of 0 and 1, and let the network consist of two links, $g_{12} = g_{23} = 1$. This network can be represented in an adjacency matrix G as follows:

	1	2	3
1	0	1	0
2	1	0	1
3	0	1	0

---

[6] Freeman (1979) shows that

$$\max_{g' \in G} \left[\sum_{i=1}^{n} [C_c(i^*; g') - C_c(i; g')] \right] = \frac{(n-2)(n-1)}{2n-3}.$$

Simple computations now reveal that G^2 is

	1	2	3
1	1	0	1
2	0	2	0
3	1	0	1

Thus there is one walk of length 2 between 1 and 1 and between 3 and 3, but two walks of length 2 between 2 and 2. There are no other walks of length 2 in this network.   △

Let $a \geq 0$ be a scalar and let I be the identity matrix. Define the matrix $M(g,a)$ as follows:

$$M(g,a) = [I - aG]^{-1} = \sum_{k=0}^{\infty} a^k G^k. \qquad (2.11)$$

This expression is well-defined so long as a is sufficiently small. The entry $m_{ij}(g,a) = \sum_{k=0}^{\infty} a^k g_{ij}^k$ counts the total number of walks in g from i to j, where walks of length k are weighted by a factor a^k. Given parameter a, the Bonacich centrality vector is defined as

$$C_{\mathrm{B}}(g,a) = [I - aG]^{-1} \cdot 1, \qquad (2.12)$$

where 1 is the (column) vector of 1s. In particular, the Bonacich centrality of player i is

$$C_{\mathrm{B}}(i; g, a) = \sum_{j=1}^{n} m_{ij}(g, a). \qquad (2.13)$$

This measure of centrality counts the total number of (suitably weighted) walks of different lengths starting from i in network g. To see this note that (2.13) can be rewritten as follows:

$$C_{\mathrm{B}}(i; g, a) = m_{ii}(g, a) + \sum_{j \neq i}^{n} m_{ij}(g, a). \qquad (2.14)$$

Since $G^0 = I$, it follows that $m_{ii}(g, a) \geq 1$ and so for every player i in any network, $C_{\mathrm{B}}(i; g, a) \geq 1$. It is exactly equal to 1 when $a = 0$.

The Bonacich centrality of a node can also be expressed as a function of the centrality of its neighbors. Let $\lambda(a)$ be the (largest) eigenvalue of the adjacency matric G. The Bonacich centrality of a node can then be defined as

$$C_{\mathrm{B}}(i; g, a) = \frac{1}{\lambda} \sum_{j \in N} g_{ij} C_{\mathrm{B}}(j; g, a). \qquad (2.15)$$

It is easy to compute Bonacich centrality measures for different networks. For instance, in the star network with three players as represented in the adjacency matrix in example 2.1, the Bonacich centrality of nodes 1 and 3 is 0.500 while that of the central player is 0.707.[7] More generally, the ratio of Bonacich centralities between the central player and the peripheral player in a star is $\sqrt{n-1}$, which is an increasing and concave function of the number of nodes n.

Clustering. We turn finally to ways of measuring the overlap in the neighborhoods across nodes. The study of overlap is motivated by a number of classical theoretical considerations: for instance, in the context of social norms it is felt that greater overlap in neighborhoods makes it easier to implement collective punishments.[8] At an individual level, the measures of overlap address the simple question, what fraction of my friends are friends of each other? Measures of clustering may be seen as a response to this question. The *clustering coefficient* for any node i (which has two or more links) in network g is

$$\mathrm{Cl}_i(g) = \frac{\sum_{l \in N_i(g)} \sum_{k \in N_i(g)} g_{lk}}{\eta_i(\eta_i - 1)}. \qquad (2.16)$$

This is simply the proportion of a node's neighbors which are neighbors of each other.

The clustering coefficient for the network g as a whole can be obtained by taking an "average" across nodes in the network. This averaging can be done in two ways. One possibility is to give each node an equal weight. Under equal weighting, the clustering coefficient for a network g is[9]

$$\mathrm{Cl}_u(g) = \frac{1}{n} \sum_{i=1}^{n} \frac{\sum_{l \in N_i(g)} \sum_{k \in N_i(g)} g_{lk}}{\eta_i(\eta_i - 1)}. \qquad (2.17)$$

In the star network the clustering level for the central node is 0 since the central node's neighbors are not neighbors of each other, while the peripheral nodes all have a single link (and clustering is not defined for such nodes). By contrast, in the complete network the clustering coefficient for each node and for the network as a whole is 1. Likewise, clustering is 1 in networks with the exclusive groups architecture. In the core–periphery network, the nodes in the core have positive clustering (which is less than 1), while clustering is not defined for peripheral nodes.

The other possibility is to take a weighted average in which a node is weighted by its number of links. The clustering coefficient of a network under this degree weighted scheme of averaging is

$$\mathrm{Cl}_w(g) = \frac{\sum_{i \in N'} \sum_{l \in N_i(g)} \sum_{k \in N_i(g)} g_{lk}}{\sum_{i \in N'} \eta_i(\eta_i - 1)}, \qquad (2.18)$$

where $N' \subset N$ is the set of nodes which have two or more neighbors.

---

[7] These numbers have been obtained with the use of the UCINET software program.

[8] See chapter 4 for a formal model which examines this idea.

[9] In the following formula it is assumed that all nodes have two or more neighbors.

The two formulas lead to the same network clustering coefficients if there is no correlation between node degree and its clustering level. On the other hand, if there is a positive correlation between node degree and its clustering, then the latter measure yields a higher estimate of network clustering, while if there is a negative correlation between node degree and its clustering, then the latter measure leads to a lower estimate of network clustering.

The study of overlap in neighborhoods can be extended to a group of nodes. Here the concern is with the following question, how self-contained or cohesive is a collection of nodes? The notion of *cliques* is one simple (and somewhat stark) way to approach this question. A *clique* is a maximal subset of nodes with the property that every pair of nodes has a link. Formally, a set of nodes $I = \{i_1, i_2, \ldots, i_k\} \subset N$, where $k \geq 3$, is said to be a clique if, for every pair $i_x, i_y \in I$, $g_{i_x i_y} = 1$ and there is no superset $I' \supsetneq I$ with this property. In the complete network, there is one clique and this comprises all nodes. In the core–periphery network, there is one clique and this consists of all nodes in the core (so long as there are three or more nodes in the core). In the exclusive groups network each component constitutes a clique.

2.3   Properties of Empirical Networks

Empirical work on networks has been a very active field of research in the last decade and this work has helped us in identifying similarities as well as differences across networks.[10] In this book, the focus is on social and economic networks and we will discuss three networks—the World Wide Web, coauthor networks, and firm networks—in detail in later chapters of the book.[11] The aim of this section is to discuss, in general terms, a few key features of empirical networks.

We start by looking at four empirical networks. Figure 2.7 presents the World Wide Web, figure 2.8 presents the coauthor network among economists, figure 2.9 presents a network of sexual relations, while figure 2.10 presents the network of collaboration among biotechnology and pharmaceutical firms.[12]

---

[10] For work on the World Wide Web, see Broder et al. (2000) and Albert, Jeong, and Barabasi (1999); for coauthor networks, see Newman (2001), Goyal, van der Leij, and Moraga (2006), and Moody (2004); for networks of sexual contacts, see Liljeros et al. (2001) and Barabasi (2002); for firm networks, see Baker, Gibbons, and Murphy (2004) and Delapierre and Mytelka (1998); for interlocking boards of directors of firms, see Davis, Yoo, and Baker (2001); for networks of friendships and romantic relations, see Bearman, Moody, and Stovel (2004). There is also a large body of work on technological networks, such as the electricity grid and airline networks, and on metabolic networks, such as protein networks. For a general survey of this empirical work, see Albert and Barabasi (2002) and Newman (2003).

[11] The World Wide Web, the coauthor networks, and firm networks are studied in chapters 8, 9, and 10, respectively.

[12] The actual number of nodes in each of these networks is very large, and the images produced here reflect the local network around a small number of nodes.

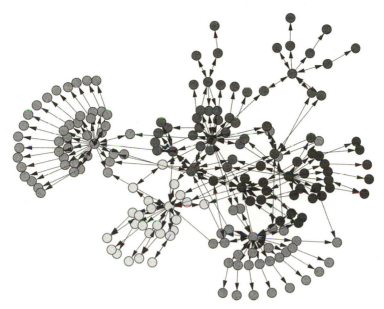

Figure 2.7. Corporate Web site with hyperlinks between pages. Reprinted with permission from Newman and Girvan, *Physical Review* E, 69, 026113, 2004. Copyright (2004) by the American Physical Society.

These networks contain a number of nodes with high degrees, the "hubs." In the World Wide Web and the coauthor network, the hubs only form links with a small fraction of all nodes and so it is reasonable to view them as central players in "local" star networks. These networks are spanned by a collection of interlinked stars. In networks with fewer nodes, such as the network of firms, the high degree nodes link with a significant fraction of all nodes (and, in some cases, with a majority of the other hubs); such networks therefore display a core–periphery architecture.

We now turn to three network properties—the degrees, the clustering, and the average distance—which have been extensively studied in the empirical literature.

(i) *Degree distribution.* Two features of the degree distribution have been high-lighted: the average degree is very small compared with the total nodes in the network ($\eta(g) \ll n$) and there is enormous variation in the degrees. This is nicely illustrated by the World Wide Web. In an early study, Broder et al. (2000) covered around 200 million Web sites and found that the average degree was only 7.5. However, the inequality was equally striking: while most Web sites had less than 10 links, there were some Web sites which had hundreds of thousands of links! Similarly, in a study of sexual contacts in Sweden, Liljeros et al. (2001) obtained data on 2810 people and observed that, while the vast majority had less than 10 partners over their lifetime, there were some who had over 100 partners.

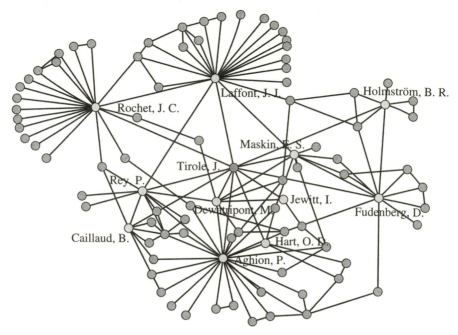

Figure 2.8. Economics coauthor network around Jean Tirole (1990s).
(From Goyal, van der Leij, and Moraga 2004.)

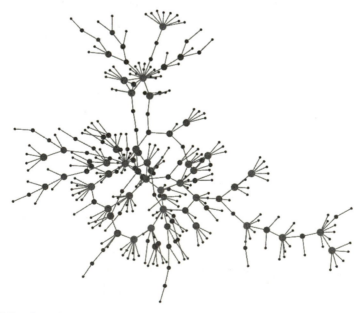

Figure 2.9. Sexual contacts network in Colorado Springs, U.S.A. (From Newman (2003),
Copyright ©2003 Society for Industrial and Applied Mathematics. Reprinted with permission.)

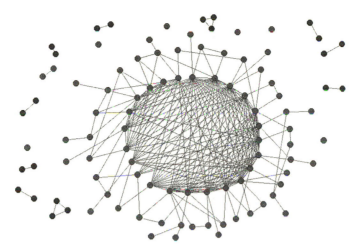

Figure 2.10. Research collaboration among firms (1973–2001). (Based on data presented in Baker, Murphy, and Gibbons (2004).)

(ii) *Clustering.* The level of clustering is significant. A natural benchmark for studying clustering is the case when links are formed at random. In a large randomly generated network g with average degree $\eta(g)$, the clustering would be given by $\eta(g)/n$ (roughly). However, in actual networks, clustering can have an altogether different magnitude. For instance, in the economics coauthor network the clustering coefficient was 0.157; this is over 7000 times the level of clustering in a random network.[13] Clustering is also high in the network among firms; however, unsurprisingly clustering is very low in the network of romantic relations as well as in the network of sexual relations.

(iii) *Average distances.* The average distance between nodes is very small. In the World Wide Web, the giant component comprised about 180 million Web sites but the average distance was only 6![14] Similarly, in the firm network there are over 4000 nodes, but the average distance is around 4.

A network with small average degrees, high clustering, and small average distances has been called a *small world* network by Watts and Strogatz (1998).[15]

We have seen that social and economic networks display some common features: they have low average degree relative to the total number of nodes, the distribution of degrees is unequal, clustering is high, and the average distance

---

[13] In this computation, we are using the weighted measure of clustering defined in expression (2.18) above.

[14] Here links on the World Wide Web are taken to be undirected.

[15] The idea of small worlds has come up in different contexts and has a colorful history; see Milgram (1967) for a pioneering experimental study and Kochen (1989) for a collection of important papers. Watts (1999) provides an excellent account of the literature.

between nodes is small. These observations, taken together with figures 2.7–2.10, lead us to the view that the star network and its variants—such as interlinked stars and core–periphery networks—capture essential elements of empirical networks. This view will inform the theoretical investigations in the chapters that follow.

3

Games on Networks

3.1 Introduction

Casual observation as well as introspection suggests that our behavior is influenced significantly by the actions of our neighbors, friends, and acquaintances. The behavior of our friends is influenced by their friends, whose behavior is in turn influenced by the behavior of their friends, and so on. We are thus led to the view that individual behavior is shaped by the entire structure of relationships that obtain in a social or economic context. The aim of this chapter is to develop a framework within which the effects of the structure of relationships on individual behavior and well-being as well as on aggregate outcomes can be examined systematically.

It is important to emphasize that the idea of neighborhood effects is not restricted to social relations; these effects are also likely to arise in a context where firms collaborate in research with each other, in the context of international relations where countries have trade treaties with each other, and in situations where buyers and sellers have informal but long-lasting ties with each other. Indeed, an important objective of the present chapter is to show how a number of "purely" economic relationships as well as the classical social relationships can be viewed within a common framework.

There are two basic building blocks of a game with relationships among players: the formal description of the pattern of relationships among individual entities, and a description of the externalities that an individual's actions create for other individuals and how these are mediated by the pattern of ties between them.

Relationships among individual entities have a number of different dimensions. The first task is therefore to find a conceptual framework within which the patterns can be described and then measured in a meaningful manner. We also need a language within which variations of relationships can be naturally expressed. Networks address these requirements very well: a network describes a collection of nodes and links between them. The basic concepts about networks were described in the previous chapter.

We now discuss the ways in which networks mediate the effects of others' actions on an individual's payoffs. The critical idea here is that the same action carried out by two players with different locations vis-à-vis player i will have a different effect on player i's payoffs. For example, it is generally agreed that a friend's choices about smoking have a much greater effect on a teenager's decision on whether or not to smoke compared with the choices of the people whom she does not know personally. Similarly, people tend to first learn the language spoken in their own locality, i.e., the language spoken by their neighbors, colleagues, and family. In the context of research by firms, it is reasonable to expect that the efforts of research partners have more spillovers on a firm's technological capabilities.

The simplest way of formalizing these ideas is to think of effects as being either "local" or "global." A player j is said to be a *neighbor* of player i if players i and j have a direct tie. In this case the effects of the actions of player j on payoffs to player i are referred to as "local" effects. All players who are not neighbors are referred to as *nonneighbors* and are treated alike and their actions affect individual payoffs through "global" effects. Two polar cases of this model are of interest. The first polar case arises when only a neighbor's actions matter; this gives rise to a model of pure local effects. A second polar case arises when the actions of all individuals have the same effects irrespective of their network location; this yields the pure global interactions model.

There are two other aspects of the effects of the actions of others on individual payoffs that are worth noting. The first is the issue of whether an increase in actions of others raises or lowers an individual's payoffs. The following classification is useful in this regard. Actions of others are said to create *positive externality* if an increase in their value raises an individual's payoffs and they are said to create *negative externality* if an increase in others' actions lowers an individual's payoff. A second aspect has to do with the following incentives-related question: how do changes in others' actions alter an individual's returns from increasing her actions? If an increase in others' actions raises the marginal returns from one's own actions, we say that the actions are *strategic complements*, while if an increase in others' actions lowers the marginal returns from own actions, then we say that the actions are *strategic substitutes*. The effects of others' actions can also have mixed effects depending on network location. So, for instance, actions of neighbors may generate positive effects while actions of nonneighbors may generate negative effects, and vice versa. This points to the potentially complex interplay between action externalities and network location.

The study of games on networks addresses the following general questions.

(i) What are the effects of network location on individual behavior and well-being? For instance, do better connected individuals earn larger payoffs than poorly connected individuals?

(ii) How does individual behavior and well-being respond to changes—the adding of links or the redistribution of links—in a network?

(iii) Are some networks better than others for the attainment of socially desirable outcomes, and, if so, can we characterize features of socially desirable networks?

These general questions, which all pertain to aspects of network effects, have motivated a large and rapidly growing body of work in economics. Section 3.2 presents a general model of games of networks. The scope of this model is illustrated via a detailed study of three economic applications in section 3.3. The first application examines the social sharing of information which is privately collected. The second application is concerned with the relationship between social interaction and the level of criminal activity. The third application studies research collaboration among firms.

The role of interaction structures in shaping the flow of information, the diffusion of innovations and diseases, and determining the levels of social cooperation and coordination has also been studied in a number of other disciplines such as sociology, statistical physics, organization theory, and mathematical biology. As was mentioned in the introductory chapter, the relationship between the research in these subjects and in economics is close in terms of motivation, i.e., the general questions that were mentioned above also drive the research in other subjects. However, the distinctive element in an economics approach is the key role of individual incentives in an understanding of individual behavior as well as in the assessment of alternative policies.

In the framework presented in this chapter (and in the following three chapters), individuals are located on fixed nodes of the network and the interest is in the influence of their location and on the structure of the network on their behavior. In some contexts, individuals face a fixed network and they have the choice of where to locate. A well-known instance of this is choice of residence; for a pioneering study of residential choice and the emergence of segregation, see Schelling (1975), and for an interesting recent exploration of the issues, see Pancs and Vriend (2007). This class of models will not be covered in the present book.

The rest of the chapter is organized as follows. Section 3.2 develops the general model laying out the different ways in which network structures mediate the effects of actions. The basic model relates to a one-shot game among players. The discussion then turns to dynamic processes arising from games on networks. Section 3.3 presents three models of network effects that have been studied in the economics literature. Section 3.4 discusses two assumptions in the general framework: that the network is common knowledge among the players, and that a player chooses a single action in all interactions. Section 3.5 concludes.

3.2 General Model

Games on networks consist of the set of players, the actions each of the players can choose, a description of the network of relationships between the players, and a specification of how the actions and the network together define the payoffs accruing to each player. An important assumption is that all these facts about players, their actions, the network in which they are located, and the full specification of every player's payoffs are common knowledge among the players.

3.2.1 Strategies and Payoffs

The formulation of the strategies of players located in a network raises a number of considerations. Perhaps the first issue that needs to be discussed is whether players are obliged to choose the same action for all links or whether they have the freedom to choose link-specific actions. It is reasonable to model individuals as choosing a single action in some contexts, such as consumer search about product prices or other characteristics. However, in some other contexts—an example would be effort in research projects—it is clear that individuals or firms have the choice of putting different amounts of resources in different projects and frequently do exercise this option. However, the single action for all links formulation has the great merit of being very simple to work with and indeed most applications to date have worked with this formulation. These two considerations—simplicity and wide usage—lead us to focus on the single-action formulation in this section. Section 3.4 discusses the issues that arise when individuals choose link-specific actions.

Suppose each player i takes an action s_i in S, where S is a compact subset of $[0, 1]$. It will be assumed that $0, 1 \in S$ and both discrete and connected action sets are allowed. The payoff (utility or reward) to player i under the profile of actions $s = (s_1, \ldots, s_n)$ is $\Pi_i : S^n \times \mathcal{G} \to \mathcal{R}$. In the games where the action set is continuous, it will be assumed that S is also convex.[1] In what follows, $s_{-i} = (s_1, s_2, \ldots, s_{i-1}, s_{i+1}, \ldots, s_n)$ refers to the profile of strategies of all players other than player i.

We now turn to the role of networks in mediating effects of actions across players. A network has a number of different attributes—such as neighborhood size, average path length, degree distribution, clustering—and it is clear that these attributes will play more or less important roles depending on the particular context under study. So there are many different ways in which network structure can be brought into the payoff function.

Many, if not most, of the studies of network effects in economics have been inspired by the idea that individuals are more affected by the actions of those who are "close by," such as neighbors, friends, partners, and colleagues. The presentation here will therefore focus on this class of effects. Perhaps the simplest way to model this is to classify other players into two categories, *neighbors* and *nonneighbors*, and to treat members in each group alike.

---

[1] A set S is said to be convex if for every pair of elements $x, y \in S$, and for any $\lambda \in [0, 1]$, $\lambda x + (1 - \lambda)y \in S$.

Two polar cases of the above formulation have been extensively studied and it is worth elaborating on them. The first special case arises when only actions of neighbors matter and the actions of nonneighbors have no effects on an individual's payoffs. This is the case of *pure local* effects. Recall that the neighbors of a player i in network g are denoted by $N_i(g)$. Given a strategy profile, s, let $s_{N_i(g)} = (s_j)_{j \in N_i(g)}$ denote the strategy profile of player i's neighbors. Define the function $\Phi_k : S^{k+1} \to \mathcal{R}$. In this case, player i faced with profile s in network g has the following payoff:

$$\Pi_i(s \mid g) = \Phi_{\eta_i(g)}(s_i, s_{N_i(g)}). \tag{3.1}$$

Well-known applications which exhibit pure local effects include social sharing of costly information, coordination games, and prisoner's dilemma games with local interaction. The sharing of costly information is discussed in section 3.3.1 while coordination games and prisoner's dilemma games are discussed in chapter 4.

Two important ideas are implicit in the above formulation. The first idea is that the payoff functions of two players with the same degree are identical. So payoff functions depend only on degree but not on the identity of the player. This is a reasonable point to start as our interest is in delineating network effects and not in studying effects of particular types of individual heterogeneity. At a later point, specific forms of heterogeneity can be introduced depending on the particular application under study. The second idea is that the payoff function is anonymous with regard to choices of actions. This means that if s'_k is a permutation of actions in s_k, then $\Phi_{\eta_i(g)}(s_i, s'_k) = \Phi_{\eta_i(g)}(s_i, s_k)$.

The second polar case is global interactions. Here the network structure does not matter as the actions of all players have the same effects on an individual's payoff. In this case, the payoffs to player i, in network g, facing a profile of actions $s = (s_1, s_2, \ldots, s_n)$ are

$$\Pi_i(s \mid g) = \Phi_{n-1}(s_i, s_{-i}). \tag{3.2}$$

Coordination games, or prisoner's dilemma games, in which an individual plays with equal probability with all players in the population exhibit global interactions.

We now turn to a model which combines local and global effects. A simple way to model this is to suppose that actions of neighbors enter via a function $f_k : S^k \to \mathcal{R}$, where k is the degree of a player while the actions of nonneighbors enter via a function $h_k : S^{n-k-1} \to \mathcal{R}$. As usual, it will be assumed that f_k treats actions of neighbors in an anonymous manner, so that the value of $f(\cdot)$ is unchanged under permutations of neighbors' actions. It will also be assumed that the functions $f_k(\cdot)$ and $h_k(\cdot)$ are the same across individual players with the same degree. Now define $\Phi : S \times \mathcal{R}^2 \to \mathcal{R}$. In a game with both local and global effects, the payoffs to player i, in network g, faced with a strategy profile s, are

$$\Pi_i(s \mid g) = \Phi(s_i, f_{\eta_i}(s_{N_i(g)}), h_{\eta_i}(s_{k \notin N_i(g) \cup \{i\}})). \tag{3.3}$$

An important special case of this framework arises when the payoff depends simply on the sum of neighbors' actions and the sum of nonneighbors' actions:

$$\Pi_i(s \mid g) = \Phi\left(s_i, \sum_{j \in N_i(g)} s_j, \sum_{k \notin N_i(g) \cup \{i\}} s_k\right). \tag{3.4}$$

So far the discussion has focused on a model where other players can be classified into two groups—neighbors and nonneighbors—with regard to the effects that their actions have on an individual's payoffs. This formulation is tractable and most models in economics which study network effects have used this partition of players into neighbors and nonneighbors.

However, it is easy to see that actions of others can be mediated in richer ways via the network. For instance, the effect of player i's action on player j's payoff may vary smoothly with distance. Alternatively, the effects may depend on the number of common neighbors or on the number of paths between the players. The study of richer models of network effects is clearly an important and promising field for further research.

The discussion now turns to the types of effects that others' actions have on a player's payoffs. In the case of pure local effects or pure global effects, there is an elegant way to classify these different types of strategic effects across players. A game with pure local effects exhibits *positive externality* if the payoffs are increasing in actions of neighbors, and it exhibits *negative externality* if they are decreasing in actions of neighbors. Formally, we have the following definition.

Definition 3.1. A game with pure local effects exhibits positive externality if for every $k \in \{0, 1, 2, \ldots, n-1\}$, for every $s_i \in S$, and for every pair of neighbors' strategies $s_k, s_k' \in S^k$, $s_k \geq s_k'$ implies that $\Phi_k(s_i, s_k) \geq \Phi_k(s_i, s_k')$.

A game with pure local effects exhibits negative externality if for every $k \in \{0, 1, 2, \ldots, n-1\}$, for every $s_i \in S$, and for every pair of neighbors' strategies $s_k, s_k' \in S^k$, $s_k \geq s_k'$ implies that $\Phi_k(s_i, s_k) \leq \Phi_k(s_i, s_k')$.

The game exhibits *strict* externality (positive or negative) if the corresponding payoff inequalities are strict whenever $s_k \gneq s_k'$.

A game with pure local effects is said to exhibit *strategic complements* or *strategic substitutes* depending on whether the marginal returns to own action for player i are increasing or decreasing in the efforts of her neighbors.

Definition 3.2. A game with pure local effects exhibits strategic complements if for every $k \in \{0, 1, 2, \ldots, n-1\}$, every pair of own strategies $s_i > s_i'$, and for every pair of neighbors' strategies $s_k, s_k' \in S^k$, $s_k \geq s_k'$ implies that $\Phi_k(s_i, s_k) - \Phi_k(s_i', s_k) \geq \Phi_k(s_i, s_k') - \Phi_k(s_i', s_k')$.

A game with pure local effects exhibits strategic substitutes if for every $k \in \{0, 1, 2, \ldots, n-1\}$, every pair of own strategies $s_i > s_i'$, and for every pair of neighbors' strategies $s_k, s_k' \in S^k$, $s_k \geq s_k'$ implies that $\Phi_k(s_i, s_k) - \Phi_k(s_i', s_k) \leq \Phi_k(s_i, s_k') - \Phi_k(s_i', s_k')$.

The payoffs satisfy *strict* complements and substitutes if the above payoff inequalities are strict whenever $s_k \gneq s_k'$.

The definitions on payoffs above can be extended in a straightforward way to games of pure global effects. In games which exhibit a combination of local and global effects, it is possible that local actions and nonlocal actions have different and opposite effects. This is illustrated by the application on collaboration among firms in section 3.3. In that context, the efforts of neighbors create a positive externality while the actions of nonneighbors create a negative externality. The efforts of neighbors are strategic complements, while the actions of nonneighbors are strategic substitutes!

3.2.2 Solution Concept

Games on networks are solved by using the concept of Nash equilibrium. A strategy profile $s^* = (s_1^*, s_2^*, s_3^*, \ldots, s_n^*)$ is a Nash equilibrium in network g if, for each player i, given the strategies of other players s_{-i}^*, s_i^* maximizes her payoffs. Recall that $s_{-i} = (s_1, s_2, \ldots, s_{i-1}, s_{i+1}, \ldots, s_n)$ refers to the strategy profile of all players other than player i. Formally then, a strategy profile $s^* = (s_i^*, s_{-i}^*)$ is a Nash equilibrium in network g if

$$\Pi_i(s_i^*, s_{-i}^* \mid g) \geq \Pi_i(s_i, s_{-i}^* \mid g), \quad \forall s_i \in S, \forall i \in N. \tag{3.5}$$

A Nash equilibrium is said to be strict if the inequalities in the above definition hold strictly for every player.

The analysis of network effects proceeds as follows. The first step is to derive an equilibrium for a given network. The second step is to examine how equilibrium strategies of players depend on their location in the network. This allows us to address issues such as whether certain network locations lead to free riding or exploitation and if these behavioral implications correspond to the differences in payoffs. The third step in the analysis examines how altering the network, by adding links or by redistributing links, alters the equilibrium. These steps in the analysis also yield insights into the effects of networks on individual well-being and overall social welfare.

The following discussion develops conditions on players' payoff functions under which a Nash equilibrium exists. It is useful to start by defining a mixed strategy. A mixed strategy for a player i is a probability distribution on the action set S and is denoted by σ_i. A profile of mixed strategies is then denoted by $\sigma = (\sigma_1, \sigma_2, \sigma_3, \ldots, \sigma_n)$. Equipped with this definition we are now ready to state the following general result on the existence of Nash equilibria.

Theorem 3.1. *Suppose the action set of every player S is a compact, nonempty, and convex subset of $\mathcal{R}$. If the payoff function of every player is continuous with respect to strategies of all players and concave with respect to her own strategy, then there exists a Nash equilibrium in pure strategies. If the action set of every player is discrete and given by $S = \{0, x_1, x_2, \ldots, x_m\}$, then there exists a Nash equilibrium, possibly in mixed strategies.*

The proof of this result is provided in the appendix to this chapter.

3.2.3 Efficiency and Equity

The efficiency and the equity of outcomes are central normative concerns in an economics approach. There are different ways of defining and measuring them. This section discusses some of the measures which seem most relevant.

Let us first define efficiency. In network g, given a strategy profile $s \in S^n$, the payoff profile is denoted by $\Pi(s \mid g) = (\Pi_1(s \mid g), \Pi_2(s \mid g), \ldots, \Pi_n(s \mid g))$. A payoff profile $\Pi(s \mid g)$ dominates another payoff profile $\Pi(s' \mid g)$, where $s' \in S^n$, if $\Pi_i'(s' \mid g) \geq \Pi_i(s \mid g)$ for all players and there is some player j such that $\Pi_j'(s' \mid g) > \Pi_j(s \mid g)$. *A payoff profile $\Pi(s \mid g)$ is Pareto efficient if there exists no other feasible strategy profile $s' \in S^n$ such that $\Pi(s' \mid g)$ dominates $\Pi(s \mid g)$.* This notion of efficiency is appropriate when interpersonal comparisons of utility are not possible.

In the networks literature, a simpler aggregate notion of efficiency has been more widely used. Define aggregate welfare from a strategy profile $s \in S^n$, in network g, as $W(s \mid g) = \sum_{i \in N} \Pi_i(s \mid g)$. *A payoff profile is said to be efficient in network g if $W(s \mid g) \geq W(s' \mid g)$ for all $s' \in S^n$.* Clearly, any profile that maximizes aggregate payoffs is also Pareto efficient; the converse is, however, not true.

The distribution of income and the measurement of inequality have been abiding concerns of economics. These concerns have been especially prominent in the study of networks, as there has been an underlying perception that social connections serve to generate as well as perpetuate inequality.[2]

Consider again the payoff profile $\Pi(s \mid g) = (\Pi_1(s \mid g), \Pi_2(s \mid g), \ldots, \Pi_n(s \mid g))$ from strategy profile $s \in S^n$, in network g. If we interpret the payoffs as monetary payments, the inequality generated by the network can be assessed by using standard notions of inequality such as range and variance. These concepts can be defined by suitably adapting the notation for inequality in distribution of degrees which was presented in chapter 2.

---

[2] There is a large and important body of work in sociology which is concerned with the effects of social structures in creating and perpetuating economic inequality; see, for example, the classic work of Mills (1956, 1976) and the more recent work of Burt (1994). For an elegant formal model that studies inequality-generating effects of networks in the context of labor markets, see Montgomery (1991). Chapter 6 presents this model.

3.2.4 Dynamics

The discussion so far has focused on one-shot interactions between players located in a network. Many of the interactions reflected in these games actually take place repeatedly and over time. So it is important to examine how the structure of interaction mediates the dynamics of individual behavior over time. The dynamics of actions can be described as follows. Time proceeds in discrete points; at every point, an individual gets an opportunity to choose an action. In choosing her action she takes into account the past history of actions and then chooses an action which is optimal for herself. The set of actions taken together defines the profile of actions for the current period and this in turn shapes the behavior of actions in the next period.

The dynamics of the system will depend crucially on the objective function of the individuals and the information they have about the actions of other players and what they infer about the future actions of players based on this information. Almost all the research on dynamics of actions in networks carried out within economics assumes that individuals are boundedly rational.[3] This bounded rationality is embodied in two specific assumptions: the first assumption is that individuals care only about the immediate payoffs and do not care about future payoffs. This means that they do not choose an action with a view to altering payoffs in future periods. The second assumption is that a player believes that the actions of other players in the current period are the same as the actions in the immediately preceding period. This assumption yields a very simple inference rule about relevant actions of other players. Given these two assumptions on objective functions and inferences about others' actions, every player maximizes the payoffs in the current period. The actions of players generate a *myopic best-response dynamic process* through time.

This myopic best-response dynamic is used extensively throughout this book and it is important to briefly clarify the motivation for the bounded rationality embodied in it. The main reason for these assumptions is descriptive plausibility. To get a sense of the complexity of considerations that arise if players are far sighted, consider games with pure local effects. In this class of games, an individual player i's action influences the incentives of her neighbors. A change in neighbors' actions, in turn, affects the incentives of the neighbors of the neighbors, and so on. Moreover, the changes in actions of neighbors of neighbors can feedback on player i herself. The feedback effects will depend in turn on the details of the network—the length and number of paths—leading from player i to each of the other players. In a network context there also arises the major issue of incomplete information about actions of others. Indeed it is reasonable to suppose that neighbors of player i will know more about the change in her

---

[3] Exceptions to this include the work on repeated games by Haag and Lagunoff (2006) and the work on social learning by Gale and Kariv (2003). This work is discussed in chapters 4 and 5, respectively.

actions than players who are far off from player i in the network. This in turn creates substantive inference problems for these far-off players: if they observe a change in action of some player, what should they infer about the origins of these changes. The role of network-specific local private information about others' actions greatly complicates the type of inferences that an individual player has to make. These information issues are clearly important and a fuller analysis of them is an important avenue for further research.

The applications to coordination games and cooperation games in chapter 4 will study dynamics and the general ideas underlying the myopic best-response dynamics will be tailored to the specificities of those applications. The presentation of the formal dynamic models is therefore postponed to that chapter.

3.3   Applications

This section studies the effects of network structure on individual behavior and aggregate outcomes in three economic contexts: the social sharing of information which is privately costly to collect,[4] social interactions in criminal activity, and research collaboration among firms. The aim of this section is, first, to show that the above framework for games on networks offers a simple but general approach to the study of economic and social interaction in contexts where the pattern of interaction is important. The second aim is to show that the analysis of these games yields insights into the determinants of individual behavior and aggregate outcomes which are substantive and novel.

3.3.1   Sharing of Costly Information

Information sharing about the quality of products, ideas, technologies, and the prices of goods and services is a prominent feature of social life and is widely believed to have important effects on the demand of products and diffusion of new technologies. An important aspect of this influence is that in many contexts there exists a small set of individuals who are very well-informed, and that such individuals play a critical role in diffusion of new products and technologies.[5] Is there an economic explanation for the emergence of such experts and is the existence of such experts good for social welfare? This section presents a model which addresses these questions. The presentation is based on Bramoullé and Kranton (forthcoming).

---

[4] The focus in this section will be on the effects of social sharing of information on incentives to privately gather information and the analysis will be done within a static model. The dynamics of the diffusion of information is a major theme of research in economics; this subject is taken up in chapter 5.

[5] These experts are called mavens in the marketing literature. For empirical work on the importance of mavens, see, for example, Feick and Linda (1987). For a general discussion of the role of opinion leaders and experts in shaping opinions and behavior, see Gladwell (2000) and Rogers (2003).

To fix ideas we will consider a situation where individuals do not know the prices charged by firms and carry out costly search to find these prices.[6] They share this information with their friends, neighbors, and colleagues. Individuals then buy at the lowest prices they have found themselves or via others. The benefits to each player therefore depend on her own efforts and the search efforts of her neighbors.[7]

Suppose each player chooses a search intensity $s_i \in S$, where S is a compact and convex interval in $\mathcal{R}_+$. The payoffs to a player i, in network g, faced with a profile of efforts $s = (s_1, s_2, \ldots, s_n)$, are

$$\Pi_i(s \mid g) = f\left(s_i + \sum_{j \in N_i(g)} s_j\right) - cs_i, \tag{3.6}$$

where $c > 0$ is the marginal cost of effort. It is assumed that $f(0) = 0$, $f'(\cdot) > 0$, and $f''(\cdot) < 0$. It then follows that this is a game of pure local effects. Moreover, the payoffs are an increasing function of others' actions and the marginal payoffs are a decreasing function of others' actions. Therefore, this is a game of positive externality and strategic substitutes.

The action set is compact, the payoffs are continuous in the actions of all players and concave in own action, and so it follows from theorem 3.1 that a Nash equilibrium in pure strategies exists. With the existence issue resolved we can now examine how an equilibrium is sensitive to the structure of the network.

A useful first step in this study is a general property concerning the aggregate level of effort—own plus the neighborhood—enjoyed by any individual. Let $\hat{s} \in \mathcal{R}_+$ be such that $f'(\hat{s}) = c$ and also let $\bar{s}_i = \sum_{j \in N_i(g)} s_j$. From the concavity of $f(\cdot)$, it then follows that if $\bar{s}_i \geq \hat{s}$, then marginal returns to effort are lower than the marginal cost and so optimal effort is 0, while if $\bar{s}_i < \hat{s}$, then marginal returns from effort to player are strictly larger than marginal costs c and so optimal effort is positive and given by $\hat{s} - \bar{s}_i$.[8] These observations are summarized as follows.

Proposition 3.1. *A profile of actions* $s^* = (s_1, s_2, \ldots, s_n)$ *is a Nash equilibrium if and only if for every player* i *either* $\bar{s}_i^* \geq \hat{s}$ *and* $s_i^* = 0$ *or* $\bar{s}_i^* \leq \hat{s}$ *and* $s_i^* = \hat{s} - \bar{s}_i^*$.

---

[6] The prices of firms will not be explicitly considered. For a model in which firms set different prices in response to the information sharing among consumers, see Galeotti (2005).

[7] Since acquiring information is costly, its social sharing implies that individual search has the features of a local public good. The study of local public goods has a long and distinguished tradition in economics. Since individuals underestimate the social value of their efforts, they will tend to under provide such effort. The interest has been in understanding how this problem of under provision can be resolved via the design of suitable institutions and policies. For an exposition of this theory, see Cornes and Sandler (1996). The distinctive element here is the focus on the interpersonal networks in determining the distribution of efforts across players.

[8] Note that here we are suppressing, for expositional simplicity, the dependence of $\bar{s}_i$ on the underlying network.

The proof of this result is immediate from the earlier observations, and is omitted. This result tells us that in any network g in equilibrium there are potentially two types of player: those who receive aggregate effort from their neighbors in excess of $\hat{s}$ and exert no effort on their own, and those who receive less than $\hat{s}$ aggregate effort from their neighbors and contribute exactly the difference between what they receive and $\hat{s}$.

The above characterization is very useful as it implies, in particular, that an individual will choose $\hat{s}$ if and only if each of her neighbors chooses 0. This observation leads us to examine the possibility of equilibrium in which every player chooses either $\hat{s}$ or 0. We shall refer to such equilibria as *specialized equilibria*. Equilibria with this feature are of interest as they illustrate network-based experts and free riding in an especially acute form. We now examine whether such an equilibrium exists, and how its existence is related to the network structure.

The first point to note is that in the absence of a social structure for information sharing, in the empty network, there is a unique equilibrium in which every player chooses $\hat{s}$. In such a network there is no free riding. It turns out that this is the only network in which no free riding is possible.

To prove this point formally, it is useful to define the concept of *independent sets*. An *independent set* of a network g is a set of players $I \subseteq N$ such that, for any $i, j \in I$, $g_{ij} \neq 1$, i.e., no two players in I are directly linked. A *maximal independent set* is an independent set that is not contained in any other independent set.

Does there exist a maximal independent set in every network? The answer to this is yes. To see why this is so, proceed as follows. First, number the players $1, 2, \ldots, n$. Now start by placing player 1 in I, and look for players $j \notin N_1(g)$. If player 2 $\notin N_1(g)$, then include her in the independent set, I; if player 2 $\in N_1(g)$, then include her in the complement set I^c. Suppose, to fix ideas, that $1, 2 \in I$. Next consider player 3: if player 3 $\notin N_1(g) \cup N_2(g)$, then include her in I, while if player 3 $\in N_1(g) \cup N_2(g)$, then include her in I^c. Move next to player 4 and proceed likewise until you reach player n. At each stage, a player is included in the set if she is not a neighbor of any player who is already included in the set. This process is well-defined starting from player 1, and will lead to a maximal set of players I such that, for any pair of players $i, j \in I$, $g_{ij} \neq 1$. Since g was arbitrary, this also shows that a maximal independent set exists in every network g.

To get a feel for this concept, note that in the empty network there exists a unique maximal independent set and this is the set of all players N. In the complete network on the other hand, there are n distinct maximal sets, each of which contains a single player. In the star network, there are two maximal independent sets, one which contains only the central player and one which contains all the peripheral players.

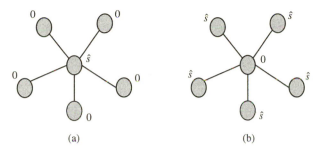

Figure 3.1. Free riders and experts in a star network: (a) center is expert and peripheries are free riders; (b) center is free rider and peripheries are experts.

Now assign the action $\hat{s}$ to every member of a maximal independent set and assign action 0 to every player who is not a member of this maximal independent set. This configuration constitutes an equilibrium in view of the characterization provided in proposition 3.1. Such an equilibrium is by construction a specialized equilibrium. Moreover, it is immediate that in any nonempty network, a maximal independent set must be a *strict* subset of the set of players N. Thus in any nonempty network there is an equilibrium with free riding. These observations are summarized in the following result.

Proposition 3.2. *There exists a specialized equilibrium in every network. In the empty network the unique equilibrium is specialized and every player chooses $\hat{s}$, so there is no free riding. In any nonempty network there exists a specialized equilibrium with experts and free riders.*

The proof of this result follows directly from the above observations, and is omitted. This result gives us a first impression of how networks matter: when we move from the empty network to any nonempty network this gives rise to the possibility of significant free riding, with a subset of players exerting maximal effort while others exert no effort at all. For instance, in the context of the star network this result tells us that there are two specialized equilibria. In one the central player chooses $\hat{s}$ and all the peripheral players choose 0, while in the other the peripheral players each choose $\hat{s}$, and the central player chooses 0. Figure 3.1 illustrates these equilibria.

We now turn to the possibility of outcomes in which everyone contributes positively. Define an equilibrium strategy profile in which all players choose positive effort as a *distributed equilibrium*. Does there exist a distributed equilibrium in every network? The answer to this question is no. The following example explains why this is the case.

Example 3.1. Suppose $n \geq 3$. In a *star* network no distributed equilibrium is possible. Note that in any distributed equilibrium it must be the case that, for each player i, $s_i > 0$ and $s_i + \bar{s}_i = \hat{s}$. Let s_c denote the central player's effort. For any peripheral player l, proposition 3.1 says that $s_l + s_c = \hat{s}$, while for the central player, $s_c + \sum_{j \neq c} s_j = \hat{s}$. These equalities cannot be simultaneously satisfied since $s_l > 0$ for every peripheral player in a distributed equilibrium. $\triangle$

Distributed equilibria, however, arise naturally in regular networks, as the following example illustrates.

Example 3.2. In any regular network with degree k, there exists a symmetric distributed equilibrium s^* such that $f'(s^* + ks^*) = c$. In other words, every regular network of degree k has a distributed equilibrium in which a player chooses $s_i^* = \hat{s}/(k+1)$. $\triangle$

Examples 3.1 and 3.2 tell us that network structure can potentially determine whether distributed equilibria exist and they highlight the point that the level of free riding varies with the structure of the network.

A recurring theme in the study of network effects has been the possibility of individuals exploiting network position to extract extra private surpluses. The discussion so far indirectly relates to this issue as it points to the role of network structures in creating experts and helping others to free ride on them. A more direct way to address the issue of network advantage is to ask if there is a systematic relation between network position and the level of equilibrium individual payoffs. The idea of network position is quite general, and it is possible to think of a number of different aspects of network location, such as centrality, betweenness, and degree, that may be important in determining payoffs. Indeed, it is reasonable to suppose that the feature of network location that matters for payoffs varies with the particular application being considered.[9]

In the present application, individual payoffs are increasing in efforts of neighbors and so it is interesting to ask if players with higher degree earn a higher payoff in equilibrium. The following example illustrates some issues that arise in addressing this question.

Example 3.3. Consider again the star network. As was noted earlier there are two specialized equilibria. One in which the center chooses $\hat{s}$ and the spokes choose 0, and a second equilibrium in which the peripheral players choose $\hat{s}$ and the center chooses 0. In the first equilibrium the center earns less than the peripheral players while in the second equilibrium it is the other way round.

Consider next the complete network. The distributed equilibrium in which every player i chooses $s_i^* = \hat{s}/n$ is clearly an equilibrium. There is also, however, a specialized equilibrium in which one player chooses $\hat{s}$ and all other players choose 0. $\triangle$

This example shows that there is no simple relation between degree and equilibrium payoffs. In the star network there exists an equilibrium with a positive

---

[9]The discussion on crime networks in the next section identifies a particular form of centrality as being key to understanding equilibrium behavior.

relation between degree and payoffs as well as an equilibrium with the converse correlation. Moreover, in the complete network there is an equilibrium in which all players with the same degree earn the same payoffs as well as an equilibrium in which one player earns much less than all the others. These observations motivate the following (weaker) question: does there always exist an equilibrium which exhibits a positive relation between degree and payoffs in every network? This appears to be an open problem.

The discussion now turns to the aggregate welfare consequences of network structures. In the present model, aggregate welfare from a strategy profile s in network g is

$$W(s \mid g) = \sum_{i \in N} \left[f\left(s_i + \sum_{j \in N_i(g)} s_j\right) - cs_i \right]. \tag{3.7}$$

The first observation with regard to efficiency is that any equilibrium in a non-empty network is inefficient. This follows directly from the observation that in any equilibrium a player chooses an action level which equates (personal) marginal effort with marginal cost. On the other hand, social welfare maximization requires that *social* marginal returns are equal to marginal costs. Social marginal returns are a sum of personal marginal returns and the marginal returns of neighbors; since by assumption $f'(\cdot) > 0$, it follows that the marginal returns for each neighbor are strictly positive and thus strictly exceed the personal marginal returns. The formal details of this result are presented in the appendix. While this result is simple, it does raise the question, are some networks better than others from the point of view of social welfare?

One way to address this question is to ask whether networks with more links attain a higher level of welfare. At first glance, adding links to a network appears to be clearly a good thing since it permits greater sharing of efforts, which, under the maintained assumption of positive marginal returns, is welfare improving. This line of reasoning is clearly valid so long as efforts are unaffected by the addition of links. To make this more concrete, consider the case of a network g and a specialized equilibrium $s^*(g)$. Now suppose a link is added between i and j, and we obtain $g' = g + g_{ij}$. Suppose that, in the equilibrium in network g, $s_i^*(g) = \hat{s}$ and $s_j^*(g) = 0$. It is easy to see that the same action profile is also an equilibrium in network g'. This example illustrates two points. First, it shows that if a link is added between a player who chooses $\hat{s}$ and another player who chooses 0, then the equilibrium in the original network is also an equilibrium in the supplemented network g'. Second, in the supplemented network g', player j has access to additional efforts from player i and under the assumption $f'(\cdot) > 0$, her payoff is strictly higher. All other players retain the old level of payoffs. Thus adding links in this particular way creates the possibility of welfare improvements.

A second situation in which adding links is clearly beneficial arises when we look at regular networks. In the distributed equilibrium mentioned in example 3.2,

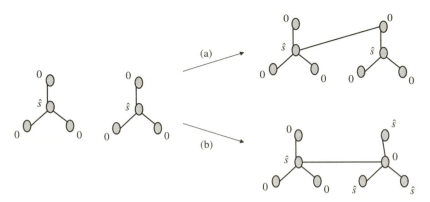

Figure 3.2. Adding a link.

the equilibrium payoff to a player in a degree k network is

$$f(\hat{s}) - \frac{\hat{s}}{k+1}c. \tag{3.8}$$

It is easy to see that as the degree k increases, the gross returns remain constant while the costs decline, and so the net payoffs increase.

How general are these findings? The following example shows that the equilibrium effects of adding a link may depend on minute details of where this link is added.

Example 3.4. Start with two stars each with three peripheral players. Fix an equilibrium in which the two centers exert action $\hat{s}$ while the peripheral players all choose 0.

First, add a link between a center and a spoke of the other star. Following the argument above, in the new network the old action profile still constitutes an equilibrium. It then follows that aggregate welfare increases on the adding of a link. Case (a) in figure 3.2 illustrates this form of network change.

Second, add a link between the centers as in case (b) of figure 3.2. Now the old profile of actions is no longer an equilibrium as the two centers do not constitute a maximal independent set any more. However, there is an equilibrium in which the center of one star and the spokes of the other star choose $\hat{s}$, and all other players choose 0. However, it is possible to show that, in this new equilibrium, aggregate welfare strictly decreases if $2c\hat{s} > f(4\hat{s}) - f(\hat{s})$.[10]   △

This section has brought out the important role of networks in shaping the distribution of effort. It has also illustrated their role in sustaining significant free riding and corresponding payoff inequality. In particular, we showed that some networks, such as the star, do not permit outcomes in which all players exert

---

[10] It is possible to check that this strategy profile yields the best equilibrium payoffs, in other words that it is second best.

positive effort and therefore imply the existence of experts and free riders. The discussion also showed that some key intuitions we have about network effects—adding links should lower effort and increase well-being—are true when we add links in particular ways (for example, between spokes and a center) and in certain types of network (e.g., regular networks). However, we also constructed examples in which these key intuitions fail, as when welfare declines upon the adding of a link between the central nodes of two-star networks, or when the central node of a star who is well-connected actually earns less than a peripheral node who is poorly connected.

An important feature of the analysis was that in some networks, such as the star and the complete network, multiple equilibria are possible, and that the equilibria exhibit very different properties. Indeed, the example on equilibria in star networks suggests that even the symmetric equilibria may differ greatly with regard to the relation between degree and payoffs. This raises the question, are some equilibria relatively more robust compared with others? A general analysis of this problem appears to be an open problem.

3.3.2 Social Interactions in Crime

The role of interaction effects in shaping the level of criminal activity has been a recurring theme in different disciplines such as sociology, psychology, and economics.[11] This work suggests that criminal activity exhibits a form of "complementarity": individual incentives to engage in such activities are increasing in the level of criminal activity of friends and family. This creates the possibility that variations in criminal activity arise out of differences in network location. This section presents a model with a view to exploring this line of reasoning. The presentation here is based on Ballester, Calvó-Armengol, and Zenou (2006).

Consider an n-player game with linear quadratic payoffs. The payoffs to player i faced with strategy profile s are

$$\Pi_i(s) = \alpha s_i + \tfrac{1}{2}\rho s_i^2 + \sum_{j \neq i} \rho_{ij} s_i s_j. \tag{3.9}$$

Assume that $\alpha > 0$, while $\rho < 0$ (this reflects concavity in own action) and the different ρ_{ij} reflect effects of others' actions on player i's payoffs (these can be positive or negative). The effects of actions on payoffs can be represented in an $n \times n$ adjacency matrix, Γ. We first show that this adjacency matrix can be decomposed into three parts reflecting an own concavity part, a uniform global effect (which is common across players), and a local pairwise effect, respectively.

---

[11] For empirical evidence on such effects, see, for example, Case and Katz (1991) and Glaeser, Sacerdote, and Scheinkman (1996). For an early theoretical model of crime and social interaction, see Sah (1999).

Define $\bar{\rho} = \max \rho_{ij}$ and $\underline{\rho} = \min \rho_{ij}$. Define $\gamma = -\min\{\underline{\rho}, 0\}$ and let $\lambda = \bar{\rho} + \gamma \geqslant 0$. Note that $\lambda > 0$ generically. Define, for $i \neq j$,

$$g_{ij} = \frac{\rho_{ij} + \gamma}{\lambda}. \tag{3.10}$$

Also set $g_{ii} = 0$, for all $i \in N$. By construction $0 \leqslant g_{ij} \leqslant 1$. There is a link between i and j if $g_{ij} > 0$ and the value of the link reflects relative complementarity.

Example 3.5. Suppose $\rho_{ij} = \rho_{ji}$, and $\rho_{ij} \in \{-1, 1\}$. Then $\bar{\rho} = 1$ and $\underline{\rho} = -1$. In this case $\gamma = 1, \lambda = 2$, and $g_{ij} \in \{0, 1\}$. The adjacency matrix G is symmetric and has entries of 0 and 1 only. $\triangle$

In this presentation, for reasons of tractability, we will focus on games in which own concavity effects are larger than cross-player effects: so assume that $\underline{\rho} < \min\{\rho, 0\}$. Given this assumption, there is a number $\beta > 0$ such that $\underline{\rho} = -\beta - \gamma$.[12] Next let I be the $n \times n$ identity matrix, U be the $n \times n$ square matrix of 1s and G be the $n \times n$ matrix with entries g_{ij}. The adjacency matrix of own action concavity and cross-player effects can be written as

$$\Gamma = \beta I - \gamma U + \lambda G. \tag{3.11}$$

In this expression, β reflects own concavity, γ reflects global uniform effects, while λ is the parameter measuring pairwise effects.

Using this decomposition, we can now rewrite (3.9) as follows:

$$\Pi_i(s \mid g) = \alpha s_i - \tfrac{1}{2}(\beta - \gamma)s_i^2 - \gamma \sum_{j=1}^{n} s_i s_j + \lambda \sum_{j=1}^{n} g_{ij} s_i s_j. \tag{3.12}$$

In the context of crime it is reasonable to suppose that the uniform global effects are negative (this reflects the idea that if others commit more crime, then there is less left for any specific player to profit from) and that pairwise local effects are positive (this captures the idea that a player gains by local sharing of information created via experience and so an increase in neighbors' actions yields positive benefits to a player).

Differentiating payoffs (3.12) with respect to s_i we get

$$\frac{\partial \Pi_i(s)}{\partial s_i} = \alpha - \beta s_i - \gamma \sum_{j=1}^{n} s_j + \lambda \sum_{j=1}^{n} g_{ij} s_j = 0. \tag{3.13}$$

Thus an interior equilibrium solves a system of n linear equations. For generic values of the parameters, there exists a unique solution to this system of equations. Under some further parameter restrictions, these solutions are positive.[13] In what follows we focus on the unique interior equilibrium.

---

[12] Relatively large own concavity (β is large) is used to establish uniqueness of equilibrium later.

[13] The details of these restrictions are presented in the appendix to this chapter.

The main result of this section concerns the relationship between network centrality and individual behavior. An individual's incentives depend on others' actions via the uniform effects term and the local pairwise terms. The uniform terms are by definition the same across players in a network. So any differences in player choices must be due to differences in pairwise local effects. An individual's payoffs are affected by the actions of her neighbors, but the choices of neighbors reflect the choices of their neighbors, and so on. Thus a player's incentives will be based on the direct and the indirect connections across the network. Indeed, the main result in this section shows that the equilibrium efforts of players are proportional to their Bonacich centrality.

Recall from chapter 2 the following definition of Bonacich centrality. Let G be the adjacency matrix of network ties, then the vector of Bonacich centralities is $C_B(g, a) = [I - aG]^{-1} \cdot \mathbf{1}$, where a is a scalar (small enough to ensure that the inverse is well-defined). Moreover, the Bonacich centrality of a player i is

$$C_B(i; g, a) = \sum_{j=1}^{n} m_{ij}(g, a), \qquad (3.14)$$

where $m_{ij}(g, a)$ is the total number of weighted walks of all lengths between players i and j, in network g. Define $\lambda^* = \lambda/\beta$ and, for any $y \in \mathcal{R}^n$, let $\tilde{y} = y_1 + y_2 + \cdots + y_n$. The following result, due to Ballester, Calvó-Armengol, and Zenou (2006), is the key finding of this section.

Proposition 3.3. *The game Γ has a unique interior Nash equilibrium $s^*(\Gamma) = (s_1^*, s_2^*, \ldots, s_n^*)$, which is given by*

$$s^*(\Gamma) = \frac{\alpha}{\beta + \gamma \tilde{C}_B(g, \lambda^*)} C_B(g, \lambda^*). \qquad (3.15)$$

Simple algebra now yields the following expression on equilibrium efforts:

$$s_i^*(\Gamma) = \frac{C_B(i; g, \lambda^*)}{\tilde{C}_B(g, \lambda^*)} \tilde{s}^*(\rho). \qquad (3.16)$$

This expression captures the key insight here: equilibrium efforts are proportional to Bonacich centrality. Recall that in a star network the central node has a higher centrality than the peripheral nodes, and this result implies therefore that the central player will exert higher criminal efforts as well. By contrast, in a cycle or a complete network all players have the same centrality and so their efforts will be equal as well.

The interest now turns to effects of adding links to a network. Let Γ' dominate Γ if $\rho'_{ij} \geq \rho_{ij}$, for all i, j, and $\rho'_{ij} > \rho_{ij}$ for some pair i, j.

Proposition 3.4. *Suppose β is large and Γ' dominates Γ. Then $\tilde{s}^{*\prime}(\Gamma') > \tilde{s}^*(\Gamma)$.*

To get some intuition for this result consider the case where the network changes via the addition of a link. Adding a link between i and j has no impact on the uniform negative externalities for any player, but it does add an additional complementarity effect for players i and j. This in turn raises their incentives for higher efforts and, via local complementarities, the incentives of their neighbors, and so on. This leads to an increase in efforts for everyone.

To summarize, the discussion in this section has generated a number of insights. First, it was shown that any game with linear quadratic payoffs can be expressed in terms of three components: an own concavity component, a uniform global effects component, and a local pairwise effects components. The analysis focused on the case where the uniform global effects were negative (reflecting substitutes) while local pairwise effects were positive (reflecting complements).

Second, the characterization of equilibrium yielded a number of insights into the relation between individual behavior and network structure. We showed that the equilibrium efforts of a player are proportional to her Bonacich centrality in the network. This result thus provides a micro-foundation for a particular measure of centrality. This is very useful as there are a number of different measures of centrality available and it is therefore important to know which measure is appropriate in which context. This result tells us that individual behavior in linear quadratic games is completely characterized by Bonacich centrality of players. A related result of interest concerns the effects of adding links in a network: we showed that a denser network leads to higher actions.

We conclude with a remark on the scope of these results. These results obtain in a game where actions of all other players have a strategic substitute effect while the actions of neighbors have in addition a strategic complements effect. Thus the results are not restricted to the application to crime. However, the quadratic-linear payoffs and the parametric restrictions with regard to the relative magnitude of own concavity and cross-player effects are crucial in the analysis. If local effects are relatively strong, then multiple equilibria can arise. In a context of multiple equilibria it is entirely possible that, in some equilibria, actions are increasing, while in others they are decreasing with the centrality of the player. The discussion of equilibria in the star network in the previous section (see figure 3.1) is an instance of how this can come about.

3.3.3 Collaboration and Market Competition

Firms increasingly choose to collaborate in research with other firms. This collaboration takes a variety of forms and is aimed both at lowering costs of production and improving product quality and introducing entirely new products. Indeed, in a recent survey, Hagedoorn (2002) argues that there has been a significant increase in the level of collaborative research among firms. Two features of this collaboration activity are worth noting. The first feature is that firms enter into a number of relationships with nonoverlapping sets of firms: in other words, that the relations are nonexclusive. The second feature is that firms often collaborate with other firms within the same market, giving rise to a complex relation which combines cooperation and competition.[14] The fact that firms collaborate with others in the same market suggests a perspective in which individual activity is shaped jointly by local networks and anonymous markets. This section presents a simple model of R&D which embodies this perspective. The presentation here is based on Goyal and Moraga (2001).[15]

Suppose that demand is linear and given by $Q = 1 - p$ and that the initial marginal cost of production in a firm is $\bar{c}$ and assume that $n\bar{c} < 1$. Each firm i chooses a level of research effort $s_i \in S = [0, \bar{c}]$. Collaboration between firms is at a bilateral level and it allows for firms to share research efforts which lower costs of production. The marginal costs of production of a firm i, in network g, facing a profile of efforts s, are

$$c_i(s \mid g) = \bar{c} - \left(s_i + \sum_{j \in N_i(g)} s_j \right). \tag{3.17}$$

It is assumed that efforts are costly and this cost is $Z(s_i) = \alpha s_i^2$, where $\alpha > 0$. In the analysis below it is assumed that α is sufficiently large so that the profit function is concave in own effort. Given costs $c = (c_1, c_2, \ldots, c_n)$, firms choose quantities to maximize profits.

Suppose that firms compete in the same market by choosing quantities. Firms choose quantities $(q_1, q_2, \ldots, q_n)$, with $Q = \sum_{i \in N} q_i$. Thus, the profits of firm i in collaboration network g are

$$\Pi_i(s \mid g) = \left[1 - q_i(g) - \sum_{j \neq i} q_j(g) - c_i(g) \right] q_i(g) - \alpha s_i^2(g). \tag{3.18}$$

Using standard arguments, it follows that equilibrium quantities in the market competition stage are $q_i = (1 - nc_i + \sum_{j \neq i} c_j)/(n + 1)$. The derivations in the appendix allow us to express the payoffs in terms of research efforts directly. In particular, the payoffs to a firm i, located in network g, faced with a research

---

[14] In the strategy literature this form of relation has been termed co-opetition. See Brandenberg and Nalebuff (1996) on the different forms of co-opetition. For a collection of papers which examine the relation between networks and markets, also see Rauch and Casella (2001).

[15] The model presented here is basic and, in recent years, it has been extended in a number of different directions, such as allowing for differentiated goods (Billand and Bravard 2002; Deroian and Gannon 2005), modeling the spillovers across noncollaborating firms (Deroian 2006), and studying international collaboration among firms that are subject to research subsidies/taxes from their governments (Song and Vannetelbosch 2005).

profile s, are

$$\Pi_i(s \mid g) = \frac{[1 - \bar{c} + s_i[n - \eta_i] + \sum_{j \in N_i(g)} s_j[n - \eta_j(g)]}{(n+1)^2}$$
$$- \alpha s_i^2(g).$$

This game exhibits a combination of local and global effects. The payoff function exhibits positive externality across neighbors' actions and negative externality across nonneighbors' actions. Moreover, actions of neighbors are strategic complements, while the actions of nonneighbors are strategic substitutes. This illustrates how a rather simple game of collaboration and competition generates a rich set of externalities. Finally, note that the effects of the efforts of neighbors and nonneighbors also depend on their degree, so that a simple "sum of efforts" specification does not capture the payoff externality adequately.

The analysis will focus on the impact of network structure on equilibrium behavior of firms. The first step then is to establish existence of equilibrium in this game. The action set is compact and convex, while payoffs are continuous in strategies of all players and for large α they are concave in own strategy. From the existence result theorem 3.1 it then follows that there exists a pure strategy equilibrium in this game.

In what follows we will focus on regular networks; such a network can be parametrized by the degree of the typical firm, $\eta \in \{0, 1, \ldots, n-1\}$. In a regular network of degree k, g^k, the payoffs to a player are

$$\Pi_i(s \mid g^k)$$
$$= \frac{[1 - \bar{c} + s_i(n - k) + \sum_{j \in N_i(g)} s_j(n - k) - \sum_{l \notin N_i(g) \cup \{i\}} s_l(k + 1)]^2}{(n+1)^2}$$
$$- \alpha s_i^2. \tag{3.19}$$

The first-order condition for an (interior) optimal solution of firm i is

$$(n - k)\left[1 - \bar{c} + s_i(n - k) + \sum_{j \in N_i(g)} s_j(n - k) - \sum_{l \notin N_i(g) \cup \{i\}} s_l(k + 1)\right]$$
$$- \alpha(n + 1)^2 s_i = 0. \tag{3.20}$$

For large α, the payoff function is concave in own strategy and so the first-order condition is necessary as well as sufficient for an (interior) optimum.

In a regular network it is reasonable to focus on a symmetric equilibrium. Invoking symmetry of research efforts, it can be shown that there is a unique (interior) equilibrium effort in a degree k network, $s_i^*(g^k)$, where

$$s_i^*(g^k) = \frac{(1 - \bar{c})(n - k)}{\alpha(n + 1)^2 - (n - k)(k + 1)} \quad \text{for } k \in \{0, 1, 2, \ldots, n - 1\}. \tag{3.21}$$

The first issue to be addressed is the relationship between degree and equilibrium effort. In the present context, this can be studied by simply looking at the derivative of the equilibrium effort s_i^* with respect to the degree k. This derivative is negative and so it follows that equilibrium efforts are declining in the degree of the network. The intuition behind this result is the following. The first effect is that an increase in degree raises the number of partner firms with which the research efforts are shared, and this lowers marginal returns. The second effect is that an increase in degree leads to more aggregate efforts arriving from partners which increases marginal returns. The third effect is that an increase in degree leads to other firms having more partners and hence lower costs, and this lowers marginal returns as well. The above computations establish that the first and third effects together dominate the second effect and the overall effect of an increase in degree on equilibrium effort levels is negative.

Individual firm efforts are declining in degree but an increase in degree also increases the sharing of individual efforts. Thus the effect of additional links on cost reduction is unclear. To examine this more closely, first note that substitution of equilibrium actions (3.21) in the cost structure (3.17) tells us that equilibrium cost is

$$c_i(g^k) = \frac{\bar{c}\alpha(n+1)^2 - 1(n-k)(k+1)}{\alpha(n+1)^2 - (n-k)(k+1)}. \tag{3.22}$$

The derivative of this cost with respect to degree can be computed and the sign of this derivative is negative if and only if the degree of the network $k < (n-1)/2$. Thus costs are initially falling and then increasing as a function of network degree and minimal costs are attained at an intermediate level of collaboration. To get some intuition for this pattern note that an increase in degree has two effects: on the one hand it leads to a fall in effort by each firm, and on the other hand it leads to a greater sharing of effort. These two effects act in opposite directions, and the sign of the derivative tells us that the second effect dominates at lower degrees, while the first effect dominates at higher degrees.

The interest now turns to the impact of degree on firm profits. Substituting the equilibrium effort levels in the profits expression (3.19) yields the following expression in a degree k network:

$$\Pi_i^*(g^k) = \frac{(1-\bar{c})^2\alpha[\alpha(n+1)^2 - (n-k)^2]}{[\alpha(n+1)^2 - (n-k)(k+1)]^2}. \tag{3.23}$$

The effect of degree on equilibrium profits can be assessed by examining the derivative with respect to degree. Straightforward computations (which are presented in the appendix) tell us that equilibrium profits are initially increasing in degree. Moreover, direct calculation shows that profits are larger in a degree $n-2$ network than in a degree $n-1$ network (i.e., the complete network). These observations suggest that equilibrium profits vary nonmonotonically with respect to degree, and that they are maximized at an intermediate degree. The result is consistent with the earlier result that cost reduction is maximal at intermediate degree levels. In sparse networks, additional links lower effort but this is more than compensated for by the sharing of resources; this leads to lower costs of production and higher profits. On the other hand, starting with a dense network, an addition of links leads to higher costs of production and this increase in costs of production more than offsets the fall in research costs, and therefore there is a fall in firm profits.

The above discussion on network effects in research collaboration is summarized in the following result, due to Goyal and Moraga (2001).

Proposition 3.5. *Consider a homogeneous good market where firms compete in quantities and suppose that firms are located in a regular network of research collaboration. The following network effects arise. (i) Research effort of a firm is decreasing in the degree. (ii) Costs are initially declining and then increasing with respect to degree. (iii) Profits are initially increasing but eventually falling with respect to degree.*

The details of the computations are presented in the appendix to the chapter.

The discussion above focused on firm profits. Collaboration networks affect costs and hence equilibrium quantities. This means that they also affect consumer surplus. What can be said about the relation between the degree and social welfare? Recall that in the linear Cournot model consumer surplus is $Q^2/2$, where Q is the aggregate output. Also note that in a symmetric equilibrium firm and hence aggregate output is falling in the cost level of the firms. It then follows that consumer surplus will initially increase and then decline, as the degree increases. From proposition 3.5 we know that profits initially increase but eventually decrease in degree. These observations taken together imply that social welfare—the sum of consumer surplus and producers profits—will initially increase but eventually decline. Thus social surplus is maximized at an intermediate level of collaboration as well.

The analysis of the model of research collaboration has brought out a number of interesting insights, which we summarize now. First, we showed how a textbook model with linear demand and cost-reducing collaboration alliances generates a very interesting mix of local and global network effects. The efforts of partners create positive externality and are strategic complements, while the efforts of nonpartners create negative externality and are strategic substitutes. Second, our analysis of this model showed how in a regular network, the effects of increasing degree are unambiguous: efforts decline, costs of production initially decline and then increase, and profits initially increase and then decline. These effects are quite different from the effects of networks that we observed in the information-sharing application as well as the criminal activity application. In our view these differences highlight the interplay between local network influences and anonymous market forces of competition.

The discussion so far has focused on regular networks. The analysis of research efforts in general networks is a complicated problem. To get a flavor of some of the issues that arise, consider the effects of adding a link to a network. Consider a six-firm cycle network in which each firm has degree 2, and let us use the convention that firms are numbered clockwise. Now it is easy to see that a single additional link can have different effects depending on where it is located. To illustrate, if firm 1 forms an additional link with firm 3, then there are four types of firm: $\{1, 3\}$, $\{4, 6\}$, $\{2\}$, and $\{5\}$. Firms 1 and 3 have an extra link compared with the rest, while the other groups differ from each other with respect to their "distance" from 1 and 3. In our model, research efforts have indirect effects which depend on the distance from the new link. For example, firm 2 is affected directly by 1 and 3 while firm 5 is indirectly affected via the changes in the efforts of firms 4 and 6. This implies that we must solve a system of four equations (in four unknowns). On the other hand, if firm 1 forms an additional link with firm 4 instead, then we have only two types of firm in the resulting network: $\{1, 4\}$ and $\{2, 3, 4, 6\}$. This implies that we have to solve a very different problem with two equations (in two unknowns). These observations suggest that the effects of an additional link will depend on where it is located in the network.

3.4 Discussion of Two Assumptions

Two key assumptions have been maintained throughout the discussion so far: complete information about the network structure, and the specification of the strategy in terms of the choice of a single action. This section examines these two assumptions.

3.4.1 Incomplete Network Knowledge

First consider the assumption that the network structure is common knowledge among the players. In reality networks are complex objects and it is likely that individuals will have only partial knowledge about the network. Indeed, empirical work suggests that individuals located in social networks generally know their own neighbors and have some idea of the neighbors of their neighbors but usually do not know a great deal more about the network (see, for example, Bondonio 1998; Casciaro 1998). Similarly, firms located in research networks or scientists in coauthor networks typically have fairly limited information on the networks. These observations motivate the study of a model of network effects in which individuals have incomplete information about the network. The presentation here draws on a recent paper by Galeotti et al. (2006).

The first thing to note is that, in principle, different aspects of a network, such as distance between players, the degree of players, and the level of clustering, may be relevant for the transmission of externalities. The examples presented in section 3.3 suggest that the number of connections is an important variable. For instance, in the case of local public goods individual payoffs depend on own efforts and the sum of neighbors' efforts. The sum of neighbors' efforts in turn depends on the levels of effort of individuals and the degree of an individual. In what follows, we sketch an approach to the study of games on networks which is based on degree distributions.

Recall that a degree distribution is a vector P, where $P(k)$ is the frequency or fraction of nodes with degree k. There are several attractions of working with degree distributions. First, the degree distribution summarizes a large amount of information about the network in a very simple and natural way. Second, it allows for a simple formalization of the ideas of adding links or redistributing links in the network. The notion of adding links to a network is formalized in terms of first-order stochastic dominance relations between the degree distributions, while the idea of redistributing links is formalized in terms of second-order stochastic dominance relations. A third advantage is that a formulation with degree distributions allows for a natural model of incomplete network knowledge. At one extreme players know only the degree distribution of the network, while at the other extreme the complete network architecture is common knowledge. In between there is a whole range of knowledge radii which can be parametrized by a number $d \geqslant 0$. Two polar cases of this are, first, incomplete information, in which each player knows the degree distribution $P(\cdot)$ and her own degree. This corresponds to $d = 1$. The second polar case is complete information and this arises when every player knows the entire network structure. This corresponds to $d = n - 1$.

In the incomplete information case, an important issue is, what do players learn about the network by observing their own degree? This depends on the assumptions on degree correlations across players. When the degrees of neighbors are independent, knowledge about own degree reveals no additional information about degrees of neighbors. By contrast, if there is a positive degree correlation, then a higher own degree signals a higher expected degree of neighbors. At a general level then, the private information about the network defines the type of a player and hence the strategic interaction among players can be studied by using the familiar apparatus of Bayesian games of incomplete information (Harsanyi 1969).

Players start with a common prior degree distribution. Each player then gets some private information on the network, which defines her type. She uses this information to update her priors about the network and arrives at a posterior belief. Given this belief she then chooses an action from the set of possible actions S, to maximize her expected payoffs. The interest is in studying how individual behavior depends on networks, and how this network effect is shaped by the nature of the game being played as well as the level of network knowledge with players.

This approach yields a number of interesting general results. We discuss two of the results informally. For simplicity, consider games with pure local effects with payoffs depending only on own actions and the sum of neighbors' actions. Moreover, assume that players have local knowledge and that there is no correlation between own degree and the degree of neighbors. Then a symmetric Bayes–Nash equilibrium is a profile of strategies $(s_1, s_2, \ldots, s_{\bar{k}})$, in which any player with degree k chooses the strategy s_k. The first result is that *equilibrium actions are increasing (decreasing) in degree if the game exhibits strategic complements (substitutes)*.[16] This result reflects our intuitions about such games. To see this consider a game with strategic complements. Consider a player with degree $k + 1$. Suppose all her neighbors followed the symmetric equilibrium strategy but her $(k + 1)$th neighbor chooses the minimal 0 action. Since only the sum of neighbors' actions matters, her best response would be identical to the equilibrium best response of a degree k player. However, in any nontrivial equilibrium, the $(k + 1)$th neighbor would be choosing, on average, a positive action. Strict complementarities imply that our player best responds with strictly higher actions than her k degree peers. A similar reasoning applies to the strategic substitutes case.

What is the relation between individual payoffs and networks? The second result responds to this concern. *In a game with incomplete information, every symmetric equilibrium has monotone increasing (decreasing) payoffs if payoffs exhibit positive (negative) externalities.* To get some intuition for this result, consider the positive externalities game, and look at a $k + 1$ degree player. Suppose, as before, that all of her neighbors follow the symmetric equilibrium strategy but her $(k + 1)$th neighbor chooses the minimal 0 action. Since payoffs only depend on the sum of neighbors' actions, our player would be able to replicate the expected payoff to a k degree player by simply using the strategy of the degree k player. However, if there is a positive probability that the $(k + 1)$th neighbor chooses a positive action, then positive externalities imply a higher expected payoff for our $k + 1$ degree player. Thus, the $(k + 1)$ degree player is assured of an expected payoff which is at least as high as that of any k degree player.

These two results provide a clean relationship between degree and effort levels and payoffs for a broad class of games. These results rely heavily on the information structure. To see this, it is worth noting that the social sharing of costly information example discussed in section 3.3.1 is a game in which payoffs depend only on own action and the sum of neighbors' actions which satisfies positive externalities and strategic substitutes. However, in that context, example 3.1 showed us that there is no such clear relationship between degree on the one hand

---

[16] If the equilibrium is in mixed strategies, then the statement can be amended to allow for distributions on actions in the natural way: for instance, the mixed strategy distribution on actions of degree $k + 1$ player first-order dominates the mixed strategy distribution on actions of degree k, for games with strategic complements.

and efforts and payoffs on the other. In a star network there is an equilibrium in which the central node chooses high effort while all the peripheral nodes choose 0. In this equilibrium clearly the central player earns a lower payoff as well. This equilibrium is not possible in a setting with incomplete information (and with no correlation between degrees of neighbors) a higher degree player has the same views as the peripheral player about the degree of her neighbors. Thus she will expect each of her neighbors to put in, on average, the same effort as the average effort expected of her neighbor, by a peripheral player. Given that efforts are strategic substitutes, this implies that the central player would choose a lower effort than the peripheral players in equilibrium.[17]

3.4.2 Link-Specific Actions

The second key assumption is that a player chooses a single/common action in interaction with all neighbors. However, in some important contexts a central issue is the allocation of resources across links. The following example illustrates this. Consider a group of firms which have entered into a set of collaboration agreements with other firms. This sharing of efforts has several potential effects: it creates economies of effort by allowing different firms to exploit the same effort; it may induce free riding since there is a divergence between individual returns and joint returns; and there are competitive effects as sharing between two firms alters their relative position vis-à-vis third parties. These effects raise a number of questions such as, how do firms allocate effort between private individual projects and different joint projects? How do incentives in specific links vary with the network characteristics of the different firms?[18]

Similar questions arise in other contexts such as resource allocation in social connections and allocation of time and effort between single-author papers and different multi-authored papers. The study of games in networks where strategies are link specific is still at an early stage; for an attempt at modeling link-specific efforts, see Goyal, Konovalov, and Moraga (2003). The presentation here draws on that paper and on Goyal (2005b).

There are $N = \{1, 2, \ldots, n\}$ players located in an undirected network g. As usual, $N_i(g)$ denotes the set of neighbors of player i and $\eta_i(g)$ the degree of player i in network g. The strategy of player i is a vector $s_i = \{s_{ii}, \{s_{ij}\}_{j \in N_i(g)}\}$, s_{ii} refers to an independent action, while s_{ij} refers to the action with respect to link g_{ij}. The strategy profile is defined as $s = (s_1, s_2, \ldots, s_n)$, as before. Figure 3.3 presents strategic options in the single action and in the link-specific actions case,

---

[17] These results extend in different ways when the degrees of neighbors exhibit correlation; see Galeotti et al. (2006) for a discussion on these extensions.

[18] Another possibility is for individuals to choose different actions across interactions. For a study of the effects of networks when individuals have the flexibility to choose different actions with different partners, see Goyal and Janssen (1997).

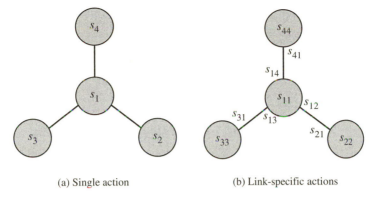

(a) Single action (b) Link-specific actions

Figure 3.3. Comparison of two models.

to illustrate the difference between the two. The payoffs to player i, located in network g, and faced with a profile s, are $\Pi_i(s \mid g)$.

The issues about the effects of others' actions on individual payoffs that were discussed in section 3.2, however, also arise here. The possibility of link-specific actions also gives rise to some new considerations which are worth mentioning briefly. To fix ideas it is useful to consider the example of research collaboration in networks. Each firm i chooses an investment in a private project, s_{ii}, and an investment level in each of its different joint projects, $\{s_{ij}\}_{j \in N_i(g)}$. This raises the issue of what is the relation between the private project efforts of a partner j and payoffs to firm i. Similarly, there are several modeling possibilities with regard to the relationship between the efforts of a partner j in project s_{jk} and the payoffs to a partner firm i. Thus allowing for link-specific efforts greatly enlarges the range of possible spillovers across actions of players located in a network. This richness is worth exploring as models of link-specific investments allow an explicit examination of the quality of links that are consistent with individual incentives.

3.5 Concluding Remarks

The starting point of this chapter was the observation that individual behavior is shaped by others who are "close by"; these "close by" others are referred to as *neighbors*. However, the behavior of these neighbors is in turn affected by the actions of their neighbors, whose actions are in turn affected by the actions of their neighbors, and so on. This line of reasoning led to the view that the overall pattern of ties between individuals plays a role in shaping individual behavior and aggregate social outcomes.

The chapter first presented a general framework for the study of games on networks. This framework consists of a description of the ties that link individuals, the strategic options available to them, and the payoffs that arise as a result of the actions that individuals take. In this context, the key idea is that the effects of a player's actions on other players is mediated by the network. Different aspects of a network can in principle come into play, and the chapter discussed some of the main network features that have been studied in the literature.

We then examined the role of networks in three interesting contexts: the social sharing of costly information, social interactions in crime, and research collaboration among firms. The models developed to study the network effects constitute special cases of the general framework developed earlier, and the discussion for each of the models was organized to address the following three questions. How does behavior depend on network features? How does it change as the network changes? And how is aggregate welfare affected by the network structure?

A number of insights were obtained on how the nature of the game—the type of externality that is generated by others' actions—and the structure of the network jointly shape individual behavior. First consider the case where a network is fixed and ask how behavior is shaped by network location. Here, the results on information sharing in a star network are worth noting: we found that there is no equilibrium in which all players exert positive effort. Moreover, there are two specialized equilibria possible, one in which the central node exerts effort while the peripheral nodes free ride, and a second equilibrium in which the reverse pattern obtains. Thus network structure can lead to the emergence of experts and free riding, but the relation between network location and free riding is not fully determined.

Next, we considered the effects of changing the network. Perhaps the simplest way to do this is to take a regular network and increase its degree. In the information-sharing example there exists a symmetric equilibrium in which effort falls, in the crime example effort increases, while in the research collaboration example effort falls with an increase in degree. This illustrates in a simple way how the type of game being played shapes outcomes. How about changing a network more generally? This is a difficult problem and the examples in the information-sharing application are illustrative. We found that the effect of adding a link depends very much on where in the network it is added.

We are thus led to two general observations: the first observation is that network structure have significant effects on individual behavior and on social welfare. The second observation is that networks are rich and complicated objects and this makes it difficult to obtain tight and general predictions regarding their effects on individual behavior.

These difficulties led to a consideration of a simpler approach to the study of network effects, which abstracts from a full description of the network and instead focuses on one facet of the network: the distribution of degrees. A model of games on networks based on degree distribution was developed. It was shown that such a model allows for a natural formulation of incomplete network knowledge among players located in networks. The analysis of such a model yields a number of general results on network effects such as a monotonic relation between degree and effort and payoffs, in different types of games.

3.6 Appendix

3.6.1 Existence of Nash Equilibria

The game on network g has a finite set of players $N = \{1, 2, \ldots, n\}$. Each player has the same strategy set, which is a compact subset of the unit interval $[0, 1]$. Two cases of the action set will be considered: the first in which $S = [0, 1]$, and the second in which $S = \{0, x_1, x_2, \ldots, x_m, 1\}$. A strategy of player i is denoted by s_i and a strategy profile is denoted by $s = (s_1, s_2, s_3, \ldots, s_n)$. The space of strategies of all players is the product of individual players' strategy sets and is S^n. The payoffs to a player i are $\Pi_i : S^n \to \mathcal{R}$.

Recall that a mixed strategy of player i, $\sigma_i : S \to \mathcal{R}_+$, is a probability distribution on the set of actions S. Let the set of probability distributions on S be denoted by Δ. A mixed strategy profile $\sigma^* = (\sigma_1^*, \sigma_2^*, \ldots, \sigma_n^*)$ is a Nash equilibrium if for each player i, given the strategies of other players σ_{-i}^*, σ_i^* maximizes her (expected) payoffs.

Theorem 3.2. *Suppose the action set of every player S is a compact, nonempty, and convex subset of $\mathcal{R}$. If the payoff function of every player is continuous with respect to strategies of all players and concave with respect to her own strategy, then there exists a Nash equilibrium in pure strategies. If the action set of every player is discrete and given by $S = \{0, x_1, x_2, \ldots, x_m, 1\}$, then there exists a Nash equilibrium, possibly in mixed strategies.*

Proof. This proof is taken from Fudenberg and Tirole (1991). The proof for the finite action set is given first. The basic idea is to define the best-response correspondence for each player, and then apply Kakutani's fixed point theorem to these correspondences.

Player i's best-response correspondence r_i maps each strategy profile σ to the set of mixed strategies that maximize her payoffs, when her opponents play according to the strategy profile σ_{-i}. Clearly, the best response of player i does not depend on σ_i, in the profile σ, but it is convenient to write the best response in this form for the purposes of using the fixed point theorem. Define $r : \Delta^n \to \Delta^n$ to be the Cartesian product of r_i. A fixed point of the correspondence is a profile σ such that $\sigma \in r(\sigma)$, so a fixed point constitutes a Nash equilibrium.

Kakutani's fixed point theorem provides a set of sufficient conditions for the existence of a fixed point for the correspondence $r : \Delta^n \to \Delta^n$.

(i) The set Δ is a compact, convex, and nonempty subset of a finite-dimensional Euclidean space.

(ii) $r(\sigma)$ is nonempty for all σ.

(iii) $r(\sigma)$ is convex for all σ.

(iv) $r(\sigma)$ has a closed graph: if a sequence $(\sigma^m, \hat{\sigma}^m) \to (\sigma, \hat{\sigma})$, with $\hat{\sigma}^m \in r(\sigma^m)$ for all m, then $\hat{\sigma} \in r(\sigma)$.

The next step is to show that the game on network g satisfies these conditions.

Since the strategy set for each player is the simplex of dimension $\#S - 1$, it is clearly compact, convex, and nonempty. The payoffs are linear and hence continuous functions of own mixed strategy, and so the payoff to every player attains a maximum. This means that $r(\sigma)$ is nonempty for all σ. Next consider convexity of $r(\sigma)$. If $r(\sigma)$ is not convex, then there is some player i such that for some σ there exist $\sigma_i', \sigma_i'' \in r_i(\sigma)$ such that $\lambda\sigma_i' + (1 - \lambda)\sigma_i'' \notin r_i(\sigma)$. However, by the linearity of payoffs in mixed strategies it follows that

$$\Pi_i(\lambda\sigma_i' + (1 - \lambda)\sigma_i'', \sigma_{-i} \mid g) = \lambda\Pi_i(\sigma_i', \sigma_{-i} \mid g) + (1 - \lambda)\Pi_i(\sigma_i'', \sigma_{-i} \mid g),$$
$$(3.24)$$

so that if both σ_i' and σ_i'' are best responses to σ, then so is every convex combination of the two. Thus the game satisfies condition (iii).

Suppose condition (iv) is violated. Then there exists a sequence $(\sigma^m, \hat{\sigma}^m) \to (\sigma, \hat{\sigma})$, with $\hat{\sigma}^m \in r(\sigma^m)$, such that $\hat{\sigma} \notin r(\sigma)$. This means that $\hat{\sigma}_i \notin r_i(\sigma)$ for some player i. But then there exists an $\epsilon > 0$ and a strategy σ_i' such that $\Pi_i(\sigma_i', \sigma_{-i} \mid g) \geq \Pi_i(\hat{\sigma}_i, \sigma_{-i} \mid g) + 3\epsilon$. Since $\Pi_i(\cdot)$ is continuous in the mixed strategies of all players, and $(\sigma^m, \hat{\sigma}^m) \to (\sigma, \hat{\sigma})$, it follows that, for sufficiently large m,

$$\Pi_i(\sigma_i', \sigma_{-i}^m \mid g) > \Pi_i(\sigma_i', \sigma_{-i} \mid g) - \epsilon$$
$$> \Pi_i(\hat{\sigma}_i, \sigma_{-i} \mid g) + 2\epsilon$$
$$> \Pi_i(\hat{\sigma}_i^m, \sigma_{-i}^m \mid g).$$
$$(3.25)$$

Thus σ_i' does strictly better than $\hat{\sigma}_i^m$, against σ_{-i}^m, which contradicts the hypothesis that $\hat{\sigma}_i^m \in r_i(\sigma^m)$.

The proof for the continuous actions case follows from similar arguments. Clearly, S satisfies the conditions on action sets. Then from continuity of payoff functions and compactness of action set it follows that the best-response correspondence is nonempty and that the graph of the correspondence is closed. The convexity of the best-response correspondence follows from the concavity in own actions of the payoff function. $\qquad\qquad\square$

3.6.2 Sharing of Costly Information

This section presents a formal proof for the observation that in any nonempty network an equilibrium is inefficient. The payoffs to player i in network g facing an action profile s are

$$\Pi_i(s \mid g) = f\left(s_i + \sum_{j \in N_i(g)} s_j\right) - cs_i, \qquad (3.26)$$

where $c > 0$ is the marginal cost of effort. It is assumed that $f(0) = 0$, $f' > 0$, and $f'' < 0$.

The following proposition is due to Bramoullé and Kranton (forthcoming).

Proposition 3.6. *In any nonempty network every Nash equilibrium is inefficient.*

Proof. Fix some nonempty network g, and let s^* be an equilibrium with $s_i > 0$, for some $i \in N$, and suppose that for some i and j, $g_{ij} = 1$. From proposition 3.1, it follows that $s^*_{N_i(g)} + s^*_i = \hat{s}$ and this implies that $f'(s^*_i + s^*_{N_i(g)}) - c = 0$. Now consider the partial derivative of social welfare with respect to s_i evaluated at s^*_i:

$$\frac{\partial W(s^* \mid g)}{\partial s_i} = \sum_{j \in \{i\} \cup N_i(g)} f'\left(s^*_j + \sum_{k \in N_j(g)} s^*_k\right) - c$$

$$= \sum_{j \in N_i(g)} f'\left(s^*_j + \sum_{k \in N_j(g)} s^*_k\right), \qquad (3.27)$$

which is strictly positive since $f'(\cdot) > 0$. So welfare can be strictly increased by increasing s_i. Thus the equilibrium is inefficient. □

3.6.3 Social Interactions and Crime

The results and their proofs in this section are taken from Ballester, Calvó-Armengol, and Zenou (2006). Recall that payoffs to player i in network game Γ, faced with strategy profile $s = (s_1, s_2, \ldots, s_n)$, are as follows:

$$\Pi_i(s) = \alpha s_i - \tfrac{1}{2}(\beta - \gamma)s_i^2 - \gamma \sum_{j=1}^n s_i s_j + \lambda \sum_{j=1}^n g_{ij} s_i s_j. \qquad (3.28)$$

Let $\mu_1(g)$ be the largest eigenvalue of G.

Proposition 3.7. *The matrix $[\beta I - \lambda G]^{-1}$ is well-defined if and only if $\beta > \lambda \mu_i(g)$. The game Γ has a unique interior Nash equilibrium $s^*(\Gamma) = (s_1^*, s_2^*, \ldots, s_n^*)$, which is characterized by*

$$s^*(\Gamma) = \frac{\alpha}{\beta + \gamma \tilde{C}_B(g, \lambda^*)} C_B(g, \lambda^*). \qquad (3.29)$$

Proof. The necessary and sufficient conditions for the matrix $[\beta I - \lambda G]^{-1}$ to be well-defined and nonnegative follow from Debreu and Herstein (1953). These conditions suffice for the existence of a unique interior equilibrium.[19]

Next consider the characterization of equilibrium. From the first-order conditions, it follows that an interior s_i^* satisfies

$$\beta s_i^* + \gamma \sum_{j=1}^{n} s_j^* - \lambda \sum_{j=1}^{n} g_{ij} s_j^* = \alpha. \tag{3.30}$$

Using matrix Γ we can rewrite this as follows:

$$[\beta I + \gamma U - \lambda G]s^* = \alpha \cdot 1. \tag{3.31}$$

The matrix $[\beta I + \gamma U - \lambda G]$ is generically nonsingular and so there is a unique generic solution in $\mathcal{R}^n$.

Recall that, for any $y \in R^n$, $\tilde{y} = y_1 + y_2 + \cdots + y_n$ and $\lambda^* = \lambda/\beta$. Now exploit $U \cdot s = \tilde{s} \cdot 1$ to rewrite the above as

$$\beta[I - \lambda^* G]s^* = [\alpha - \gamma \tilde{s}^*] \cdot 1. \tag{3.32}$$

Inverting the matrix and using the definition of $C_B(\cdot)$ we can write this as

$$\beta s^* = [\alpha - \gamma \tilde{s}^*]C_B(g, \lambda^*). \tag{3.33}$$

Simple algebra then yields

$$s^* = \frac{\alpha}{\beta + \gamma \tilde{C}_B(g, \lambda^*)} C_B(g, \lambda^*). \tag{3.34}$$

This completes the proof.   □

Recall that Γ' is said to dominate Γ if $\rho'_{ij} \geq \rho_{ij}$ for all i, j and $\rho'_{ij} > \rho_{ij}$ for some pair i, j.

Proposition 3.8. *Suppose β is large and Γ' dominates Γ. Then $\tilde{s}^{*\prime}(\Gamma') > \tilde{s}^*(\Gamma)$.*

Proof. Define $\Gamma' = \Gamma + \lambda D$, where $d_{ij} \geq 0$ for all i, j, and strictly positive for some pair i, j. Suppose β is large enough so that proposition 3.7 holds. Then in equilibrium,

$$-\Gamma s^*(\Gamma) = -\Gamma' s^*(\Gamma') = \alpha \cdot 1. \tag{3.35}$$

Now exploit symmetry of Γ and we get

$$\alpha \tilde{s}^{*\prime}(\Gamma') = -s^{*\prime\prime}(\Gamma')\Gamma s^*(\Gamma) = \alpha \tilde{s}^*(\Gamma) + \lambda s^{*\prime\prime}(\Gamma)D s^*(\Gamma). \tag{3.36}$$

Given that $\alpha, \lambda > 0$, it follows that $\tilde{s}^{*\prime}(\Gamma') > \tilde{s}^*(\Gamma)$.   □

---

[19] No corner equilibria exist in this model; for details of the proof, see Ballester, Calvó-Armengol, and Zenou (2006).

3.6.4   Collaboration and Market Competition

The results and the proofs in this section are taken from Goyal and Moraga (2001). We start by deriving the payoffs for firms. Suppose that firms compete in the same market by choosing quantities. Firms choose quantities $(\{q_i\}_{i \in N})$, with $Q = \sum_{i \in N} q_i$; demand is assumed to be linear and given by $Q = 1 - p$, $1 > n\bar{c}$. Thus, the profits of firm i in collaboration network g are

$$\Pi_i(s \mid g) = \left[1 - q_i(g) - \sum_{j \neq i} q_j(g) - c_i(g) \right] q_i(g) - \alpha s_i^2(g). \qquad (3.37)$$

Using standard arguments, it follows that equilibrium quantities are $q_i = (1 - nc_i + \sum_{j \neq i} c_j)/(n + 1)$. Substituting for the equilibrium value of $q_i(g)$ in the above function yields the following expression:

$$\Pi_i(s \mid g) = \frac{[1 - nc_i(s \mid g) + \sum_{j \neq i} c_j(s \mid g)]^2}{(n + 1)^2} - \alpha s_i^2(g). \qquad (3.38)$$

Now substituting for the role of effort in defining costs yields the following expression:

$$\Pi_i(s \mid g) = \left[1 - \bar{c} + n \left[s_i + \sum_{j \in N_i(g)} s_j \right] - \sum_{l \neq i} \left[s_l + \sum_{m \in N_l(g)} s_m \right] \right] - \alpha s_i^2(g). \tag{3.39}$$

Next note that the effort of firm x, s_x, affects its costs as well as the costs of $\eta_x(g)$ other firms. Using this property, equation (3.39) can be rewritten in terms of actions of neighbors and nonneighbors as follows:

$$\Pi_i(s \mid g) = \frac{\begin{array}{c}[1 - \bar{c} + s_i[n - \eta_i(g)] + \sum_{j \in N_i(g)} s_j[n - \eta_j(g)] \\ - \sum_{l \in N \setminus \{i\} \cup N_i(g)} s_l[1 + \eta_l(g)]]^2\end{array}}{(n + 1)^2}$$
$$- \alpha s_i^2(g). \qquad (3.40)$$

In a regular network of degree k, g^k, the payoffs to firm i are

$$\Pi_i(s \mid g^k)$$
$$= \frac{[1 - \bar{c} + s_i(n - k) + \sum_{j \in N_i(g)} s_j(n - k) - \sum_{l \in N \setminus \{i\} \cup N_i} s_l(k + 1)]^2}{(n + 1)^2}$$
$$- \alpha s_i^2(g). \qquad (3.41)$$

The following result, due to Goyal and Moraga (2001), summarizes the analysis of network effects.

Proposition 3.9. *Consider a homogeneous good market where firms compete in quantities and suppose that firms are located in a regular network of collaboration.*

The following network effects obtain. (i) Research effort of a firm is decreasing in the degree. (ii) Costs are initially declining and then increasing with respect to degree. (iii) Profits are initially increasing but eventually falling with respect to degree.

Proof. The first-order condition for an interior optimal solution of firm i is

$$(n-k)\left[1 - \bar{c} + s_i(n-k) + \sum_{j \in N_i(g)} s_j(n-k)\right.$$
$$\left. - \sum_{l \in N\setminus\{i\}\cup N_i(g)} s_l(k+1)\right] - \alpha(n+1)^2 s_i = 0. \quad (3.42)$$

For large α the second derivative is negative, and so the first-order condition is necessary as well as sufficient for an interior optimum. Invoking symmetry, i.e., $s_i = s_l = s_m = s(g^k)$, and solving for $s(g^k)$, it follows that the interior equilibrium effort level is

$$s^*(g^k) = \frac{(1 - \bar{c})(n-k)}{\alpha(n+1)^2 - (n-k)(k+1)}. \quad (3.43)$$

A simple way to examine the effects of changing degree on equilibrium actions is by looking at the sign of the derivative of equilibrium action with respect to degree. Simple computations yield the following expression for this derivative:

$$\frac{\partial s^*(g^k)}{\partial k} = (1 - \bar{c})\frac{(n-k)^2 - \alpha(n+1)^2}{[\alpha(n+1)^2 - (n-k)(k+1)]^2}. \quad (3.44)$$

The numerator is negative for large α, while the denominator is always positive and so it follows that equilibrium efforts are declining in the degree of the network. This proves part (i).

To examine the effect of degree on cost reduction, proceed similarly. Equilibrium costs can be expressed as follows:

$$c(g^k) = \frac{\bar{c}\alpha(n+1)^2 - (n-k)(k+1)}{\alpha(n+1)^2 - (n-k)(k+1)}. \quad (3.45)$$

The derivative of equilibrium costs with respect to degree is

$$\frac{\partial c(g^k)}{\partial k} = \frac{(2k+1-n)\alpha(n+1)^2(1-\bar{c})}{[\alpha(n+1)^2 - (n-k)(k+1)]^2}. \quad (3.46)$$

This is negative if and only if $k < (n-1)/2$. Thus costs are initially falling and then increasing as a function of network degree and minimal costs are attained at an intermediate level of collaboration. This proves part (ii).

Substituting the equilibrium effort levels in the profits expression (3.19) yields the following expression for equilibrium profits in a degree k network:

$$\Pi_i^*(g^k) = \frac{(1 - \bar{c})^2 \alpha [\alpha(n + 1)^2 - (n - k)^2]}{[\alpha(n + 1)^2 - (n - k)(k + 1)]^2}. \tag{3.47}$$

The derivative of equilibrium profits with respect to degree is

$$\frac{\partial \Pi_i^*(g^k)}{\partial k} = \frac{2\alpha(1 - \bar{c})^2 [n - k][\alpha(n + 1)^2 - (n - k)(k + 1)]^2}{[\alpha(n + 1)^2 - (n - k)(k + 1)]^4}$$

$$- \frac{2\alpha(1 - \bar{c})^2 [\alpha(n + 1)^2 - (n - k)^2]}{[\alpha(n + 1)^2 - (n - k)(k + 1)][2k + 1 - n]}{[\alpha(n + 1)^2 - (n - k)(k + 1)]^4}. \tag{3.48}$$

The denominator is positive. In the numerator, all the expressions are positive except $2k + 1 - n$, which is negative if and only if $k < (n - 1)/2$. This implies that equilibrium profits are increasing in degree initially. Direct calculation shows that profits are larger in a degree $n - 2$ network than in a degree $n - 1$ network (i.e., the complete network). These observations taken together complete the proof of part (iii). □

4

Coordination and Cooperation

4.1 Introduction

Social coordination and cooperation are two recurring themes in the study of strategic interaction and an important reason for this is that they arise in both social and economic contexts. The problem of coordination arises in its simplest form when, for an individual, the optimal course of action is to conform to what others are doing. The following three examples illustrate how coordination problems arise naturally in different walks of life.

(i) *Adoption of new information technology.* Individuals decide on whether to adopt a fax machine without full knowledge of its usefulness. This usefulness depends on the technological qualities of the product but clearly also depends on whether others with whom they communicate adopt a similar technology. Empirical work suggests that there are powerful interaction effects in the adoption of information technology (Economides and Himmelberg 1995).

(ii) *Language choice.* Individuals choose which language to learn at school as a second language. The rewards depend on the choices of others with whom they expect to interact. Empirical work suggests that changes in the patterns of interactions among individuals—for instance, a move from a situation in which groups are relatively isolated with little across-group interaction to one in which individuals are highly mobile and groups are more integrated—has played an important role in the extinction of several languages and the dominance of a few languages (see, for example, Watkins 1991; Brenzinger 1998).

(iii) *Social norms.* Individuals choose whether to be punctual or to be casual about appointment times. The incentives for being punctual are clearly sensitive to whether or not others are punctual. Casual observation suggests that in some countries punctuality is the norm while in others it is not.[1] Similarly, the decision on whether to stand in a queue or to jump it is very

---

[1] For a formal model of punctuality as a social norm, see Basu and Weibull (2002).

much shaped by the choices of others. Likewise the arrangement of cutlery on a table is governed by norms which have evolved spatially and across time (for a study, see Elias (1978)). These examples illustrate the role of interaction externalities in shaping social outcomes.

The problem of cooperation arises when individual incentives lead to an outcome which is socially inefficient or undesirable. Such conflicts between individual incentive-driven behavior and social goals are common in many situations. The following two examples illustrate this.

(i) *Provision of public goods.* Individuals have the choice of exerting effort which is privately costly but yields benefits to themselves as well as to others. A simple example of this is proper maintenance of a personal garden which is also enjoyed by others. Another example is the participation of parents in school monitoring associations, such as governing bodies. In such contexts, it is often the case that the personal costs exceed the personal benefits but are smaller than the social benefits. Theoretical work argues that the structure of interaction between individuals—in particular, whether one's acquaintances know each other—can be crucial in determining levels of public goods provision (see, for example, Coleman 1988).

(ii) *Informal insurance.* Social insurance systems offer relatively modest protection against income shocks in many developing countries. Families are obliged therefore to rely on systems of informal risk sharing. Loans do not come with a formal contract, and so it is possible for a borrower to default on a loan without the fear of legal sanctions. However, anticipating this incentive for default, lenders will not lend money and so potentially important insurance will not be provided. There is therefore a conflict between individual incentives and socially desirable outcomes. Empirical work suggests that the performance of informal insurance systems depends on the level of trust in a society and that this is related to the structure of social connections (see, for example, Fafchamps 2003, 2004; Dercon 2004).

This chapter examines the relationship between networks of personal interaction and the prospects for social coordination and cooperation.

We will start by studying games of coordination and cooperation within a static framework which was presented in the previous chapter, i.e., individuals make their choices once and simultaneously. Moreover, the games studied in this chapter will exhibit pure local effects. In this context, we will address two questions.

• Are there features of networks that facilitate or hinder the adoption of socially efficient actions?

• What are the structural features of networks that help sustain diversity of actions?

A number of results will be derived to illustrate the different ways in which network structure can matter for individual behavior and social outcomes. The static model, however, will also tell us that these games of social coordination and cooperation often have multiple equilibria; this is a finding which motivates an enquiry into the relative robustness of different outcomes. We will then formulate a dynamic model and ask:

- How does the network of interaction shape the dynamics of individual behavior?

The study of coordination and cooperation problems has a long and distinguished tradition in economics. The problem of coordination has been approached in two different ways, broadly speaking. One approach views this to be a static game between players, and tries to solve the problem through introspective reasoning; Schelling (1960) introduced the notion of focal points in this context.[2] The second approach takes a dynamic perspective and seeks solutions to coordination problems via the gradual accumulation of precedent. This approach has been actively pursued in recent years; see Young (1998) for a survey of this work. The present chapter also takes a dynamic approach and the focus here is on how the network of interaction shapes the process of learning to coordinate.

The conflict between behavior driven by personal interest and social good has been a central theme in economics (and game theory). One approach to the resolution of this problem focuses on the role of repeated interaction between individuals. A self-interested individual may be induced to act in the collective interest in the current game via threats of punishments in the future from other players. This line of reasoning has been explored in models of increasing generality over the years and a number of important results have been obtained. For a survey of this work, see Mailath and Samuelson (2006). Most of this work takes the interaction between individuals to be centralized (an individual plays with everyone else) or assumes that interaction is based on random matching of players. A second approach to this problem focuses on the role of nonselfish individual preferences and nonoptimizing rules of behavior. This approach uses empirical and experimental evidence as a motivation for the study of alternative models of individual behavior. The role of altruism, reciprocity, fairness, and inequity

---

[2] For recent work in this tradition, see Bacharach (2006) and Sugden (2004). Also see Lewis (1969) for an influential study of the philosophical issues relating to conventions as solutions to coordination problems.

On the applied side, the theory of network externalities is closely related to the problem of social coordination. This theory arose out of the observation that in many markets the benefits of using a product are increasing in the number of adopters of the same product (examples include fax machines and word processing packages). In this literature, the focus was on the total number of adopters and an important issue was whether these consumption externalities will inhibit the adoption of new products. For a survey of this work, see Besen and Farrell (1994) and Katz and Shapiro (1994). The models of social coordination with local interaction presented in section 4.2 can be seen as an elaboration of this line of research.

aversion has been investigated in this line of work. Camerer (2003) and Fehr and Schmidt (2003) provide surveys of this research. The present chapter takes a dynamic approach to the study of cooperation and the interest is in understanding how decision rules and networks of interaction jointly shape individual behavior.

This chapter is organized as follows. Section 4.2 studies games of coordination, while section 4.3 studies a contribution problem which is similar to a prisoner's dilemma game. Section 4.4 concludes. Complete proofs of the results are provided in the appendix to the chapter.

4.2 Coordination Games

It is useful to start with a description of a two-action coordination game among two players. Denote the players by 1 and 2 and the possible actions by α and β. The rewards to a player depend on her own action and the action of the other player. These rewards are summarized in the following payoff matrix:

1 & 2	α	β
α	a,a	d,e
β	e,d	b,b

At the heart of coordination games are two basic ideas: first, there are gains from individuals choosing the same action, and, second, rewards may differ depending on which actions the two players coordinate on. These considerations motivate the following restrictions on the payoff parameters:

$$a > d; \qquad b > d; \qquad d > e; \qquad a + d > b + e. \qquad (4.1)$$

These restrictions imply that there are two (pure strategy) Nash equilibria of the game, $\{\alpha, \alpha\}$ and $\{\beta, \beta\}$, and that coordinating on either of them is better than not coordinating at all.[3] The assumption that $a + d > b + e$ implies that if a player places equal probability on her opponent playing the two actions, then it is strictly better for her to choose α. In other words, α is the *risk-dominant* action in the sense of Harsanyi and Selten (1988). It is important to note that α can be risk-dominant even if it is not efficient (that is, even if $b > a$). Indeed, one of the important considerations in the research to date has been the relative salience of riskiness versus efficiency. Given the restrictions on the payoffs, the two equilibria are *strict* in the sense that the best response in the equilibrium yields a strictly higher

---

[3] In principle, players can want to coordinate on action combinations $\{\alpha, \beta\}$ or $\{\beta, \alpha\}$; games with such equilibria may be referred to as anti-coordination games. See Bramoullé (2007) for a study of network effects in this class of games.

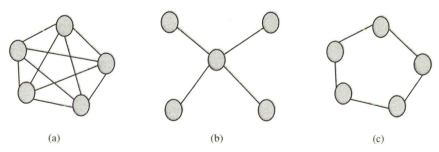

Figure 4.1. Simple networks: (a) complete network;
(b) star network; (c) local interaction on a circle.

payoff than the other option. It is well-known that strict equilibria are robust to standard refinements of Nash equilibrium (see, for example, van Damme 1991).

The focus of the analysis is on the effects of local interactions. We study local interaction in terms of neighborhoods within a model of networks. Suppose, as before, that the $N = \{1, 2, \ldots, n\}$ players are located on the nodes of an undirected network $g \in \mathcal{G}$, where $\mathcal{G}$ is the set of all possible undirected networks on n nodes. We will assume that a player i plays the coordination game with each of her neighbors. Recall that $N_i(g) = \{j \in N \mid g_{ij} = 1\}$ refers to the set of players with whom i is linked in network g. Three networks of interaction—the complete network, the star, and local interaction among players located around a circle—will be extensively used in this chapter. For easy reference they are presented in figure 4.1.

As before, s_i denotes the strategy of player i and $S_i = \{\alpha, \beta\}$ the strategy set. Let $\prod_{i \in N} S_i = S$ denote the set of all strategy profiles in the game and let $s \in S$ refer to a typical member of this set. In the two-player game, let $\pi(x, y)$ denote the payoffs to player i when this player chooses action x, while her opponent chooses action y. The payoffs to a player i in network g, from a strategy s_i, given that the other players are choosing s_{-i}, are

$$\Pi_i(s_i, s_{-i} \mid g) = \sum_{j \in N_i(g)} \pi(s_i, s_j). \tag{4.2}$$

This formulation reflects the idea that a player i interacts with each of the players in the set $N_i(g)$. The players N, their interactions summarized by a network g, the set of actions for each player $S_i = \{\alpha, \beta\}$, and the payoffs (4.2) (where $\pi(x, y)$ satisfies (4.1)) together define a social coordination game.[4]

---

[4] In some important contexts—an instance is social protest movements—individuals have thresholds for actions: choose protest if at least x others choose to protest, and choose to stay at home otherwise. Suppose that there is a distribution of these thresholds in the population. The question is, under what distributions will a social protest take place? The distribution of thresholds may be interpreted as a form of individual heterogeneity with regard to preference for coordination. For an early study of this question, see Granovetter (1978). Knowledge that individuals have about each others' thresholds will naturally play

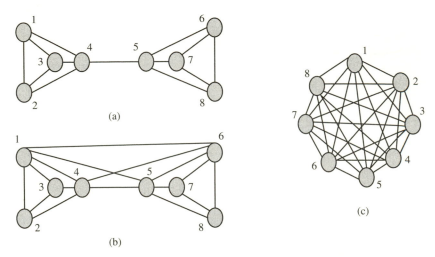

Figure 4.2. Levels of network integration: (a) integration level 1;
(b) integration level 2; (c) full integration.

4.2.1   Multiple Equilibria

This section starts by describing some Nash equilibria that can arise under different network structures. First, note that the strategy profile $s_i = x$ for all $i \in N$,
where $x \in \{\alpha, \beta\}$, is a Nash equilibrium for every possible network structure.
This is easily checked given the restrictions on the payoffs. Are there other types
of equilibria which display diversity of actions and how is their existence affected
by the structure of interaction? To get a sense of some of the forces driving conformism and diversity, it is useful to consider a class of societies in which there
are several groups and intra-group interaction is more intense than inter-group
interaction. Figure 4.2 presents network structures with two groups which capture
this idea. The number of cross-group links reflects the level of integration of the
society. Simple calculations reveal that equilibria with a diversity of actions are
easy to sustain in societies with low levels of integration, but that such equilibria
cannot be sustained in a fully integrated society, i.e., in the complete network.

The above observations are summarized in the following result.

Theorem 4.1. *Consider a social coordination game. A strategy profile in which
everyone plays the same action is a Nash equilibrium for every network $g \in \mathcal{G}$. If
the network is complete, then these are the only possible Nash equilibria. If the
network is incomplete, then there may exist equilibria with a diversity of actions
as well.*

---

an important role in shaping the prospects of social action. In a recent paper, Chwe (2000) examines the
role of social networks in conveying information about these thresholds. His interest is in characterizing
network structures which facilitate the emergence of social action.

This result yields two insights: multiple equilibria with social conformism exist for every possible network of interaction; and social diversity can arise in equilibrium, but the possibility of such outcomes depends on the network architecture.

These observations lead to an examination of the robustness of different equilibria and how this is in turn related to the structure of interaction.

4.2.2 Dynamic Stability and Equilibrium Selection

The dynamic model will take time to be a discrete variable and indexed by $t = 1, 2, 3, \ldots$. In each period, with probability $p \in (0, 1)$, a player gets an opportunity to revise her strategy. Faced with this opportunity, player i chooses an action which maximizes her payoff, under the assumption that the strategy profile of her neighbors remains the same as in the previous period. If more than one action is optimal, then the player persists with the current action. Denote the strategy of a player i in period t by s_i^t. If player i is not active in period t, then set $s_i^t = s_i^{t-1}$. This simple best-response strategy revision rule generates, for every network g, a transition probability function, $P_g(ss') : S \times S \rightarrow [0, 1]$, which governs the evolution of the state of the system s^t. A strategy profile (or state), s, is absorbing if the dynamic process cannot escape from the state once it reaches it, i.e., $P_g(ss) = 1$.[5] The interest is in the relation between absorbing states and the structures of local interaction.

The first step in the analysis is the following convergence result and the characterization of the limiting states.

Theorem 4.2. *Consider a social coordination game. Starting from any initial strategy profile, s^0, the dynamic process s^t converges to an absorbing strategy profile in finite time, with probability 1. There is an equivalence between the set of absorbing strategy profiles and the set of Nash equilibria of the static social game.*[6]

The equivalence between absorbing states and Nash equilibria of the social game of coordination is easy to see. The arguments underlying the convergence result are as follows. Start at some state s^1. Consider the set of players who are not playing a best response. If this set is empty, then the process is at a Nash equilibrium profile and this is an absorbing state of the process, as no player has an incentive to revise her strategy. Suppose therefore that there are some players who are currently choosing action α but would prefer to choose β. Allow them

---

[5] For a rigorous exposition of the probability theory underlying the dynamic processes discussed in this book, see Billingsley (1985).

[6] The relation between the Nash equilibria of the social coordination game and the equilibria of the original 2×2 game has been explored in Mailath, Samuelson, and Shaked (1997). They show that the set of Nash equilibria of the static social game is equivalent to the set of correlated equilibria of the 2×2 game. Ianni (2001) studies convergence to correlated equilibria under myopic best-response dynamics.

to choose β, and let s^1 be the new state of the system (this transition occurs with positive probability, given the decision rules used by individuals). Now examine the players choosing α in state s^1 who would like to switch actions. If there are some such players, then have them switch to β and define the new state as s^2. Clearly, this process of having the α players switch will end in finite time (since there are a finite number of players in the society). Let the state with this property be $\hat{s}$. Either there will be no players left choosing α or there will be some players choosing α in $\hat{s}$. In the former case the process is at a Nash equilibrium. Consider the second possibility next. Check if there are any players choosing β in state $\hat{s}$ who would like to switch actions. If there are none, then the process is at an absorbing state. If there are some β players who would like to switch, then follow the process as outlined above to reach a state in which there is no player who wishes to switch from β to α. Let this state be denoted by $\bar{s}$. Next observe that no player who chose α (and did not want to switch actions) in $\hat{s}$ would be interested in switching to β. This is true because the game is a coordination game and the set of players choosing α has (weakly) increased in the transition from $\hat{s}$ to $\bar{s}$. Hence the process has arrived in finite time (with positive probability) at a state in which no player has any incentive to switch actions. This is an absorbing state of the dynamics; since the initial state was arbitrary, and the above transition occurs with positive probability, the theory of Markov chains says that the transition to an absorbing state will occur in finite time, with probability 1.

An early result on convergence of dynamics to a Nash equilibrium in regular networks (where every player has the same number of neighbors) is presented in Anderlini and Ianni (1996). In their model a player is randomly matched to play with one other player in her neighborhood. Moreover, every player gets a chance to revise her move in every period. Finally, a player who plans to switch actions can make an error with some probability. They refer to this as noise on the margin. With this decision rule, the dynamic process of choices converges to a Nash equilibrium for a class of regular networks. The result presented here holds for all networks and does not rely on mistakes for convergence. Instead, the above result exploits inertia of individual decisions and the coordination nature of the game to obtain convergence.

Theorem 4.2 shows that the learning process converges. This result also says that every Nash equilibrium (for a given network of interaction) is an absorbing state of the process. This means that there is no hope of selecting across the variety of equilibria identified earlier in proposition 4.1 with this dynamic process. This finding motivates a study of relative stability of different equilibria with respect to small but repeated perturbations, i.e., stochastic stability of outcomes.

The ideas underlying stochastic stability can be informally described as follows. Suppose that s and s' are the two absorbing states of the best-response dynamics described above. Given that s is an absorbing state, a movement from s to s' requires an error or an experiment on the part of one or more of the players. Similarly, a movement from s' to s requires errors on the part of some subset of players. We will follow standard practice in this field and refer to such errors/experiments as *mutations*. The state s is said to be stochastically stable if it requires more mutations to move from s to s' than to move from s' to s. If it takes the same number of mutations to move between the two states, then they are both stochastically stable.

Formally, suppose that players occasionally make mistakes, experiment, or simply disregard payoff considerations in choosing their strategies. Assume that, conditional on receiving a revision opportunity at any point in time t, a player chooses her strategy at random with some small *mutation* probability $\epsilon > 0$. Given a network g, and for any $\epsilon > 0$, the mutation process defines a Markov chain that is aperiodic and irreducible and, therefore, has a unique invariant probability distribution; denote this distribution by μ_g^ϵ.[7] The analysis will study the support of μ_g^ϵ as the probability of mistakes becomes very small, i.e., as ϵ converges to 0. Define $\lim_{\epsilon \to 0} \mu_g^\epsilon = \hat{\mu}_g$. A state s is said to be *stochastically stable* if $\hat{\mu}_g(s) > 0$. This notion of stability identifies states that are relatively more stable with respect to such mutations.[8]

We will now examine the effects of the network of interaction, g, on the set of stochastically stable states. We will consider the complete network, local interaction around the circle, and the star network.

Example 4.1 (the complete network). This example considers the complete network in which every player is a neighbor of every other player. Suppose that player 1 is deciding on whether to choose α or β. It is easy to verify that at least $k = (n-1)(b-d)/[(a-e)+(b-d)]$ players need to choose α for α to be optimal for player 1 as well. Similarly, the minimum number of players needed to induce player 1 to choose β is $l = (n-1)(a-e)/[(a-e)+(b-d)]$. Given the assumption that $a + d > b + e$, it follows that $k < l$. If everyone is choosing α, then it takes l mutations to transit to a state where everyone is choosing β; likewise, if everyone is choosing β, then it takes k mutations to transit to a state where everyone is choosing α. From the general observations on stochastic stability above, it then follows that in the complete network everyone choosing the risk-dominant action α is the unique stochastically stable outcome.

$\triangle$

Example 4.2 (local interaction around a circle). This example considers local interaction with immediate neighbors around a circle and is taken from Ellison (1993). Suppose that at time $t - 1$ every player is choosing β. Now suppose that

---

[7] This follows from standard results in the theory of Markov chains (see, for example, Billingsley 1985).

[8] These ideas have been applied extensively to develop a theory of equilibrium selection in game theory. The notion of stochastic stability was introduced into economics by Kandori, Mailath, and Rob (1993) and Young (1993).

two adjacent players i and $i + 1$ choose action α at time t, due to a mutation in the process. It is now easy to verify that, in the next period $t + 1$, the immediate neighbors of i and $i + 1$, players $i - 1$ and $i + 2$, will find it optimal to switch to action α (this is due to the assumption that α is risk-dominant and $a + d > b + e$). Moreover, in period $t + 2$ the immediate neighbors of $i - 1$ and $i + 2$ will have a similar incentive, and so there is a process under way which leads to everyone choosing action α, within finite time. On the other hand, if everyone is choosing α, then $n/2$ players must switch to β to induce a player to switch to action β. To see why this is the case, note that a player bases her decision on the actions of immediate neighbors, and so long as at least one of the neighbors is choosing α the optimal action is to choose α. It then follows that everyone choosing the risk-dominant action α is the unique stochastically stable state. $\triangle$

The simplicity of the above arguments suggests the following conjecture: the risk-dominant outcome obtains in all networks. This conjecture is false, as the following example illustrates.

Example 4.3 (the star network). This example considers interaction on a star; recall that a star is a network in which one player has links, and hence interacts, with all the other $n - 1$ players, while the other players have no links between them. This example is taken from Jackson and Watts (2002). Suppose that player 1 is the central player of the star network. The first point to note about a star network is that there are only two possible equilibrium configurations, both involving social conformism. A study of stochastically stable actions therefore involves a study of the relative stability of these two configurations. However, it is easily verified that in a star network a perturbation which switches the action of player 1 is sufficient to get a switch of all the other players. Since this is also the minimum number of mutations possible, it follows that both states are stochastically stable! $\triangle$

Examples 4.1–4.3 show that network structure has an important bearing on the nature of stochastically stable states. They also raise two types of questions. The first question pertains to network structure. Is it possible to identify general features of networks that sustain conformism and diversity, and tell which type of conformism a network favors? The second question relates to the decision rules. Is the role of interaction structures sensitive to the formulation of decision rules and the probability of mutations? The first question appears to be an open one;[9] section 4.2.3 takes up the second question.

We conclude this section by discussing the effects of the network of interaction on the rates of convergence of the dynamic process. From a practical point of view, the invariant distribution $\hat{\mu}_g$ is only meaningful if the rate of convergence of the

---

[9] There is a small experimental literature on coordination games which studies specific structures of local interaction (see, for example, Cassar, forthcoming; Berninghaus, Ehrhart, and Keser 2002; My, Willinger, and Ziegelmeyer 1999).

dynamics is relatively quick. In the above model the dynamics are Markovian
and if there is a unique invariant distribution, then standard mathematical results
suggest that the rate of convergence is exponential. In other words, there is some
number $\rho < 1$ such that the probability distribution of actions at time t, μ^t,
approaches the invariant distribution μ^* at a rate approximately given by ρ^t.
While this result is helpful, it is easy to see that this property allows a fairly wide
range of rates of convergence, depending on the value of ρ. If ρ is close to 1,
then the process is essentially determined by the initial configuration for a long
period, while if ρ is close to 0, then initial conditions play a less important role and
dynamics shape individual choices quickly. The work of Ellison (1993) directed
attention to the role of interaction structure in shaping the rate of convergence. He
argued that in a complete network transition between strict Nash equilibria based
on mutations would take a very long time in large populations since the number
of mutations needed is of the order of the population. By contrast, as example 4.2
showed under local interaction around a circle, a couple of mutations (followed by
best responses) are sufficient to initiate a transition to the risk-dominant action.
Thus local interaction leads to dramatically faster rates of convergence to the
risk-dominant action.[10]

4.2.3   Related Themes

The study of social coordination with local interaction has been a very active field
of research and a number of themes have been explored. This section discusses two
strands of this work. One, we consider other decision rules and two, we discuss
the implications of imposing restrictions on initial configurations of actions.

Alternative decision rules.   In the discussion above, we started with a myopic
best-response decision rule. We then complemented it with small but persistent
mutations and looked at what happens as the probability of mutations becomes
small. We now discuss alternatives to the best-response rule with equiprobable
mutations. A first step in this exercise is to consider an alternative formulation
of decision rules in which individual experimentation is more sensitive to payoff
losses. In any period t, an individual i located in network g is drawn at random
and chooses α (say) according to a probability distribution, $p_i^\gamma(\alpha \mid s^t, g)$, where
$\gamma > 0$ and s^t is the strategy profile at time t:

$$p_i^\gamma(\alpha \mid s^t, g) = \frac{e^{\gamma \Pi_i(\alpha, s^t_{-i} \mid g)}}{e^{\gamma \Pi_i(\alpha, s^t_{-i} \mid g)} + e^{\gamma \Pi_i(\beta, s^t_{-i} \mid g)}}. \tag{4.3}$$

This is referred to as the log-linear response rule; in the context of coordination
games, this rule was first studied by Blume (1993). Note that for large values
of γ the probability distribution will place most of the probability mass on the

---

[10] For a general result on rates of convergence in networks, see Young (2005).

best-response action. Define $\Delta_i(s \mid g) = \Pi_i(\beta, s_{-i} \mid g) - \Pi_i(\alpha, s_{-i} \mid g)$. Then for large γ the probability of action α is

$$p_i^\gamma(\alpha \mid s^t, g) = \frac{e^{-\gamma \Delta_i(s^t \mid g)}}{1 + e^{-\gamma \Delta_i(s^t \mid g)}} \cong e^{-\gamma \Delta_i(s^t \mid g)}. \qquad (4.4)$$

This expression says that the probability of not choosing the best response is exponentially declining in the payoff loss from the deviation. The analysis of local learning in coordination games when individuals use the log-linear decision rule is summarized in the following result, due to Young (1998).

Theorem 4.3. *Consider a social coordination game on a connected network g. Suppose that in each period one individual is picked at random to revise choices. In revising choices this individual uses the log-linear response rule. Then the stochastically stable outcome is a state in which every player chooses the risk-dominant action.*

This result tells us that if the mutation probabilities are payoff sensitive in a strong form—the probability of choosing an action is exponentially declining in payoff losses associated with it—then the network structure has no effect on the long-run distribution of actions. To get some intuition for the result it is useful to discuss the dynamic process in the star network. In that example, the simplest way to get a transition is via a switch in the action of the central player. In the standard model, with payoff-insensitive mutations, the probability of the central player making a switch from α to β is the same as the other way around. By contrast, under the log-linear response rule, matters are very different. If there are many peripheral players, then there is a significant difference in the payoff losses involved and the probability of switching from α to β is significantly smaller than the probability of switching from β to α. This difference is crucial for obtaining the above result.

The mutation structure has been the subject of considerable research over the years. In an influential paper, Bergin and Lipman (1996) showed that any outcome could be supported as stochastically stable under a suitable mutation structure. This "anything is possible" result has provoked several responses and two of them are worth discussing here. The first response interprets mutations as errors, and says that these errors can be controlled at some cost. This argument has been developed in van Damme and Weibull (2002). This paper shows that incorporating this cost structure leads back to the risk-dominant equilibrium. This line of research has been further extended to cover local interaction on general weighted graphs by Baron et al. (2002). A second response is to argue that risk dominance obtains for any possible mutation rule, if some additional conditions are satisfied. In this vein, a recent paper by Lee, Szeidl, and Valentinyi (2003) argues that, given any state-dependent mutation process, under local interaction on a two-dimensional torus, the dynamics select for the risk-dominant action, provided the number of players is sufficiently large.

We turn next to a consideration of decision rules that are different in a more fundamental way from the best-response principle. A simple and widely studied rule of thumb is *imitation*: *choose an action that yields the highest payoffs, among all the actions that are currently chosen by all others.*[11] Robson and Vega-Redondo (1996) study this rule in the context of social coordination games, and show that, taken together with random matching, it leads to the efficient action being the unique stochastically stable action. The study of imitation dynamics in a model with local interaction and suitable informational constraints appears to be an open problem.

Restrictions on the initial configuration. In the discussion of the dynamics above, no restrictions were placed on the initial configuration of actions. A number of papers have examined the nature of dynamics under restrictions on initial configuration. Two approaches will be discussed here as they illustrate quite different types of restrictions on initial conditions. The first one uses a random process to determine the initial configuration: every individual independently chooses an action with some probability. This random choice determines the starting point of the dynamic process. Lee and Valentinyi (2000) study the spread of actions on a two-dimensional lattice starting with this random assignment of initial actions. They show that if individuals use the best-response rule, then all players eventually choose the risk-dominant action.

The second approach considers the following problem. If we start with a small group of players choosing an action, what are the features of the network that allow for this behavior to be taken up by the entire population?[12] Morris (2000) shows that maximal contagion occurs when local interaction is sufficiently uniform and there is slow neighbor growth, i.e., the number of players who can be reached in d steps does not grow exponentially in d.

4.3 Games of Conflict

This section studies effects of interaction structure in situations where incentives of individuals are in conflict with socially desirable outcomes. Potential conflict between incentives of individuals and socially desirable outcomes is clearly an important dimension of social and economic life and the importance of this problem has motivated an extensive literature on the evolution of social norms. This literature spans the fields of biology, computer science, philosophy, and political science, in addition to economics.[13] However, it seems that few analytical results with regard to the effects of network structure on social cooperation have been

---

[11] This rule is also used in the study of altruism in section 4.3.

[12] See Goyal (1996) for a discussion of specific networks and some case studies.

[13] For a survey, see, for example, Ullman-Margalit (1977), Axelrod (1997), and Nowak and May (1992).

obtained. The presentation here will be based on Eshel, Samuelson, and Shaked (1998).[14]

The provision of local public goods illustrates the economic issues very well: every individual contributes to an activity and all the individuals in her neighborhood benefit from it.[15] Suppose there are $N = \{1, 2, \ldots, n\}$ players (where n is assumed to be large) and each player has a choice between two actions C (contribute) and D (defect or not contribute). Let $s_i = \{C, D\}$ denote the strategy of player i and as usual let $s = (s_1, s_2, s_3, \ldots, s_n)$ refer to the strategy profile of the players. Define $n_i(C, s_{-i} \mid g)$ to be the number of neighbors of player i in network g who choose C given the strategy profile s_{-i}. The payoffs to player i, in network g, from choosing C, given the strategy profile s_{-i}, are

$$\Pi_i(C, s_{-i} \mid g) = n_i(C, s_{-i} \mid g) - e, \qquad (4.5)$$

where $e > 0$ is the cost associated with the (contribution) action C. On the other hand, the payoffs to player i from action D are

$$\Pi_i(D, s_{-i} \mid g) = n_i(C, s_{-i} \mid g). \qquad (4.6)$$

Since $e > 0$, it follows that action D strongly dominates action C. So, if players are payoff optimizers, then they will never choose C. Thus it is necessary to have at least some players using alternative decision rules if there is to be any chance of action C being adopted.

4.3.1   Imitation and Altruism

Suppose that all players use an *imitate the best action* rule: compare the average payoffs from the two actions in the neighborhood and choose the action that attains the higher average payoff. Moreover, if everyone chooses the same action, then payoffs across different actions cannot be compared and an individual persists with the current action.

As in the previous sections consider a dynamic model in which time is discrete and indexed by $t = 1, 2, \ldots$. Suppose that in each period a player gets a chance to revise her strategy with some probability $p \in (0, 1)$. This probability is independent across individuals and across time. Let the strategy profile at time t be denoted by s^t. The above decision rule along with an initial action profile, s^1, define a Markov process where the states of the process are the strategy profiles. Recall that a state (or a set of states) is said to be absorbing if the process cannot escape from the state once it is reached. The interest is in the relation between the interaction structure and the nature of the absorbing state (or set of states) of the dynamic process.

---

[14] For an alternative approach to this problem, see Mobius and Szeidl (2006).

[15] Clearing the snow in front of one's house, having the night-light on, playing music at reasonable hours and at a low volume, and trimming the hedges and maintaining a garden are some everyday activities that fit the description of local public goods.

Consider first the complete network. If both actions are being chosen in a society, then it follows from simple computations that the average payoffs from choosing D are larger than the payoffs from choosing C.[16] This means that the outcome in which everyone chooses action D will obtain. Thus *starting from any initial configuration (except the extreme case where everyone is doing C), the dynamic process will converge to a state in which everyone chooses D.* This negative result on the prospects of contribution under the complete network leads to an exploration of local interaction.

So consider next the contribution game with local interaction around a circle.[17] Let $N_i(g) = \{i-1, i+1\}$ be the neighborhood of player i and let this interaction network be denoted by g^{circle}. The payoffs to player i in g^{circle} are $n_i(C, s_{-i} \mid g^{\text{circle}}) - e$ if player i chooses C and $n_i(C, s_{-i} \mid g^{\text{circle}})$ if she chooses action D.

In the following discussion, to focus attention on an interesting range of costs, it will be assumed that $e < \frac{1}{2}$. Suppose that there is a string of three players choosing action C, and they are surrounded on both sides by a population of players choosing D. Given the decision rule, any change in actions can only occur at the boundaries. What are the payoffs observed by the player choosing action C on the boundary? Well, she observes one player choosing D with a payoff of 1, while she observes one player choosing action C with payoff $2 - e$. Moreover, she observes her own payoff of $1 - e$, as well. Given that $e < \frac{1}{2}$, it follows that she prefers action C. On the other hand, the player on the boundary choosing action D observes one player choosing action D, with payoff 0, one player choosing action C with payoff $1-e$, and herself with a payoff 1. Given that $e < \frac{1}{2}$, she prefers to switch to action C. This suggests that the region of altruists will expand. Note, however, that if everyone except one player is choosing action C, then the player choosing D will get a payoff of 2 and since this is the maximum possible payoff, this will induce her neighbors to switch to action D. However, as they expand, this group of egoists will find that their payoffs fall (as the interior of the interval can no longer free ride on the altruists). These considerations suggest that a long string of players choosing action C can be sustained, while a long string of players choosing D will be difficult to sustain. These arguments are summarized in the following result, due to Eshel, Samuelson, and Shaked (1998).

Theorem 4.4. *Consider the contribution game with local interaction around a circle and suppose that $e < \frac{1}{2}$. Absorbing sets are of two types: they contain*

---

[16] Note that, in a complete network, with a strategy profile where K players choose C, the average payoffs to a C player are $K - 1 - e$, while the average payoffs to a D player are K.

[17] Tieman, Houba, and van der Laan (2000) consider a related model of cooperative behavior with local interaction in games with conflict. In their model, players are located on a network and play a generalized (many-action) version of the prisoner's dilemma. They find that with local interaction and a tit-for-tat-type decision rule, superior payoff actions which are dominated can survive in the population, in the long run.

a singleton state in which all players choose either action C *or action* D*; they contain states in which there are strings of* C *players of length 3 or more which are separated by strings of* D *players of length 2. In the latter case, at least 60% of the players choose action* C.

It is worth commenting on the relative proportions of C players in mixed configurations. First note that a string of D players cannot be of size 3 or longer (in an absorbing state). If it is, then the boundary D players will each have two players choosing C on one side and a player choosing D who is surrounded by D players. It is easy to show that these boundary players will switch to C. Likewise, there have to be at least three players in each string of C players; otherwise, the boundary players will switch to D. These considerations put together yield the proportions mentioned in the result above.

Given the above arguments, it is easily seen that in any initial string of five players who are choosing C at least three players will remain with action C, forever. If players strategies are randomly chosen initially, then it follows that the probability of such a string of C players can be made arbitrarily close to 1, by suitably increasing the number of players. This idea is summarized in the following result, due to Eshel, Samuelson, and Shaked (1998).

Theorem 4.5. *Consider the contribution game with local interaction around a circle and suppose that* $e < \frac{1}{2}$. *Suppose that players' initial strategy choices are determined by independent and identically distributed variables where the probability of* C *and* D *is positive. Then the probability of convergence to an absorbing set containing states with at least 60% of* C *players goes to* 1, *as* n *gets large.*

This result shows that, with local interaction around a circle, in large societies a majority of individuals will contribute, in the long run.[18]

So far the discussion on network effects has been restricted to the case of pure local interaction among agents located on a circle. This raises the question, how likely is contribution in more general structures of interaction? In the case of pure local interaction around a circle, the persistence and spread of cooperative behavior appears to be related to the presence of C players who are protected from D players and therefore earn sufficiently high payoffs so that other C players on the boundary persist with action C as well. In higher-dimensional interaction (e.g., k-dimensional lattices) or asymmetric interaction (as in a star) this protective wall can be harder to create and this may make altruism more vulnerable. The following example illustrates this.

Example 4.4 (altruism in a star network). First note that mixed configurations in which some individuals choose C while others choose D are not possible in

---

[18] Eshel, Samuelson, and Shaked (1998) also study stochastic stability of different absorbing sets. They show that the states identified in the above proposition are also the stochastically stable ones.

a star. Therefore only the two pure strategy configurations—everyone choosing C or everyone choosing D—are possible in an absorbing state. What is the relative robustness of these two absorbing states? As in the previous section, let us examine the stochastic stability of the two states. It is possible to move from a purely altruistic society to a purely egoist society, via a switch by the central player, followed by imitation by the rest. The reverse transition requires switching of action by at least three players, the central player and two peripheral players. Thus if interaction is on a star network, then all individuals will choose D and contribution will be zero, in the stochastically stable outcome.   △

These arguments taken along with the earlier discussion on the pure local interaction model suggest that the structure of interaction has profound effects on the levels of contribution that can be sustained in a society. These observations also lead back to a general question posed in the introduction: are some interaction structures better than others at sustaining contributions (and hence efficient outcomes), and what is the relation between interaction structures and diversity of actions?

Existing work on this subject seems to be mostly based on simulations (Buskens 1996; Nowak and May 1992; Nowak and Sigmund 2005).[19] This work suggests that, in the absence of mutations, altruism can survive in a variety of interaction settings. There is also an extensive literature in evolutionary biology on the emergence and persistence of altruistic traits in different species. In this work the spread of altruistic traits is attributed to greater reproductive success. This success leads to the larger set of altruists spilling into neighboring areas and this in turn leads to a growth of the trait over time (see, for example, Wynne-Edwards 1986; Eshel and Cavalli-Sforza 1982).

4.3.2 Related Themes

In the discussion above it was assumed that individuals were engaged in a one-shot interaction. In practice, many of the contribution games are repeated over time among the same set of individuals. While the literature on repeated games is very large, it seems that there is relatively little on repeated games with local interaction.[20] In a recent paper, Haag and Lagunoff (2006) examine a setting in which players play the repeated prisoner's dilemma game with their immediate neighbors. They examine the network architectures which support high cooperation, when discount factors vary across players. Their main result shows that a cooperative action is facilitated by an interaction structure with the following

---

[19] There is also a small experimental literature which examines cooperative behavior in games with local interaction (see Mobius, Quoc-Anh, and Rosenblat (2004) and Cassar (forthcoming) for some recent work).

[20] For analysis of repeated games among players who are randomly matched, see Ellison (1994) and Kandori (1992). For an early model of reputations in social networks, see Raub and Weesie (1990).

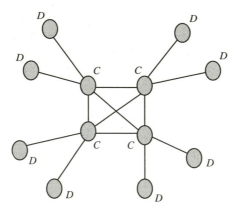

Figure 4.3.   Cooperative core plus defecting peripheral players.

properties: *there is a clique of patient players (who are fully linked among them-selves) each of whom is linked to a small set of impatient players.* Figure 4.3 presents an example of such a network.

In equilibrium, each of the players in the clique of patient players chooses the cooperative action while the impatient players at the periphery all choose to play the defect action. The players in the core of the network play cooperatively in spite of the defection of the periphery players because they are patient and their cooperative play is reciprocated by other patient players in the core group. This optimal structure may be interpreted as supporting the role of network closure—the property that a player's neighbors know each other—in sustaining cooperation. Network closure has been a prominent theme in the literature on trust and social capital since the early work of Coleman (1988).

4.4   Concluding Remarks

This chapter examined the effects of patterns of connections on the prospects of social coordination and cooperation.

We began with a study of games of coordination. The first finding was that multiple equilibria in which individuals all choose the same action obtain in all networks; however, the interaction structure plays a crucial role in determining whether diversity of actions is sustainable. This finding led to a study of stochastic stability of different actions. The second finding was that if individuals choose best responses and perturbations to actions are random and equiprobable, then the stochastic stability of different actions depends on the interaction structure. How-ever, a characterization of interaction structures which support different stochas-tically stable outcomes remains an open problem. These arguments motivated a model of choice in which the probability of different actions is exponentially declining in the payoff losses associated with them. The third finding was that with this decision rule, known as the log-linear rule, the risk-dominant action obtains for all networks. This finding, however, leads to the following two questions. What are reasonable models of decision making? Are different modes of decision making better suited to specific networks of interaction? The above three findings pertain to the relation between network structure and long-run outcomes. The long-run outcome is only meaningful if it obtains relatively soon and this led to a discussion on rates of convergence. The fourth finding was that the pattern of connections plays a crucial role in determining the speed of convergence to the risk-dominant action.

Games of conflict cover an important class of decision situations but there appears to be relatively little analytical work on the role of interaction structures in shaping individual behavior. The presentation in this chapter focused on a game of contribution with local interaction. In this game it is a dominant strategy for each individual not to contribute but this led to the socially inefficient outcome. The first finding was that a combination of imitation-based decision making and pure local interaction was needed to ensure high levels of contribution. The second finding was that pure local interaction among individuals located around a circle also supported a diversity of actions, with some individuals making positive contributions while others make no contributions. However, a discussion of some other interaction structures, such as the star, suggested that these findings are sensitive to the precise model of local interaction. Thus the possibility of cooperative behavior in more general networks of interaction remains an open question.

4.5 Appendix

4.5.1 Coordination Games

Recall that s_i denotes the strategy of player i and $S_i = \{\alpha, \beta\}$ is the strategy set. Let $\prod_{i \in N}$ denote the set of all strategy profiles in the game and let s refer to a typical member of this set. In the two-player game, let $\pi(x, y)$ denote the payoffs to player i when she chooses action x while her opponent chooses action y. The payoffs to a player i from a strategy s_i, given that the other players are choosing s_{-i}, are then

$$\Pi_i(s_i, s_{-i} \mid g) = \sum_{j \in N_i(g)} \pi(s_i, s_j). \tag{4.7}$$

The following result gives a first impression of the effects of networks on equilibrium play in a coordination game.

Theorem 4.6. *Consider a social coordination game. A strategy profile in which everyone plays the same action is a Nash equilibrium for every network $g \in \mathcal{G}$. If the network is complete, then these are the only possible Nash equilibria. If the* *network is incomplete, then there may exist equilibria with a diversity of actions as well.*

Proof. If everyone chooses an action then it is clearly optimal to choose the same action, irrespective of the network of interaction. So the existence of equilibrium with complete conformism is straightforward in games of coordination. It is now shown that in a complete network these are the only possible outcomes. Suppose that players are in a complete network and $1 \leqslant k < n$ players are choosing action α, while $n - k$ players are choosing β. Since this is an equilibrium it must be the case that for an α player the payoff from α must exceed the payoff from choosing β:

$$(k - 1)a + (n - k)d \geqslant (k - 1)e + (n - k)b.$$

Similarly, for a player choosing β the payoffs from action β must exceed the payoffs from action α:

$$ke + (n - k - 1)b \geqslant ka + (n - k - 1)d.$$

It is easily checked that these two inequalities cannot be simultaneously satisfied.

The simplest way to sustain diverse actions is to consider a society constituted of two distinct components, C_1 and C_2. It is clearly an equilibrium for players in C_1 to choose α, while players in C_2 choose β. The incentives in these distinct components can be generalized and also hold when the two components have a few connections between them. To see this consider the case illustrated in figure 4.2. There exists a range of values for which the following configuration is an equilibrium: players 1, 2, 3, and 4 choose action α, while players 5, 6, 7, and 8 choose action β. Clearly, it is optimal for players 1, 2, and 3 to choose action α, since all their potential partners choose α. Player 4 will choose action α so long as $3(a - e) \geqslant b - d$. Similarly, action β is clearly optimal for players 6, 7, and 8, while it is optimal for player 5 if $3(b - d) \geqslant a - e$. It is easily seen that the incentives of players 4 and 5 are compatible for a range of values. $\square$

Theorem on the log-linear decision rule.   This result exploits the concept of a potential function. A game has a potential if there exists a real-valued function $F(x, y)$ and a rescaling of the utility functions such that, whenever a player deviates unilaterally, the change in payoff equals the change in the potential. For a symmetric two-player game, this means that there exists a symmetric function $F(x, y) = F(y, x)$ such that for some rescaling of utilities, π_i, and for all $x, x', y \in S_i$,

$$\pi_i(x, y) - \pi_i(x', y) = F(x, y) - F(x', y). \qquad (4.8)$$

Next note that if a symmetric two-player game admits a potential, then so does the corresponding social game on a network g. To see this let x be a profile of actions in the social game, and suppose that player i deviates by choosing x_i'. Let $x' = (x_i', x_{-i})$. Then

$$
\begin{aligned}
\Pi_i(x \mid g) - \Pi_i(x' \mid g) &= \sum_{j \in N_i(g)} [\pi_i(x_i, x_j) - \pi_i(x_i', x_j)] \\
&= \sum_{j \in N_i(g)} [F(x_i, x_j) - F(x_i', x_j)] \\
&= \sum_{g_{h,k}=1} F(x_h, x_k) - \sum_{g_{h,k}=1} F(x_h', x_k'), \qquad (4.9)
\end{aligned}
$$

where $g_{h,k} = 1$ refers to all links that are present in network g. It follows that a potential for the social game is

$$
F^*(x \mid g) = \sum_{g_{h,k}=1} F(x_h, x_k). \qquad (4.10)
$$

Now suppose that in every period an individual is picked with equal probability to revise her actions. Player i uses the log-linear decision rule in revising her action. This rule says that the probability of choosing action α is

$$
p_i^\gamma(\alpha \mid s^t, g) = \frac{e^{\gamma \Pi_i(\alpha, s_{-i}^t \mid g)}}{e^{\gamma \Pi_i(\alpha, s_{-i}^t \mid g)} + e^{\gamma \Pi_i(\beta, s_{-i}^t \mid g)}}, \qquad (4.11)
$$

where $\gamma > 0$.

Given a network g, let P_g^γ be the probability transition matrix corresponding to the dynamic process and the log-linear decision rule with some $\gamma > 0$. The following result on long-run behavior of the system, due to Young (1998), can now be stated and proved.

Theorem 4.7. *Consider a symmetric two-person game with potential function F. Let g be an undirected graph. For every $\gamma > 0$, the adaptive process P_g^γ has the unique stationary distribution,*

$$
\mu_g^\gamma = \frac{e^{\gamma F^*(x \mid g)}}{\sum_{z \in S} e^{\gamma F^*(z \mid g)}}, \qquad (4.12)
$$

where $F^*(x \mid g)$ is defined as in (4.10). The stochastically stable states of the social game are those that maximize $F^*(x \mid g)$. In the social coordination game considered earlier, this implies the stochastically stable outcome is a state in which every player chooses the risk-dominant action.

Proof. For simplicity write μ instead of μ_g^γ and P instead of P_g^γ. The detailed balanced condition states

$$
\mu(x) P(xy) = \mu(y) P(yx) \quad \text{for all } x, y \in S. \qquad (4.13)
$$

It is shown that μ satisfies this detailed balance condition. First observe that $P(xy) > 0$ only if either $x = y$ or x and y differ for exactly one player. Note that any player is chosen with probability $1/n$. This means that

$$\mu(x)P(xy) = \frac{1}{n}\left[\frac{e^{\gamma F^*(x|g)}}{\sum_{z\in S} e^{\gamma F^*(z|g)}}\right]\left[\frac{\exp(\gamma \sum_{j\in N_i} \pi_i(y_i, x_j))}{\sum_{z_i\in S_i} \exp(\gamma \sum_{j\in N_i} \pi_i(z_i, x_j))}\right]. \tag{4.14}$$

Define

$$\lambda = \frac{1}{n}\left[\frac{1}{\sum_{z\in \mathcal{S}} e^{\gamma F^*(z|g)}}\right]\left[\frac{1}{\sum_{z_i\in S_i} \exp(\gamma \sum_{j\in N_i} \pi_i(z_i, x_j))}\right]. \tag{4.15}$$

This allows us to rewrite equation (4.14) as

$$\mu(x)P(xy) = \lambda \exp\left[\gamma\left[\sum_{g_{h,k}=1} F(x_h, x_k) + \sum_{j\in N_i(g)} \pi_i(y_i, x_j)\right]\right]$$

$$= \lambda \exp\left[\gamma\left[\sum_{g_{h,k}=1} F(x_h, x_k)\right.\right.$$

$$\left.\left. + \sum_{j\in N_i(g)} [\pi_i(x_i, x_j) - F(x_i, x_j) + F(y_i, x_j)]\right]\right]$$

$$= \lambda \exp\left[\gamma\left[\sum_{g_{h,k}=1} F(y_h, y_k) + \sum_{j\in N_i(g)} \pi_i(x_i, x_j)\right]\right]$$

$$= \mu(y)P(yx). \tag{4.16}$$

This proves that $\mu(\cdot)$ satisfies the detailed balanced condition. Given that the detailed balance condition holds, it then follows that

$$\sum_{x\in S} \mu(x)P(xy) = \sum_{x\in S} \mu(y)P(yx) = \mu(y)\sum_{x\in S} P(yx) = \mu(y). \tag{4.17}$$

Thus μ is an invariant distribution, and since the process is irreducible it is the unique invariant distribution. The claim on stochastically stable states now follows from the behavior of μ as $\gamma \to \infty$.

Note next that there exists a potential function in the coordination game:

$$F(\alpha, \alpha) = a - e, \qquad F(\alpha, \beta) = F(\beta, \alpha) = 0, \qquad F(\beta, \beta) = b - d.$$

Next define $w_\alpha(x)$ ($w_\beta(x)$) as the total number of player pairs who choose α (β) in profile x. Then it follows that the probability of profile x in the invariant distribution $\mu(x)$ is proportional to $e^{(a-e)w_\alpha + (b-d)w_\beta}$. If α is risk-dominant, then $a - e > b - d$ and it follows that $\mu(\cdot)$ places all probability mass on the state where everyone chooses the risk-dominant action. $\qquad\square$

4.5.2 Games of Conflict

The following payoffs are exploited in the proofs: the payoff to a boundary C player in a string of three Cs will be $1 - e$, while the payoff to the adjoining C player will be $2 - e$, and the payoff to the adjoining (boundary) D player will be 1 if she faces one C player and 2 if she faces two C players. Note also that the payoff to an isolated C player is $-e$, while the payoff to an isolated D player is 2.

Theorem 4.8. *Consider the contribution game with local interaction around a circle and suppose that $e < \frac{1}{2}$. Absorbing sets are of two types: they contain a singleton state in which all players choose either action C or action D; they contain states in which there are strings of C players of length 3 or more which are separated by strings of D players of length 2. In the latter case, at least 60% of the players choose action C.*

Proof. It is clear that pure states in which everyone does C or D are absorbing states, under the imitation decision rule. So the proof focuses on the mixed states.

Consider initial strings of Cs. If this string is a singleton, then clearly it does worse than the neighboring Ds and so it will disappear. Similarly, a string of two Cs will disappear. Moreover, a simple enumeration of different possibilities shows that they will not create any new C converts in the process either.

Consider next a string of three Cs. This string can either expand, by the conversion of neighboring Ds or shrink by the conversion of Cs. Note from payoffs that such a string can only expand if there are three or more Ds next it. This implies that two C strings cannot merge. Thus the number of strings of three or more Cs will either remain fixed or shrink; moreover, no new strings of Cs can emerge.

Putting these facts together we get the following. There exists a time τ such that at this time the number of strings of Cs is equal to or less than the number of C strings at the start. Moreover, the number of C strings at all points after τ is equal to the number at time τ. Finally, all C strings are of length 3 or more.

Consider next the length of the D strings after time τ. The first observation is that the number of such strings is equal to the number of C strings. Next note that a D string of length 1 expands by 2, a string of length 2 stays put, while a string of length 3 or more shrinks by 2. So after a point there will only be strings of D of length 2, under the assumption that $p < 1$. Thus starting from any mixed initial state at point τ the system will arrive at a situation in which every C string has length 3 or more, while every D string is of length 2. Given that the number of strings choosing different actions are equal, the statement on proportion of C types follows. $\qquad\square$

Theorem 4.9. *Consider the contribution game with local interaction around a circle and suppose that $e < \frac{1}{2}$. Suppose that players' initial strategy choices are* *determined by independent and identically distributed random variables where the probability of each strategy is positive. Then the probability of convergence to an absorbing set containing states with at least 60% of C players goes to 1, as n gets large.*

Proof. Note that if the initial profile has a string of five or more C players, then there will be a string of at least three Cs forever. This is because any shrinkage (from a size of five or more) in the C string means that there are two or more neighboring Ds (next to this shorter C string). However, from arguments in the proof of theorem 4.8 above it follows that such a string of Ds cannot expand any further. Thus if the process starts with a string of five or more Cs, then there will always exist a string of at least three. The argument is completed by noting that, in an independent and identically distributed draw where all actions have positive probability, the probability of having a string of five or more Cs goes to 1, as n gets large.   □

5
Social Learning

5.1 Introduction

We often have to choose among alternatives without knowing their relative advantages. In arriving at a decision we make use of our past experience as well as the experience of others, especially those who are *close* to us. Two individuals may be said to be close if they know each other very well or if they have several common acquaintances. This type of closeness is important because the costs of communication with close acquaintances or friends are lower and also because an individual may find it easier to trust someone whom he knows. A second possible interpretation of "closeness" is in terms of similarity of preferences or needs. We are especially keen to know the experience of others who have similar tastes or face similar economic constraints. These ideas are clarified via the following examples.

- *Consumer choice.* A consumer buying a computer chooses a brand without being fully informed about the different options. Since a computer is a major purchase, potential buyers also discusses the pros and cons of different alternatives with close friends, colleagues, and acquaintances. The importance of opinion leaders and mavens in the adoption of consumer goods has been documented in a number of studies (see, for example, Feick and Price 1987; Kotler and Armstrong 2004).

- *Medical innovation.* Doctors have to decide on new treatments for ailments without complete knowledge of their efficacy and side-effects; they read professional magazines and peer-reviewed journals as well as exchange information with other doctors in order to determine whether to prescribe a new treatment. Empirical work suggests that location in interpersonal communication networks affects the timing of prescription while the structure of the connections between physicians influences the speed of diffusion of new medicines (for a pioneering study on this, see Coleman, Katz, and Mentzel (1966)). There is also evidence that medical practices vary widely across countries and part of this difference is explained by the relatively weak communication across countries (see, for example, Taylor 1979).

• *Agricultural practices.* Farmers decide on whether to switch crops and adopt new seeds and alternative farming packages without full knowledge of their suitability for the specific soil and weather conditions they face. Empirical work shows that individuals use the experience of similar farmers in making critical decisions on adoption of new crops as well as input combinations (see, for example, Munshi 2004; Griliches 1957; Conley and Udry 2005).

In these examples the patterns of information flow between people can potentially have a decisive impact on their choices. This chapter develops a theoretical framework to study the effects of local information flows on the process of social learning.

We suppose that individuals are located on nodes of a network and the links between the nodes reflect information flows between them. At regular intervals, individuals choose an action from a set of alternatives. Since they are uncertain about the rewards from different actions they use their own past experience as well as gathering information from their *neighbors*. We will address the following questions:

(i) Are there features of networks that facilitate or hinder the adoption of optimal actions?

(ii) What are the structural features of networks that help sustain diversity of actions?

Repeated choice among alternatives whose relative advantages are imperfectly known is a common feature of many real life decision problems. Actions often yield outcomes which are informative and so the process of learning optimal actions has been extensively studied in the economics and decision theory literatures. The initial models focused on a the prospects of a single decision maker learning the optimal action in the long run (see, for example, Berry and Fristedt 1985; Rothschild 1974; Easley and Kiefer 1988). In many of the applications (as in the examples mentioned earlier in the introduction) experimentation with different alternatives is expensive and it is natural to suppose that individuals will use the experience of others in making their own choices. However, if the outcomes of individual trials yield information which is shared with others, individual experimentation becomes a public good and so choice takes on a strategic aspect, even though actions of others do not matter for individual payoffs. This motivates a study of the dynamics of strategic experimentation; for an elegant analysis of this issue, see, for example, Bolton and Harris (1999). In this line of research the actions and outcomes of any individual are commonly observed by everyone. By contrast, the focus of this chapter is on the differences in what individuals observe and how these differences affect the process of social learning.

A study of social learning yields insights into the diffusion process in networks. Diffusion in networks has been extensively studied in sociology, mathematical biology, statistical physics, and more recently in computer science. This is a vast body of work and it is not possible to discuss the different literatures here.[1] It is important, however, to reiterate a general point concerning the relationship between the economics approach to the study of diffusion in networks, which will be developed here, and the other approaches. There are two distinctive elements to an economics approach and they will figure prominently in the framework presented in this chapter: (i) an explicit model of individual beliefs, objectives, and optimal decision rules; and (ii) a concern with the attainment of socially efficient outcomes.

This chapter is organized as follows. Section 5.2 introduces a basic model of social learning. Section 5.3 presents the main analytical results, while section 5.4 discusses related themes that have been explored in the literature. Section 5.5 concludes. The proofs of the results are presented in the appendix.

5.2 Theoretical Framework

This section presents a model of social learning: an individual's reward depends only on his own actions; the rewards from different actions, however, are unknown and own actions as well as actions of others generate valuable information concerning the relative attractiveness of different actions. It is convenient to present the model in three parts: the first part lays out the decision problem faced by individuals, the second part introduces notation concerning directed networks, while the third part discusses the dynamics. The presentation here is based on the work of Bala and Goyal (1998, 2001).[2]

Decision problem. Suppose that time proceeds in discrete steps, and is indexed by $t = 1, 2, \ldots$. There are $n \geqslant 3$ individuals in a society who each choose an action from a finite set of alternatives, denoted by S_i. It is assumed that all individuals have the same choice set, i.e., $S_i = S_j = A$, for every pair of individuals i and j. Denote by $a_{i,t}$ the action taken by individual i in time period t. The payoffs from an action depend on the state of the world θ, which belongs to a finite set Θ. This state of the world is chosen by nature at the start of the process and remains fixed across time. If θ is the true state and an individual

---

[1] See Bailey (1975) for an early discussion in mathematical biology, Pastor-Satorras and Vespignani (2001, 2002) for recent work in statistical physics, and Kempe, Kleinberg, and Tardos (2003) for recent work in computer science.

[2] In an early paper, Allen (1982) studied technology adoption by a set of individuals located on nodes of a graph, who are subject to local influences. This is close in spirit to the motivation behind the framework developed here. Her work focused on invariant distributions of actions, while the interest in this chapter is on the dynamic processes of learning that arise in different networks.

chooses action $a \in A$, then he observes an outcome $y \in Y$ with conditional density $\phi(y, a; \theta)$ and obtains a reward $r(a, y)$. For simplicity, take Y to be a subset of $\mathcal{R}$, and assume that the reward function $r(a, \cdot)$ is bounded. In some examples Y will be finite and we will interpret $\phi(y, a; \theta)$ as the probability of outcome y, under action a, in state θ.

Individuals do not know the true state of the world; their private information is summarized in a prior belief over the set of states. For individual i this prior is denoted by $\mu_{i,1}$. The set of prior beliefs is denoted by $\mathcal{P}(\Theta)$. To allow for the possibility that individuals can learn about the true state of the world, it will be assumed that prior beliefs are interior, i.e., $\mu_{i,1}(\theta) > 0$, $\forall \theta$ and $\forall i \in N$. Given belief μ, an individual's one-period expected utility from action a is

$$u(a, \mu) = \sum_{\theta \in \Theta} \mu(\theta) \int_Y r(a, y) \phi(y, a; \theta) \, \mathrm{d}y. \tag{5.1}$$

The expected utility expression has a natural analogue in the finite Y case. In the basic model, it will be assumed that individuals have similar preferences which are reflected in a common reward function $r(\cdot, \cdot)$. Learning among neighbors with heterogeneous preferences will be taken up subsequently.

Given a belief, μ, an individual chooses an action that maximizes (one-period) expected payoffs. Formally, let $B : \mathcal{P}(\Theta) \to A$ be the one-period optimality correspondence:

$$B(\mu) = \{a \in A \mid u(a, \mu) \geq u(a', \mu), \ \forall a' \in A\}. \tag{5.2}$$

For each $i \in N$, let $b_i : \mathcal{P}(\Theta) \to A$ be a selection from the one-period optimality correspondence B. Let δ_θ represent point mass belief on the state θ; then $B(\delta_\theta)$ denotes the set of optimal actions if the true state is θ. A well-known special case of this decision problem is the two-armed bandit.

Example 5.1 (the two-armed bandit). Suppose $A = \{a_0, a_1\}$, $\Theta = \{\theta_0, \theta_1\}$, and $Y = \{0, 1\}$. In state θ_1, action a_1 yields Bernoulli distributed payoffs with parameter $\pi \in (\frac{1}{2}, 1)$, i.e., it yields 1 with probability π, and 0 with probability $1 - \pi$. In state θ_0, action a_1 yields a payoff of 1 with probability $1 - \pi$, and 0 with probability π. Furthermore, in both states, action a_0 yields payoffs which are Bernoulli distributed with probability $\frac{1}{2}$. Hence action a_1 is optimal in state θ_1, while action a_0 is optimal in state θ_0. The belief of an individual is a number $\mu \in (0, 1)$, which represents the probability that the true state is θ_1. The one-period optimality correspondence is

$$B(\mu) = \begin{cases} a_1 & \text{if } \mu \geq \frac{1}{2}, \\ a_0 & \text{if } \mu \leq \frac{1}{2}. \end{cases} \tag{5.3}$$

$\triangle$

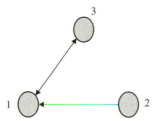

Figure 5.1. Directed information network.

An individual chooses an action $b_i(\mu_{i,1})$ and observes the outcome of his action; he also observes the actions and outcomes obtained by a subset of the others, namely, his *neighbors*. The notion of neighborhoods and related concepts are defined next.

Directed networks. Each individual is located (and identified with) a distinct node of a network. A link between two individuals i and j is denoted by g_{ij}, where $g_{ij} \in \{0, 1\}$. In the context of information networks, it is natural to allow for the possibility that individual i observes individual j, but the reverse does not hold. This motivates a model of links which are *directed*: if $g_{ij} = 1$, then there is flow of information from j to i, but we will allow for $g_{ji} = 0$ even when $g_{ij} = 1$. In figure 5.1, there are three players, 1, 2, and 3, and $g_{13} = g_{31} = g_{21} = 1$. A directed link from i to j, $g_{ij} = 1$, is represented as an arrow that ends at j.

There is a *directed* path from j to i in g either if $g_{ij} = 1$ or there exist distinct players $j_1, \ldots, j_m$ different from i and j such that $g_{ij_1} = g_{j_1 j_2} = \cdots = g_{j_m j} = 1$. For example, in figure 5.1 there is a directed path from player 3 to player 2, but the converse is not true. The notation "$j \xrightarrow{g} i$" indicates that there exists a (directed) path from j to i in g. Define $N_i(g) = \{k \mid i \xrightarrow{g} k\} \cup \{i\}$ as the set of players that i accesses either directly or indirectly in g, while $\eta_i(g) \equiv |N_i(g)|$ is the number of people accessed. The length of a path between i and j is simply the number of intervening links in the path. The distance from j to i in network g refers to the length of the shortest directed path between them in the network g, and is denoted by $d_{ij}(g)$.

Let $N_i^d(g) = \{k \in N \mid g_{ik} = 1\}$ be the set of individuals with whom i has a direct link in network g. This set $N_i^d(g)$ will be referred to as the *neighbors* of i in network g. Define $\eta_i^d(g) \equiv |N_i^d(g)|$ as the *out-degree* of individual i.[3] Analogously, let $N_{-i}^d(g) = \{k \in N \mid g_{ki} = 1\}$ be the set of people who observe i and define $\eta_{-i}^d(g) \equiv |N_{-i}^d(g)|$ as the *in-degree* of individual i.

A network g is said to be connected[4] if there exists a path between any pair of players i and j. The analysis will focus on connected networks. This is a natural

---

[3] The notation being defined here for directed networks differs from the notation defined for undirected networks in chapter 2. We use this directed networks notation in chapters 7 and 8 also.

[4] Some authors refer to this property as strongly connected.

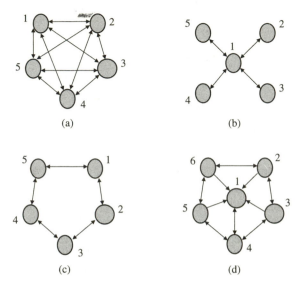

Figure 5.2. Simple information networks: (a) complete network; (b) star;
(c) local observation on a circle; (d) local plus common observation.

class of networks to consider since any network which is not connected can be
viewed as consisting of a set of connected sub-networks, and then the analysis
we present can be applied to each of the connected sub-networks. Figure 5.2
presents four simple examples of connected networks: the complete network,
a star network, local observation on a circle, and a network which combines
local and common observations. This last network reflects a situation in which
individuals gather information from their local neighborhoods and supplement it
with information from a common source. The star represents a situation in which
the in-degree and out-degree of an individual are equal, but the in-degree of the
central node is higher than that of the peripheral node. By contrast, the network
in figure 5.2(d) represents a situation in which there is significant asymmetry
between the in-degree and the out-degree of the central node, while the other
nodes have in-degree equal to the out-degree. The central individual only observes
one other node but is observed by five others.

Over the years, a number of studies have been done on the architecture of
information networks in different contexts ranging from small villages to the
World Wide Web (see, for example, Rogers 2003; Rogers and Kincaid 1981;
Broder et al. 2000). In spite of their very different contexts, these networks exhibit
some striking similarities. The first feature is the very unequal distribution of
connections. For instance, most Web sites (over 90%) have fewer than ten other
Web sites linking to them (this is their in-degree), but at the same time there exist
Web sites, such as google.com, bbc.co.uk, and cnn.com, which have hundreds
of thousands of in-coming links. Communication networks in rural communities

have been found to exhibit a similar inequality: most people in a village talk to their relatives and neighbors and to a small set of highly connected villagers leading to a skewed distribution of in-degrees (Rogers 2003). Empirical work suggests that the out-degree distribution also exhibits significant inequality.

The second feature is the asymmetry between in-degree and out-degree of a node. In many contexts, there exist a small set of nodes which have a very large in-degree and relatively small out-degree, while most other nodes have an out-degree which is larger than their in-degree. This pattern of connections arises naturally if individuals have access to local as well as some common or public source of information. For instance, in agriculture, individual farmers observe their neighboring farmers and all farmers observe a few large farms and agricultural laboratories. Similarly, in academic research, individual researchers keep track of the work of other researchers in their own narrow field of specialization and also try and keep abreast of the work of pioneers and intellectual leaders in their subject more broadly defined.

Dynamics. In period 1 each individual starts by choosing an action $b_i(\mu_{i,1})$: in other words, we assume that individuals are myopic in their choice of actions. This myopia assumption is made for simplicity: it allows us to abstract from issues concerning strategic experimentation and to focus on the role of the network in shaping social learning.[5] At the end of the period, every individual i observes the outcome of his own actions. He also observes the actions and outcomes of each of his neighbors, $j \in N_i^d(g)$. Individual i uses this information to update his prior $\mu_{i,1}$ and arrive at the prior for period 2, $\mu_{i,2}$. He then makes a decision in period 2, and so on.

In principle, the choices of an individual $j \in N_i^d$ reveal something about the priors (and hence private information) of that individual and over time will also reveal something about the actions and experience of his neighbors. However, in updating his priors, it will be assumed that an individual does not take into account the fact that the actions of his neighbors potentially reveal information about what these neighbors have observed about their neighbors. The main reason for this assumption is tractability. The study of social learning in the presence of inferences about the neighbors of neighbors is an important subject; see section 5.4 for a discussion of recent research on this topic.

We now introduce the space of outcomes and the probability space within which the dynamics occur as the notation is needed for stating the results. The details of the construction are provided in the appendix. The probability space is denoted by $(\Omega, \mathcal{F}, P^\theta)$, where Ω is the space of all outcomes, $\mathcal{F}$ is the σ field,

---

[5] We conjecture that the arguments developed in theorems 5.1–5.3 carry over to a setting with far-sighted players, so long as optimal decision rules exhibit a cutoff property in posterior beliefs (as identified, for instance, in example 5.1). The recent work of Gale and Kariv (2003) on observational learning with fully rational individuals is related to this concern; see section 5.4 for a discussion of this work.

and P^θ is a probability measure if the true state of the world is θ. Let P^θ be the probability measure induced over sample paths in Ω by the state $\theta \in \Theta$.

Let Θ be endowed with the discrete topology, and suppose $\mathcal{B}$ is the Borel σ-field on this space. For rectangles of the form $\mathcal{T} \times H$, where $\mathcal{T} \subset \Theta$ and H is a measurable subset of Ω, let $P_i(\mathcal{T} \times H)$ be given by

$$P_i(\mathcal{T} \times H) = \sum_{\theta \in \mathcal{T}} \mu_{i,1}(\theta) P^\theta(H) \tag{5.4}$$

for each individual $i \in N$. Each P_i extends uniquely to all $\mathcal{B} \times \mathcal{F}$. Since every individual's prior belief lies in the interior of $\mathcal{P}(\Theta)$, the measures $\{P_i\}$ are pairwise mutually absolutely continuous. All stochastic processes are defined on the measurable space $(\Theta \times \Omega, \mathcal{B} \times \mathcal{F})$.

A typical sample path is of the form $\omega = (\theta, \omega')$, where θ is the state of nature and ω' is an infinite sequence of sample outcomes,

$$\omega' = ((y_{i,1}^a)_{a \in A, i \in N}, (y_{i,2}^a)_{a \in A, i \in N}, \dots), \tag{5.5}$$

with $y_{i,t}^a \in Y_{i,t}^a \equiv Y$. Let $C_{i,t} = b_i(\mu_{i,t})$ denote the action of individual i in period t, $Z_{i,t}$ the outcome of this action, and let $U_{i,t} = u(C_{i,t}, \mu_{i,t})$ be the expected utility of i with respect to his own action at time t. Given this notation the posterior beliefs of individual i in period $t + 1$ are

$$\mu_{i,t+1}(\theta \mid g) = \frac{\prod_{j \in N_i^d(g) \cup \{i\}} \phi(Z_{j,t}; C_{j,t}; \theta) \mu_{i,t}(\theta)}{\sum_{\theta' \in \Theta} \prod_{j \in N_i^d(g) \cup \{i\}} \phi(Z_{j,t}; C_{j,t}; \theta) \mu_{i,t}(\theta)}. \tag{5.6}$$

The interest is in studying the influence of the network g on the evolution of individual actions, beliefs, and utilities, $(a_{i,t}, \mu_{i,t}, U_{i,t})_{i \in N}$, over time.

5.3   Learning from Neighbors

Individual actions are an optimal response to beliefs, which in turn evolve in response to the information generated by actions. Thus the dynamics of actions and beliefs feed back on each other. Over time, as an individual observes the outcomes of own actions and the actions and outcomes of neighbors, his beliefs will evolve depending on the particularities of his experience. However, it seems intuitive that, as time goes by and his experience grows, additional information should have a smaller and smaller effect on his views of the world. This intuition is captured by the following result, due to Bala and Goyal (1998), which shows that the beliefs and utilities of individuals converge.

Theorem 5.1. *The beliefs of individuals converge in the long run. More precisely, there exists $Q \in \mathcal{B} \times \mathcal{F}$ satisfying $P_i(Q) = 1$ for all $i \in N$, and random vectors $\{\mu_{i,\infty}\}$ such that $\omega \in Q \Rightarrow \lim_{t \to \infty} \mu_{i,t}(\omega) = \mu_{i,\infty}(\omega)$.*

The proof is presented in the appendix. This result follows as a corollary of a well-known mathematical result, the martingale convergence theorem (see, for example, Billingsley 1985).

In what follows, we will take θ_1 to be the true state of nature. Note that

$$Q^{\theta_1} = \{\omega = (\theta, \omega') \mid \theta = \theta_1\} \tag{5.7}$$

has P^{θ_1} probability 1.[6] It will be assumed that the strong law of large numbers holds on Q^{θ_1}.[7] All statements of the form "with probability 1" are with respect to the measure P^{θ_1}.

The discussion now turns to the effects of network structure on the diffusion of information in a society. The first question is, do individuals attain the same utility level in the long run? The following result, due to Bala and Goyal (1998), responds to this question.

Theorem 5.2. *The utilities of individuals converge:* $\lim_{t \to \infty} U_{i,t}(\omega) = U_{i,\infty}(\omega)$ *for every* $i \in N$, *with probability 1. If the society is connected, then every individual gets the same long-run utility:* $U_{i,\infty}(\omega) = U_{j,\infty}(\omega)$ *for every pair of individuals* $i, j \in N$, *with probability 1.*

The proof of this result is presented in the appendix. Consider the convergence result first. Let $A_i(\omega)$ be the set of actions that are chosen infinitely often by individual i along sample path ω. Note that, since the set of actions is finite, this set is always nonempty. It is intuitive that an action $a \in A_i(\omega)$ must be optimal with respect to the long-run beliefs. Moreover, since the different states in the limiting beliefs are not distinguished by the actions, these actions must yield the same utility in each of the states that are in the support of the limit belief $\mu_{i,\infty}(\omega)$. These observations yield the convergence of utilities result.

Now consider the equal utilities result. The key observation here is that if i observes the actions and outcomes of j, then he must be able to do as well as j in the long run. While this observation is intuitively plausible, the formal arguments underlying the proof are quite complicated. The principal reason for the complication is that individual i observes the actions and corresponding outcomes of a neighbor j, but does *not* observe the actions and outcomes of the neighbors of j. The claim that i does as well as j if he observes j then rests on the idea that all payoff-relevant information that j has gathered is (implicitly) reflected in the choices that he makes, over time. In particular, if j chooses a certain action in the long run, then this action must be the best action for him, conditional on all his information. However, individual i observes this action and the corresponding outcomes and can therefore do as well as j by simply imitating j.

The next step in the proof shows that this payoff-improvement property must also be true if person i observes j indirectly, via a sequence of other persons,

---

[6] There is a slight abuse of notation here; the domain of the definition of P^{θ_1} is Ω and not $\Theta \times \Omega$.

[7] For a statement of the strong law of large numbers, see, for example, Billingsley (1985).

$i_1, i_2, \ldots, i_m$. The above argument says that i does as well as i_1, who does as well as i_2, and so on until i_m does as well as j. The final step is to note that in a connected society there is an information path from any player i to any player j.

This result shows that in any connected society, local information transmission is sufficient to ensure that every person gets the same utility in the long run. Connected societies cover a wide range of possible societies and this result is therefore quite powerful. However, it leaves open the question of whether individuals are choosing the optimal action and earning the maximal possible utility in the long run.

To study this question it is useful to fix a true state and an optimal action. Let θ_1 be the true state of the world and let $B(\delta_{\theta_1})$ be the set of optimal actions corresponding to this state. Social learning is said to be *complete* if, for all $i \in N$, $A_i(\omega) \subset B(\delta_{\theta_1})$, on a set of sample paths which has probability 1 (with respect to the true state θ_1). The analysis of long-run learning rests on the informativeness of actions. An action is said to be fully informative if it can help an individual distinguish between all the states: if, for all $\theta, \theta' \in \Theta$, with $\theta \neq \theta'$,

$$\int_Y |\phi(y; a, \theta) - \phi(y; a, \theta')| \, dy > 0. \tag{5.8}$$

By contrast, an action a is uninformative if $\phi(\cdot, a; \theta)$ is independent of θ. In example 5.1, action a_0 is uninformative while action a_1 is fully informative.

In any investigation of whether individuals choose the optimal action in the long run, it is necessary to restrict beliefs. To see why this is so, consider example 5.1. If everyone has priors such that the uninformative action is optimal, then there is no additional information emerging in the society and so individual posterior beliefs will be equal to the prior beliefs and everyone will therefore choose the suboptimal action forever. Optimism by itself is, however, not sufficient. The structure of connections is also important for learning to take place. This is illustrated with the help of the following two examples.

Example 5.2 (incomplete learning). Suppose that the decision problem is as in example 5.1 and suppose that everyone is optimistic, i.e., $\mu_{i,1}(\theta_1) > \frac{1}{2}$. Moreover, for concreteness, assume that beliefs satisfy the following condition:

$$\inf_{i \in N} \mu_{i,1} > \frac{1}{2}, \qquad \sup_{i \in N} \mu_{i,1} < \frac{1}{1 + x^2}, \tag{5.9}$$

where $x = (1 - \pi)/\pi \in (0, 1)$. These restrictions incorporate the idea that individuals are optimistic about the unknown action but there is an upper bound on their optimism. From the optimality correspondence formula given in expression (5.3), it follows that every person chooses a_1 in period 1. Suppose that individuals are arranged around a circle and observe their neighbors and a set of common

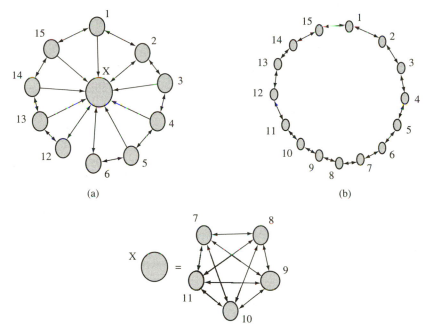

Figure 5.3. Local plus common information: (a) local plus
common observation; (b) local observation only.

individuals: i.e., $N_i^d = \{i-1, i+1\} \cup \{7, 8, 9, 10, 11\}$. Figure 5.3(a) illustrates
such a society.[8]

We now show that *there is a strictly positive probability of incomplete learning*
in this society. The argument is quite simple: suppose that every person in the
commonly observed set is unlucky in the first period and gets an outcome of 0.
Consider any individual i and note that this person can get at most three positive
signals from his immediate neighborhood. Thus any person in this society will
have a minimum residual of two negative signals on the true state. Given the
assumptions on the priors, this negative information is sufficient to push the
posteriors below the critical cutoff level of $\frac{1}{2}$ and this will induce a switch to action
a_0 in period 2, for everyone. From then on no further information is generated and
so everyone chooses the suboptimal action a_0 forever. Notice that this argument
does not use the size of the society and so there is an upper bound on the probability
of learning, which is smaller than 1, *irrespective of the size of the society.*   △

To appreciate the failure of information aggregation implicit in the above example, note that if θ_1 is the true state, then, in a large society, roughly a fraction π
(where $\pi > \frac{1}{2}$) of individuals will receive a payoff of 1 from the action a_1 and a

---

[8] This figure is only illustrative of the general structure and must be interpreted with care: in particular,
individual 6 observes 5 and 7–11, 7 observes 6–11, individuals 8–10 only observe 7–11, while individual
11 observes 7–12.

fraction $(1 - \pi)$ (where $1 - \pi < \frac{1}{2}$) of people will receive a payoff of 0. Example 5.2 thus illustrates how a few common signals can block out and overwhelm a vast amount of locally available positive information on action a_1. One way of exploring the role of network structure is by altering the relative size of local and common information. This is the route taken in the next example.

Example 5.3 (complete learning). Consider again the decision problem as in example 5.1 and suppose that information flows via observation of immediate neighbors who are located around a circle: for every i, $N_i^d = \{i - 1, i + 1\}$. Thus this society is obtained from the earlier one in example 5.2 by deleting a large number of communication connections. Figure 5.3(b) illustrates this new society. What are the prospects of learning in such a society? First, fix an individual i and note that, since θ_1 is the true state of the world, action a_1 is optimal. This means that there is a positive probability that a sequence of actions a_1 will on average generate positive information forever. This means that starting with optimistic priors, individual i will persist with action a_1, forever, if he were isolated, with positive probability.

Analogous arguments show that similar sequences of actions can be constructed for each of the neighbors of player i, $i - 1$, and $i + 1$. Exploiting independence of actions across players, it follows that the probability of the three players $i - 1, i$, and $i + 1$ receiving positive information on average is strictly positive. Denote this probability by $q > 0$. Hence the probability of individual i choosing the suboptimal action a_0 is bounded above by $1 - q$. Finally, note that along this set of sample paths, the experience of other individuals outside the neighborhood cannot alter the choices of individual i. So we can construct a similar set of sample paths for individual $i + 3$, whose information neighborhood is $\{i + 2, i + 3, i + 4\}$. From the independent and identical nature of the trials by different individuals, it can be deduced that the probability of this sample of paths is $q > 0$ as well. Note next that, since individuals i and $i + 3$ do not share any neighbors, the two events, $\{i$ does not try optimal action$\}$ and $\{i + 3$ does not try optimal action$\}$, are independent. This in turn means that the joint event that *neither of the two try the optimal action* is bounded above by $(1 - q)^2$. In a society where $N_i^d = \{i - 1, i + 1\}$, and given that $q > 0$, it now follows that learning can be made arbitrarily close to 1, by suitably increasing the number of individuals. $\triangle$

Example 5.3 illustrates in a simple way how the architecture of connections between individuals in a society can determine whether a society adopts the optimal action in the long run. It also helps in developing a general property of networks that facilitates learning of optimal actions. In the society of example 5.2 (see figure 5.3(a)) with a set of commonly observed individuals, the positive information generated on the optimal actions in different parts of the society is overturned by the negative information generated by this common observed group. By contrast, in a society with only local ties, negative information does arise over time but it cannot overrule the positive information generated in different parts of the society. This allows the positive local information to gain a foothold and eventually spread across the whole society.

The critical feature of the society in example 5.3 (in figure 5.3(b)) is the existence of individuals whose immediate neighborhood is distinct. This leads naturally to the idea of *local independence*. Two individuals i and j are locally independent if $\{N_i^d(g) \cup \{i\}\} \cap \{N_j^d(g) \cup \{j\}\} = \emptyset$. Recall that a player i has optimistic prior beliefs if the set of optimal actions under the prior belief $B(\mu_{i,1}) \subset B(\delta_{\theta_1})$. The following general result on networks and social learning, due to Bala and Goyal (1998), can now be stated.

Theorem 5.3. *Consider a connected society. In such a society the probability that everyone chooses an optimal action in the long run can be made arbitrarily close to 1 by increasing the number of locally independent optimistic players.*

The proof of this result is provided in the appendix. The arguments in the proof extend the intuition underlying example 5.3, to allow for an arbitrary number of actions as well as more general outcomes spaces.

Theorem 5.3 and examples 5.2 and 5.3 have a number of interesting implications which are worth elaborating. The first remark is about the relation with the strength of weak ties hypothesis due to Mark Granovetter (see Granovetter 1973). In Granovetter's theory, society is visualized as consisting of a number of groups which are internally tightly linked but have few links across them. In one interpretation, the links across the groups are viewed as weak ties and Granovetter's idea is that weak ties are strong in the sense that they are critical for the flow of new ideas and innovations across the groups in a society. The above result can be interpreted as showing that in societies with this pattern of strong ties (within groups) and weak ties (across groups), the weak ties between the groups do carry valuable information across groups and therefore play a vital role in sustaining technological change and dynamism in a society.

The second remark is about what examples 5.2 and 5.3 and theorem 5.3 tell us about the generation and diffusion of information in real-world networks. Our description of information networks in section 5.2 suggests that they exhibit very unequal distribution of in-degrees. It is intuitively plausible that in networks with such unequal in-degree distribution a few highly connected nodes have the potential to start off waves of diffusion of ideas and technologies. The formal arguments presented above suggest, somewhat disturbingly, that these waves can lead to mass adoption of actions or ideas whose desirability is contradicted by large amounts of locally collected information. Moreover, due to the broad adoption of such actions, information generation about alternative actions is seriously inhibited and so suboptimal actions can persist for a long time.

The third remark is about the impact of additional links on the prospects of diffusion of a desirable action. On the one hand, examples 5.2 and 5.3 together show that adding links in a network can actually lower the probability of a society learning to choose the optimal action. However, if links are added to the network in figure 5.3(a) we will eventually arrive at the complete network: clearly, in a complete network, the probability of adopting optimal action can be increased to 1 by simply increasing the number of nodes. These observations suggest that the impact of additional links depends very much on the initial network and how the links are added. Can we say anything about the marginal value of different links in a network? The above discussion about strength of weak ties suggests that links which act as *bridges* between distinct groups in a society will be very valuable. However, an assessment of the marginal value of links in more general networks appears to be an open question.

The fourth remark is about a potential trade-off between the possibility of learning and the speed of learning. A society with a common pool of observations has quick but inefficient convergence, whereas the society with pure local learning exhibits a slower speed of learning but the probability of learning is higher. A similar trade-off is also present in Ellison and Fudenberg (1993), who study a spatial model of learning, in which the payoffs are sensitive to location. They suppose that there is a continuum of individuals arranged along a line. Each individual has a window of observation around himself (this is similar to the pure local learning network considered above). They consider a choice between two technologies, and suppose that technology A (B) is optimal for all locations to the right (left) of 0. For individual i, the window is an interval $[i - w, i + w]$, for some $w \in \mathcal{R}_+$. Each individual chooses the action which yields a higher average payoff in this window. Suppose that, at the start, there is a boundary point $x_0 > 0$, with technology A being adopted to the right of x_0, and technology B being adopted to the left of x_0. Ellison and Fudenberg show that the steady-state welfare is decreasing in the size of the interval. Thus smaller intervals are better from a long-term welfare point of view. However, if w is small, then the boundary moves slowly over time and if the initial state is far from the optimum, then this creates a trade-off: increasing w leads to a short-term welfare gain but a long-term welfare loss.

Diversity. The discussion now turns to the third question posed in the introduction: what is the relation between the structure of connections and the prospects for diversity of actions in a society? Theorem 5.2 says that in a connected society all individuals will obtain the same utility. If there is a unique optimal action for every state, this implies that all individuals will choose the same action as well. When there are multiple optimal actions, however, the result does not say anything about conformism and diversity. To get an impression of the issues involved, start with a society which is split into distinct complete components. Now the level of integration of the society can be measured in terms of the number of cross-group links. Figure 5.4 presents three such societies, with varying levels of integration.

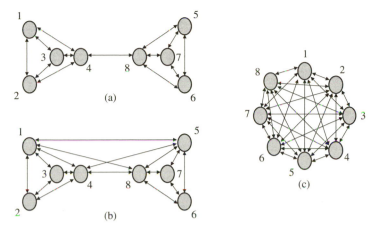

Figure 5.4. Network integration and social conformism:
(a) integration level 1; (b) integration level 2; (c) full integration.

Bala and Goyal (2001) study the probability of diversity as a function of the level of integration. They find that diversity can occur with positive probability in a partially integrated society but that the probability of diversity is zero in a fully integrated society (i.e., the complete network). A characterization of networks which allow for diversity appears to be an open problem.

Preference heterogeneity. This result on conformism, and indeed all the results reported so far, are obtained in a setting where individuals have identical preferences. However, individuals often have different preferences which are reflected in a different ranking of products or technologies. This raises the question, what are the implications of individual preference heterogeneity on the three results, theorems 5.1–5.3, obtained above?

It is easy to see that the considerations involved in theorem 5.1 do not depend in any way on the structure of interaction, so the convergence of beliefs and utilities will obtain in the more general setting with differences in preferences as well. This leads to a study of the long-run distribution of utilities. In a society with individuals who have different preferences, the analogue of theorem 5.2 would be as follows: *in a connected society, all individuals with the same preferences obtain the same utility.* Bala and Goyal (2001) show that this conjecture is false. They construct an example in which preference differences can create information blockages that impede the transmission of useful information and thereby sustain different utility levels (and therefore also different actions) for individuals with similar preferences.

This example motivates a stronger notion of connectedness: *group-wise* connectedness. A society is said to be group-wise connected if for every pair of individuals i and j of the same preference type, either j is a neighbor of i or there exists a path from j to i with all members of the path being individuals having the same preference as i and j. Bala and Goyal (2001) then show that the conjecture on equal utilities for members of the same preference type obtains in societies which satisfy this stronger connectedness requirement. In a setting with a unique optimal action for every preference type, this result also implies conformity in actions within preference types.

5.4   Related Themes

In the framework of section 5.2, learning takes place in a context where every player has a fixed set of neighbors and it has been assumed that individuals observe actions as well as the outcomes of actions of these neighbors. Moreover, everyone is given the chance to revise their decisions in each period. This section briefly discusses models of social learning which make alternative assumptions in these three respects.

5.4.1   Random Sampling

The framework developed in section 5.2 was motivated by the idea that social proximity is an important factor in determining the sources of information that individuals rely upon in making decisions. While this motivation appears to be sound and is supported by a range of empirical work, the framework developed above to study social learning is a little rigid in the following sense. In many situations, individuals get aggregate data on the relative popularity of different actions in the population at large. Measures of popularity are potentially useful because they may yield information on average quality of the product. This type of information is not considered by the above analysis. One way to model this idea is to suppose that individuals get to observe a sample of other people chosen at random. They use the information obtained from the sample—which could relate to the relative popularity of different actions or actions and outcomes of different actions—in making his choices. This approach has been explored by Ellison and Fudenberg (1993, 1995), among others. In this approach the attention has been on the size of the sample, the type of information extracted from the sample, and the nature of the decision rule which maps this information into the choice of individuals.

Changes in decision rules will have an impact on the learning process and the outcomes may well be different with non-Bayesian rules of thumb such as imitation of the best or popularity weighted schemes. In a recent paper, Chatterjee and Xu (2004) explore learning from neighbors under alternative boundedly rational decision rules.[9]

---

[9] For an analysis of the dynamics of different decision rules in the context of social coordination and cooperation, see chapter 4.

5.4.2 Observational Learning

In the framework studied in section 5.2, it was assumed that an individual observes all the actions as well as the outcomes of the actions of his direct neighbors. While this appears to be a reasonable assumption in situations where individuals are engaged in personal communication, it does require a fairly detailed description of personal experience. There is a very large literature that has studied an alternative formulation in which individuals observe actions of their cohorts only. For early work on this approach see, for example, Banerjee (1992) and Bikhchandani, Hirshliefer, and Welch (1992). In the basic model, there is a single sequence of privately informed individuals who take one action each. Before making his choice an individual gets to observe the actions of all the people who have made a choice earlier. The actions of his predecessors potentially reveal their private information. An individual can therefore use the information revealed via the actions of others along with his own private information to make decisions.

In recent work, Gale and Kariv (2003) have extended this model to a setting in which fully rational individuals get a private signal at the start and in subsequent periods get to observe the actions of their neighbors, who in turn observe the actions of their neighbors and so on. In this setting, the choice of actions can potentially communicate the private information generated at the start of the process. Individual actions, however, do not generate fresh information, unlike the model discussed in section 5.2. However, full rationality of individuals makes the inference problem quite complicated and they are obliged to focus on small societies to get a handle on the dynamics of learning. Their main results are closely related to theorems 5.1 and 5.2 presented earlier. In particular, they show that beliefs and utilities of individuals converge. This finding is similar to theorem 5.1 reported above. They also show that in a connected society every individual chooses the same action and obtains the same utility. Thus social conformism obtains in the long run. The ideas behind this result mirror those discussed in theorem 5.2 above.

The above references on observational learning assume that individuals are fully rational. In an interesting recent paper, De Marzo, Vayanos, and Zwiebel (2003) study the process of opinion formation in contexts where individuals are subject to *persuasion bias*. In the context of networks the problem of persuasion bias arises naturally as follows. Suppose person A observes two other people, B and C, choosing the same action. In a context where he does not know the sources of information on which B and C base their action, one possibility is that A supposes that the choices of B and C reflect distinct sources of information. To the extent that B and C may have based their decision on a common observation of person D, this inference of A is biased. The authors show how this bias creates the possibility of social influence: a situation in which a person influences public opinion not only due to the accuracy of his information but also due to his location in a social network.

5.5   Concluding Remarks

This chapter considered situations where individual rewards depend only on personal actions, but the payoffs from different actions are not known. In such a situation the experience of others—such as friends, colleagues, and acquaintances—is useful since it can yield valuable information on alternative actions. The aim of this chapter was to develop a theoretical framework to study the effects of neighborhood structure on the process of social learning.

The chapter focused on a class of societies that are connected. The first finding was that in such societies every person earns the same payoffs and chooses the same action (except when there are several payoff equivalent actions), in the long run. Connected societies can, however, take on a variety of forms and examples were developed to illustrate how some of them get locked into suboptimal actions while others are always able to choose the optimal action in the long run. These examples brought out the following idea: information blockages arise due to the presence of individuals who observe few others but are observed by a great many other people. This pattern of linkages is of practical interest as it is observed in actual information networks such as the World Wide Web and social communication networks.

These examples lead to the study of network features that facilitate social learning. The principal finding was that an information network in which individuals learn the optimal actions and earn the maximum payoffs has two general properties. The first property is *local independence*. Local independence captures the idea that individuals have distinct sources of information and that these distinct sources are relatively important compared with common sources of information. Local independence facilitates experimentation and gathering of new information. The second property is the existence of links that act as *bridges* between the distinct sources of information. These links facilitate the diffusion of useful information across a society.

The analysis also suggests that there may be a trade-off between the speed of learning and the possibility of complete learning: structures that speed up learning may discourage adequate experimentation. This trade-off has potentially important implications for the design of optimal communication networks.

These findings were obtained under the assumption that individuals have the same preferences. The analysis of learning when individuals have different preferences is still at a preliminary stage and only a few general results are available. This work does suggest, however, that heterogeneous preferences can easily generate information blockages and this can lead to individuals of the same type choosing different actions with unequal payoffs, even in a connected society. From an individual perspective this raises the question, whom should I observe and learn from? This question motivates the theory of network formation, which is developed in chapters 7–10.

5.6 Appendix

This section provides complete proofs of the three theorems presented in section 5.3.

We first construct the probability space within which the processes take place. Recall that the probability space is denoted by $(\Omega, \mathcal{F}, P^\theta)$, where Ω is the space of all outcomes, $\mathcal{F}$ is the σ-field, and P^θ is a probability measure if the true state of the world is θ. Let Θ be the set of possible states of the world and fix $\theta \in \Theta$ in what follows. For each individual $i \in N$, action $a \in A$, and time periods $t = 1, 2, \ldots,$ let $Y^a_{i,t}$ be the set of possible outcomes. For each $t = 1, 2, \ldots,$ let $\Omega_t = \prod_{i \in N} \prod_{a \in A} Y^a_{i,t}$ be the space of tth period outcomes across all individuals and all actions. For simplicity, we will assume that $Y^a_{i,t} = Y$. Ω_t is endowed with the product topology. Let $H_t \subset \Omega_t$ be of the form

$$H_t = \prod_{i \in N} \prod_{a \in A} H^a_{i,t}, \tag{5.10}$$

where $H^a_{i,t}$ is a Borel subset of Y, for each $i \in N$ and $a \in A$. Define the probability P^θ_t of the set H_t as

$$P^\theta_t(H_t) = \prod_{i \in N} \prod_{a \in A} \int_{H^a_{i,t}} \phi(y; a, \theta) \, dy. \tag{5.11}$$

P^θ extends uniquely to the σ-field on Ω_t generated by the sets of the form H_t. Let $\Omega = \prod_{t=1}^\infty \Omega_t$. For cylinder sets $H \subset \Omega$, of the form

$$H = \prod_{t=1}^T H_t \times \prod_{t=T+1}^\infty \Omega_t, \tag{5.12}$$

let $P^\theta(H)$ be defined as $P^\theta(H) = \prod_{t=1}^T P^\theta_t(H_t)$. Let $\mathcal{F}$ be the σ-field generated by sets of the type given by (5.12). P^θ extends uniquely to the sets in $\mathcal{F}$. This completes the construction of the probability space $(\Omega, \mathcal{F}, P^\theta)$.

Let Θ be endowed with the discrete topology, and suppose $\mathcal{B}$ is the Borel σ-field on this space. For rectangles of the form $\mathcal{T} \times H$, where $\mathcal{T} \subset \Theta$, and H is a measurable subset of Ω, let $P_i(\mathcal{T} \times H)$ be given by

$$P_i(\mathcal{T} \times H) = \sum_{\theta \in \Theta} \mu_{i,1}(\theta) P^\theta(H) \tag{5.13}$$

for each individual $i \in N$. Each P_i extends uniquely to all $\mathcal{B} \times \mathcal{F}$. Since every individual's prior belief lies in the interior of $\mathcal{P}(\Theta)$, the measures $\{P_i\}$ are pairwise mutually absolutely continuous.

The σ-field of individual i's information at the beginning of period 1 is $\mathcal{F}_{i,1} = \{\emptyset, \Theta \times \Omega\}$. For every time period $t \geqslant 2$, define $\mathcal{F}_{i,t}$ as the σ-field generated by the past history of individual i's observations of his own and his neighbors' actions and outcomes, $(C_{j,1}, Z_{j,1})_{j \in N_i^d(g) \cup \{i\}}, \ldots, (C_{j,t-1}, Z_{j,t-1})_{j \in N_i^d(g) \cup \{i\}}$. Individuals only use the information on actions and outcomes of their neighbors, so the set classes $\mathcal{F}_{i,t}$ are the relevant σ-fields for our study. We shall denote by $\mathcal{F}_{i,\infty}$ the smallest σ-field containing all $\mathcal{F}_{i,t}$ for $t \geqslant 2$.

Recall that the objects of study are the optimal actions, $C_{i,t}$, the beliefs, $\mu_{i,t}$, and the individual expected utilities, $U_{i,t}$.

The first theorem concerns convergence of beliefs.

Theorem 5.4. *There exists $Q \in \mathcal{B} \times \mathcal{F}$ satisfying $P_i(Q) = 1$, for all $i \in N$, and random vectors $\{\mu_{i,\infty}\}$ such that $\omega \in Q \Rightarrow \lim_{t\to\infty} \mu_{i,t}(\omega) = \mu_{i,\infty}(\omega)$.*

Proof. For each $\theta \in \Theta$, the belief $\mu_{i,t}(\theta)$ of individual i at the beginning of time t can be regarded as a version of the conditional expectation $E[I_{\theta \times \Omega} \mid \mathcal{F}_{i,t}]$, where the expectation is taken with respect to the measure P_i. Since this sequence of random variables is a uniformly bounded martingale (see Easley and Kiefer 1988), with respect to the increasing sequence of σ-fields $\{\mathcal{F}_{i,t}\}$, the martingale convergence theorem applies, so that $\mu_{i,t}$ converges almost surely to the $\mathcal{F}_{i,\infty}$ measurable limit belief $\mu_{i,\infty}$. Let Q_i be the set of sample paths on which individual i's beliefs converge, where $P_i(Q_i) = 1$. Since the measures are pairwise mutually absolutely continuous and the set of players is at most countable, the set $Q = \bigcap_{i \in N} Q_i$ also has P_i measure 1 for each i. $\square$

In what follows, fix θ_1 to be the true state of nature. Note that

$$Q^{\theta_1} = \{\omega = (\theta, \omega') \mid \theta = \theta_1\} \tag{5.14}$$

has P^{θ_1} probability 1. It will be assumed that the strong law of large numbers holds on Q^{θ_1}. All statements of the form "with probability 1" are, from now on, with respect to the measure P^{θ_1}.

The following result establishes convergence of utilities and also shows that an action that is chosen in the long run must be optimal with respect to the limiting beliefs. Recall that there is a finite set of actions and so along every sample path there is a set of actions that is chosen infinitely often. Let $A_i(\omega)$ be the set of actions that is chosen infinitely often by individual i along sample path ω.

Lemma 5.1. *Suppose $\omega \in Q^{\theta_1}$.*

(i) *If $a' \in A_i(\omega)$, then $a' \in \operatorname{argmax}_{a \in A} u(a, u_{i,\infty}(\omega))$.*

(ii) *There exists a real number $U_{i,\infty}(\omega)$ such that $\{U_{i,t}(\omega)\} \to U_{i,\infty}(\omega)$. Furthermore, $U_{i,\infty}(\omega) = u(a', \mu_{i,\infty}(\omega))$, where a' is any member of $A_i(\omega)$.*

Proof. Since $a' \in A_i(\omega)$ there exists a subsequence $\{t_k\}$ such that

$$u(a', \mu_{i,t_k}(\omega)) \geq u(a, \mu_{i,t_k}(\omega)).$$

Taking limits and using continuity of u on the set $\mathcal{P}(\Theta)$, we get

$$u(a', \mu_{i,\infty}(\omega)) \geq u(a, \mu_{i,\infty}(\omega)).$$

Since a was arbitrary, this proves statement (i). Statement (ii) follows from statement (i) and the maximum theorem.[10] $\qquad\square$

The above result says that an action that is chosen in the long run must be optimal with respect to the limiting beliefs. However, actions reveal information about the true state and so every action that is taken in the long run, i.e., chosen infinitely often, must yield no information that can distinguish the states of the world which are in the support of the limiting distribution. The following lemma generalizes this observation to all actions an individual observes over time.

Lemma 5.2. *Suppose $j \in N_i^d(g)$ and $\omega \in Q^{\theta_1}$. If $\theta \in \text{supp}(\mu_{i,\infty}(\omega))$, for $\theta \neq \theta_1$, then $u(a, \delta_\theta) = u(a, \delta_{\theta_1})$ for all $a \in A_{j \in N_i^d(g)}(\omega) \cup A_i(\omega)$.*

Proof. Suppose there is some $a \in A_{j \in N_i^d(g)}(\omega) \cup A_i(\omega)$ and some $\theta \neq \theta_1$, with $\theta \in \text{supp}(\mu_{i,\infty}(\omega))$ such that $u(a, \delta_{\theta_0}) \neq u(a, \delta_{\theta_1})$. This immediately implies that

$$\int_Y |\phi(y; a, \theta_1) - \phi(y; a, \theta)| \, dy > 0. \tag{5.15}$$

Since a is chosen infinitely often by individual i or one of his neighbors, this implies that individual i observes infinite, independent, and identically distributed draws of a random variable, which allows us to exploit the strong law of large numbers and to conclude that $\mu_{i,\infty}(\omega)(\theta) = 0$, so that θ is not in the support of the limit distribution $\mu_{i,\infty}$. This contradiction establishes the result. $\qquad\square$

Equipped with the above lemmas, we can prove the following result.

Theorem 5.5. *The utilities of individuals converge: $\lim_{t \to \infty} U_{i,t}(\omega) = U_{i,\infty}(\omega)$, for every $i \in N$, with probability 1.*
Suppose that a society is connected. Then $U_{i,\infty}(\omega) = U_{j,\infty}(\omega)$, for all $i, j \in N$, with probability 1.

---

[10] For an exposition of the maximum theorem, see Debreu (1959).

Proof. The convergence of utilities has already been proved in lemma 5.1. Consider the equal utilities statement. The crucial observation is that if j observes i, then in the long run j must do as well as i. The argument is then completed by simply noting that in a connected society every player observes everyone else directly or indirectly and exploiting transitivity. It therefore suffices to establish the following property of limiting utilities: if $i \in N_j^d(g)$, then $U_{j,\infty}(\omega) \geq U_{i,\infty}(\omega)$ on $\omega \in Q^{\theta_1}$.

It will be shown that if $a' \in A_j(\omega)$, then $u(a', \delta_{\theta_1}) \geq u(a, \delta_{\theta_1})$ for all $a \in A_i(\omega)$. This will suffice for the proof since from lemma 5.2 we have

$$U_{j,\infty}(\omega) = u(a', \mu_{j,\infty}(\omega)) = u(a', \delta_{\theta_1}) = u(a', \delta_\theta) \quad \text{for all } \theta \in \text{supp}(\mu_{j,\infty}) \tag{5.16}$$

and

$$U_{i,\infty}(\omega) = u(a, \mu_{i,\infty}(\omega)) = u(a, \delta_{\theta_1}) = u(a, \delta_\theta) \quad \text{for all } \theta \in \text{supp}(\mu_{j,\infty}). \tag{5.17}$$

There are two cases we need to consider. If $\mu_{j,\infty}(\omega) = \delta_{\theta_1}$, the result follows directly from lemma 5.1. So suppose there exist $\theta \neq \theta_1$ and $\theta \in \text{supp}(\mu_{j,\infty}(\omega))$. The argument is by contradiction. Assume that $u(a', \delta_{\theta_1}) < u(a, \delta_{\theta_1})$. Since $\theta \in \text{supp}(\mu_{j,\infty}(\omega))$, lemma 5.2, together with the facts that $a' \in A_j(\omega)$ and $a \in A_i(\omega)$, implies that $u(a', \mu_{j,\infty})(\omega) < u(a, \mu_{j,\infty})(\omega)$. However, this contradicts lemma 5.1. This proves that if $a' \in A_j(\omega)$, then $u(a', \delta_{\theta_1}) \geq u(a, \delta_{\theta_1})$ for all $a' \in A_i(\omega)$. $\square$

Our interest now turns to the conditions on networks that ensure that long-run actions are optimal. First observe that since the action set is finite and the utility function is continuous with respect to beliefs, there exists a number $\bar{d} < 1$ such that if $\mu(\theta_1) \geq \bar{d}$, then the set of optimal actions $B(\mu) \subset B(\delta_{\theta_1})$.

The following lemmas are used in the proof of the theorem on learning of optimal actions.

Lemma 5.3. *Fix some individual $i \in N$ with $|N_i^d(g)| + 1 \leq K$. For any $\lambda \in (0, 1)$, there exists a set of sample paths W_i satisfying $P^{\theta_1}(W_i) \geq \lambda$ and $d(\lambda) \in (0, 1)$ such that if $\mu_{i,1}(\theta_1) \geq d(\lambda)$ then*

$$\omega \in W_i \Rightarrow A_i(\omega) \subset B(\delta_{\theta_1}). \tag{5.18}$$

Proof. Consider individual i in isolation first and suppose that he only chooses action a for $t - 1$ periods and observes a sequence $\{y_{i,\tau}^a\}_{\tau=1}^{t-1}$, where each $y_{i,\tau}^a \in Y$. Individual i's information about state $\theta \neq \theta_1$ can then be summarized by the product likelihood ratio:

$$r_{i,t}^{a,\theta}(\omega) = \frac{\prod_{\tau=1}^{t-1} \phi(y_{i,\tau}^a(\omega); a, \theta)}{\prod_{\tau=1}^{t-1} \phi(y_{i,\tau}^a(\omega); a, \theta_1)}. \tag{5.19}$$

(If $t = 1$, then we follow the convention that $r_{i,t}^{a,\theta} = 1$.) It follows from an application of the strong law of large numbers that $r_{i,t}^{a,\theta} \to \bar{r}_i^{a,\theta}$, where $\bar{r}_i^{a,\theta} < \infty$ almost surely (see, for example, DeGroot 1970). Since this is true for all $\theta \neq \theta_1$ and all $a \in A$, there exists a number σ and a set W_i^σ of sample paths defined as

$$W_i^\sigma = \prod_{a \in A} \left(\max_{\theta \in \Theta \backslash \theta_1} \sup_{t \geq 1} r_{i,t}^{a,\theta} \leq \sigma \right) \times \prod_{t=1}^{\infty} \prod_{j \in N \backslash i} Y^{|A|} \qquad (5.20)$$

such that $P^{\theta_1}(W_i^\sigma) \geq \delta$, where $\delta = \lambda^{1/K} > 0$. It follows from our convention $r_{i,t}^{a,\theta} = 1$ that $\sigma \geq 1$. Intuitively, this tells us that the bad information concerning state θ_1 arising from individual i's own actions is bounded above by $\sigma^{|A|}$.

Now exploiting the assumption that trials of the same action by different individuals are identically distributed, it follows that for each $j \in N_i^d(g)$ there is a similar set of sample paths W_j^σ with $P^{\theta_1}(W_j^\sigma) = P^{\theta_1}(W_i^\sigma)$. Define the set $W_i = \bigcup_{j \in N_i^d(g)} W_j^\sigma \cup W_i^\sigma$. Using the assumption that the realizations of actions across individuals are independent, it now follows that

$$P^{\theta_1}(W_i) \geq \delta^{|N_i^d|+1} \geq \delta^K = \lambda, \qquad (5.21)$$

where we use the assumption that $|N_i^d(g)| + 1 \leq K$. Note that individual i's posterior belief about state θ_1 at time t can be written as

$$\mu_{i,t}(\theta_1)(\omega) = \frac{\mu_{i,1}(\theta_1)(\omega)}{\mu_{i,1}(\theta_1)(\omega) + \sum_{\theta \neq \theta_1} \prod_{j \in N_i^d \cup \{i\}} \prod_{a \in A} r_{j,t}^{a,\theta}(\omega) \mu_{i,1}(\theta)(\omega)}, \qquad (5.22)$$

where $r_{j,t}^{a,\theta}(\omega)$ now refers to the product likelihood ratio along the sample path when actions $\{C_{j,t}\}$ are chosen. For $\omega \in W_i$, we have

$$\mu_{i,t}(\theta_1)(\omega) \geq \frac{\mu_{i,1}(\theta_1)(\omega)}{\mu_{i,1}(\theta_1)(\omega) + \sum_{\theta \neq \theta_1} \sigma^{K|A|} \mu_{i,1}(\theta)(\omega)} \qquad (5.23)$$

by construction of the set W_i.[11]

Let $\bar{d}$ be the number defined prior to the lemma statement above. Since the expression on the right-hand side of equation (5.23) is independent of t, it is evident that there will exist a number $d(\lambda) \in (0, 1)$ such that if $\mu_{i,1}(\theta_1) > d(\lambda)$ and $\omega \in W_i$, then $\mu_{i,t}(\theta_1)(\omega) \geq \bar{d}$ for all $t \geq 1$. By the definition of $\bar{d}$ this means $B(\mu_{i,t}(\omega)) \subset B(\theta_1)$ for each t. Since $C_{i,t}(\omega) \in B(\mu_{i,t}(\omega))$ for each t, the proof follows. $\qquad \square$

Thus for an individual whose prior $\mu_{i,1}(\theta_1) \geq d(\lambda)$ there is a set of sample paths W_i with probability λ such that i will choose an optimal action for ever on sample paths $\omega \in W_i$. Theorem 5.2 tells us that in a connected society all

---

[11] Note that if a person chooses action a for the kth time on ω, then he observes the kth realization along the sample path, $y_{j,k}^a(\omega)$.

individuals get the same expected utility. So, if i plays an optimal action for ever, then so will everyone else in the long run. The next lemma formalizes this idea.

Lemma 5.4. *Suppose that the society is connected. If for some $\omega \in Q^{\theta_1}$ there is an individual $i \in N$ such that $A_i(\omega) \subset B(\delta_{\theta_1})$, then, for every $j \in N$, $A_j(\omega) \subset B(\delta_{\theta_1})$.*

Proof. Let $a \in A_i(\omega)$, so that $a \in B(\delta_{\theta_1})$. From arguments in lemmas 5.2 and 5.3 it follows that $U_{i,\infty}(\omega) = u(a, \delta_{\theta_1})$. Fix $j \in N$. Connectedness implies, and here theorem 5.2 is being used, that $U_{i,\infty}(\omega) = U_{j,\infty}(\omega)$. Hence $U_{j,\infty}(\omega) = u(a, \delta_{\theta_1})$. Let $a' \in A_j(\omega)$. Using arguments in lemma 5.3 again it follows that $U_{j,\infty}(\omega) = u(a', \delta_{\theta_1})$ and so $u(a', \delta_{\theta_1}) = u(a, \delta_{\theta_1})$. Since $a \in B(\delta_{\theta_1})$ it follows that $a' \in B(\delta_{\theta_1})$ as well. Since a' and j were arbitrary, the argument is complete. $\square$

We are now ready to prove our main result on learning. Recall that two individuals i and j are said to be *locally independent* if $\{N_i^d(g) \cup \{i\}\} \cap \{N_j^d(g) \cup \{j\}\} = \emptyset$. A pairwise locally independent group of individuals is a subset of N such that any two persons i, j in the set are mutually locally independent. Fix a number $K > 0$ and a $\bar{\lambda} > 0$. Let $\bar{d} = d(\bar{\lambda})$ be the corresponding value whose existence is guaranteed by lemma 5.3. Consider the collection of individuals $i \in N$ such that $|N_i^d| \leq K$ and satisfying $\mu_{i,1}(\theta_1) \geq \bar{d}$. Let $N_{K,\bar{d}}$ be a maximal group of pairwise locally independent individuals chosen from this collection, i.e., a subset of the above collection which has the highest cardinality. We are now ready to state and prove the following learning result.

Theorem 5.6. *Consider a connected society. Let $\bar{\lambda} > 0$, $\bar{d} = d(\bar{\lambda})$, and $N_{K,\bar{d}}$ be defined as above. Then*

$$P^{\theta_1}\left(\bigcup_{i \in N} \{A_i(\omega) \not\subset B(\delta_{\theta_1})\} \right) \leq (1 - \bar{\lambda})^{|N_{K,\bar{d}}|}. \tag{5.24}$$

In particular, if for some $\bar{\lambda} > 0$ and $\bar{d} = d(\lambda)$, $|N_{K,\bar{d}}| \to \infty$, then the probability of everyone choosing the optimal action goes to 1.

Proof. Let $i \in N_{K,\bar{d}}$ and let W_i be the set of sample paths specified in lemma 5.3 corresponding to $\bar{\lambda}$, so that $P^{\theta_1}(W_i) \geq \bar{\lambda}$. By definition, $i \in N_{K,\bar{d}}$ implies that $\mu_{i,1}(\theta_1) \geq \bar{d}$. Applying lemma 5.3 and lemma 5.4 we get $W_i \subset \bigcap_{j \in N} \{A_j(\omega) \subset B(\delta_{\theta_1})\}$. Since $i \in N_{K,\bar{d}}$ is arbitrary, we have

$$\bigcup_{i \in N_{K,\bar{d}}} W_i \subset \bigcap_{j \in N} \{A_j(\omega) \subset B(\delta_{\theta_1})\} \tag{5.25}$$

as well. Hence,

$$\bigcup_{j \in N} \{A_j(\omega) \not\subset B(\delta_{\theta_1})\} \subset \bigcap_{i \in N_{K,\bar{d}}} W_i^c, \tag{5.26}$$

where W_i^c is defined as being complementary to W_i. However, as the individuals in $N_{K,\bar{d}}$ are pairwise locally independent, the events $\{W_i^c\}_{i \in N_{K,\bar{d}}}$ are independent. Thus

$$P^{\theta_1}\left(\bigcup_{j \in N}\{A_j(\omega) \not\subset B(\delta_{\theta_1})\}\right) \leq P^{\theta_1}\left(\bigcap_{i \in N_{K,\bar{d}}} W_i^c\right) \leq (1 - \bar{\lambda})^{|N_{K,\bar{d}}|}, \quad (5.27)$$

where we have used the fact that $P^{\theta_1}(W_i) \geq \bar{\lambda}$. $\qquad\square$

6

Social Networks in Labor Markets

6.1 Introduction

Workers like jobs that suit their skills and location preferences, while firms are keen to hire workers who have the right abilities. However, workers do not know which firms have vacancies, and finding the right job takes time and effort. Similarly, firms do not know which workers are looking for a job. Faced with this lack of information, workers look for job advertisements in newspapers, magazines, and online. They also spread the word among their friends and acquaintances that they are looking for a job, and indeed there is substantial evidence that they often get information on job vacancies via their personal connections.[1]

A second type of information problem concerns the ability of workers: a person generally knows more about his own ability than does a potential employer. Indeed, this asymmetry in information leads workers to invest in signals of their quality (such as educational degrees, certificates, and licenses), and it leads potential employers to ask for references and recommendation letters.[2] Empirical work also shows that referrals—references and recommendation letters—are widely used in the process of matching workers and firms. A letter of reference is only valuable in so far as the employer can trust the writer of the letter; this suggests that the structure of personal connections is likely to play an important role in matching workers and firms.

These observations lead us to examine how the pattern of social contacts affects the flow of information about jobs and about the abilities of workers. The flow of information across persons will influence how quickly workers are matched with jobs which will in turn shape the level of employment. The patterns of social connections will also determine who gets information and when; this in turn may determine who gets a job and who is left unemployed, which will in turn have a bearing on the distribution of earnings and overall inequality in a society.

This chapter presents two theoretical models of social networks in labor markets to examine these issues. In the first model, the interest is in the transmission of

---

[1] The empirical work on sources of job vacancies is discussed in section 6.4.

[2] For a classical study of the effects of asymmetric information on the functioning of markets, see Akerlof (1970).

information on job vacancies, while in the second model the focus is on the use of referrals by firms to hire workers whose ability is unknown.

The model of information transmission on job vacancies is built on the following ideas. Individual workers have personal connections and these connections taken together define a social network. Information about new jobs arrives randomly to individuals. If they are unemployed, they take up the job; if they are employed and do not need the job, they send this information to their unemployed friends and acquaintances. There is also a chance that someone who is employed may lose his job. The process of job loss, arrival of new job information, the transmission of this information via the network, and the matching of worker with this job defines a dynamic process the outcome of which is summarized in terms of employment status of different individuals at any point in time. The interest is in understanding how the properties of the social network affect the employment prospects of individuals.

The analysis of this model yields two main insights. The first insight is that the employment status of individuals in a social network is positively correlated. Empirical work suggests that there is significant correlation in employment status within social communities or geographically contiguous city districts (see, for example, Conley and Topa 2002; Topa 2001). Geographical proximity overlaps highly with social connections and so this first insight provides a theoretical account of how local information sharing can generate such correlations in employment status. The second insight is that the probability of finding a job is declining with the duration of unemployment. Duration dependence of unemployment has been widely documented (see, for example, Heckman and Borjas 1980). The reason that duration dependence arises in a context of social information sharing is that a longer spell of unemployment reveals that a person's social contacts are less likely to be employed, which in turn makes it less likely that they will pass on information concerning vacancies. This in turn lowers the probability of the individual moving out of unemployment and into employment.

In the first model, social networks act as a conduit for information on job vacancies. The friends and acquaintances of a person also have information on her ability and employees may find it profitable to use such information. The second model examines this role of social networks. The starting point of the model is that workers know their own ability, while potential employers do not know it. However, working in a firm reveals to the firm information about the ability of the worker. Now consider a firm who needs to hire a new worker. This firm can place an advertisement in the newspapers and/or it can ask its current employees if they know someone who is suitable for the job. Empirical work suggests that there is considerable similarity in attributes between workers who know each other (see, for example, Rees 1966; Marsden 1988). This motivates the idea that a firm with high-ability workers expects its current workers to recommend someone of higher ability on average, compared with a firm whose current employee is of low ability. This difference in expectation may lead some firms to use referrals while others go to the market. If some firms hire via referrals and these firms pick out the higher-ability workers on average, then the ability of workers who go to the market will be lower on average. These differences are reflected in the wages that different workers make. The model explores these ideas and brings out the aggregate implications of social connections for wage inequality and firm profits.

The analysis of this model yields two key insights. The first insight is that workers with more connections will earn a higher wage and that firms who hire through contacts (of their existing high-quality workers) will earn higher profits. The reason for this relation between connections and wages is simple: more connections implies a higher number of referral wage offers from firms (on average) and this translates into a higher accepted wage (on average). The reason that firms which hire through contacts earn higher profits is that when a firm makes a referral wage offer the competition between firms for this worker is imperfect (due to a positive probability of a person receiving only one offer); on the other hand, firms hiring workers in the open market are perfect competitors and therefore make zero profits. The second insight is that an increase in the density of social connections raises the inequality in wages. This is a reflection of the lemons effect: an increase in social ties means that more high-ability workers are hired via referrals, and this lowers the quality of workers who go into the open market, thereby pushing down their wage, relatively.

The frictions in the matching of workers and firms have traditionally been studied within a framework where individual and firms are anonymous and search for the best match. The essential trade-off here is that on the one hand greater search is costly in terms of effort and time spent, while on the other hand it generates benefits in terms of a better quality match. This approach has been developed in several directions and has generated a number of insights; for recent surveys of this line of research, see, for example, Mortenson (2003) and Rogerson, Shimer, and Wright (2005). The emerging body of work on social networks in labor markets departs in one crucial way from the work on search and matching: *the workers are no longer anonymous.* For instance, in the model on sharing of job information individual workers share information with some workers but not with others. Similarly, in the model of referrals, firms get information on the quality of workers who are linked to their current employees. Thus the research on networks should be seen as complementary to the existing body of work on search and matching in markets. In particular, the interest is in understanding how workers who are homogeneous in skills, endowments, and preferences may nonetheless fare very differently due to differences in their connections.

Section 6.2 develops a model in which information about job vacancies flows via a social network. Section 6.3 presents a model of referrals in labor markets. We then present evidence on the use of social networks in labor markets in section 6.4.

Section 6.5 concludes. The proofs of the main results are presented in an appendix at the end of the chapter.

6.2   The Social Transmission of Job Information

This section develops a model of the transmission of job vacancy information through social networks. This presentation here is based on Calvó-Armengol and Jackson (2004).

Consider a set of N individuals/workers who all have the same skills. Time evolves in discrete periods $t = 1, 2, \ldots$. At the end of time t a worker is either employed, $s_{i,t} = 1$, or unemployed, $s_{i,t} = 0$. The vector $s_t = \{s_{1t}, \ldots, s_{nt}\}$ describes the employment status of everyone at end of time t. By convention, the employment status at the start of time $t + 1$ is set equal to the employment status at the end of time t.

A period t starts with new information on jobs arriving. A worker hears about the jobs with a probability $a \in (0, 1)$. This probability is identical and independent across workers. If the worker is unemployed, he takes the job; if he is employed, then he passes on the information to one of his contacts who is unemployed. This is the point at which the pattern of personal connections becomes important. If a worker knows no one and is employed, then the information is wasted. By contrast, if he knows many people, then it is more likely that one of them will be unemployed and therefore more likely that the information can be useful.

The pattern of connections is captured in an (undirected) network g. The probability that a worker j gets a job that worker i originally heard about is

$$
p_{ij}(s) = \begin{cases} a & \text{if } s_i = 0 \text{ and } i = j, \\ \dfrac{a}{\sum_{k:s_k=0} g_{ik}} & \text{if } s_i = 1, \ s_j = 0, \text{ and } g_{ij} = 1, \\ 0 & \text{otherwise.} \end{cases}
$$

Notice that, in the above formulation, information only travels one link; however, it is important to note that the existence of other workers in the network does have an important bearing on a worker's employment prospects. This is because of two possible effects. The first effect is competitive. If i knows other workers who are unemployed, then this lowers the probability of worker j getting the information. In other words, the existence of other workers creates greater competition for worker j. The second effect goes in the opposite direction. The existence of other workers linked to worker i also means that it is more likely that i will get information from them on jobs, which in turn means that it is more likely that he will pass on to worker j information about jobs which he receives. More generally, the pattern of connections across the society will influence the employment prospects of individual j. This idea leads us to define the concept of path connectedness of workers. A pair of workers i and j are said to be path-connected in network g if there exists a path between them in network g.

The last event within a period is the possibility that a worker loses his job; this happens with probability $b \in (0, 1)$. This probability is also identical and independent across individual workers.

To summarize, at the start of period t, the employment status of workers is a vector s_{t-1}. During period t, workers receive information on new jobs, which is shared via the social network. Some workers may lose jobs and these factors together define a new employment status, s_t, at the end of the period. The interest is in understanding how the network g influences the evolution of employment status of workers over time.[3]

6.2.1 Dynamics of Employment

The first result concerns the relationship between employment status of workers in the same network. As discussed earlier, there are two forces at work here. Two workers i and k who are linked to the same worker j compete for the information of worker j, and this may induce a negative correlation between the employment status of i and k. On the other hand, worker k receives information on jobs as well, and this information may be used by worker j to get a job. This in turn may allow worker j to pass on information on jobs to worker i, which may lead to a positive correlation between the employment status of i and k. In the long run, the second effect dominates. The following example illustrates this in the context of a simple four-worker economy.

Consider an example with $n = 4$, and let $a = 0.100$ and $b = 0.015$.[4] We look at four possible networks: the empty network (g^e), the network with one link (g^1), the cycle network with four links (g^{cycle}), and the complete network with six links (g^c). Table 6.1 was taken from Calvó-Armengol and Jackson (2004) and it presents the probability of being employed and the correlations in employment status across workers in a network. In this table, note that workers 1 and 2 are directly connected in networks g^1, g^{cycle}, g^c, while workers 1 and 3 are indirectly connected in network g^{cycle} and directly connected in g^c.

In the empty network, there is no information sharing on jobs and this means that every worker has the same probability of unemployment, 0.132. As links are added in the social network and more information is shared on jobs among the

---

[3] The model presented here has deliberately been kept very simple to bring out the essential implications of the network transmission of information. It is possible to generalize the model to allow for heterogeneity in skills, indirect transmission of information, as well as to make the transmission of information sensitive to the wages that different workers are earning. For an exposition of the general model, see Calvó-Armengol and Jackson (2007).

[4] If we interpret these as weekly estimates, then a worker gets information on a new job once every 10 weeks, and loses his job on average every 67 weeks.

Table 6.1. Employment levels in a network.

g	$\Pr(s_1 = 0)$	$\text{Corr}(s_1, s_2)$	$\text{Corr}(s_1, s_3)$
g^e	0.132	—	—
g^1	0.083	0.041	—
g^{cycle}	0.063	0.025	0.019
g^c	0.050	0.025	0.025

workers, the probability of being unemployed falls: it is 0.083 in the single-link network, 0.063 in the cycle network, and 0.050 in the complete network. This suggests that a worker in a more connected network faces better employment prospects over time. The next point to note is about the correlation between the employment prospects of different workers. First, we note that the correlation is positive across all workers. Second, we note that the correlation is positive and higher for directly linked workers 1 and 2 compared with the indirectly linked workers 1 and 3 in the cycle network.

The positive correlation across employment status of workers in a social network is a general property. To state this result formally, we need to introduce some new notation. For any network g, with workers' population N, arrival probability $a \in (0, 1)$, and breakdown probability $b \in (0, 1)$, define a finite-state irreducible and aperiodic Markov process $\mathcal{M} = (g, a, b)$. From standard results in the theory of Markov chains it then follows that there exists a unique invariant distribution μ (see, for example, Billingsley 1985). The process can be split up into finer periods simply by dividing through by a common number T and this yields a corresponding process $\mathcal{M}^T = (g, a/T, b/T)$. Correspondingly, define the unique long-run distribution by μ^T.

We are now in a position to state the following general result on correlation across employment statuses of workers, due to Calvó-Armengol and Jackson (2004).

Theorem 6.1. *Consider the Markov process of employment status of workers* $\mathcal{M}^T$. *There exists a* $\hat{T}$ *such that, for all* $T \geqslant \hat{T}$, *the long-run distribution* μ^T *is unique and in this distribution the employment status of path-connected workers is positively correlated.*

The intuition underlying this result is simple: if a group of workers are employed, then it is more likely that they will share information on new jobs, which in turn makes it more likely that their friends and neighbors will be employed.[5]

---

[5] This result is consistent with the empirical evidence discussed in section 6.4. In particular, the work of Topa (2001) shows that there is a positive correlation between employment statuses of workers in the same neighborhoods of the city of Chicago. This result is also consistent with the empirical findings of Conley and Topa (2002) that there is a positive correlation in employment for workers who are close to each other in other socioeconomic metrics such as ethnicity and occupation.

Table 6.2. Duration dependence in employment.

g	1 period	2 periods	10 periods	limit
g^e	0.099	0.099	0.099	0.099
g^l	0.176	0.175	0.170	0.099
g^c	0.305	0.300	0.278	0.099

The positive correlation noted in the above result also obtains across time. The following result, due to Calvó-Armengol and Jackson (2004), makes this precise.

Theorem 6.2. *Consider the Markov process of employment status of workers $\mathcal{M}^T$. There exists a $\hat{T}$ such that, for all $T \geqslant \hat{T}$, starting from the long-run distribution μ^T the employment status of any two path-connected workers is positively correlated across arbitrary time periods.*

We now turn to the question of how the duration of unemployment affects future employment prospects. In other words, how does the probability of getting employment vary with the duration of unemployment? To get some intuition for the forces at work here, let us again consider the four-worker economy discussed earlier in this section. Table 6.2 presents the probability of being employed conditional on 1, 2, and 10 periods of unemployment.

In the empty network, the probability of getting employed depends solely on getting information on a new job. These events do not depend on the duration of unemployment and this explains the constant figure in the first row of table 6.2. However, as the network gets denser, a longer duration of unemployment tells us more about the status of the other workers: in particular, that the other workers are not employed. This negative information in turns means that the other workers are less likely to share any information they will get, and this implies that a longer duration of unemployment lowers the probability of getting a job in the near future.

Positive duration dependence is a general property of labor markets in which job vacancy information is transmitted across social networks. The following result, due to Calvó-Armengol and Jackson (2004), summarizes our discussion.

Theorem 6.3. *Consider the Markov process of employment status of workers $\mathcal{M}^T$. There exists a $\hat{T}$ such that, for all $T \geqslant \hat{T}$, starting from the long-run distribution μ^T the conditional probability that a worker will be employed in a given period is decreasing with the length of their observed unemployment spell.*

The intuition underlying this result is as follows. The longer the duration of unemployment of an individual, the more likely it is that his neighbors, and the neighbors of his neighbors, are also unemployed. In other words, a longer duration of unemployment reveals that a worker's environment is poor, which in turn also leads to low forecasts for future employment of the worker in question.

The analysis of job-information sharing in networks yields two insights: (i) that social transmission of job information provides a natural explanation for spatial and community-level variations in employment prospects; and (ii) that the use of social connections in obtaining job information helps us to understand duration dependence in unemployment at the individual level.

In the model presented the structure of links is kept very general. It can be argued that the links vary with the status or ethnicity of workers: it may be easier for two employed people to maintain a tie compared with an employed and an unemployed person keeping a tie. These ideas broadly suggest a type of *inbreeding bias* in links. Buhai and van der Leij (2006) argue that such an inbreeding bias in links can help sustain very unequal wages across communities. Bramoullé and Saint-Paul (2004) show that, in a dynamic context, if linking is more likely between persons with the same employment status, then duration dependence arises in a strong form. A longer duration of unemployment leads to fewer employed contacts, and this lowers access to job information, which in turn prolongs unemployment.

6.3   Adverse Selection and Referrals

A worker generally knows more about his own ability compared to a potential employer. This asymmetry in information has been used to interpret educational degrees, certificates, and licenses as signals that workers may use to convey information about their ability to potential employers.[6] This asymmetry in information also leads potential employers to ask for personal references and recommendation letters. The discussion of empirical work in section 6.4 suggests that referrals— personal references and recommendation letters—are widely used in the process of matching workers and firms. This section develops a model of a labor market in which both workers and firms choose between being matched in a formal decentralized market or via a system of referrals. Referrals operate via personal connections, and so the model allows for an explicit examination of the role of social structure in shaping wage inequality and firm profits. The exposition here is based on Montgomery (1991).[7]

6.3.1   A Simple Model of Referrals

The model has two periods and there are a large number of firms and workers. In each period a firm hires one worker. The output of a firm is equal to the ability of the worker who works for the firm. Workers know their ability while firms do not know their ability. In period 1, all firms therefore have an expectation of the average ability of worker, and pay wages corresponding to this average. During

---

[6] For a seminal study of signalling in markets, see Spence (1974).

[7] Also see Saloner (1985) for an interesting model of social networks as a screening device.

period 1, a firm learns the ability of its worker. At the start of period 2, it has a choice between asking the period 1 worker for the name of a potential worker and offering a referral wage or simply posting a wage in the market, which can be taken up by any of the large number of workers. There are a large number of firms competing for workers and so market wages are equal to expected ability and *ex ante* (at the start of period 1) expected profits of firms are equal to zero. We now get into the details of the model.

Workers. There are a large number of workers and workers live for one period. The number of workers is equal in each period. There are two types of worker: High and Low. It is assumed that there is an equal number of both types in each period and this number is N. Next suppose that the productivity of a High type is 1, while the productivity of a Low type is 0. Workers know their own ability, but workers of different ability are observationally equivalent to the firms.

Firms. There are a large number of firms and every firm employs one worker in each period. The profit of a firm is equal to the productivity of the worker less the wage which is paid to the worker. Wages are set at the start of each period, and it is assumed that firms cannot offer fully contingent contracts. A simple way to model this is to suppose that wages are set before learning the productivity of workers.

Social structure. Each period 1 worker knows at most one period 2 worker, possessing a social tie with probability $r \in [0, 1]$. The specific individual for the link is selected as follows. First it is assumed that conditional upon holding a tie, the period 1 worker knows a period 2 worker of his own type with probability $\alpha > \frac{1}{2}$. The assumption that $\alpha > \frac{1}{2}$ reflects the idea that it is more likely that a worker knows someone with the same ability as himself. The social structure is thus defined by the two parameters, r reflecting the density of links and α reflecting the inbreeding bias in the links. Since links are randomly assigned it is possible that some period 2 workers have many connections while others have none. Thus the model allows a very simple formulation of the idea that there is inequality in the distribution of connections.

Timing of offers. At the start of period 1, firms hire period 1 workers through the market, which clears at wages given by w_{M1}. In period 1, production occurs. During the process of production, each firm learns the ability of its worker. At the start of period 2, a firm decides whether to offer a referral wage or to hire and offer a wage on the anonymous market. If a firm decides to offer a referral wage, then this is denoted by w_{Ri}. These wages are communicated via social contacts to workers in period 2. The workers in period 2 compare wage offers and accept one of the referral offers. If a worker rejects all offers, then he goes to the market. Similarly, if a firm's referral offer is rejected, then it goes to the market as well. The decentralized anonymous market in period 2 clears at a wage denoted by w_{M2}.

The interest is in the level of market wages w_{M1}, w_{M2}, and the referral wages, w_{Ri}, and how they relate to the parameters of social structure r and α. These wages in turn define the level of inequality that arises in the market.

6.3.2   Social Connections and Wage Inequality

It is useful to start by noting that in the absence of a social structure, learning about period 1 workers will give no information on period 2 workers, and so the two periods will be identical and separate. In such a world the probability that a firm hires a High type worker is equal to $\frac{1}{2}$, and this will also be the market clearing wage. This is the benchmark to bear in mind in the following discussion.

In a world where $r > 0$ and $\alpha > \frac{1}{2}$, learning about the period 1 worker gives the firm some information on the ability of a contact that its period 1 worker has: in particular, if period 1 worker has ability High, then the firm expects that a worker contacted via a referral is more likely to be a High type rather than a Low type. The converse is true if the period 1 worker has Low ability.[8] It is then intuitive that a firm will want to hire via referral only if its period 1 worker is of High ability. Standard arguments from the theory of search now yield a simple structure of wages: each firm using referral will offer prices drawn from a distribution which has support on the interval $[w_{M2}, \bar{w}_R]$, where $\bar{w}_R$ refers to the maximal referral wage offered by any firm and w_{M2} refers to the market wage in period 2. Moreover, again from standard considerations, it can be shown that the probability density is positive for all wages in the interval. Suppose that there is an interval of wage levels $[\underline{w}, \bar{w}] \subset [w_{M1}, \bar{w}_R]$, the probability of which is zero. It then follows that the firm offering a referral wage $\bar{w}$ can lower the wage slightly. This will have no effect on the probability of acceptance but will increase the surplus of the firm (upon acceptance). In other words, a wage offer of $\bar{w}$ cannot be optimal, contradicting the hypothesis.[9]

In period 2, a majority of the workers receiving (and accepting) the referral wages will be the High type workers, which implies that those who go on to the decentralized market will on average be lower ability than $\frac{1}{2}$: in other words there is a *lemons effect* created by the use of social connections for referral wages.

In equilibrium wages will then be a function of ability only indirectly: via the inbreeding bias that is being assumed in social connections. In particular, wages would be equal to $\frac{1}{2}$ for all workers in the absence of this inbreeding bias.

Next consider the profits of firms. In period 2, a firm which has a High type worker can hope to make positive profits. This is because it will use referral wages, and there is imperfect competition between firms who use referrals. So,

---

[8] Note that, in this model, a low-ability worker cannot refer a high-ability worker to his firm. Thus it is the ability of the worker rather that what he says about the contact that is critical for the assessment of the firm.

[9] This line of reasoning is taken from the search literature (see, for example, Burdett and Judd 1983).

expected profits are positive (and constant) across the wages in the support of the distribution $[w_{M1}, \bar{w}_R]$. However, there is free entry in the market for firms, and so expected profits in the two periods must be zero. In period 2, firms with High type workers will earn positive profits, but not the others. To compensate for this possibility of positive profits, firms have to set wages w_{M1} which are higher than expected ability of workers in period 1, $\frac{1}{2}$. These findings are summarized in the following result, due to Montgomery (1991).

Theorem 6.4. *Consider the model of referrals.*

(i) *A firm makes a referral offer in period 2 if and only if it employs a High type worker in period 1.*

(ii) *Referral wage offers are dispersed over the interval $[w_{M2}, \bar{w}_R]$ and the density of the referral wage is positive over the interval.*

(iii) *Period 2 wages are characterized by a lemons effect: $w_{M2} < \frac{1}{2}$.*

(iv) *An increase in the density of links, r, or in the inbreeding bias, α, leads to a fall in w_{M2} as well as an increase in the maximal referral wage $\bar{w}_R$.*

The intuition for the effects of changes in density of connections r and inbreeding bias α is as follows. An increase in either r or α strengthens the lemons effect: a greater proportion of High type workers are employed via referrals. This in turn lowers the average ability of workers who enter the decentralized market and this lowers w_{M2}. Turning next to the maximal referral wage, note that an increase in r increases the number of offers a period 2 workers receives, which increases competition and pushes up wages. Similarly, an increase in α increases the average type of a worker via referrals, which also pushes up the maximal referral wage. Thus an increase in either r or α leads to a greater wage dispersion, in the sense of lowering the minimum wage and increasing the maximal wage.

As was noted above, the presence of social connections implies that market wages in period 1, w_{M1}, are larger than the expected productivity of workers, $\frac{1}{2}$. An increase in r or in α drives up profits of firms who make a hire through referrals. The zero profit market equilibrium condition then implies that wages in period 1 must adjust to account for this. In other words, an increase in r or in α pushes up the first period market wage w_{M1}. Since expected profits are zero in equilibrium, this in turn implies a redistribution from period 2 workers to period 1 workers.

The social structure of contacts has powerful implications for wage inequality among period 2 workers. In equilibrium, a period 2 worker's wage is determined by the number and ability of ties he holds. A Low-ability period 2 worker is likely to have ties mostly with Low type period 1 workers; by contrast a High type period 2 worker is more likely to have ties with High type worker. This suggests that a High period 2 worker is more likely to receive referral wage offers, and will be at an advantage compared with a situation in which the social structure was absent. Moreover, even among High type workers, those who have more links with period 1 High type workers will receive more offers and therefore will land up getting higher wages. These observations highlight the implications of including social connections in a straightforward manner.

In the referral model a High type worker has no way of signaling his ability. In labor markets, workers can use mechanisms such as certificates and educational degrees to communicate their ability. This raises the question, what is the role of social connections in a context where workers also have access to such signaling mechanisms? Cassella and Hanaki (2006, forthcoming) study this question by using an extension of the model of referrals discussed above. The model contrasts signals and networks in the following plausible way: a signal can be bought at a cost and it offers a proof of ability which is valid across all potential employers, while a personal contact allows access to a single employer, and communicates ability via the assortative tie hypothesis (as in the referral model above). Their analysis yields the following insight: in a context where certificates are imperfect signals of ability, for signals to work well they must be costly to acquire. However, if they are costly to acquire, then social ties (which are cheap) become attractive and signals are not used. These contradictory pressures on signals imply that social networks are quite resilient even in the presence of "anonymous" mechanisms, such as educational certificates, which signal ability.

6.4   The Use of Social Networks: Empirical Evidence

Empirical work on the sources of information about jobs and about workers has a long and distinguished history; influential contributions include Rees (1966), Myers and Schultz (1951), Rees and Schultz (1970), and Granovetter (1973). These early studies presented evidence for specific geographical locations and/or particular occupations; in recent years, the research has covered a wider range of professions and skill levels and a number of countries as well. Taken together, this research establishes that social networks are used extensively across skill levels and across countries in labor markets.

This work has looked at the use of contacts by both employees and employers. With regard to the use of personal contacts by workers, the literature has focused on three themes. To what extent do workers rely on personal sources of information in obtaining jobs? How does the use of personal contacts vary with the nature of the job and across countries? How productive is this reliance upon contacts in terms of wages of the jobs obtained?

Early work by Rees (1966), Myers and Schultz (1951), and Granovetter (1973) first explored the extensive use of social connections in obtaining information about jobs. Myers and Schultz (1951) in a study of textile workers showed that

Table 6.3. Sources of job information.

Source	Contacts	Application	Employment agency	Ads	Other	Sample size
1. Rees and Schultz (1970)						
Typist	37.3	5.5	34.7	16.4	6.1	343
Keypunch operator	35.3	10.7	13.2	21.4	19.4	280
Accountant	23.5	6.4	25.9	26.4	17.8	170
Janitor	65.5	13.1	7.3	4.8	9.3	246
Janitress	63.6	7.5	5.2	11.2	12.5	80
Truck driver	56.8	14.9	1.5	1.5	25.3	67
Tool and die maker	53.6	18.2	1.5	17.3	9.4	127
2. Granovetter (1973)						
Professional	56.1	18.2	15.9	—[a]	9.8	132
Technical	43.5	24.6	30.4	—	1.4	69
Managerial	65.4	14.8	13.6	—	6.2	81
3. Corcoran, Datcher, and Duncan (1980)						
White males	52.0	—[b]	5.8	9.4	33.8	1499
White females	47.1	—	5.8	14.2	33.1	988
Black males	58.5	—	7.0	6.9	37.6	667
Black females	43.0	—	15.2	11.0	30.8	605

This table is based on information provided in Montgomery (1991). Rees and Schultz (1970) used data from the Chicago labor market, Granovetter (1973) used a sample of professional and managerial workers living in Newton, Massachusetts, while Corcoran, Datcher, and Duncan (1980) used data from the Panel Study on Income Dynamics (11th wave) which followed 5000 families in the 1970s in the United States. [a]Agencies and advertisements are collected together and are reported under employment agencies. [b]Gate applications are included under "other."

almost 62% of those surveyed obtained their first job via personal contacts, in contrast to only 15% who obtained their job from agencies and advertisements. Similarly, in a widely cited study, Granovetter (1973) showed that almost one half of the people he surveyed received information about their current job from a personal acquaintance.

These findings have inspired an extensive body of empirical research over the years. Table 6.3, which is based on information in Rees and Schultz (1970), Montgomery (1991), Corcoran, Datcher, and Duncan (1980), and Granovetter (1973), summarizes some of the evidence that has been collected for the United States. The extensive use of personal contacts in finding jobs has also been reported in other countries; see Harris (1987) and Fevre (1989) for studies of job information in Britain, and Watanabe (1987) for a study of the Japanese labor market. Granovetter (1994a) and Pellizzari (2004) provide an extensive set of references on information sources of job vacancies across countries.

The empirical work on variations in use of contacts across types of jobs suggests that personal contacts are used less often for higher salary jobs: there exists a negative correlation between age, education, and occupational status and the likelihood of finding one's job through personal contacts. This finding is observed in the 1978 Panel Study on Income Dynamics (Corcoran, Datcher, and Duncan 1980), the study of Indianapolis labor market (Marsden and Campbell 1990), and the 1970 Detroit area study (Marsden and Hurlbert 1988). These studies all pertain to the United States; a similar negative correlation is also observed across European countries (Pellizzari 2004).

A number of papers study the effectiveness of personal contacts both with regard to the success of finding a job and well as with regard to the wages obtained in jobs which are found via contacts. The studies use different methods and have different concerns, so it is difficult to compare them directly. However, a number of the studies find that personal contacts are an efficient way of finding jobs: a higher proportion of jobs found via contacts are likely to be accepted (Blau and Robins 1990; Holzer 1988). With regard to the relation between relative wages of jobs found via personal contacts, the evidence here is mixed. Early work by Ullman (1966) suggested that there is a positive relation between wages and hiring via contacts. In more recent work, Pellizzari (2004) finds that in some countries such as Austria, Belgium, and the Netherlands there exists a wage premium for jobs found via personal contacts, while in others countries such as Greece, Italy, Portugal, and the United Kingdom there exists a wage penalty for jobs obtained via contacts.

Moving on to the other side of the market, there is also evidence on employers using referrals in their recruitment. Indeed, a study by Holzer (1987) found that over 35% of the firms interviewed filled their last vacancy via referral. Similarly, Marsden and Campbell (1990) in their study of 53 Indiana establishments (in the United States) found that roughly 51% of the jobs had been filled through referrals.

Another major theme in the empirical work has been the distinction between strong and weak ties. In his classical account of social networks in labor markets, Granovetter (1973) presented evidence that individuals frequently obtain information on jobs from others who are not close friends or relatives but from casual acquaintances and other people whom they know only slightly. The distinction between close friends and relatives and casual acquaintances has been formalized in terms of the concept of strong and weak ties. This finding of the frequent use of slight acquaintances led to the coining of the well-known phrase, the *strength of weak ties*. This hypothesis has motivated a very large body of work over the years.

In short, Granovetter's argument proceeds as follows: strong ties are *transitive*; this means that if two individuals have a common close friend, then it is unlikely that they have no relationship at all. Therefore, strong ties cover close-knit networks, where "a friend of my friend is also my friend." On the other hand, weak ties are much less transitive, and therefore weak ties cover a larger but less dense area. Weak ties are more likely to be *bridges*: crucial ties that interconnect different subgroups in the social network. The suggested network structure implies that information from a strong tie is likely to be very similar to the information one already has. On the other hand, weak ties are more likely to open up information sources very different from one's own. Also, a society with few weak links is likely to be scattered into separate cliques with little communication between cliques. Granovetter's arguments may be viewed as an aspect of a more general theory of social structure: the idea that the social world is a collection of groups which are internally densely connected via strong links, and there are a few weak links connecting the groups.

This line of reasoning has led to two quite distinct strands of empirical enquiry. One strand of the research examines the relation between earnings in jobs obtained via strong and weak ties. One way to approach this question is to ask if, on average, the earnings in a job obtained via weak ties are higher than the earnings obtained via a strong tie. The evidence on this is mixed; while some authors such as Bridges and Villemez (1986) find negative correlation between strength of tie and earnings, others such as Bian and Ang (1997) argue that in East Asian countries job seekers rely heavily on *strong* ties in their job search. For theoretical attempts at understanding the relation between strength of tie and wages, see Lin (1990) and Montgomery (1992).[10]

A second strand of research examines the empirical properties of actual networks with a view to testing if strong ties are more transitive than weak ties and how this affects the criticality of weak and strong ties in bridging the network. The structural implications of Granovetter's hypothesis of strength of weak ties can be formulated in terms of two testable statements: that strong ties are transitive, and that weak ties are more important in reducing shortest path lengths between actors. These hypotheses have been examined by Friedkin (1980) and Borgatti and Feld (1994) for small networks and by van der Leij and Goyal (2006) for large networks.

The empirical work on the role of social networks in labor networks is nicely summarized by Granovetter (1994a):

> Despite modernization, technology, and the dizzying pace of social change, one constant in the world is that where and how we spend our working hours, the largest slice of life for most adults, depends very much on how we are embedded in networks of social contacts—the relatives, friends, and acquaintances that are not banished by the never-ending proposals to pair people to jobs by some automatic technical procedures such as national computerized matching.

---

[10] Also see Calvó-Armengol, Verdier, and Zenou (2007) for a recent attempt at studying the effects of strong and weak links on employment and crime.

6.5   Concluding Remarks

The matching between workers and their employers is characterized by imperfections in information. The study of these information problems has been at the heart of work on labor markets. The standard approach has concentrated on search and matching frictions and assumes that players are anonymous. The study of networks in labor markets departs from this tradition by relaxing the anonymity assumption: in particular, the focus is on how the pattern of social ties between individual workers shapes the matching process and thereby determines the level of employment as well as the inequality in wages.

Two types of information are especially prominent in labor markets: the information on the location of job vacancies and the information on the ability of workers. This chapter has presented formal models which incorporate these information imperfections and the analysis of these models illustrated how social networks can influence the determination of employment status, create duration dependence in unemployment, and generate inequality in incomes.

While these models reflect important progress in the study of the role of social networks in the functioning of labor markets, many questions remain open. For instance, in the context of information sharing on job vacancies the research has obtained some implications of information sharing. However, we know relatively little of how features of the network such as clustering, the diameter of the network, or the degree distribution of the network matter. In a context where workers are looking for jobs, it is natural to suppose that they will also carry out searches on their own. It is therefore important to develop models in which traditional search takes place alongside the informal sharing of information in networks.

6.6   Appendix

6.6.1   Social Transmission of Job Information

The presentation starts with the introduction of some mathematical concepts and relationships that are used in the proofs. The exposition here is based on Calvó-Armengol and Jackson (2004).[11]

Let S_i be a simple random variable which takes on values 1 or 0, reflecting the states of employment and unemployment, respectively. Let $S = \{S_1, S_2, S_3, \ldots, S_n\}$ denote the vector of random variables and let $s = (s_1, s_2, \ldots, s_n)$ denote a realization of this vector of random variables. Recall that our interest is in the relationship between the employment states of different workers who are connected via an information network. The central concept in this analysis is

---

[11] It is possible to establish analogous results using results from the theory of interactive particle systems; for an outline of proofs which use these techniques, see Mobius (2006); for a general introduction to the theory of particle systems, see Liggett (1985).

association. Let μ be a joint probability distribution on S. The joint distribution μ is said to be associated if, for any pair of nondecreasing functions $f : \{0, 1\}^n \to \mathcal{R}$ and $g : \{0, 1\}^n \to \mathcal{R}$, $\mathrm{Cov}_\mu(f, g) \geq 0$, where $\mathrm{Cov}_\mu(f, g) = E_\mu[f(s)g(s)] - E_\mu(f(s))E_\mu(g(s))$ is the covariance. Note that if the joint distribution of S is associated, then we say that the random variables are associated. In particular, association implies that any two random variables S_i and S_j are positively correlated.

The notion of *strong association* is a natural extension of the above definition. In the present context interest will center on the strong correlation between the employment states of workers who are in the same component of the network. Let $\mathcal{C} = \{C_1, C_2, \ldots, C_k\}$ be the partition of workers into distinct components of a network g. A distribution μ is strongly associated with respect to $\mathcal{C}$ if it is associated and for any component $C_l \in \mathcal{C}$, and nondecreasing functions f and g, $\mathrm{Cov}_\mu(f, g) > 0$, if f is increasing in s_i and g is increasing in s_j and i and j are in the same component C_l.

The second concept which will be used extensively is *domination*. The distribution μ *dominates* a distribution ν if for any nondecreasing function f it is the case that $E_\mu(f) \geq E_\nu(f)$. The domination is said to be strict if the inequality is strict for some nondecreasing function f. Note that, for $n = 1$, domination reduces to the idea of first-order stochastic dominance.

The following mathematical result shows that if μ dominates ν then there exists a probability transition function with a specific property—dilation—which relates the two distributions. Let $\mathcal{P}(\{0, 1\}^n)$ be the set of all probability distributions on $\{0, 1\}^n$. A probability transition function $\phi : \{0, 1\}^n \to \mathcal{P}(\{0, 1\}^n)$ is a dilation if $\phi_{ss'} > 0$ implies that $s' \geq s$.

Lemma 6.1. *Consider two distributions μ and ν on $\{0, 1\}^n$. The distribution μ dominates ν if and only if there exists a Markov probability transition function ϕ such that $\mu(s') = \sum_s \phi_{ss'}\nu(s)$, where ϕ is a dilation. Strict domination holds if $\phi_{ss'} > 0$ for some $s' \neq s$.*

The proof of this result follows as a corollary to theorem 18.40 in Aliprantis and Border (1999) and is omitted.

In the analysis the following alternative characterization of the dominance relation across distributions will also be used. Define $\mathcal{E} = \{E \subset \{0, 1\}^n \mid s \in E, s' \geq s \Rightarrow s' \in E\}$. In other words, $\mathcal{E}$ is a collection of sets (of employment states) with the property that if a state s is in a set E, then so is every state s' which dominates s. The following mathematical result presents a relation between dominance and association and the probability of such sets E.

Lemma 6.2. *Consider two distributions μ and ν on $\{0, 1\}^n$. $\mu(E) \geq \nu(E)$ for every $E \in \mathcal{E}$ if and only if μ dominates ν. Strict domination holds if and only if the inequality is strict for some $E \in \mathcal{E}$. The probability measure μ is associated if* *and only if* $\mu(EE') \geq \mu(E)\mu(E')$, *where* $E, E' \in \mathcal{E}$. *The association is strong (relative to a partition* $\mathcal{C}$*) if the inequality is strict whenever* E *and* E' *are both sensitive to some* $C_k \in \mathcal{C}$.[12]

The proof of this result is given in Calvó-Armengol and Jackson (2004) and Esary, Proschan, and Walkup (1967). This completes the presentation of the mathematical background required for the proofs of theorems 6.1 and 6.2.

The following intermediate result is useful in the proofs of the theorems. The proof is simple and is omitted.

Lemma 6.3. *Let* μ *be associated and have full support on* S. *If* f *is a nondecreasing function which is increasing in* S_i *for some* i, *and* g *is a nondecreasing function which is increasing in* S_j *for some* j, *and* $\mathrm{Cov}_\mu(S_i, S_j) > 0$, *then* $\mathrm{Cov}_\mu(f, g) > 0$.

Recall that an economy $\mathcal{M} = \{g, a, b\}$. Let P^T denote the matrix of transitions under a T period division of the dynamics: $\mathcal{M}^T = \{g, a/T, b/T\}$. So $P_{ss'}^T$ is the probability that $s_t = s'$ conditional on $s_{t-1} = s$. Define $P_{sE}^T = \sum_{s' \in E} P_{ss'}^T$ to be the transition probability from the state s to the set E.

Consider two possible states today, s and s'. If the employment status of workers in state s' is better than that in state s, then the next period state following from s' should be better than the next period state following from s, under the process P^T, as it is more likely that information on new jobs will be shared. The following result formalizes this intuition.

Lemma 6.4. *Consider an economy* $\mathcal{M} = (g, a, b)$. *Consider* s *and* s' *with* $s' \geq s$. *Then, for all* T *and* $E \in \mathcal{E}$, $P_{s'E}^T \geq P_{sE}^T$. *Moreover, if* $s' \neq s$, *then the inequality is strict for some* $E \in \mathcal{E}$.

Proof. Let states s and s' differ in the status of one worker l only and suppose that $s_l' = 1$, while $s_l = 0$. The argument presented below shows that $P_{s'E}^T \geq P_{sE}^T$. It is clear that the argument extends directly to cover $s' \geq s$ which differ by more than one worker, by a sequence of similar pairwise comparisons.

Recall that $p_{ij}(s)$ is the probability that information about a job arrives at i and lands up with j. By hypothesis $s_k = s_k'$ for all $k \neq l$ and so it follows that $p_{ij}(s') \geq p_{ij}(s)$ for all $j \neq l$ and for all i. Moreover, for worker l, $s_l' > s_l$ and so the probability of worker l being employed following on s' is larger than the probability of being employed following on s. Putting together these observations we get that $\mathrm{Pr}_{s'}^T(S_t)$ dominates $\mathrm{Pr}_s^T(S_t)$ (where $\mathrm{Pr}_s^T(\cdot)$ is the probability distribution conditional on state $s_{t-1} = s$). The result now follows by an application of lemma 6.2.

---

[12] The set E is sensitive to C_l if its indicator function is sensitive. A nondecreasing function $f : \{0, 1\}^n \to \mathcal{R}$ is sensitive to $C_l \in \mathcal{C}$ if there exist s and $\tilde{s}_C$ such that $f(s) \neq f(s_{-C}, \tilde{s}_C)$, and s, $(s_{-C}, \tilde{s}_C)$ are in the support of μ.

The strict domination part follows from the observation that starting at s there is a strictly positive probability of player l being unemployed in the interim state before the firing stage, while the probability of worker l being unemployed at this stage is equal to zero starting at state s'. $\qquad\square$

The above result concerns the effects of starting at higher employment states. We now establish a similar result with regard to initial distributions of states of employment. Given a probability distribution μ on $\{0, 1\}^n$, let μP^T be the induced distribution in the next period.

Lemma 6.5. *Consider an economy* $\mathcal{M} = (g, a, b)$ *and two measures* μ *and* ν. *If* μ *dominates* ν, *then* μP^T *dominates* νP^T *for all* T. *Moreover, if* μ *strictly dominates* ν, *then* μP^T *strictly dominates* νP^T *for all* T.

Proof. For any $E \in \mathcal{E}$ we wish to show that

$$[\mu P^T](E) - [\nu P^T](E) = \sum_s P_{sE}^T [\mu_s - \nu_s] \geq 0. \tag{6.1}$$

By lemma 6.1 we rewrite this as

$$[\mu P^T](E) - [\nu P^T](E) = \sum_s P_{sE}^T \left(\sum_{s'} \nu_{s'} \phi_{s's} - \nu_s \right), \tag{6.2}$$

where ϕ is a dilation function. The right-hand side of this equation can be rewritten as

$$\sum_s \sum_{s'} \nu_{s'} \phi_{s's} P_{sE}^T - \sum_s \nu_s P_{sE}^T, \tag{6.3}$$

which, since the second term depends only on s, can in turn be rewritten as

$$\sum_{s'} \left[\sum_s \nu_{s'} \phi_{s's} P_{sE}^T - \nu_{s'} P_{s'E}^T \right]. \tag{6.4}$$

Note now that ϕ is a dilation, and so $\phi_{s's} > 0$ only if $s \geq s'$. This allows us to say that

$$[\mu P^T](E) - [\nu P^T](E) = \sum_{s'} \nu_{s'} \left[\sum_{s \geq s'} \phi_{s's} P_{sE}^T - P_{s'E}^T \right]. \tag{6.5}$$

Lemma 6.4 then implies that $P_{sE}^T \geq P_{s'E}^T$ whenever $s \geq s'$. Since $\phi_{s's} \geq 0$ and $\sum_{s \geq s'} \phi_{s's} = 1$, the desired inequality obtains.

Suppose next that μ strictly dominates ν. Then from lemma 6.1 this implies that there exists some $s \neq s'$ such that $\phi_{s's} > 0$. From lemma 6.4 this implies that there exists some $E \in \mathcal{E}$ such that $P_{sE}^T > P_{s'E}^T$. It then follows that $[\mu P^T](E) > [\mu P^T](E)$, for such E, and from lemma 6.2 this implies that μP^T strictly dominates νP^T. $\qquad\square$

Theorem 6.5. *Consider the Markov process of employment status of workers* $\mathcal{M}^T$. *There exists a* $\hat{T}$ *such that for all* $T \geqslant \hat{T}$, *the long-run distribution* μ^T *is unique and in this distribution, the employment status of path-connected workers is positively correlated.*

Proof. The proof of this theorem involves a number of arguments and it is useful to present them in separate steps.

Step 1. For any T, P^T is an irreducible and aperiodic Markov chain, so it has a unique invariant/steady-state distribution μ^T. Moreover, the steady-state distributions μ^T converge to a unique limit distribution as T grows, i.e., $\lim_{T \to \infty} = \mu^*$ (for a proof of this, see Young (1998)).

The transition matrix P^T is based on the arrival rates of information a, the rate of firing b, as well as the network g. In general, the probability of two players receiving information on a job will be correlated. For example, if i and j are both neighbors of k, and unemployed, then the probability of i receiving information from k is negatively related to the probability of j receiving this information. It is, therefore, much simpler to work with a modified dynamic process $\bar{P}^T$, in which the probability of i receiving information about a job is $p_i(s) = \sum_{j \in N} p_{ji}(s)$ and it is assumed that p_i is independent of p_j, for any pair of players. Again, from standard considerations, it follows that the process has a unique invariant distribution. Let $\bar{\mu}^T$ be this invariant distribution and let $\bar{\mu}^* = \lim_{T \to \infty} \bar{\mu}^T$. The next step relates the invariant distribution of the original process and the invariant distribution of this modified process.

Step 2. $\bar{\mu}^* = \mu^*$. As a first step in the proof of this equality, it is useful to derive an expression for the probability of any state s under the invariant distribution. Let $\mathcal{Z}$ be a finite-state space and let P be an irreducible and aperiodic Markov process on this state space. A z-tree is a weighted directed tree on vertices $\mathcal{Z}$, with a unique directed path from every state $z' \neq z$ to z. The weight of a link zz', where $z \neq z'$, is $P_{zz'}$. Denote the set of all z-trees by T_z. Define

$$p_z = \sum_{\tau \in T_z} \left[\prod_{z', z'' \in \tau} P_{z'z''} \right]. \tag{6.6}$$

The following result is due to Freidlin and Wentzel (1984). *If P is a transition matrix for an aperiodic and irreducible Markov chain on $\mathcal{Z}$, then its unique invariant distribution μ is described by*

$$\mu(z) = \frac{p_z}{\sum_{z' \in \mathcal{Z}} p_{z'}}. \tag{6.7}$$

Given some state $s \in S$, consider the set of s-trees in which every adjacent node is an adjacent state,[13] and denote it by T_s^*. Now note that as T grows large,

---

[13] Two states are said to be adjacent if there is one and only one worker $l \in \{1, 2, \ldots, n\}$ such that $s_l \neq s_l'$ and $s_i = s_i'$ for all $i \neq l$.

$P^T_{s,s'}$ goes to 0 at rate $1/T$ if s and s' are adjacent, and goes to 0 at rate at least $1/T^2$ for nonadjacent states. The above characterization on invariant distribution can now be used to argue that for sufficiently large T, $\mu^T(s)$ can be approximated by

$$\mu(s) = \frac{\sum_{\tau \in T^*_s} \prod_{s',s'' \in \tau} P^T_{s',s''}}{\sum_{\hat{s}} \sum_{\tau \in T^*_{\hat{s}}} \prod_{s',s'' \in \tau} P^T_{s',s''}}. \tag{6.8}$$

For large T, and adjacent s and s', $P^T_{s,s'} = b/T + o(1/T^2)$ for the case where one fewer worker has a job, and $P^T_{s,s'} = p_i(s)/T + o(1/T^2)$ for the transition where one additional worker has a job. (Here $o(1/T^2)$ refers to the terms which go to zero at rate $1/T^2$.) Now define $\hat{P}^T_{s,s'} = b/T$ for $s > s'$ and $\hat{P}^T_{s,s'} = p_i(s)/T$ for $s < s'$. The probability under the limit distribution μ^* can now be written as

$$\mu^*(s) = \lim_{T \to \infty} \frac{\sum_{\tau \in T^*_s} \prod_{s',s'' \in \tau} \hat{P}^T_{s',s''}}{\sum_{\hat{s}} \sum_{\tau \in T^*_{\hat{s}}} \prod_{s',s'' \in \tau} \hat{P}^T_{s',s''}}. \tag{6.9}$$

The proof of step 2 is completed by noting that the limit $\bar{\mu}^*$ is defined analogously. We next turn to the properties of this limit distribution.

Step 3. $\bar{\mu}^*$ *is associated.* First note from above that

$$\bar{\mu}^*(s) = \lim_{T \to \infty} \frac{\sum_{\tau \in T^*_s} \prod_{s',s'' \in \tau} \hat{P}^T_{s',s''}}{\sum_{\hat{s}} \sum_{\tau \in T^*_{\hat{s}}} \prod_{s',s'' \in \tau} \hat{P}^T_{s',s''}}. \tag{6.10}$$

Multiplying numerator and denominator of the right-hand side of the above equation by T, we get

$$\bar{\mu}^*(s) = \frac{\sum_{\tau \in T^*_s} \prod_{s',s'' \in \tau} \bar{P}^T_{s',s''}}{\sum_{\hat{s}} \sum_{\tau \in T^*_{\hat{s}}} \prod_{s',s'' \in \tau} \bar{P}^T_{s',s''}}, \tag{6.11}$$

where $\bar{P}^T_{s,s'} = b$ for $s > s'$ and $\bar{P}^T_{s,s'} = p_i(s)$ for $s < s'$ and $\bar{P}^T_{s,s'} = 0$ for nonadjacent states.

Suppose that for T and any associated μ, $\mu \bar{P}^T$ is associated. From this, it follows that if we start from an associated μ_0 at time 0, then $\mu_0(\bar{P}^T)^k$ is associated for any k. Since $\bar{\mu}^T = \lim_k \mu_0(\bar{P}^T)^k$ for any μ_0 and association is preserved under (weak) convergence,[14] this implies that $\bar{\mu}^T$ is associated for all T. Since $\bar{\mu}^* = \lim_{T \to \infty} \bar{\mu}^T$, analogous reasoning implies that $\bar{\mu}^*$ is associated. So the claim is proved if we show that $\nu = \mu \bar{P}^T$ is associated.

From lemma 6.2 it is sufficient to show that

$$\nu(EE') - \nu(E)\nu(E') \geq 0 \tag{6.12}$$

---

[14] For a treatment of convergence issues, see Szekli (1995).

for any $E, E' \in \mathcal{E}$. This expression can be rewritten as

$$v(EE') - v(E)v(E') = \sum_s \mu(s)[\bar{P}^T_{sEE'} - \bar{P}^T_{sE}v(E')]. \qquad (6.13)$$

Now note that conditional on $S_{t-1} = s$, S_t is independent, and so it is also associated. Thus

$$\bar{P}^T_{sEE'} \geqslant \bar{P}^T_{sE}\bar{P}^T_{sE'}. \qquad (6.14)$$

Substituting in equation (6.12) yields

$$v(EE') - v(E)v(E') \geqslant \sum_s \mu(s)[\bar{P}^T_{sE}\bar{P}^T_{sE'} - \bar{P}^T_{sE}v(E')]. \qquad (6.15)$$

This inequality can be rewritten as

$$v(EE') - v(E)v(E') \geqslant \sum_s \mu(s)\bar{P}^T_{sE}[\bar{P}^T_{sE'} - v(E')]. \qquad (6.16)$$

Now note that both $\bar{P}^T_{sE}$ and $[\bar{P}^T_{sE'} - v(E')]$ are increasing functions of s. Since μ is associated it follows from (6.16) that

$$v(EE') - v(E)v(E') \geqslant \left[\sum_s \mu(s)\bar{P}^T_{sE}\right]\left[\sum_s \mu(s)(\bar{P}^T_{sE'} - v(E'))\right]. \quad (6.17)$$

From the definition of v, it follows that the second term on the right-hand side of the inequality is 0. This completes the proof of step 3.

Step 4. $\bar{\mu}^*$ is strongly associated. The aim is to establish that for any pair of functions f and g which are increasing in s_i and s_j, respectively, where i and j are path connected, $\mathrm{Cov}_{\bar{\mu}^*}(f, g) > 0$. From lemma 6.3 it is sufficient to show that $\mathrm{Cov}_{\bar{\mu}^*}(S_i, S_j) > 0$.

For any probability transition matrix P, let

$$P_{sij} = \sum_{s'} P_{ss'}s'_is'_j \quad \text{and} \quad P_{si} = \sum_{s'} P_{ss'}s'_i.$$

Define

$$\mathrm{Cov}^T_{ij} = \sum_s \bar{\mu}^T(s)\bar{P}^T_{sij} - \sum_s \bar{\mu}^T(s)\bar{P}^T_{si}\sum_{s'}\bar{\mu}^T(s')\bar{P}^T_{s'j}. \qquad (6.18)$$

Thus it is sufficient to show that $\mathrm{Cov}^T_{ij} > 0$ for large T.

The diagonal entries in the transition matrix $\bar{P}^T$ tend to 1 while the nondiagonal entries tend to 0 as $T \to \infty$. Define a new but closely related transition matrix in which some nondiagonal entries do not tend to 0 as follows:

$$\underline{P}^T_{s,s'} = \begin{cases} T\bar{P}^T_{s,s'} & \text{if } s \neq s', \\ 1 - \sum_{s'' \neq s} T\bar{P}^T_{s''} & \text{if } s = s'. \end{cases}$$

It is easily verified that the invariant distribution under this transition matrix is identical to the invariant distribution under $\bar{P}^T$. This then implies that

$$\text{Cov}_{ij}^T = \sum_s \bar{\mu}^T(s) \underline{P}_{sij}^T - \sum_s \bar{\mu}^T(s) \underline{P}_{si}^T \sum_{s'} \bar{\mu}^T(s') \underline{P}_{s'j}^T. \tag{6.19}$$

Moreover, the transitions across time are still independent under $\underline{P}^T$. This implies that starting from any s, the distribution $\underline{P}_s^T$ is associated and so

$$\underline{P}_{sij}^T \geqslant \underline{P}_{si}^T \underline{P}_{sj}^T. \tag{6.20}$$

This implies that

$$\text{Cov}_{ij}^T \geqslant \sum_s \bar{\mu}^T(s) \underline{P}_{si}^T \underline{P}_{si}^T - \sum_s \bar{\mu}^T(s) \underline{P}_{sj}^T \sum_{s'} \bar{\mu}^T(s') \underline{P}_{s'j}^T. \tag{6.21}$$

It follows that $\underline{P}_{si}^T$ converges to $\tilde{P}_{si}$, where $\tilde{P}_{si}$ is a rescaled version of $\hat{P}$ as defined in step 3 above. In other words,

$$\tilde{P}_{s,s'}^T = \begin{cases} T \hat{P}_{s,s'}^T & \text{if } s \neq s', \\ 1 - T \hat{P}_{s,s'}^T & \text{if } s = s'. \end{cases}$$

This allows us to state that

$$\lim_{T \to \infty} \text{Cov}_{ij}^T \geqslant \sum_s \bar{\mu}^*(s) \tilde{P}_{si} \tilde{P}_{sj} - \sum_s \bar{\mu}^*(s) \tilde{P}_{si} \sum_{s'} \bar{\mu}^*(s') \tilde{P}_{s'j}. \tag{6.22}$$

It is now shown that the right-hand side of the above inequality is strictly positive. Note that $\tilde{P}_{si}$ and $\tilde{P}_{sj}$ can be viewed as functions of s, and that they are both nondecreasing functions and so it is sufficient to show that $\text{Cov}(\tilde{P}_{si}, \tilde{P}_{sj}) > 0$.

First recall from step 3 that $\bar{\mu}^*$ is associated. Second, consider the case that $g_{ij} = 1$. Observe that $\tilde{P}_{si}$ is increasing in s_i and also in s_j (since $g_{ij} = 1$). Moreover, $\tilde{P}_{sj}$ is also increasing in s_j. It then follows, from lemma 6.3, that $\text{Cov}(\tilde{P}_{si}, \tilde{P}_{sj}) > 0$. This argument can be extended in a natural way to cover the case where the connection between two workers i and k is indirect. This completes the proof that $\lim_{T \to \infty} \text{Cov}_{ij}^T > 0$. The proof of theorem 6.1 is now completed by observing that $\bar{\mu}^T \to \bar{\mu}^*$. $\qquad\square$

Theorem 6.6. *Consider the Markov process of employment status of workers $\mathcal{M}^T$. There exists a $\hat{T}$ such that for all $T \geqslant \hat{T}$, starting from the long-run distribution μ^T the employment status of any two path-connected workers is positively correlated across arbitrary time periods.*

Proof. Step 4 from the proof of theorem 6.1 says that $\bar{\mu}^*$ is strongly associated. The result then follows by repeated application of lemma 6.5, and taking T large enough so that $\bar{\mu}^T$ is close enough to $\bar{\mu}^*$ (for the desired strict inequalities to hold). $\qquad\square$

Theorem 6.7. *Consider the Markov process of employment status of workers* $\mathcal{M}^T$. *There exists a* $\hat{T}$ *such that, for all* $T \geq \hat{T}$, *starting from the long-run distribution* μ^T *the conditional probability that a worker will be employed in a given period is decreasing with the length of their observed unemployment spell.*

Proof. It will be shown that, for any worker i, the probability of securing employment after a k-period spell of unemployment is larger than the probability of unemployment after a $(k+1)$-period of unemployment.

For $t > t' \geq 0$, let $h_{i0}^{t',t}$ be the event that $S_{it'} = \cdots = S_{i,t-1} = S_{i,t} = 0$ and let $h_{i1}^{t',t}$ be the event that $S_{it'} = 1$ and $S_{it'+1} = \cdots = S_{i,t-1} = S_{i,t} = 0$. In other words the two events $h_{i0}^{t',t}$ and $h_{i1}^{t',t}$ differ only in the outcome in period t'. It will be shown that

$$P(S_{i,t+1} = 1 \mid h_{i0}^{0,t}) < P(S_{i,t+1} = 1 \mid h_{i0}^{1,t}). \tag{6.23}$$

Observe that $P(S_{i,t+1} = 1 \mid h_{i0}^{1,t})$ is a weighted average of $P(S_{i,t+1} = 1 \mid h_{i0}^{0,t})$ and $P(S_{i,t+1} = 1 \mid h_{i1}^{0,t})$. We need to show that

$$P(S_{i,t+1} = 1 \mid h_{i0}^{0,t}) < P(S_{i,t+1} = 1 \mid h_{i1}^{0,t}). \tag{6.24}$$

From Bayes's rule the expressions for these probabilities are

$$P(S_{i,t+1} = 1 \mid h_{i0}^{0,t}) = \frac{P(S_{i,t=1} = 1, h_{i0}^{0,t})}{P(S_{i,t=1} = 1, h_{i0}^{0,t}) + P(S_{i,t=1} = 0, h_{i0}^{0,t})}, \tag{6.25}$$

$$P(S_{i,t+1} = 1 \mid h_{i1}^{0,t}) = \frac{P(S_{i,t+1=1} = 1, h_{i1}^{0,t})}{P(S_{i,t+1=1} = 1, h_{i1}^{0,t}) + P(S_{i,t+1=1} = 0, h_{i1}^{0,t})}. \tag{6.26}$$

Substituting these two expressions in (6.24) yields the requirement that

$$\frac{P(S_{i,t+1} = 1, h_{i0}^{0,t})}{P(S_{i,t+1} = 1, h_{i0}^{0,t}) + P(S_{i,t+1} = 0, h_{i0}^{0,t})}$$
$$< \frac{P(S_{i,t+1} = 1, h_{i1}^{0,t})}{P(S_{i,t+1} = 1, h_{i1}^{0,t}) + P(S_{i,t+1} = 0, h_{i1}^{0,t})}. \tag{6.27}$$

Rearranging this inequality we get

$$P(S_{i,t+1} = 1, h_{i0}^{0,t}) P(S_{i,t+1} = 0, h_{i1}^{0,t})$$
$$< P(S_{i,t+1} = 1, h_{i1}^{0,t}) P(S_{i,t+1} = 1, h_{i0}^{0,t}). \tag{6.28}$$

For any time period x, let E_{i0}^x be the set of states in which $s_{i,x} = 0$ and let E_{i1}^x be the states in which $s_{i,x} = 1$. Recall that μ^* is the unique steady-state distribution and divide (6.28) by $\mu^*(E_{i0}^0)\mu^*(E_{i1}^0)$ to obtain

$$\frac{P(S_{i,t+1} = 1, h_{i0}^{0,t})}{\mu^*(E_{i0}^0)} \frac{P(S_{i,t+1} = 0, h_{i1}^{0,t})}{\mu^*(E_{i1}^0)}$$

$$< \frac{P(S_{i,t+1} = 1, h_{i1}^{0,t})}{\mu^*(E_{i1}^0)} \frac{P(S_{i,t+1} = 0, h_{i0}^{0,t})}{\mu^*(E_{i0}^0)}. \qquad (6.29)$$

To establish this inequality it suffices to show that

$$\frac{P(S_{i,t+1} = 1, h_{i0}^{0,t})}{\mu^*(E_{i0}^0)} < \frac{P(S_{i,t+1} = 1, h_{i1}^{0,t})}{\mu^*(E_{i1}^0)}, \qquad (6.30)$$

$$\frac{P(S_{i,t+1} = 0, h_{i1}^{0,t})}{\mu^*(E_{i1}^0)} < \frac{P(S_{i,t+1} = 0, h_{i0}^{0,t})}{\mu^*(E_{i0}^0)}. \qquad (6.31)$$

We establish inequality (6.30); the proof for (6.31) is analogous and omitted. First observe that the left-hand side of (6.30),

$$\frac{P(S_{i,t+1} = 1, h_{i0}^{0,t})}{\mu^*(E_{i0}^0)}$$

$$= \sum_{s^0 \in E_{i0}^0} \sum_{s^1 \in E_{i0}^1} \cdots \sum_{s^{t+1} \in E_{i1}^{t+1}} \frac{\mu^*(s^0)}{\mu^*(E_{i0}^0)} P_{s^0 s^1} P_{s^1 s^2} \cdots P_{s^t s^{t+1}}, \qquad (6.32)$$

which may be rewritten as follows:

$$\frac{P(S_{i,t+1} = 1, h_{i0}^{0,t})}{\mu^*(E_{i0}^0)}$$

$$= \sum_{s^0 \in E_{i0}^0} \sum_{s^1 \in E_{i0}^1} \cdots \sum_{s^{t+1} \in E_{i0}^{t+1}} \mu^*(s^0 \mid E_{i0}^0) P_{s^0 s^1} P_{s^1 s^2} \cdots P_{s^t s^{t+1}}. \qquad (6.33)$$

Similarly, the right-hand side can be written as

$$\frac{P(S_{i,t+1} = 1, h_{i1}^{0,t})}{\mu^*(E_{i1}^0)}$$

$$= \sum_{s^0 \in E_{i1}^0} \sum_{s^1 \in E_{i1}^1} \cdots \sum_{s^{t+1} \in E_{i1}^{t+1}} \mu^*(s^0 \mid E_{i1}^0) P_{s^0 s^1} P_{s^1 s^2} \cdots P_{s^t s^{t+1}}. \qquad (6.34)$$

From theorem 6.1 it follows that $\mu^*(s^0 \mid E_{i1}^0)$ dominates $\mu^*(s^0 \mid E_{i0}^0)$, with some strict inequalities for some states s^0 (since i is connected to at least one other agent). Inequality (6.30) now follows from the above equations and repeated application of lemma 6.5, across time periods $1, 2, \ldots, t + 1$. $\qquad \square$

6.6.2 Adverse Selection

Theorem 6.8. *Consider the model of referrals.*

(i) *A firm makes a referral offer in period 2 if and only if it employs a High-ability worker in period 1.*

(ii) *Referral wage offers are dispersed over the interval $[w_{M2}, \bar{w}_R]$ and the density of the referral wage is positive over the interval.*

(iii) *Period 2 wages are characterized by a lemons effect: $w_{M2} < \frac{1}{2}$.*

(iv) *An increase in the density of links, r, or in the inbreeding bias, α, leads to a fall in w_{M2} as well as an increase in the maximal referral wage $\bar{w}_R$.*

Proof. We will compute w_{M2}, the profits of firms offering referral wages, the nature of w_{M1}, and the nature of the distribution of referral offers.

We start with a consideration of the decision problem of a High type worker H, faced with a referral wage w_{Ri}:

$$\Pr\{\text{H accepts } w_{Ri}\} = \Pr\{\text{H receives no higher offer } w_{Rj} \; \forall j \neq i\}$$

$$= \prod_{j \neq i} \Pr\{\text{H receives no higher offer } w_{Rj}\}$$

$$= \prod_{j \neq i}(1 - \Pr\{\text{H receives } w_{Rj} > w_{Ri}\}), \qquad (6.35)$$

where

$$\Pr\{\text{H receives } w_{Rj} > w_{Ri}\}$$
$$= \Pr\{\text{firm } j \text{ makes an offer}\}\Pr\{\text{offer } w_{Rj} > w_{Ri}\}. \qquad (6.36)$$

Suppose $F(\cdot)$ is the distribution of referral wages. Then this expression is equal to

$$\left(\frac{\alpha r}{N}\right)(1 - F(w_{Ri})), \qquad (6.37)$$

where we have used the fact that there are N High type workers.

Substituting into the above expression yields

$$\Pr\{\text{H accepts } w_{Ri}\} = \left(1 - \left(\frac{\alpha r}{N}\right)(1 - F(w_{Ri}))\right)^{N-1}. \qquad (6.38)$$

From standard considerations, it follows that

$$\lim_{N \to \infty} \Pr\{\text{H accepts } w_{Ri}\} = e^{-\alpha r(1 - F(w_{Ri}))}. \qquad (6.39)$$

Similarly, for N large,

$$\Pr\{\text{L accepts } w_{Ri}\} = e^{-(1-\alpha)r(1 - F(w_{Ri}))}. \qquad (6.40)$$

In what follows we will implicitly be assuming that N is equal to infinity.

Note that

$$\Pr\{\text{H accepts } w_{Ri}\} < \Pr\{\text{L accepts } w_{Ri}\} \tag{6.41}$$

because a High type worker is more likely to receive more offers, since $\alpha > \frac{1}{2}$.

Note next that

$$\Pr\{\text{market} \mid \text{H}\} = \Pr\{\text{H accepts } w_{M2}\} = e^{-\alpha r}, \tag{6.42}$$

$$\Pr\{\text{market} \mid \text{L}\} = \Pr\{\text{L accepts } w_{M2}\} = e^{-(1-\alpha)r}. \tag{6.43}$$

We now exploit the assumption of infinite N to derive the expected productivity of workers in the period 2 market:

$$\Pr\{\text{H} \mid \text{market}\} = \frac{\Pr\{\text{market} \mid \text{H}\} \Pr\{\text{H}\}}{\Pr\{\text{market} \mid \text{H}\} \Pr\{\text{H}\} + \Pr\{\text{market} \mid \text{L}\} \Pr\{\text{L}\}}$$

$$= \frac{e^{-\alpha r}}{e^{-\alpha r} + e^{-(1-\alpha)r}}. \tag{6.44}$$

In this derivation we have used the assumption that $\Pr\{\text{H}\} = \Pr\{\text{L}\} = \frac{1}{2}$.

Note that we use actual α and r, not realized values. (This is not a problem since we are assuming that N is equal to infinity.) Now note that due to competition, wages will be equal to average productivity of workers in the market. Hence market wages in the second period are

$$w_{M2} = \frac{e^{-\alpha r}}{e^{-\alpha r} + e^{-(1-\alpha)r}}. \tag{6.45}$$

Notice that $w_{M2} < \frac{1}{2}$, and that this means that market wage is less than the average period 2 productivity! It is possible to check that w_{M2} is falling in α and r.

What is the profit earned by a firm that has a period 1 High-ability worker and that chooses to offer a referral wage?

$$E(\Pi \mid w_R) = \Pr\{\text{H hired} \mid w_R\}(1 - w_R) + \Pr\{\text{L hired} \mid w_R\}(-w_R), \tag{6.46}$$

$$\Pr\{\text{H hired} \mid w_R\} = \Pr\{\text{offer made to H}\} \Pr\{\text{H accepts } w_R\}$$

$$= \alpha r e^{-\alpha r(1 - F(w_R))}. \tag{6.47}$$

Similarly,

$$\Pr\{\text{L hired} \mid w_R\} = (1 - \alpha) r e^{-(1-\alpha)r(1 - F(w_R))}. \tag{6.48}$$

Thus

$$E(\Pi_H \mid w_R) = \alpha r e^{-\alpha r(1 - F(w_R))}(1 - w_R) + (1 - \alpha) r e^{-(1-\alpha)r(1 - F(w_R))}(-w_R). \tag{6.49}$$

Firms must be earning the same profits for all wage offers $w_R \in [w_{M2}, \bar{w}_R]$:

$$\alpha r e^{-\alpha r(1 - F(w_R))}(1 - w_R) + (1 - \alpha) r e^{-(1-\alpha)r(1 - F(w_R))}(-w_R) = c \quad \forall w_R. \tag{6.50}$$

Substituting for $w_R = w_{M2} = e^{-\alpha r}/(e^{-\alpha r} + e^{-(1-\alpha)r})$:

$$c(\alpha, r) = \frac{(2\alpha - 1)r}{e^{-\alpha r} + e^{-(1-\alpha)r}}. \tag{6.51}$$

$c(\alpha, r) > 0$ since $\alpha > \frac{1}{2}$. Thus such a firm will always offer referral wages. It may be checked that $c(\cdot)$ is increasing in both α and r.

We next derive $\bar{w}_R$. By definition, $F(\bar{w}_R) = 1$:

$$\alpha r(1 - \bar{w}_R) + (1 - \alpha)r(-\bar{w}_R) = \frac{(2\alpha - 1)r}{e^{-\alpha r} + e^{-(1-\alpha)r}}$$

$$\implies \quad \alpha r - r(\bar{w}_R) = \frac{(2\alpha - 1)r}{e^{-\alpha r} + e^{-(1-\alpha)r}}$$

$$\implies \quad r(\alpha - \bar{w}_R) = \frac{(2\alpha - 1)r}{e^{-\alpha r} + e^{-(1-\alpha)r}}$$

$$= c(\alpha, r). \tag{6.52}$$

Hence,

$$\bar{w}_R = \alpha - c/r. \tag{6.53}$$

It is possible to verify that this wage is increasing in α and also in r.

We now show that firms hiring an L-type worker in period 1 will not offer a referral wage:

$$E(\Pi_L \mid w_R) = (1 - \alpha)re^{-\alpha r(1 - F(w_R))}(1 - w_R)$$
$$+ \alpha re^{-(1-\alpha)r(1 - F(w_R))}(-w_R), \tag{6.54}$$

$$\frac{\partial E(\Pi_L \mid w_R)}{\partial w_R} = (1 - \alpha)re^{-\alpha r(1 - F(w_R))}(1 - w_R)\alpha r(F'(w_R))$$
$$+ (1 - \alpha)re^{-\alpha r(1 - F(w_R))}(-1)$$
$$+ \alpha re^{-(1-\alpha)r(1 - F(w_R))}(-w_R)\alpha r(-F'(w_R))$$
$$+ \alpha re^{-(1-\alpha)r(1 - F(w_R))}(-1), \tag{6.55}$$

$$\frac{\partial E(\Pi_H \mid w_R)}{\partial w_R} = \alpha re^{-\alpha r(1 - F(w_R))}(1 - w_R)\alpha r(F'(w_R))$$
$$+ \alpha re^{-\alpha r(1 - F(w_R))}(-1)$$
$$+ (1 - \alpha)re^{-(1-\alpha)r(1 - F(w_R))}(-w_R)\alpha r(-F'(w_R))$$
$$+ (1 - \alpha)re^{-(1-\alpha)r(1 - F(w_R))}(-1). \tag{6.56}$$

It can be checked that

$$\frac{\partial E(\Pi_L \mid w_R)}{\partial w_R} < \frac{\partial E(\Pi_H \mid w_R)}{\partial w_R}. \tag{6.57}$$

The latter is zero for all $w \in (w_{M2}, \bar{w}_R)$, since all referral offers yield the same profits.

So $E(\Pi_L \mid w_R)$ is maximized at w_{M2}. It can be checked that

$$E(\Pi_L \mid w_{M2}) = \frac{(1 - 2\alpha)e^{-r}}{e^{-\alpha r} + e^{-(1-\alpha)r}} < 0 \tag{6.58}$$

since $\alpha < \frac{1}{2}$. Going to the market can ensure that $E\Pi_L = 0$. Hence a firm with an L-type worker in period 1 will *not make a referral offer*.

Given free entry in period 1, firms set wages equal to expected ability in period 1 plus expected profits in period 2:

$$w_{M1}(\alpha, r) = \frac{1}{2} + \frac{1}{2}c(\alpha, r) = \frac{1}{2}(1 + c(\alpha, r)). \tag{6.59}$$

$\square$

7

Strategic Network Formation: Concepts

7.1 Introduction

The first part of the book argued that the network structure has profound effects on individual behavior and payoffs as well as on aggregate social outcomes. In particular, we observed that individuals occupying certain positions in a network have access to substantial advantages. In the context of interfirm alliances, for instance, collaborations create cost advantages which increase market share and profits. Similarly, we found that in labor markets, two workers with the same ability would earn different wages depending on the number of their personal connections.[1] These advantages suggest that individual entities—firms, workers, managers, or countries—will have an incentive to form connections with others to shape the network in ways that are advantageous to themselves. These general considerations suggest an economic approach in which individuals will trade off the costs and benefits of forming connections. This economic theory of network formation has been extensively studied in the past ten years. The aim of this chapter is to present an overview of the basic elements of the theory. The next three chapters will present a number of applications, with a view to illustrating how this theory can be used to examine interesting economic questions.

The strategic aspect of link formation arises from the observation that links between a pair of individual entities influence the payoffs to others, i.e., generates externalities, in ways that are sensitive to the structure of the network. A game of network formation specifies a set of players, the link formation actions available to each player and the payoffs to each player from the networks that arise out of individual linking decisions. There are a number of different possibilities with regard to how a model of network formation can be developed. Two issues are especially worth noting: the specification of the individual and social values arising from networks, and the decision power of different individuals in determining links.

Let us first discuss the issue of individual and social values. In chapter 3 we studied social sharing of information. One of the main findings was that changing

---

[1] See chapters 3 and 6 for discussion on network advantages for firms and workers, respectively.

the network structure has a significant effect on individual payoffs. In particular, we showed that a link between a peripheral player in a star and a central player in another star can lead to very asymmetric effects on the payoffs to the two players. The modeling question is, how should the returns to a player i from a link with player j be defined? There are a number of different ways in which this can be done. One possibility is to suppose that no transfers are possible and every player pays her share of the costs of linking. However, given that the returns are asymmetric, it would also be reasonable to derive the division of costs of linking from a bargaining process between the firms. The choice of the payoff allocation rule will have a bearing on the incentives of firms and will in turn shape the network of collaboration.

Next consider the issue of decision power. Which firms should have the power to decide on a link between two firms i and j? A simple way to proceed is to assume that any one firm can decide to form the link with another firm. A second possibility is to suppose that only the two firms directly involved have a say in the matter. However, a link between i and j alters the payoffs to others, and it seems reasonable to suppose that the other firms, especially the existing current partners of firms i and j, should have some say in the formation of a link between i and j. The rules defining the decision power on link formation are likely to have a bearing on which links will form.

A network is said to be strategically stable or in equilibrium if there are no incentives for individual players—either acting alone or in groups—to form or delete links and thereby alter the network. The research on network formation has focused on single- or two-player incentives. One of the principal attractions of networks is that they are amenable to subtle and quick transformations via local, and small-scale, linking and de-linking activity. In line with this observation, it has been felt that invoking the incentives, coordination, and agreements among large groups is not the "right" way to approach a positive theory of network formation. Another important reason is tractability; networks are complicated objects and even with single- or two-person moves the analysis of network formation is quite intricate and general characterization results have been difficult to obtain.

Bearing in mind the complexity of the network formation game, we start with a consideration of the simplest scenario: each player can form links with any subset of players. The payoffs to a player depend on her own links as well as the links that other players form. The primary motivation for a study of one-sided link formation is methodological: it leads to a simple model of link formation which captures essential economic trade-offs and it can be analyzed with the help of familiar concepts such as Nash equilibrium. In some important instances—such as forming links on the World Wide Web, citations, making gifts, and investing in observing the actions of others—one-sided link formation is also descriptively appropriate. We start with a description of a static game and define Nash equilibrium in such contexts. We then present a model of dynamic network formation and briefly discuss absorbing networks and the relation between absorbing networks and Nash equilibrium networks.

We then turn to a model of network formation in which a link between i and j requires the assent of both the individuals. The analysis of bilateral link formation games requires concepts that go beyond single-person deviation and hence beyond Nash equilibrium. We present the main concepts that have been developed in increasing order of complexity: starting with pairwise stability, which looks at incentives to add or delete a single link, all the way to networks that are stable with respect to addition and deletion of several links by many players. This is followed with a brief discussion of the dynamics of network formation with two-sided link formation.

The origins of an economic approach to network formation can be traced to the early work of Boorman (1975), Aumann and Myerson (1988), and Myerson (1991).[2] Boorman (1975) studied a setting in which individuals choose to allocate a fixed set of resources across links; these links yield information on jobs. Larger resource allocation to a link makes it stronger, which in turn yields more information (on average). However, an increase in the number of links of a person implies that each of her contacts has a lower probability of receiving information. Hence link formation involves private resources and generates externalities on other players. The main finding of Boorman's analysis was that individual linking can generate an inefficient flow of information about jobs and this has implications for the level of employment in an economy. The model studied by Boorman is quite specific but it captures the following general ideas: link formation has costs and benefits for the individual and it also generates externalities on others. These two ideas and the principle of individual optimization together constitute the key conceptual elements in the economic theory of network formation.

Aumann and Myerson (1988) introduced an extensive form game of link formation with the following rules. Pairs of players are ordered and in each period one pair is given the opportunity to form a link. Linking is irreversible. Once every pair of players has had a chance and decided on whether or not to form a link, the game ends. Aumann and Myerson examined some examples to illustrate that subgame perfect equilibrium networks of this process may be socially inefficient. More recently, Myerson (1991) proposed the following simultaneous link formation model: every player announces a subset of links which she intends to form and a link between two players is formed if and only if both players involved express a wish to form a link.

Issues relating to group formation have been a central concern in economics. The traditional approach to the problem of group formation has used a framework of *coalitions*. In this framework, a player can be a member of one and only

[2] In recent years, the study of network formation has been a very active field of study in economics and a number of different questions have been explored; Demange and Wooders (2005) and Dutta and Jackson (2003) are excellent sources for references.

one group. Coalitional membership therefore partitions the set of players into mutually exclusive groups. Initial work on coalition formation was carried out within the tradition of cooperative game theory.[3] In recent years, a lot of effort has gone into developing a noncooperative theory of coalition formation (see, for example, Bloch 1995; Maskin 2006; Ray and Vohra 1997; Yi 1997). For a survey of this work, see Bloch (1997). The network approach differs from the coalition approach in two ways. One, the network approach considers two-player or bilateral relationships. In this respect it is restrictive compared with the coalition framework, which allows for groups of arbitrary size. Two, the network approach allows for a player to be a member of more than one group at the same time. In particular, the network approach allows for structures such as stars and interlinked stars, core–periphery structures as well as cycles, which are not permitted in the coalitions framework. As we noted in chapter 2 (and chapters 8–10 will present more detailed empirical evidence on this), such structures are widely observed in practice. The first part of the book also showed that these structures have important implications for individual behavior and aggregate social welfare. It is therefore important to develop a framework within which the emergence of such structures can be formally studied.

The formation of networks is a complicated process and is clearly subject to a variety of technological, economic, and social forces. This richness of the process has meant that over the years a number of different approaches have been used in the study of network formation. Early work on network formation used random link formation and led to the classical results of Erdős and Rényi (1960) (for a survey of their findings and the theory of random graphs, see Bollobás (1998)). There is also a rich literature in mathematical sociology which studies the dynamics of networks under different link formation rules (see Doreian and Stokman (2001) for a survey of this work). More recently, computer scientists, physicists, and business strategists have been studying network formation as well. Roughgarden (2005) is a recent book surveying the computer science research, Barabasi (2002) and Watts (1999) provide accessible surveys of the work in physics, while Gulati, Nohria, and Zaheer (2000) discuss the major issues in network formation in the context of business strategy.

The distinctive feature of the economics approach is its emphasis on individual incentives in shaping link formation decisions and therefore in understanding how a network arises out of purposeful individual actions. The central role of individual choice requires that we explicitly take into account the preferences, the knowledge, and the rationality of individuals. This explicit formulation in turn permits the examination of a number of normative questions such as whether the

---

[3] For an interesting model of link formation in this tradition, see Dutta, van den Nouweland, and Tijs (1998); for a survey of cooperative games of link formation, see Slikker and van den Nouweland (2001b).

networks that arise are good or bad and if something should be done to modify individual incentives to facilitate the emergence of other (better) networks.[4]

The rest of the chapter is organized as follows. Section 7.2 presents the model of one-sided link formation, while section 7.3 presents the model of two-sided link formation. Section 7.4 discusses efficiency and equity in networks, while section 7.5 concludes. The proof of existence of pairwise stable networks is presented in the appendix.

7.2 One-Sided Links

This section presents a particularly simple model of network formation. There are n players and each of them can unilaterally form links with any subset of the other players. The payoffs to a player depend on the links she forms as well as the links that others have formed. What is the architecture of the resulting network? The presentation in this section is based on Bala and Goyal (2000a).[5]

Let $N = \{1, \ldots, n\}$, with $n \geq 3$, be the set of players and let i and j be typical members of this set. A strategy of player $i \in N$ is a (row) vector $s_i = (s_{i1}, \ldots, s_{ii-1}, s_{ii+1}, \ldots, s_{in})$, where $s_{ij} \in \{0, 1\}$ for each $j \in N \backslash \{i\}$. Player i has a *link* with j if $s_{ij} = 1$. The set of (pure) strategies of player i is denoted by $\mathcal{S}_i = \{0, 1\}^{n-1}$. A strategy profile for all players is denoted by $s = (s_1, s_2, s_3, \ldots, s_n)$, with the set of all strategies being given by $\mathcal{S} = \prod_{i=1}^{n} \mathcal{S}_i$. There is an equivalence between a strategy profile and a directed network. Let $\mathcal{G}$ be the set of directed networks on n nodes. In what follows we will use the network notation when discussing payoffs and incentives.

We shall say that $N_i^d(g) = \{j \in N \mid g_{ij} = 1\}$ is the set of players with which player i forms a link and define $\eta_i^d(g) = |N_i^d(g)|$ as the number of connections of player i in network g. Similarly, define $N_{-i}^d(g) = \{j \in N \mid g_{ji} = 1\}$ as the set of players who form a link with player i and define $\eta_{-i}^d(g) = |N_{-i}^d(g)|$ as the number of players who form links with player i. Recall that $\eta_i^d(g)$ is the out-degree and $\eta_{-i}^d(g)$ the in-degree of player i in network g. In the directed network g, let $\mathcal{N}_i(g) = \{k \mid i \xrightarrow{g} k\}$ be the set of players to whom player i has a path. We follow the convention that a player accesses herself, and so the number of players accessed by player i in network g is $n_i(g) \equiv |\mathcal{N}_i(g)| + 1$.

The one-way flow model due to Bala and Goyal (2000a) is an example of a network formation game with one-sided link formation.

---

[4] The relationship between research in different subjects is discussed in the introductory chapter of the book. The models of network formation used in computer science, statistical physics, and economics are similar in some respects and this relationship will be discussed in chapter 8.

[5] This paper subsumes Goyal (1993), which introduced the static link formation model, and Bala (1997), which introduced the study of the dynamics of link formation. The dynamics are presented in the next subsection.

Example 7.1 (one-way flow model). The interest is in situations in which there are advantages from being able to access a larger number of people, and where links are costly to maintain. Denote the set of nonnegative integers by $\mathbb{Z}_+$. Let $\phi : \mathbb{Z}_+^2 \to \mathcal{R}$ be such that $\phi(x, y)$ is strictly increasing in x and strictly decreasing in y. Define each player's payoff function $\Pi_i : \mathcal{G} \to \mathcal{R}$ as

$$\Pi_i(g) = \phi(n_i(g), \eta_i^d(g)). \tag{7.1}$$

Given the above properties of ϕ, $n_i(g)$ can be interpreted as the "benefit" that player i receives from the network, while $\eta_i^d(g)$ measures the "cost" associated with maintaining her links. Note that the assumptions on the payoff function $\phi(\cdot, \cdot)$ allow for both increasing and decreasing marginal returns from connections. $\triangle$

In some instances, the links may be formed by a single player but the benefits of the link accrue to both the individuals involved in the link. Consider the case of telephone conversation. Player i calls player j and they share some information, which is mutually advantageous. In this case, player i pays for the link, while both players gain via the exchange of information. In such situations, it is useful to work with the undirected path between i and j in the directed network g. Define $\hat{g} = \max\{g_{ij}, g_{ji}\}$. Then we can suitably relabel the ideas of neighbors and paths as follows. Let $\hat{N}_i^d(g) = \{j \in N \mid \hat{g}_{ij} = 1\}$ and $\hat{\eta}_i^d(g) = |\hat{N}_i^d(g)|$. There is an undirected path from i and j, with $i \neq j$, in network g if there exists a set of distinct players $i_1, i_2, \ldots, i_n$ such that $\hat{g}_{ii_1} = \hat{g}_{i_1 i_2} = \cdots = \hat{g}_{i_n j} = 1$. Define $\hat{\mathcal{N}}_i(g) = \{k \mid i \xrightarrow{g} k\}$ and, using the convention that a player always accesses herself, we define the number of players accessed by player i, in network g, as $\hat{n}_i(g) \equiv |\hat{\mathcal{N}}_i(g)| + 1$.

The two-way flow model due to Bala and Goyal (2000a) illustrates a network formation game in which links are unilaterally formed but the flow of benefits is independent of who paid for the link.

Example 7.2 (two-way flow model). As before, define the function $\phi : \mathbb{Z}_+^2 \to \mathcal{R}$. The payoff to player i given strategy profile g is

$$\Pi_i(g) = \phi(\hat{n}_i(g), \eta_i^d(g)). \tag{7.2}$$

Assume that ϕ is increasing in the first argument and decreasing in the second argument. The interpretation is that an increase in players accessed via (undirected) paths increases payoffs while links are costly and so forming more links lowers payoffs. $\triangle$

What is the architecture of networks that will arise in examples 7.1 and 7.2, and more generally under games of one-sided link formation? Games of unilateral link formation are solved by using the concept of Nash equilibrium strategies.

Chapter 8 provides a characterization of (strict) Nash equilibrium networks for these examples.[6]

7.2.1 Dynamics

Networks change as individuals add and delete links over time: does the process of link formation lead to specific networks? What is the relation between the networks that arise in the long run and the networks that are Nash equilibria of the static network formation game. These questions constitute the primary motivation for the study of the dynamics of network formation.

Perhaps the simplest way to approach the dynamics of networks is to think of a world in which individuals periodically get an opportunity to revise their links, form links with some new players, maintain some of the existing links, and delete some of the other links. Decisions on linking at any point in time will be guided by a number of considerations. The structure of the existing network will determine the potential rewards from linking with different players and this will clearly be important. Similarly, the possibility that current linking activity will alter incentives for others and hence shape future linking activity will be an important factor as well. The importance of this latter issue will depend on how quickly the network changes as well as how patient players are.

The simplest and best understood case is the one in which players are assumed to be perfectly impatient: they care only about the immediate returns and ignore the second consideration mentioned above. This leads to the myopic best-response model of dynamics. The myopic best-response model and the dynamic process that is generated by it were described in chapter 5. In the present context we supplement the description there with a rule for behavior in case of indifference: if two link strategies are equally attractive, then we require that a player choose each of the strategies with strictly positive probability. For expositional purposes it is convenient to briefly summarize the key features of the dynamic process using the notation introduced in this chapter.

Time is a discrete variable, and is indexed by $t = 1, 2, 3, \ldots$. Let g^t be the network/strategy profile at the start of time t. In each period, with probability $p \in (0, 1)$, a player gets an opportunity to revise her strategy. She is assumed to know the network that exists at that point in time, and she chooses a profile of links which maximize her payoff, under the assumption that the links of all other players do not change. If more than one action is optimal, then a player randomly picks one of the optimal strategies. Denote the strategy of a player i in period t by g_i^t. If player i is not active in period t, then it follows that $g_i^t = g_i^{t-1}$. This simple best-response strategy revision rule generates a transition probability function $P_{gg'} : \mathcal{G} \times \mathcal{G} \rightarrow [0, 1]$, with $\sum_{g'} P_{gg'} = 1$, for every $g \in \mathcal{G}$. The dynamics of networks g^t obey this transition probability function. A strategy profile (or

---

state), g, is absorbing if the dynamic process cannot escape from the state once it reaches it, i.e., $P_{gg} = 1$.

In some cases the process may not converge; in such cases, we will talk of absorbing set(s) of networks. An absorbing set is a collection of networks such that once the process reaches one of the networks in this set, then it remains within this set forever after.[7]

The analysis in chapter 8 will show that in some applications, such as examples 7.1 and 7.2, there exist multiple absorbing states. This will lead us to investigate the relative stability of different networks. As in chapter 4, we will use the ideas of stochastic stability in this study. Chapter 8 illustrates the power of stochastic stability analysis in selecting among absorbing networks.

Practically all the research on dynamic models of network formation assumes that players are myopic. Individual linking is costly and alters the incentives for linking by others. This suggests that players may like to wait or preempt others in linking decisions and this leads naturally to strategic intertemporal considerations. The characterization of networks which arise when links are one-sided and players are far-sighted appears to be an open problem.

7.3   Two-Sided Links

This section considers the case where a link between two players requires the approval of both the players involved. This is the natural way to think about link formation in a number of social and economic contexts such as the formation of friendship ties, coauthorships, collaborations between firms, trading links between buyers and sellers, and free trade agreements between nations.[8] The simplest way to think of two-sided link formation is to imagine an announcement game along the lines of the game sketched by Myerson (1991). Each player announces a set of *intended* links. An intended link is a binary variable, $s_{ij} \in \{0, 1\}$, where $s_{ij} = 1$ ($s_{ij} = 0$) means that player i intends to (does not intend to) form a link with player j. A (pure) strategy for player i is $s_i = \{s_{ij}\}_{j \in N \setminus \{i\}}$, with $\mathscr{S}_i$ denoting the strategy set of player i. A strategy profile for all players is denoted by $s = (s_1, s_2, s_3, \dots, s_n)$, with the set of all strategies being given by $\mathscr{S} = \prod_{i=1}^{n} \mathscr{S}_i$. Define $g_{ij} = \min\{s_{ij}, s_{ji}\}$. Clearly, $g_{ij} = 1$ if and only if $s_{ij} = s_{ji} = 1$. Every strategy profile $s = (s_1, s_2, \dots, s_n)$ therefore induces a corresponding *undirected* network $g(s)$.[9] In the (undirected) network g, let $\mathscr{N}_i(g) = \{k \mid i \xrightarrow{g} k\}$ be the set of players to whom player i has a path. Define $\Pi_i : \mathscr{S} \to \mathscr{R}$ as the payoff function of a player i in network g.

---

[7] Note that the set of all networks is clearly an absorbing set of the process.

[8] Chapter 9 studies models of social connections, coauthorships, trading links, and free trade networks, while chapter 10 examines a model of interfirm collaboration networks.

[9] We will use the same notation for directed and undirected networks; the context of the model should make it clear which type of network is being referred to.

The connections model due to Jackson and Wolinsky (1996) provides a simple example of such a payoff function.

Example 7.3 (connections model). Let $\delta \in [0, 1]$ be the rate of decay in value as it moves across links. Given a strategy profile s, the payoffs to player i in a network $g(s)$ are

$$\Pi_i(s) = 1 + \sum_{j \in \mathcal{N}_i(g(s)) \setminus \{i\}} \delta^{d(i,j;g(s))} - \eta_i(g(s))c, \qquad (7.3)$$

where $c > 0$ is the cost of forming a link. It is worth noting that player i incurs the cost of a link g_{ij} only if this link is actually formed, i.e., both players announce an intention to form a link. Setting a value of $\delta = 0$ implies that there is full decay and no flow of value, while a value of $\delta = 1$ reflects the absence of any decay. The payoff function here captures the idea that links facilitate the flow of benefits such as information or social favors, but for values of $\delta \in (0, 1)$ there is some decay or delay in flow as paths between players get longer. This will induce players to form links with others to shorten paths to others, an incentive which has to be balanced by the costs of forming links. $\triangle$

What is the architecture of networks that will arise in such contexts? In a context where links are two sided there are elements of "cooperation" involved in the formation of a link, and so solving such games calls for new concepts.

It is useful to begin with the discussion of the familiar notion of Nash equilibrium as this will illustrate some of the conceptual issues that arise in the study of network formation with two-sided links. Recall that a strategy profile $s^* = (s_1^*, s_2^*, \ldots, s_n^*)$ is a Nash equilibrium if $\Pi_i(g(s_i^*, s_{-i}^*)) \geq \Pi_i(g(s_i, s_{-i}^*))$ for all $s_i \in S_i$ and for all $i \in N$. In the present model a link is formed only if both players acquiesce in the formation of the link. It then follows directly that if every player announces that she wants to form no links, then a best response of player i is to announce that she also wants to form no links. In other words, the empty network is a Nash equilibrium for any network formation game. More generally, for any pair i and j, it is always a best response for the players to offer to form no link. While the possibility of coordination failures in announcements is a genuine issue, in many economic applications that will be considered—such as coauthorship, collaboration among firms, trade agreements among countries—it seems more natural to suppose that pairs of players can communicate and agree to form a link as long as they both benefit from doing so.

The concept of pairwise stability due to Jackson and Wolinsky (1996) formalizes this idea of two-person deviation in the following simple way.

Definition 7.1. A network g is pairwise stable if

(i) for every $g_{ij} = 1$, $\Pi_i(g) \geq \Pi_i(g - g_{ij})$ and $\Pi_j(g) \geq \Pi_j(g - g_{ij})$;

(ii) for $g_{ij} = 0$, $\Pi_i(g + g_{ij}) > \Pi_i(g) \implies \Pi_j(g + g_{ij}) < \Pi_j(g)$.

Pairwise stability looks at the attractiveness of links in network g *one at a time*. The first condition requires that every link which is present in a stable network must be (weakly) profitable for the players involved in the link. The second condition requires that for every link which is not present in the network it must be the case that if one player strictly gains from the link, then the other player must be strictly worse off.

The principal appeal of pairwise stability is its great simplicity. For any network it is relatively easy to check whether the two conditions are satisfied. Moreover, in some applications—see, for example, collaboration among firms discussed in chapter 10—it turns out that the requirement of pairwise stability is also quite powerful as it rules out all but a few network architectures. Given the extensive use of the concept of pairwise stability it is useful to know whether a pairwise stable network always exists.

The notion of improving path is useful in this context. Formally, we have the following definition.

Definition 7.2. An improving path from a network g to a network g' is a finite sequence of networks $g^1, g^2, \ldots, g^k$, with $g^1 = g$ and $g^k = g'$ such that, for every $l \in \{1, 2, \ldots, k - 1\}$, either

(i) $g^{l+1} = g^l - g_{ij}$ for some $g_{ij}^l = 1$ and $\Pi_k(g^l - g_{ij}) > \Pi_k(g^l)$ for $k \in \{i, j\}$

or

(ii) $g^{l+1} = g^l + g_{ij}$ for some $g_{ij}^l = 0$ and $\Pi_i(g^l + g_{ij}) > \Pi_i(g^l)$ and $\Pi_j(g^l + g_{ij}) \geqslant \Pi_j(g^l)$.

A set of networks $\hat{\mathcal{G}} \subset \mathcal{G}$ forms a *cycle* if for any $g, g' \in \hat{\mathcal{G}}$ (which includes $g = g'$) there exists an improving path from g to g'.

A sufficient condition for the existence of pairwise stable networks is that there does not exist an improving path starting from every network; in a game with a finite number of players (and therefore also a finite number of networks) a sufficient condition for this is that there are no cycles of improving paths in the network. Jackson and Watts (2001) develop conditions on payoff functions in network formation games which rule out cycles. Speaking loosely, these conditions require that payoffs should exhibit a form of monotonicity. These conditions are formally derived in the appendix to this chapter.

While pairwise stability is a useful first check for strategic stability, only a relatively small set of possible deviations are ruled out and there is a real possibility that in applications this concept does not yield precise predictions (the model of structural holes in chapter 9 provides an instance of this). We now consider a number of directions in which this solution concept can be strengthened.

First, note that in pairwise stability only the deletion of a single link *or* the addition of a single link is considered. It is easy to construct games in which a deletion or an addition of a link by itself is not profitable, but the deviation in which several links are deleted together is profitable. This possibility is illustrated by the following example.

Example 7.4 (deleting a subset of links). Suppose $n = 4$. Assume that the payoffs satisfy $\Pi_i(g^c) = 10$ for all players, while $\Pi_i(g) = 15$ in every network g in which player i has no links. In a network g where two players have three links each and two players have two links each, the payoffs to players with three links are 9 while the payoffs with two links are 8. The complete network is clearly pairwise stable, since no player has an incentive to delete a single link. However, a player would strictly profit from deleting all links. $\triangle$

The notion of pairwise equilibrium addresses this concern directly by supplementing the idea of Nash equilibrium with the requirement that no pair of players wishes to form an additional link. This is a natural extension to the idea of pairwise stability and was discussed informally in Jackson and Wolinsky (1996). Pairwise equilibrium was formally defined in Goyal and Joshi (2006b) and Belleflamme and Bloch (2004).[10]

Definition 7.3. A network g^* can be sustained in a pairwise equilibrium if

(i) there is a Nash equilibrium s^* which yields g^*;

(ii) for any $g_{ij}(s^*) = 0$, $\Pi_i(g(s^*) + g_{ij}) > \Pi_i(g(s^*)) \implies \Pi_j(g(s^*) + g_{ij}) < \Pi_j(g(s^*))$.

Observe that the second requirement in the above definition is different from the refinement of (trembling hand) perfection. The latter rules out Nash equilibrium in weakly dominated strategies; by contrast the requirement that no pair of players wants to form a link is a local condition and so in settings with negative spillovers across links there can exist perfect equilibrium networks which do not satisfy the pairwise stability requirement. The following example illustrates this possibility.

Example 7.5 (perfect equilibrium and pairwise equilibrium). Suppose $n = 3$. Payoffs are symmetric and are as follows: $\Pi_i(g^e) = \Pi_i(g^c) = 10$; $\Pi_i(g^s) = 5$ and $\Pi_j(g^s) = 0$ for the central player and peripheral players in the star network, respectively, while $\Pi_i(g) = 15$ and $\Pi_j(g) = 0$ are payoffs to the linked players and isolated player, respectively, in the network with a single link. In this game, the empty network can be sustained in a perfect equilibrium, but it is not a pairwise equilibrium.[11] $\triangle$

---

[10] For a systematic study of refinements on Nash equilibrium with respect to pairwise deviations, see Gilles and Sarangi (2004) and Gilles, Chakrabarti, and Sarangi (2005).

[11] Calvó-Armengol and Ilkilic (2004) examine the relationship between Nash equilibrium and pairwise equilibrium and proper equilibrium, and obtain conditions on marginal returns from link formation under which the three concepts yield identical network outcomes.

Second, an important feature of pairwise stability is that deviations in which a pair of players each deletes one or more links *and/or* adds a link in a coordinated manner are not allowed. In some games it is possible that deleting a subset of links is not profitable for any single player *and* adding a link is not profitable for any pair of players either, but it is profitable for a pair of players to simultaneously delete a subset of their current links and add a link. The following example illustrates this possibility.

Example 7.6 (simultaneous deletion and addition of a link). Consider a game with $n = 4$. Assume the following payoffs: any isolated player earns 0; in a line network, the two central players earn 25 each while the end-players earn 10 each; in a cycle network every player earns 20 each; in a network with a cycle and an additional link the payoffs to the players with two links each are 20, while the payoffs to the three-link players are 15 each. Then it follows that the cycle is a pairwise equilibrium. However, if players can delete links and add a link at the same time, then two players in the cycle can make a coordinated move—which yields a line network with themselves as the central players—and thereby increase their payoffs. Thus the cycle is not stable with respect to coordinated deviations.

△

The notion of bilateral equilibrium addresses these concerns. Define s_{-i-j} as the strategy profile s less the strategies of players i and j, i.e., $s_{-i-j} = (s_1, \ldots, s_{i-1}, s_{i+1}, \ldots, s_{j-1}, s_{j+1}, \ldots, s_n)$. The following definition is due to Goyal and Vega-Redondo (forthcoming).

Definition 7.4. A network g^* is a *bilateral equilibrium* if

(i) there is a Nash equilibrium strategy profile s^* which yields g^*;

(ii) for any pair of players $i, j \in N$, and every strategy pair (s_i, s_j),

$$\Pi_i(g(s_i, s_j, s^*_{-i-j})) > \Pi_i(g(s^*_i, s^*_j, s^*_{-i-j}))$$
$$\Rightarrow \Pi_j(g(s_i, s_j, s^*_{-i-j})) < \Pi_j(g(s^*_j, s^*_j, s^*_{-i-j})). \qquad (7.4)$$

Thus a given network can be supported in a "bilateral equilibrium" if no player or pair of players can deviate (unilaterally or bilaterally, respectively) and benefit from the deviation (at least one of them strictly). While the terminology of "bilateral equilibrium" is introduced in Goyal and Vega-Redondo (forthcoming), the ideas behind the bilateral equilibrium are quite old. It is simply a special case of strong equilibrium in which only two-player deviations are allowed. Strong equilibrium was introduced in Aumann (1959). The characterization of conditions on payoffs for the existence of a bilateral equilibrium appears to be an open problem.

Coordinated deviations by two players are potentially subject to further deviation by individual players. It is possible, as in example 7.6, that players find it profitable to delete some of their existing links and form a link with each other; this would mean that the network g is not a bilateral equilibrium. However, conditional on player 2 carrying out her deletion of links, it may be strictly profitable for player 1 not to delete one of the links she has agreed to delete in the coordinated move with player 2. The following example illustrates this possibility.

Example 7.7 (credible deviations). Suppose $n = 6$. Keep the payoffs specified as in example 7.6; in addition assume the following payoffs for other networks. In the star network, the central player earns 40 while the spokes earn 10 each; in a network which has a three-player line and an isolated player, the spokes earn 10 each while the center earns 20. Finally, in a network with three players constituting a triangle and a fourth player being a spoke with respect to one of the vertices of the triangle, the players with two links earn 15, the player with one link earns 10, and the player with three links earns 30. In example 7.6 we argued that the cycle network is not a bilateral equilibrium since it is open to a two-person coordinated deviation which leads to a line. However, an inspection of the payoffs shows that the deviation considered is subject to a profitable further deviation: one player does not actually carry out the agreed upon deviation, and instead retains the link that she was suppose to delete. This further deviation yields her a payoff of 30 as against a payoff of 25 (which she would earn in the line). △

The above example motivates a notion of stability which requires coordinated deviations to be robust to further profitable deviations by single players, and leads to the notion of bilateral-proof equilibrium.

Definition 7.5. A network g^* can be supported in a *bilateral-proof equilibrium* if

(i) there is a Nash equilibrium profile s^* which yields g^*;

(ii) for any pair of players $i, j \in N$, and every strategy pair (s_i, s_j) with

$$\Pi_i(g(s_i, s_j, s^*_{-i-j})) > \Pi_i(g(s^*_i, s^*_j, s^*_{-i-j})),$$

one of the following two conditions hold:

(a) $\Pi_j(g(s_i, s_j, s^*_{-i-j})) < \Pi_j(g(s^*_i, s^*_j, s^*_{-i-j}))$;

(b) if $\Pi_j(g(s_i, s_j, s^*_{-i-j})) \geq \Pi_j(g(s^*_i, s^*_j, s^*_{-i-j}))$, then $\exists k, \ell \in \{i, j\}$, $k \neq \ell$, and some $\tilde{s}_k \in S_k$ such that

$$\Pi_k(g(\tilde{s}_k, s_\ell, s^*_{-k-\ell})) > \Pi_k(g(s_k, s_\ell, s^*_{-k-\ell}))$$

and

$$\Pi_l(g(\tilde{s}_k, s_\ell, s^*_{-k-\ell})) < \Pi_l(g(s^*_k, s^*_\ell, s^*_{-k-\ell})).$$

This notion of stability is developed in Goyal and Vega-Redondo (forthcoming). Note that the first condition in the definition is the standard Nash requirement; the second condition has two parts. The first part says that, starting from network g, if player i increases payoffs by forming a link with player j, then it must be the case that the payoffs to j fall. The second part takes up the case where both i and j gain by forming a link. In this case, for g to be bilateral-proof stable it must be the case that at least one of them, player i (say), can then profitably deviate once the link is formed and that this deviation makes player j worse off than the initial network g.

Bilateral-proof equilibrium is the two-player version of coalition-proof equilibrium (which allows for deviations by any subset of players). For an introduction to the study of coalition-proof equilibrium, see Bernheim, Peleg, and Whinston (1987).

The solution concepts discussed above take into account one- and two-player deviations. There are two general directions in which this framework can be extended: (i) allowing for groups of players to shape pairwise links, and (ii) allowing for many-player links.

Consider first the issue of larger group deviations within a pairwise link context. Suppose that a group of players of any size can determine the nature of networks among them, as well as determine the links between members of the group and the players who are not in the group. Group-level incentives are traditionally studied by using notions of strong equilibrium and coalition equilibrium. Jackson and van den Nouweland (2005) study strongly stable networks and derive conditions for the existence of such networks. Dutta and Mutuswami (1997) present an extensive discussion of alternative stronger solution concepts in the context of network formation.

At a more fundamental level there is the issue of why links should be bilateral. Indeed, in some well-known applications, such as coauthoring, collaboration between firms, and free trade agreements between countries, links often involve more than two players. This suggests that the level of linking should itself be viewed as endogenous. Allowing for groups of arbitrary size as well as allowing for nonexclusive membership of groups would therefore yield a general framework for studying coalitions as well as networks. This general framework would also permit a study of endogenous group size and exclusivity.

7.3.1 Dynamics

The study of network dynamics forms a natural complement to the study of stable networks, which were discussed above. The discussion starts with dynamics that are driven by myopic players adding and deleting links and then moves on to dynamics that involve far-sighted players.

As before, suppose that time is discrete, $t = 1, 2, 3, \ldots$. In each period, a single pair of players gets a chance to revise their link: they can form a link if none exists, they can delete a link if one exists, or they can let the link remain in its current state. Suppose that the probability of any pair being picked is the same and does not change over time, i.e., $p_{ij} = 2/n(n-1)$ for all t. Moreover, assume that this probability is independent across periods. The basic decision rule for players is that faced with network g, a pair of players forms a link if

$$\Pi_i(g + g_{ij}) > \Pi_i(g) \quad \text{and} \quad \Pi_j(g + g_{ij}) \geqslant \Pi_j(g),$$

while a player i deletes the link g_{ij} if

$$\Pi_i(g - g_{ij}) > \Pi_i(g).$$

This decision rule reflects a myopic best response to existing networks, and is in line with the dynamics defined in the one-sided links case.

The process of adding and deleting links generates a dynamic process of network formation. The interest is in whether this process converges and if so what are the limit networks. Observe that every pairwise stable network is an absorbing state of this dynamic process, and that if the process converges, then the limit must be a pairwise network. In many applications, there are multiple pairwise stable networks and the question arises of whether they are all equally robust to small perturbations in addition and deletion of links. This concern motivates the study of stochastically stable networks.

The ideas underlying stochastic stability were discussed in chapter 4 and are similar to those for the one-sided link formation model. The only difference is that in the two-sided link context, we assume that there is a small probability $\epsilon > 0$ that a single link is deleted or formed at random. This perturbation is small but it does imply that there is a positive probability of moving from any network g to any network g'. Applying standard results in Markov chain theory we then conclude that there is an invariant probability distribution on the set of networks $\mathcal{G}$. Any network which lies in the support of this distribution is termed a stochastically stable network.

A critical assumption in most of the research on dynamic processes of network formation with two-sided links is that players are myopic. In some applications the addition of a link by a single player is not by itself worthwhile but it becomes profitable if other players step in and also form links subsequently. This suggests that patient far-sighted players may have different incentives to form and delete links compared with myopic players. The formulation of a dynamic model with far-sighted players is an important subject and raises a number of interesting theoretical issues in the two-sided links setting. For models of network formation with far-sighted players, see Dutta, Ghosal, and Ray (2005) and Page, Wooders, and Kamat (2005).

7.4   Efficiency and Equity

In the study of network formation an important concern will be the relation between equilibrium or stable networks and socially desirable networks. Two aspects of social desirability will be touched upon: efficiency and equity.

There are different ways of defining efficiency. For our purposes two definitions are most relevant: Pareto efficiency and aggregate efficiency. These concepts were defined in chapter 2. For easy reference, they are restated here briefly. A network g yields a profile of individual payoffs $\Pi(g) = (\Pi_1(g), \Pi_2(g), \ldots, \Pi_n(g))$. A network g is said to Pareto dominate another network g' if $\Pi_i(g) \geqslant \Pi_i(g')$ for all players and there is some player j such that $\Pi_j(g) > \Pi_j(g')$. A network g is Pareto efficient if there is no other network $g' \in \mathcal{G}$, which Pareto dominates it.

In the networks literature, a simpler and more aggregate notion of efficiency has been more widely used. Define aggregate welfare from a network g as $W(g) = \sum_{i \in N} \Pi_i(g)$. A network g is said to be efficient if $W(g) \geqslant W(g')$ for all $g' \in \mathcal{G}$.

Consider next the issue of equity. If we interpret the payoffs as monetary payments, the inequality generated by network can be assessed by using standard notions of inequality such as range, variance, and Gini-coefficient or Lorenz curves. We will use the range in the following chapters and for easy reference it is presented here:

$$R(g) = \max_{i \in N} \Pi_i(g) - \min_{j \in N} \Pi_j(g), \tag{7.5}$$

where "max" refers to the maximum individual payoff and "min" refers to the minimum payoff level in the network g.[12]

7.5   Concluding Remarks

This chapter presented the principal concepts in the strategic approach to the formation of networks. The next three chapters apply these concepts to a number of different contexts. These applications highlight how a strategic approach to network formation helps us in understanding the origins of different network architectures. In addition, these applications also illustrate the value of using an approach founded on individual utilities and payoffs as this enables us to assess the normative properties—the efficiency as well as the distributional implications—of different networks.

In what follows, I discuss two substantive assumptions which have been so far maintained in this chapter.

The first assumption is about information: the framework discussed above assumes that individual players know the network they are located in and therefore

---

[12] Also see chapter 2 for other measures of dispersion and inequality.

can calculate the costs and benefits from different links precisely. However, networks are complicated objects and even with a few players a great many structures can arise. Moreover, the fact that networks are subject to subtle transformations that are typically carried out at a local level suggests that it will be difficult for players to know the precise structure of the network at any point in time. These considerations suggest an urgent need for a model of network formation with incomplete information. In the face of incomplete information about the network structure, and more generally about the value of connecting with others, individuals may want to search or experiment and so the existing framework can be extended in a number of interesting directions.[13]

The second assumption is about the nature of links: in the framework presented in this chapter, and in most of the work to date, it is assumed that links are binary variables, either they are present or they are absent. However, it is clear that in many contexts, it is not just the existence of a link but the quality of the link that is critical. Indeed, a number of classical theories about social networks, such as Granovetter's strength of weak ties and Boorman's theory of labor market networks, rest on the importance of the quality of the link. The formulation of a theory of network formation where individuals choose the quality of links is an important area for future work.[14]

7.6 Appendix

This section develops conditions for the existence of pairwise stable networks. It is convenient to write a network formation game slightly more generally as follows. There is a set of players $N = \{1, 2, \ldots, n\}$, a value function $V : \mathcal{G} \to R$, which defines the aggregate value generated by any network g, and an allocation function $\Pi : \mathcal{G} \to R^n$, which specifies, for each network g, the payoff accruing to every player in the network.

Recall the definition of a pairwise stable network.

Definition 7.6. A network g is pairwise stable if

   (i) for every $g_{ij} = 1$, $\Pi_i(g) \geqslant \Pi_i(g - g_{ij})$ and $\Pi_j(g) \geqslant \Pi_j(g - g_{ij})$;

   (ii) for $g_{ij} = 0$, $\Pi_i(g + g_{ij}) > \Pi_i(g) \implies \Pi_j(g + g_{ij}) < \Pi_j(g)$.

We will exploit the ideas of improving paths and cycles, due to Jackson and Watts (2001). An improving path is a sequence of networks that can emerge when individuals form or sever links based on individual payoff considerations.

---

[13] In a recent paper, McBride (2006b) makes a start in the study of network formation with incomplete network knowledge; chapter 8 discusses this model.

[14] See Goyal (2005b) for a discussion of the importance of modeling strength of links; for recent studies of strength of ties, see, for example, Bloch and Dutta (2005), Brueckner (2003), Goyal, Konovalov, and Moraga (2003), van der Leij and Goyal (2005), Rogers (2005), and Skyrms and Pemantle (2000).

Definition 7.7. An improving path from a network g to a network g' is a finite sequence of networks $g^1, g^2, \ldots, g^k$, with $g^1 = g$ and $g^k = g'$ such that, for every $l \in \{1, 2, \ldots, k - 1\}$, either

(i) $g^{l+1} = g^l - g_{ij}$ for some $g^l_{ij} = 1$ and $\Pi_k(g^l - g_{ij}) > \Pi_k(g^l)$ for $k \in \{i, j\}$ or

(ii) $g^{l+1} = g^l + g_{ij}$ for some $g^l_{ij} = 0$ and $\Pi_i(g^l + g_{ij}) > \Pi_i(g^l)$ and $\Pi_j(g^l + g_{ij}) \geq \Pi_j(g^l)$.

A set of networks $\hat{\mathcal{G}}$ forms a *cycle* if, for any $g, g' \in \hat{\mathcal{G}}$ (which includes $g = g'$), there exists an improving path from g to g'. A cycle $\hat{\mathcal{G}}$ is *maximal* if it is not a proper subset of any other cycle, while a cycle $\hat{\mathcal{G}}$ is *closed* if no network in $\hat{\mathcal{G}}$ lies on an improving path leading to a network which does not lie in $\hat{\mathcal{G}}$.

It follows from the definition of an improving path that a network is pairwise stable if and only if there is no improving path leading away from it. So the existence of pairwise stable networks is intimately related to the existence of cycles of improving paths. The following result, due to Jackson and Watts (2001), provides a first result on existence.

Proposition 7.1. *For any value function V and any allocation function Π, there exists at least one pairwise stable network or a closed cycle of networks.*

Proof. Start with a network g. If it is pairwise stable, then the proof is done. So suppose it is not pairwise stable. This means there exists an improving path leading away from it. If this improving path ends at some network, that network is a pairwise stable network, and the proof is done. So suppose that there is no end network: given the finiteness of the game there must exist a cycle. Thus there exists a pairwise stable network or a cycle. So suppose there exists no pairwise stable network. First, note that since G is finite there must exist a maximal cycle. Second, consider the set of maximal cycles, and note that at least one of them must have no path leaving it. If all maximal cycles had paths leaving them, then there would be a larger cycle containing two or more of such cycles, which would be a contradiction to the hypothesis that these cycles are maximal. Thus at least one maximal cycle must be closed. □

Ruling out closed cycles is one simple way to guarantee the existence of pairwise stable networks. The following terminology is used in the next result. For a given game of network formation, denote the existence of an improving path from g to g' by $g \to g'$. Clearly, "$\to$" is a transitive relation, and so it follows that there are no cycles if and only if $\to$ is asymmetric. Two networks g and g' are *adjacent* if they differ by only one link. V and Π exhibit no indifference if, for any two adjacent networks g and g', either g defeats g' or vice versa.[15] The following

---

[15] A network g defeats another network g' if there is an improving path from g' to g.

result, due to Jackson and Watts (2001), provides a useful characterization result on the existence of cycles.

Theorem 7.1. *Fix a value function V and an allocation function Π. If there exists a function $W : \mathcal{G} \to \mathcal{R}$ such that $[g'$ defeats $g] \Leftrightarrow [W(g') > W(g)$ and g and g' are adjacent$]$, then there are no cycles. Conversely, if V and Π exhibit no indifference, then there are no cycles only if there exists a function $W : \mathcal{G} \to R$ such that $[g'$ defeats $g] \Leftrightarrow [W(g') > W(g)$ and g' and g are adjacent$]$.*

Proof. Consider the first statement. This is equivalent to saying that if there exists a cycle, then there cannot exist such a W. Suppose not and there exists such a W function. Then by transitivity of $>$, it follows that $W(g) > W(g)$, which is impossible. So the existence of cycles precludes any W function which satisfies the properties mentioned.

Consider the second statement. Assume that there are no cycles and also that, for any adjacent pair of networks g and g', either g defeats g' or vice versa. The proof shows that there exists such a W satisfying the desired properties. This step exploits proposition 3.2 in Kreps (1988), which is stated below for easy reference. A binary relation "b" is negative transitive if the converse relation "*not-b*" is transitive.

Lemma 7.1. *If X is a finite set and b is a binary relation, then there exists $W : X \to R$ such that $W(x) > W(y) \Leftrightarrow x b y$ if and only if b is asymmetric and negatively transitive.*

Since there are no cycles, the binary relation "$\to$" is acyclic and therefore asymmetric. The relation "$\to$" is transitive by the definition of an improving path. However, the relation "$\not\to$" is not necessarily transitive. Therefore, a relation b has to be constructed such that (i) $g \to g'$ implies that $g' b g$, (ii) if g and g' are adjacent, then $g \to g'$ if and only if $g' b g$, and (iii) b is asymmetric and negatively transitive. Then the above lemma can be applied to obtain a W, and the theorem 7.1 follows from property (ii). The construction of b is now presented.

Case 1. For every distinct pair of networks g and g', at least one of the following holds: $g \to g'$ or $g' \to g$. Set $g' b g$ if and only if $g \to g'$. We show that this relation is negatively transitive. Define $g \, nb \, g'$ if $g \, b \, g'$ fails to obtain. Suppose that $g \, nb \, g'$ and $g' \, nb \, g''$. Given the definition of b, this means that $g' \, b \, g$ and $g'' \, b \, g'$. It then follows from the transitivity of b that $g'' \, b \, g$, which in turn implies, by asymmetry of b and definition of nb, that $g \, nb \, g''$.

Case 2. There exist distinct g and g' (which are not adjacent) such that $g \not\to g'$ and $g' \not\to g$. Define the binary relation b_1 as follows. Let $g'' \, b_1 \, g'''$ if and only if $g''' \to g''$, except on g and g', where we set $g' \, b_1 \, g$. Note that by construction (i) and (ii) are satisfied and also note that b_1 is acyclic (and hence asymmetric). To see the acyclicity of b_1, note that if there is a cycle then it would have to include g and g', as this is the only point at which b_1 and $\to$ disagree. However, the existence of such a cycle would imply that $g' \to g$, which is a contradiction. Next define b_2 by taking all the transitive implications of b_1. Again, (i) and (ii) are true of b_2. By construction b_2 is transitive. Next it is shown that b_2 is acyclic. This is shown by construction. Add one implication from b_1 and transitivity at a time and verify acyclicity at each step. Consider the first new implication that is added and suppose that there exists a cycle. Let g''' and g'' be the networks in question. So $g'' \ b_1 \ g'''$ and $g''' \ n b_1 \ g''$, but $g''' \ b_2 \ g''$, and there exists a sequence of networks $\{g_0, g_1, \ldots, g_r\}$ such that $g''' \ b_1 \ g_0 \ b_1 \ g_1 \ \cdots \ b_1 \ g_r \ b_1 \ g''$. This implies that there exists a cycle under b_1, which is a contradiction. Iterating this argument implies that b_2 is acyclic.

Now consider cases 1 and 2 when b_2 is substituted for $\to$. Iterations on this process lead to a relation where b_k has been constructed and relative to b_k this is then case 1. Iterating on the argument under case 2 it follows that (i) and (ii) will be true of b_k and b_k will be transitive and asymmetric. Then by the argument under case 1, b_k will be negatively transitive. Set $b = b_k$ and the proof is complete. $\square$

8

One-Sided Link Formation

8.1 Introduction

This chapter presents a theory of network formation in which players can form links unilaterally. Interest will center on the following model: there are n individuals, each of whom can form a link with any subset of the remaining players. Link formation is unilateral: an individual i can decide to form a link with any player j by paying for the link. While there are some interesting practical examples of this type of link formation—such as forming links across Web pages, citations, telephone calls, the sending of gifts in the context of social relations—it must be emphasized that the principal appeal of this model is its simplicity. This simplicity is an important virtue as it permits an exploration of a number of important questions concerning the process of network formation and its welfare implications in a straightforward manner.

A second feature of the model is that it allows for a fairly general description of payoffs. Individual payoffs are assumed to be increasing in the number of other people accessed via the network and they are decreasing in the number of links formed by an individual; no assumptions are made on the curvature of the returns to linking.

A third attractive feature of the model is that it yields sharp predictions on the architecture of networks. It will be shown that equilibrium networks can be completely characterized. In particular, simple network architectures, such as stars, and variants of the star, such as interlinked stars, arise naturally and the economic intuition underlying their emergence is easily conveyed. Moreover, it turns out that equilibrium networks have striking efficiency and distributional properties: stars are efficient but exhibit significant payoff inequality.

The simplicity of the model and the sharpness of its predictions have motivated an extensive theoretical literature which seeks to examine their robustness. The basic model assumes that all players are homogeneous in terms of value as well as costs of forming links. Individual heterogeneity in these dimensions is clearly an important feature of real world settings and theoretical work has looked at the implications of heterogeneity for equilibrium networks. Another important assumption in the basic model is that value flows without any frictions across paths in a network. In many contexts flow in value is likely to be negatively affected by a number of factors, prominent among them being the distance between players. For example, it is reasonable to suppose that the value of information flow between two individuals is likely to fall as the length of the path between them grows. This leads to an examination of the role of decay in shaping network formation. A number of new results are obtained. The general message of these results is that the prominence of star networks, their efficiency, and their payoff inequalities are robust features of equilibrium networks.

These theoretical findings have also led to a number of experimental investigations of network formation. These experiments have looked at the likelihood of the emergence of stars in games of network formation. These experiments reveal that in settings with homogeneous players stars are unlikely to emerge, though networks which are almost stars (differ from the star in only one link) do arise. The main explanation for this failure of star formation is that they exhibit sharp payoff inequality. This experimental finding suggests that fairness considerations play an important role in network formation. However, the experiments also show that in settings with heterogeneous players, where some players are more valuable to connect with, stars are much more likely to emerge. This suggests that in making linking decisions players are trading off the gains from connecting with a highly valuable player against the payoff inequality this potentially leads to. If the efficiency gains are large, then players are willing to tolerate the inequality and this leads to the emergence of stars in which peripheral players pay for all the links.

In recent years, a number of studies have examined the empirical properties of the World Wide Web, citation networks, and telephone calling. This work has highlighted the following features: the average number of connections is typically very small compared with the number of nodes, the average distance between players is very small, and there is significant inequality in the number of connections across players. It is natural to ask if the theoretical findings are consistent with these empirical regularities. An examination of empirical evidence suggests that stars and variations of stars, such as interlinked stars, arise in many contexts. We are thus led to the view that this simple model of strategic network formation captures essential aspects of linking activity in a variety of environments.

The rest of the chapter is organized as follows. Section 8.2 sets out the basic model of link formation and derives a first set of results on equilibrium architectures, payoffs distribution, and social efficiency. Section 8.3 extends the basic model to include decay and heterogeneity. Section 8.4 discusses the experimental work on this model of network formation and also examines the relationship between the predictions of the theoretical model and the empirical patterns observed in actual networks. Section 8.5 places this model in perspective by relating it to recent research on network formation in physics and computer science.

Section 8.6 concludes. The proofs of the main results are presented in an accompanying appendix.

8.2 A Simple Model of Link Formation

This model of network formation is based on the notion that links are formed by individual decisions that trade off the costs of forming and maintaining links against the rewards from doing so. A link with another individual allows access, in part and in due course, to the benefits available to the latter via her own links. Thus links generate externalities and define the economic background for the network formation process. This section will study the two-way flow model presented in chapter 7. The presentation here follows Bala and Goyal (2000a).

Recall that $N = \{1, \dots, n\}$, with $n \geq 3$, is the set of players. A strategy of player $i \in N$ is a (row) vector $s_i = (s_{i1}, \dots, s_{ii-1}, s_{ii+1}, \dots, s_{in})$, where $s_{ij} \in \{0, 1\}$ for each $j \in N \setminus \{i\}$. Player i has a *link* with j if $s_{ij} = 1$. The set of (pure) strategies of player i is denoted by $\mathcal{S}_i$. A strategy profile for all players is denoted by $s = (s_1, s_2, s_3, \dots, s_n)$. There is an equivalence between the set of strategy profiles $\mathcal{S}$ and the set of all directed networks on n nodes $\mathcal{G}$. In what follows we will use the network notation. In this framework, links are *one-sided* in the sense that they can be formed on individual initiative and the individual forming the link incurs the costs of forming links. A natural interpretation of links is that they are information channels.

Benefits flow between two players so long as one of the two has formed a link with the other.[1] To capture this two-way flow define $\hat{g}_{ij} = \max\{g_{ij}, g_{ji}\}$. Given the strategy profile g it is now straightforward to define a corresponding network $\hat{g}$, using the above operation. The link $\hat{g}_{ij} = 1$ is represented by an *edge* between i and j: a filled circle lying on the edge near player i indicates that it is this player who has initiated the link. Figure 8.1 presents an example of such a network. Player 1 has formed links with player 2 and 3, player 3 has formed a link with player 1 while player 2 does not link up with any other player.[2] Every strategy profile g has a unique representation in the manner shown in the figure.

Denote the set of nonnegative integers by $\mathbb{Z}_+$. Let $\phi : \mathbb{Z}_+^2 \to \mathcal{R}$ be a real-valued function. Define each player's payoff function $\Pi_i : \mathcal{G} \to R$ as

$$\Pi_i(g) = \phi(\hat{n}_i(g), \eta_i^d(g)), \tag{8.1}$$

---

[1] An example of this is a telephone call between two players. A second example is that of a social relation, which involves the exchange of gifts and reciprocal favors.

An alternative is to suppose that benefits flow from i to j only if j has invested in a link with i. This approach leads to the one-way flow model which was presented in chapter 7, and is analyzed in section 8.3.

[2] Since players choose strategies independently of each other, two players may simultaneously initiate a two-way link, as seen in the figure.

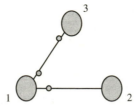

Figure 8.1.   Network representation of $\hat{g}$.

where $\hat{n}_i(g)$ is the number of players accessed by player i in the (undirected version of) network g and $\eta_i^d(g)$ is the number of links formed by player i in network g. We follow the convention that a player accesses herself, and so

$$\hat{\mathcal{N}}_i(g) = \{ j \in N \mid j \xrightarrow{\hat{g}} i \} \quad \text{and} \quad \hat{n}_i(g) = |\hat{\mathcal{N}}_i(g)| + 1.$$

We will make the following assumption about the payoff function.

Assumption 8.1. *The function $\phi(\hat{n}_i(g), \eta_i^d(g))$ is strictly increasing in $\hat{n}_i(g)$ and strictly decreasing in $\eta_i^d(g)$.*

In view of assumption 8.1, it is natural to interpret $\hat{n}_i(g)$ as the number of people that player i accesses in the network, while $\eta_i^d(g)$ measures the cost associated with maintaining her links. This assumption about the payoff function $\phi(\cdot, \cdot)$ is quite mild, and, in particular, allows for decreasing marginal returns from links as well as increasing marginal costs of links.

To develop intuition and illustrate the ideas underlying the main theorems, the following example of linear payoffs is useful:

$$\Pi_i(g) = \hat{n}_i(g) - \eta_i^d(g)c. \tag{8.2}$$

Clearly, the linear payoffs satisfy assumption 8.1. The parameter ranges $c \in (0, 1)$, $c \in (1, n-1)$, and $c > n-1$ have an important role in this model. If $c \in (0, 1)$, then player i will be willing to form a link with player j for the sake of j's value alone. When $c \in (1, n-1)$, player i will require j to access some additional players to induce her to form a link with j. Finally, if $c > n-1$, then the cost of link formation exceeds the total access benefit available from the rest of society. In this case, it is optimal for player i not to form a link with any player, irrespective of what the other players do.

An important general property of all equilibrium networks is derived in the following result, which is due to Bala and Goyal (2000a).

Theorem 8.1. *Suppose that the payoffs are given by (8.1) and that they satisfy assumption 8.1. Then a Nash network is either minimally connected or empty.*[3]

---

[3] Note that here a minimally connected network g has one and only one "undirected" path between every pair of players.

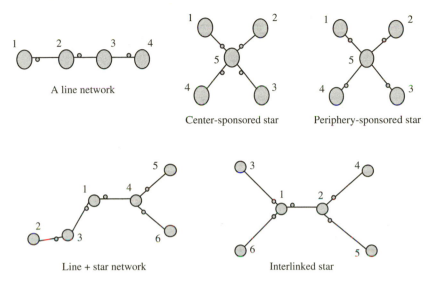

Figure 8.2. Minimally connected networks.

Minimality is a direct consequence of the assumption that the advantages that player i enjoys from accessing player j in a network do not depend on the lengths of the paths in the network. Partially connected networks are ruled out due to positive externalities created by links and the symmetry across players. To see this, consider a network with two components (each with two or more players). Then there is at least one player in each component who forms a link. Number the players 1 and 2 and suppose without loss of generality that player 1 earns weakly higher payoffs. If player 2 imitates the linking strategy of player 1, then she will be able to access all the players that player 1 is accessing plus player 1 herself, while she will form the same number of links as player 1. Given that payoff functions for players are the same and that $\phi(\cdot, \cdot)$ is strictly increasing in the number of players accessed it follows that player 2 can strictly increase her payoff by deleting all her existing links and instead imitating player 1. Thus a network with two or more components cannot be an equilibrium.

A number of networks satisfy the requirement of minimal connectedness. Figure 8.2 illustrates some of them. A center-sponsored star is a directed network with $n - 1$ links which are all formed by a single player, who is the center of the star. A periphery-sponsored star is a directed network with $n - 1$ links, in which $n - 1$ players each form one link with the same player, who is therefore the center of the star.

These networks have very different structures (and correspondingly varied payoff distributions) and this raises the question, are they equally robust? An examination of the line network suggests that player 1 would be indifferent between linking with 2 or 3. In a dynamic context, this suggests that society may move out

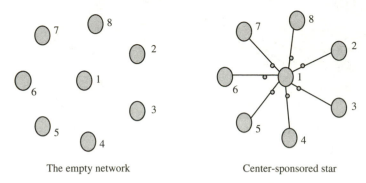

The empty network   Center-sponsored star

Figure 8.3.   Strict equilibrium networks.

of the line network, purely by chance. This possibility raises a number of questions: are there networks which are not vulnerable to such a switching argument, and if individuals revise links over time, then does the process converge, and if yes, then what are the stable networks?

The notion of strict equilibrium addresses the first question: a Nash equilibrium is strict if every player is playing a strategy which yields payoffs that are strictly higher than the payoffs from any alternative strategy. The following result, due to Bala and Goyal (2000a), provides a complete characterization of the architecture of strict Nash networks.

Theorem 8.2. *Suppose that the payoffs are given by (8.1) and that they satisfy assumption 8.1. Then a strict Nash network is either a center-sponsored star or the empty network.*

Figure 8.3 depicts these equilibrium networks for $n = 8$. In particular, in the linear payoffs case, the center-sponsored star (empty network) is the unique strict equilibrium if $0 < c < 1$ ($c > 1$). This result tells us that strategic considerations in link formation lead to networks with small average degree, an unequal degree distribution, and short average distances between players.

The proof of this result rests on a simple switching argument which we now explain. If player i has a link with j, then no other player can have a link with j. If player j did have a link with some player k, then i will be indifferent between forming a link with k or forming a link with j. This would mean that the strategy which involves a link with j is not strictly better than all other strategies. This means that such a pattern of links cannot be supported in a strict Nash equilibrium. Next note that by a further application of the switching argument it follows that no one else can form links with player i. However, since the network is nonempty, from theorem 8.1 we know that it must be connected. So it follows that player i must form links with all the players, in other words, the network is a center-sponsored star.

Theorem 8.2 shows that individual incentives restrict the range of possible network architectures quite dramatically. This characterization of equilibrium networks, however, leads us to the second question raised above: how do individuals choose links if they start with some other network and is there some pressure moving the network to the equilibrium networks identified above? In other words, will individuals learn to coordinate their link formation activity and arrive at a star network?

The dynamic process is defined by the myopic best-response rule, as discussed in chapter 7. Recall, briefly, that in every period an individual gets an opportunity to revise her strategy with positive probability $p \in (0, 1)$. Since $p < 1$, a player exhibits inertia with positive probability. Moreover, it is assumed that if more than one strategy is optimal for some individual, then she *randomizes* across the optimal strategies. These rules generate a Markovian dynamic process in which the probability of moving from a state g at time t to a state g' at time $t + 1$ depends only on the state at time t, and is given by a function $P_{gg'} : \mathcal{G} \times \mathcal{G} \to [0, 1]$, with $\sum_{g'} P_{gg'} = 1$ for every $g \in \mathcal{G}$.

The following result, due to Bala and Goyal (2000a), shows that the dynamics are well-behaved and provides a partial characterization of the absorbing networks.

Theorem 8.3. *Suppose that the payoffs are given by (8.1) and that they satisfy assumption 8.1. Let g be some initial network. If $\phi(x + 1, y + 1) > (<) \phi(x, y)$ for all $y \in \{0, 1, \ldots, n - 2\}$ and $x \in \{y + 1, y + 2, \ldots, n - 1\}$, then the dynamic process converges to the center-sponsored star (empty network) in finite time, with probability 1.*

In the context of the linear model represented in equation (8.2), this result says the following: if $0 < c < 1$, then the process converges to the center-sponsored star, and if $c > 1$, then the process converges to the empty network. The proof uses three general arguments. The first illustrates the power of positive externality generated by individual linking activity: starting with any network, the dynamics either converge to the empty network or a minimally connected network. The second argument reflects agglomeration pressures: starting from any minimally connected network, peripheral players de-link from "remote" players and move towards a central player. This process results in a network with short average distance. The third argument then relies on a miscoordination in link formation among players: miscoordination in linking arises when two players i and j who are linked to a common player k get an opportunity to revise their links and simultaneously choose to delete their link with k and instead form a link with each other instead. This leads to i and j forming a redundant link among themselves as well as isolating themselves from k. This form of coordination failure facilitates the sponsoring of additional links by player k, which, in due course, leads to the emergence of a center-sponsored star.

Efficient networks. We examine the nature of networks that maximize aggregate welfare (recall that this is equal to the sum of individual payoffs). The first observation is that efficient networks are minimal. Minimality follows from the assumption that access benefits do not depend on the length of the path between players. A characterization of efficient networks is, however, complicated by the fact that partially connected networks can be efficient for some payoff functions. This is illustrated with the following simple example.

Example 8.1 (efficiency and connectedness). Suppose $n = 3$. The payoff function takes on the following values: $\phi(1, 0) = 6.4$, $\phi(2, 0) = 7$, $\phi(3, 0) = 7.1$, $\phi(2, 1) = 6$, $\phi(3, 1) = 6.1$, $\phi(3, 2) = 0$. Note that this function satisfies assumption 8.1. Then a network g in which $g_{1,2} = 1$ and $g_{l,k} = 0$ for all other pairs of players is efficient.   △

However, if the payoff function is such that the marginal gains from accessing a player are greater than the marginal costs of forming the link, then clearly an efficient network is connected. This consideration leads us to the following result, due to Bala and Goyal (2000a).

Proposition 8.1. *Suppose that the payoffs are given by (8.1) and that they satisfy assumption 8.1. Any efficient network is minimal. If $\phi(x + 1, y + 1) \geqslant \phi(x, y)$ for all $y \in \{0, 1, \ldots, n - 2\}$ and $x \in \{y + 1, y + 2, \ldots, n - 1\}$, then an efficient network is connected.*

A complete characterization of efficient networks is, however, available for the linear model. In that case, simple calculations can be used to conclude that an efficient network must be either minimally connected or empty. Then it follows by direct calculation that a minimally connected network is efficient for $c < n$, while the empty network is efficient for $c > n$. A comparison of this characterization of efficient networks with theorem 8.2 leads to two remarks: (i) the star is efficient as well as an equilibrium network for low costs of forming links ($c < 1$), and (ii) that the equilibrium network—the empty network—is under-connected relative to efficient networks for moderate and large costs of link formation, $1 < c < n$. The intuition behind this under-connectedness is that individual links generate positive externalities for others and this leads individuals to underestimate the social value of links.

Distributional properties. There are two aspects of the distribution that are worth noting. (i) The center pays for all the links and therefore gets a much lower payoff than the peripheral players. In the linear model, this means that the center earns $(n - 1)(1 - c) + 1$, while the peripheral players each earn n. For large values of c and n the payoff difference can therefore be very large. (ii) The central player is worse off than the peripheral players. On the one hand, this suggests that in some settings the central players may actually be losing out because they pay for all the links which make them central. This is an intriguing possibility. On the other hand, this aspect of the result also seems to run counter to the intuition that players form connections to exploit network advantage and so central players should be earning higher payoffs than peripheral players.

To summarize, the analysis of the basic model of link formation yields sharp predictions on the architecture of (strict) equilibrium networks: they are stars or they are empty. Moreover, equilibrium networks may be under-connected relative to efficient networks and they exhibit significant payoff inequality.

8.3 Extensions

The above results are obtained for a general class of payoffs from connecting with others. In particular, no specific concavity or convexity assumptions were used in proving the main results. However, they are restrictive in two important respects. First, these payoff functions assume that the flow of benefits between player i and player j depends only on the existence of a path between these players and does not depend on the length of the path between the players. In other words, there is no decay. Second, it is assumed that all players have the same payoff functions; in other words, players are symmetric. This section examines the effects of introducing heterogeneity and decay in the two-way flow model discussed in section 8.2.

8.3.1 Decay

In communication networks, for instance, it is reasonable to expect that the flow of information from one person to another takes time and also involves noise. Both these factors are likely to lower the value of information to person i if it has to pass through a number of people before it reaches person j. Similarly, in exchange or trading networks, we expect that a longer path of intermediaries between i and j will lower payoffs that i and j can hope to make.[4] This section examines the implications of decay for equilibrium networks.

The standard formulation of decay considers the linear model summarized in equation (8.2). In this context, decay is modeled as a geometric fall in value as it passes from one person to another. This decay is measured by the parameter $\delta \in [0, 1]$. So $\delta = 0$ corresponds to the case of complete decay, while $\delta = 1$ corresponds to the case of no decay. Define $\hat{d}(i, j; g)$ as the length of the shortest path between two nodes i and j in the (undirected version of) network g. Following Bala and Goyal (2000a) the payoffs to player i in network g can be

---

[4] See chapter 9 for a model of exchange in which payoffs for a pair of players i and j decline in the number of (essential) intermediaries between them.

written as

$$\Pi_i(g) = 1 + \sum_{j \in \hat{\mathcal{N}}_i(g)} \delta^{\hat{d}(i,j;g)} - \eta_i^d(g)c. \tag{8.3}$$

At an intuitive level the effects of decay are quite straightforward. Decay introduces incentives for players to reduce the lengths of paths between themselves. This means that the star network is even more attractive than before. However, the introduction of decay also means that cycles can be sustained in equilibrium. As an example consider a society with n players and suppose that $0 < c < \delta - \delta^2$. Then the complete network is the unique Nash network. To get a first impression of the issues it is useful to start with the case of small decay, i.e., δ close to 1. The following discussion draws on the analysis in Bala and Goyal (2000a).

The first point to note is that if $c < 1$, then in the presence of small decay, a periphery-sponsored star is a strict equilibrium network (along with other star networks). In the periphery-sponsored star, the central player clearly has no incentive to form any additional links, and the peripheral players have no incentive to delete their link or to form an additional link given that δ is close to 1. Moreover, since $\delta < 1$, a peripheral player has a strict incentive not to switch the single link with the central player and instead connect with a peripheral player. Does this mean that the switching argument developed in the context of theorem 8.2 is basically an artifact of the absence of decay in the basic model? The answer to this question is no. The discussion in the next paragraph illustrates how a variant of the switching argument can be used to construct profitable deviations and thereby pin down equilibrium network architectures in the presence of decay.

If $1 < c < n - 1$, then it is not worth forming a link with an isolated player; so the empty network is clearly an equilibrium. However, it is possible to show that the *periphery-sponsored star is the only other equilibrium network*.[5] The arguments underlying this finding turn out to be quite general and it is therefore worth elaborating on them. First, note that, due to positive externalities created by individual linking, an equilibrium network is either connected or empty. Second, note that due to small decay the equilibrium network must be minimal. Third, consider two players i and j who are at a distance of 3 or more in such a minimal network g. Since $c > 1$ it follows that each of them must be sponsoring their connection in g. Suppose that player j earns a (weakly) higher payoff than player i and let j have a link with player k on the unique path between i and j. Since the distance between i and j in g is greater than 2, it must be true that player i does not have a link with k. Player i can earn a strictly higher payoff if she deletes her current link and instead forms a link with player k: this is because she will be at the same distance from all players as player j in the original network, and,

---

[5]To be precise, the periphery-sponsored star is only a strict equilibrium for $n \geqslant 4$; for $n = 3$, a peripheral player is indifferent between linking with the center and the other spoke player, so a periphery-sponsored star is not an equilibrium.

in addition, she will be closer to j in the new network than in g. This argument shows that the distance between any two players in an equilibrium network cannot be greater than 2. The final step in the argument is to note that the star is the only minimal network where every pair of players is at a distance of 2 or less.

The above observations indicate that even a small amount of decay can have profound implications for the nature of equilibrium networks. Nonempty networks can be strict equilibria for a whole range of values, $1 < c < n - 1$; if there is decay, by contrast, the empty network is the unique equilibrium in the absence of decay. Moreover, the architecture of the nonempty network— periphery-sponsored star—is also of great interest: they exhibit low average degree, unequal degree distribution, and short average distances. How do the periphery-sponsored stars compare with center-sponsored stars? The two types of network share three features: a low average degree, an unequal distribution of links, and small average distances. However, the big difference between the two networks is in the sponsorship of links. In the periphery-sponsored star all players but one form a single link each, while in the center-sponsored star only one player forms links, and $n - 1$ players free ride. This difference has powerful implications for the distribution of payoffs: in the center-sponsored star the peripheral players earn a larger payoff than the central player, while it is the other way around in periphery-sponsored stars. These findings motivate a more general examination of equilibrium networks under decay.

A characterization of equilibrium networks along the lines of theorem 8.2 is an open problem. To get a sense of why this is a difficult problem, note that a number of different architectures can be sustained in equilibrium, for general levels of decay. Figure 8.4 presents some of these equilibrium networks to illustrate the nature of this problem. Researchers have responded to this multiplicity in equilibrium networks in two ways. The first approach has been to study stochastically stable networks in the presence of decay.[6] The second approach proceeds by placing stronger restrictions on the payoffs to rule out a number of networks. These two approaches are now briefly discussed.

The stochastic stability of networks, in the presence of decay, has been studied by Feri (2005), who shows that, in a game with payoffs given by (8.3), the following result holds.[7]

(i) If $c < \delta - \delta^2$, then the stochastically stable network is complete.

(ii) If $\delta - \delta^2 < c < \delta$, then, for large n, a stochastically stable network is a star.

---

[6] The basic ideas underlying the theory of stochastic stability are discussed in chapter 4.

[7] The result Feri (2005) obtains is slightly stronger than what is stated here: for $\delta - \delta^2 < c < \delta - \delta^3$, stars are stochastically stable networks (along with possibly other networks), while for $\delta - \delta^3 < c < \delta$, stars are the only stochastically stable networks.

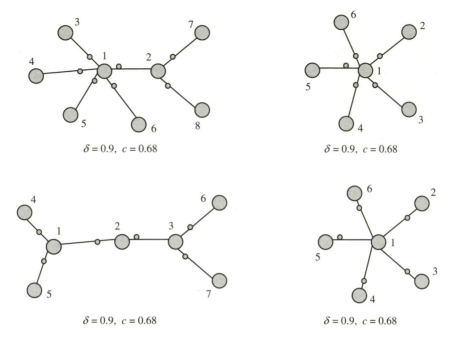

Figure 8.4.   Equilibrium networks with decay.

(iii) If $c > \delta$, then there exists $\hat{c}$ such that, for $\delta < c < \hat{c}$, a stochastically stable network is either a periphery-sponsored star or the empty network, while for $c > \hat{c}$ the stochastically stable network is empty.

The arguments underlying part (ii) of the result are of general interest and are now discussed. The first step is to note that a mutation in the strategy of a single individual is sufficient to engineer a transition from a network g to the center-sponsored star. Start with a network g and suppose that due to a mutation, player i forms a link with all players. The best response of each of the other players moving in sequence is now to delete all their links and this results in the center-sponsored star. The second step shows that it is possible to transit from one star to another star via a sequence of one-player mutations. Consider two star networks, g and g': in network g player 1 is the center and forms a link with player 2, and in network g' player 1 is the center and player 2 forms the link with player 1. It is possible to move from network g to g' if player 1 deletes the link with player 2 as part of a mutation. The best response of player 2 is then to form a link with player 1. This shows, roughly speaking, that all stars are equally robust to mutations. Since one is the minimum number of possible mutations, these steps put together imply that it requires (weakly) more mutations for the transition away from a star to a nonstar network than does a transition from a nonstar network to a star. The theory of stochastic stability then implies that stars are stochastically stable for $\delta - \delta^2 < c < \delta$.

The second approach to resolving the problem of multiple equilibrium networks proceeds by placing restrictions on the payoff function. This approach is developed by Hojman and Szeidl (2006). Let $\hat{\eta}_i^k(g)$ be the number of individuals who are at (geodesic) distance k from individual i in (the undirected network associated with) network g. The payoffs to individual i in network g are

$$\Pi_i(g) = f(a_1 \hat{\eta}_i^1(g) + \cdots + a_{n-1} \hat{\eta}_i^{n-1}(g)) - \eta_i^d(g)c, \qquad (8.4)$$

where $a_1 \geqslant a_2 \geqslant a_3 \geqslant \cdots \geqslant a_d$, and this reflects the idea that increasing distance (weakly) reduces payoffs, while $c > 0$, which reflects a positive cost of forming links, and $f(\cdot)$ is an increasing and concave function. Hojman and Szeidl (2006) impose two restrictions on the payoffs. The first is that communication can only take place between individuals who are within a certain distance of each other: there is some $D < n$ such that $a_{d'} = 0$ for all $d' \geqslant D$. The second restriction is that there are eventually strongly diminishing returns to communication: there is some M such that, for $m \geqslant M$, $f(m) - f(m/2) \leqslant c$. Their main result is that *if the number of players is large enough, relative to M and D, and if $a_2 > a_3$, then the periphery-sponsored star is the unique equilibrium network.*

The arguments establishing that a periphery-sponsored star is an equilibrium (which were mentioned above) carry over to this setting. The bounds on decay D and on change in value of $f(\cdot)$, reflected in M, together guarantee uniqueness. To see their role, consider first the bounds on decay: in the absence of decay ($a_1 = a_2 = \cdots = a_n = 1$), other minimal networks can arise in equilibrium.[8] Consider next the role of strongly decreasing returns: in the absence of such bounds, a center-sponsored star, among other networks, can be an equilibrium for small values of c.

Efficient networks. The key idea in the analysis of efficient networks here is that decay creates a pressure for the reduction in path lengths. The following result, due to Bala and Goyal (2000a), provides a complete characterization of efficient networks.

Theorem 8.4. *Suppose payoffs are given by (8.3). The unique efficient network is*

  (i) *the complete network if* $0 < c < 2[\delta - \delta^2]$,

  (ii) *the star network if* $2[\delta - \delta^2] < c < 2\delta + (n-2)\delta^2$, *and*

  (iii) *the empty network if* $2\delta + (n-2)\delta^2 < c$.

The important aspect of the above result is the sharp transitions in network architectures and corresponding number of links as costs cross certain thresholds.

---

[8] Fix a cost $c > 0$ and suppose that $n = 2k + 1$, where k is a sufficiently large integer. A network with player 1 at the center and $2k$ other players split up to into pairs with each pair constituting a two-player long "spoke" is an equilibrium network.

For example, if $c < 2[\delta - \delta^2]$, an efficient network has $n(n-1)/2$ links, while if $2[\delta - \delta^2] < c < 2\delta + (n-2)\delta^2$, an efficient network has only $n-1$ links, and if $2\delta + (n-2)\delta^2 < c$, an efficient network has zero links. These features point to an important feature of star networks: in the class of connected networks they minimize the number of links since they are minimally connected and at the same time they have very low average distance as well. In the model of links under consideration, both links and distance are costly and it is therefore not a surprise that stars are attractive from an efficiency point of view.

The study of decay yields a number of insights. The first insight is that, for a wide range of values, periphery-sponsored stars arise in equilibrium, something which was not possible in the absence of decay. The second insight pertains to the efficiency of equilibrium networks. In the basic model the empty network was the unique equilibrium network for all values of $c > 1$. By contrast, with decay, periphery-sponsored stars can be sustained in equilibrium so long as $c < \delta + (n-2)\delta^2$, and this means that efficient networks are sustainable in equilibrium over a much wider range of parameters. The third insight concerns the payoff distribution: in periphery-sponsored stars the peripheral players form all the links and therefore earn lower payoffs than the central player. This is the reverse of the direction of inequality in the center-sponsored star, where the center earns a lower payoff than the peripheral players.

8.3.2 Decay and Heterogeneity

In this section we further enrich the two-way flow model by incorporating heterogeneity. There are different ways in which player heterogeneity can be studied. Here, we examine the effects of heterogeneity in costs of linking. We will consider an *insider–outsider* model of link formation: individuals in a society are divided into prespecified groups, and the costs of forming links within a group are lower than the costs of forming links across groups. The exposition here is based on Galeotti, Goyal, and Kamphorst (2006).[9]

Consider a society composed of two groups. Let $n_l = |N_l|$ be the size of group l, with $l = 1, 2$.[10] For expositional simplicity, suppose that the value to player $i \in N$ of accessing player j, $V_{ij} = 1$ for all $j \in N$. The cost of linking for

---

[9] Galeotti, Goyal, and Kamphorst (2006) consider a general insider–outsider model which allows for heterogeneities in value and person-specific differences in costs of linking. They obtain results on how different types of heterogeneity matter for equilibrium networks.

For an early treatment of player heterogeneities in network formation, see Johnson and Gilles (2000). They present a model of two-sided link formation in which the costs of forming links depend on spatial differentiation among players. In a recent paper, Jackson and Rogers (2005) present an islands model of two-sided link formation in which linking within an island is cheaper than linking across islands. Their model is also an example of an insider–outsider model.

[10] The assumption of two groups is made for expositional simplicity; the analysis extends to a finite number of groups.

two players in the same (different) group is c_L (c_H), where $c_H > c_L > 0$. Define $N_i^{d,k}(g) = \{j \in N_k \mid g_{ij} = 1\}$ for $k = 1, 2$ and let $\eta_i^{d,k}(g) = |N_i^{d,k}(g)|$.

The payoffs to player i in group l can be rewritten as follows:

$$\Pi_i(g) = 1 + \sum_{j \in \hat{N}_i(g)} \delta^{\hat{d}(i,j;g)} - \eta_i^{d,l} c_L - \eta_i^{d,k} c_H, \tag{8.5}$$

where $l, k = 1, 2$ and $l \neq k$.

The following result, due to Galeotti, Goyal, and Kamphorst (2006), covers the case where decay is small. A network in which each group constitutes a star and a single player i of group l forms a link with the central player j of group $k \neq l$ is referred to as an interlinked group-stars network. If each star is center-sponsored (periphery-sponsored), we will say that the network is an interlinked center-sponsored (periphery-sponsored) group-stars network. A one-group periphery-sponsored star is a partially connected network where one group forms a periphery-sponsored star while the members of the other group remain isolated.

Proposition 8.2. *Suppose (8.5) holds, $n_l = \bar{n}$ for $l = 1, 2$, and that decay is small (δ is close to 1).*

(1) *Suppose $c_L \in (0, 1)$. Then*

    (1a) *if $c_H \in (c_L, \bar{n})$, any interlinked group-stars network is a strict equilibrium;*

    (1b) *if $c_H > \bar{n}$, any unconnected group-stars network is a strict equilibrium.*

(2) *Suppose $c_L \in (1, \bar{n})$. Then*

    (2a) *if $c_H \in (c_L, \bar{n})$, the interlinked periphery-sponsored group-stars and the empty network are the only strict equilibria;*

    (2b) *if $c_H > \bar{n}$, then, in an equilibrium, each group is either a periphery-sponsored star or empty.*

(3) *If $c_L > \bar{n}$, the empty network is the unique strict equilibrium.*

Figure 8.5 illustrates an interlinked group-stars network. Proposition 8.2 highlights the salience of local stars and interlinked stars across a wide range of cost parameters. When decay is small an equilibrium network will be minimal. First consider the case $c_L < 1$: members of the same group must be accessing each other. If $c_H < \bar{n}$, then there will be links across groups and so an interlinked group-stars network is an equilibrium. If $c_H > \bar{n}$, then a link across groups is not worthwhile and if c_L is not too large, then clearly each group constituting a star is an equilibrium. If $c_L > 1$ and decay is small, then equilibrium networks must be minimal and peripheral players must be sponsoring their links. The uniqueness

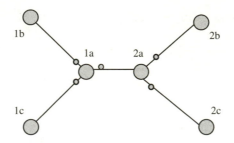

Figure 8.5.   Interlinked group-stars network.

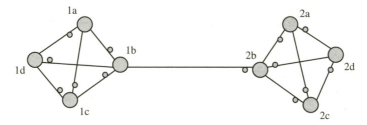

Figure 8.6.   Network with low insider costs and high decay.

of this equilibrium follows from arguments analogous to those used in showing uniqueness of periphery-sponsored stars with low levels of decay (in section 8.3.1 above).

General results in a model with heterogeneity and significant levels of decay are not available. The image of society as constituted of a set of highly clustered local communities with a few intercommunity links is a familiar one. The following example shows that such a social network is one possible equilibrium in a model of network formation with heterogeneity and significant decay.

Example 8.2 (an equilibrium network with significant decay). Suppose (8.5) holds, $n_l = \bar{n}$ for $l = 1, 2$. If $0 < c_L < \delta - \delta^2$ and $\delta - \delta^2 + (\bar{n} - 1)(\delta^2 - \delta^3) < c_H < \delta + (\bar{n} - 1)\delta^2$, then a network in which each group is a complete component and there is one link across the groups is the unique strict equilibrium.[11] Since $c_L < \delta - \delta^2$ it follows that there must be a direct link between every pair of players from the same group. The conditions on c_H imply that one and only link between the groups is individually profitable. Figure 8.6 illustrates an equilibrium of this type for a society in which $\bar{n} = 4$.   △

Proposition 8.2 and example 8.2 highlight two possible types of equilibrium network. The first type is interlinked group-stars; the second type is a group-wise complete network which exhibits some degree inequality, short average distances, and high clustering.

---

[11] Jackson and Rogers (2005) obtain a similar result in the context of an islands model of network formation.

8.3.3 Related Themes

In recent years, strategic network formation has been a very active area of research, and a number of themes have been explored. The two-way flow model presented in section 8.2 offers a simple and general framework within which these themes can be discussed and this section introduces three of these themes: local network knowledge, imperfect reliability of links, and alternative models of benefit flow.

8.3.3.1 Local Knowledge of the Network

In the basic model of connections, individuals choose links simultaneously, and once links are in place everyone can observe the entire network. In such a setting, it seems reasonable to focus on Nash equilibrium. However, in many applications—such as the World Wide Web, coauthor networks, networks of friends—the number of players is very large and individuals have at best only local knowledge about the network. Indeed, empirical work suggests that individuals typically know their own neighbors, but have only limited knowledge of the pattern of links beyond this immediate circle (see, for example, Kumbasar, Romney, and Batchelder 1994; Casciaro 1998). This raises the following question. *Does limited knowledge lead individuals to form very different networks than they would form under global knowledge?* This question has been studied by McBride (2006a,b).

To get a sense of the issues that arise suppose that payoffs are given by equation (8.2) and for simplicity assume that $c < 1$. In the full information case, a Nash network is minimally connected while a strict Nash network is a center-sponsored star (see theorems 8.1 and 8.2). McBride (2006b) shows that, with local knowledge of the network structure, cycles as well as partially connected networks can be supported in equilibrium. Thus local knowledge can lead to equilibrium networks which may be over-connected as well as under-connected relative to the equilibrium networks under full information. McBride (2006b) also shows that a variation of the switching argument developed in theorem 8.2 can be used to show that any strict equilibrium with local information is also a center-sponsored star.

8.3.3.2 Reliability

In the basic model, it is assumed that a link conveys benefits with certainty. In many contexts, e.g., social communication or flow of traffic over the Internet, there is the possibility that a link may not function perfectly. Reliability of links is an important consideration and is likely to have a bearing on equilibrium outcomes as well as socially optimal structures. Bala and Goyal (2000b) formulated the problem of reliability in terms of a probability $r \in [0, 1]$ that a link works. Assume that the probability of successful link operation is independent across links. Using this assumption, given that a network g is in place, the probability of a network $g' \subset g$ being operational or being realized is simply

$$\lambda(g' \mid g) = r^{L(g')}(1 - r)^{L(g)-L(g')}, \tag{8.6}$$

where $L(\cdot)$ is the number of links in a network. The payoffs to individual i from network g can now be written as follows:

$$\Pi_i(g) = \sum_{g' \subset g} \lambda(g' \mid g)\hat{n}_i(g') - \eta_i^d(g)c. \tag{8.7}$$

Bala and Goyal (2000b) showed that for fixed p equilibrium networks and efficient networks will be *super-connected*[12] if the number of players is large enough. The intuition behind this result can be seen from a consideration of the star network: in this network a peripheral player depends on a single link for accessing the entire network. Given p and a cost of forming links c, the marginal value from linking with another peripheral player is clearly larger than the cost of the link, for large enough n. A similar argument also implies that efficient networks are super-connected. The results obtained by Bala and Goyal (2000b) should be seen as the first steps in the analysis of network formation in the presence of imperfectly reliable links; this is clearly an area in which further work is needed.[13]

The above arguments also illustrate how the implications of imperfect reliability are quite distinct from those of decay. In the presence of decay, the star is an equilibrium and also efficient for a large range of parameters, while imperfect reliability of links calls for cycles and this makes the star less attractive.

The possibility of imperfect reliability suggests the possibility that players may be able to affect the quality of the link by investing different amounts of resources in them. In recent years a number of authors have developed models to study link-specific investments (see, for example, Bloch and Dutta 2005; Goyal, Konovalov, and Moraga 2003; Brueckner 2003). Bloch and Dutta (2005) study efficient weighted networks in the context of an extension of the link formation model presented above. Brueckner (2003) studies a model where raising investments increases the probability of a link being formed. Goyal, Konovalov, and Moraga (2003) study a setting where links are cost-cutting R&D projects between firms.

8.3.3.3 *Flow of Benefits*

The discussion so far has focused on the case where flow of benefits are two-way. In some settings—examples include links on the World Wide Web, investments

---

[12] A network is said to be super-connected if it remains connected upon the deletion of any single link.

[13] There is a large body of research on reliability in the field of operations research and management; see Ball, Colburn, and Provan (1995) for a survey of this work. This work is mostly concerned with issues such as the computation of reliability levels in given networks and the design of networks which attain a certain prespecified level of reliability.

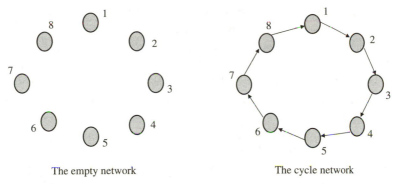

Figure 8.7.   Strict equilibrium networks with one-way flow.

to observe actions of others—observation benefits accrue mainly to players who incur the cost for setting up the link. This leads to a model with one-way flow of benefits. Recall from chapter 7 that the payoff to player i, $\Pi_i : \mathcal{G} \to \mathcal{R}$, is

$$\Pi_i(g) = \phi(n_i(g), \eta_i^d(g)). \tag{8.8}$$

We will make the following assumption about the payoff function.

Assumption 8.2.   *The payoff function $\phi(n_i(g), \eta_i^d(g))$ is strictly increasing in $n_i(g)$ and strictly decreasing in $\eta_i^d(g)$.*

The linear payoff function is an example which satisfies assumption 8.2:

$$\Pi_i(g) = n_i(g) - \eta_i^d(g)c. \tag{8.9}$$

In words, player i's payoffs are the number of players she observes less the total cost of link formation.

A cycle is a connected directed network in which each player forms exactly one link. The following result, due to Bala and Goyal (2000a), provides a complete characterization of strict equilibrium networks in the one-way flow model.

Theorem 8.5.   *Suppose that the payoffs are given by (8.8) and that they satisfy assumption 8.2. Then a strict Nash network is either the cycle or the empty network.*

Figure 8.7 depicts these equilibrium networks for $n = 8$.[14] In particular, in the context of the linear model, the cycle is the unique equilibrium network if $c < 1$, the cycle and the empty network are the only equilibria for $1 < c < n - 1$, while the empty network is the unique network for $c > n - 1$.

There are two main arguments in the proof of theorem 8.5. The first argument exploits positive externalities from individual links and the symmetry of payoffs to

---

[14] Note that in this figure a link formed by player i with player j is represented by a line joining i and j and the arrow points towards j. This is consistent with the representation of directed networks in chapter 5.

show that a Nash network is either connected or empty. There are, however, a large number of connected networks with a wide range of architectures. For example, the star and the cycle are both connected networks which can be supported in equilibrium. The second argument exploits the refinement of strictness to rule out all connected networks other than the cycle. The following variant of the switching argument is used here: if two players i and j have a link with the same player k, then player i will be indifferent between forming a link with k or instead forming a link with j. This means that every player has one and only one player who initiates a link with her. This means that in the one-way flow model a (nonempty) strict Nash network has exactly n links. From the first argument in the proof we know that a nonempty equilibrium network is connected; since the cycle is the only connected (directed) network with exactly n links, the result follows.

In this model it is easy to see that an efficient network must be either minimally connected or empty. In the class of minimally connected networks, the cycle minimizes the number of links and hence the total cost of forming links. Thus an efficient network is either empty or the cycle. In particular, for the linear model the cycle is the unique efficient network for $0 < c < n$, while the empty network is efficient for $c > n$. This implies that for $0 < c < n - 1$ and $c > n$ an efficient network is sustainable as a Nash equilibrium, while for $n - 1 < c < n$ an efficient network is not sustainable in equilibrium. There is, therefore, a wide range of cost values for which the set of equilibrium and efficient networks coincide. Finally, note that the cycle is perfectly symmetric in terms of number of links as well as payoffs.

A comparison of theorems 8.2 and 8.5 shows that assumptions on flow of benefits have powerful implications for the architecture, payoff distribution, and the efficiency of equilibrium networks.[15]

8.4 Experiments and Empirical Regularities

The theoretical models yield a number of predictions concerning (strict) Nash equilibrium networks. In the model with no decay, a center-sponsored star network is the unique equilibrium structure. In the presence of decay, center-sponsored stars and periphery-sponsored stars can both arise in equilibrium. However, for large societies and under reasonable concavity restrictions on payoffs, periphery-sponsored stars are the unique network architectures in equilibrium. How do these predictions fare in experiments and are they consistent with empirical regularities in real-world networks?

---

[15] In a recent paper, Galeotti (2006) examines an extension of the one-way flow model to allow for heterogeneity in valuations and benefits.

The theoretical work has motivated a number of experiments (see, for example, Callander and Plott 2005; Falk and Kosfeld 2005; Goeree, Riedl, and Ule 2005; Pantz and Zeigelmeyer 2003).[16] The experimental setups differ in the details but the general framework is very close to the dynamic model studied in section 8.2. Individuals can form links at discrete periods of time; they can observe the network that formed in the previous period and can revise their links. The interest has centered on the question of whether individuals settle on a specific network over time (the issue of convergence) and also whether this network is the star.

The experimental work yields the following general finding: in settings with homogeneous players—i.e., all individuals have the same value and the same costs of linking with others—star networks arise very rarely. However, even in these settings, the process does get close to stars in the sense that it reaches networks which differ from a star in one link only. By contrast, in a setting with player heterogeneity—especially in a situation in which linking to one player is more worthwhile than others—stars arise frequently. Moreover, in experiments with many rounds, the long-run network is almost always a star network (see Falk and Kosfeld 2005; Goeree, Riedl, and Ule 2005). How can these findings be explained?

These papers develop an explanation based on the idea of inequity aversion. Recall that in a star network the payoff distribution is unequal. These papers argue that, in a setting with homogeneous players, inequity aversion prevails and stars rarely emerge; in cases where they emerge, they are not stable over time. On the other hand, in the presence of player heterogeneity, with one player being more valuable than the others, it is especially attractive to directly link with this player (in the presence of decay). In other words, there are payoff advantages to having the high value player as the center of a star. The experimental work suggests that players trade off this efficiency gain against the potential inequality the star entails. If the efficiency gains are large enough, then players overcome their inequity aversion and the star network arises and is stable over time.

The experimental work uses specific levels of heterogeneity in value, and this raises the issue of how much *ex ante* inequality is needed to generate periphery-sponsored stars. In this context, it is worth noting a theoretical result due to Hojman and Szeidl (2006). They show that even a small difference in value between players guarantees that the highly valued player will constitute the central player. They interpret this result as saying that network formation has the effect of greatly exacerbating *ex ante* inequalities. When set in the context of the experimental work discussed in this section, this result suggests the need for a closer examination of the relation between *ex ante* player heterogeneity and equilibrium payoff inequality.

---

[16] Kosfeld (2004) provides a survey of this work.

Table 8.1. Data on directed networks.

Period	Telephone	World Wide Web
Total nodes	53×10^6	200×10^6
Giant component as percentage		0.90
Average degree	3.16	7.5
Clustering coefficient		n.a.
Average distance		6
Diameter		28

The data for the World Wide Web are from 1999 and are taken from Broder et al. (2000). The numbers for giant component, average distance, and diameter are derived by assuming that links are undirected. This is in the spirit of the two-way flow model. If we take the links to be directed, then the giant component will comprise about 28% of all the Web sites while the average distance will be around 16. The data on the telephone network are taken from Aiello, Chung, and Lu (2000). The nodes are telephone numbers, while the links are directed (going from the caller to the receiver). The network is constructed by using data from long-distance calls made during a single day.

8.4.1 Empirical Findings

In recent years a lot of empirical research has been done on the architecture of large social, technological, and economic networks; see chapter 2 for references to this literature. This work has helped identify a number of key empirical regularities in large real-world networks. Interest has centered on a few variables such as the number and distribution of connections (the degree distribution), the proximity between different nodes (average distance in the network), and the extent of overlap between connections (the clustering coefficient of the network). Table 8.1 presents statistics on these variables for the World Wide Web and for a telephone call network.[17]

These data highlight the following features.

Number of connections. The average number of connections is very small relative to the total number of nodes. Broder et al. (2000) identified over 200 million pages and 1.5 billion links using Altavista crawls of the World Wide Web in 1999. They also discovered that the average degree of pages was a mere 7.5. Similarly, in a study of telephone call networks, Aiello, Chung, and Lu (2000) identified over 50 million nodes (telephone numbers) and found that the average degree was only 3.16.

Average distance. The average distance between nodes is very small. For instance, on the World Wide Web, Broder et al. (2000) explored links between 200 million documents, and found that the average path length was only 6.[18]

---

[17] We have presented data on these networks in this chapter as they are directed networks; the data on coauthor networks are presented in chapter 9, while the data on interfirm networks are presented in chapter 10.

[18] Here links on the World Wide Web are taken to be undirected.

Unequal connections. The key to reconciling the small number of connections and small average distance is the striking inequality in the degree distribution. For instance, on the World Wide Web the average degree in the whole network was 7.5, but there are sites which have hundreds of thousands of links.

How do these properties match with the features of equilibrium networks obtained in sections 8.2 and 8.3.1? The average degree in a star is (approximately) 2, which is relatively speaking very small in networks with large n; the central player has $(n - 1)$ links while each of the peripheral players has only 1 link each, implying a range of $n - 2$, which is enormous if a network has large n. Finally, the average distance in a star network is less than 2 and this is independent of the number of players; this average distance is tiny when seen in the context of the low average degree and the large number of players. This leads to the conclusion that the equilibrium star network and their variations, such as the interlinked star, share a number of features with empirical networks.

The network formation model studied in sections 8.2 and 8.3 is very simple and does not incorporate competition among players, congestion effects, or incomplete information about the network, features which are likely to be important in different applications. Viewed in this light, the similarity between the equilibrium and the empirical networks is quite striking and suggests that the basic model—in which payoffs are increasing in the number of players accessed and falling in the number of links—captures key elements of network formation processes in a wide range of environments.

8.5   Research in Other Subjects

The model of link formation discussed above is perhaps the simplest way to formalize ideas about network formation. It is therefore not surprising that models with similar features have also been studied in other subjects which are interested in network formation. This section briefly relates the two-way flow model of network formation with major developments in statistical physics and computer science.

The research on network formation in statistical physics has been especially concerned with developing models that generate networks which are consistent with real-world networks discussed in section 8.4 (as well as in chapters 2, 9, and 10).[19] In particular, physicists have been especially interested in explaining the scale-free or power-law degree distribution in these networks.[20] Perhaps the simplest model of network formation which explains the scale-free degree distribution and short average distances is the one proposed by Barabasi and Albert

---

[19] For surveys of this work, see Barabasi (2002), Newman (2003), and Watts (1999).

[20] A power-law degree distribution takes the form $f(k) = \alpha k^{-\beta}$, with $\alpha > 0$ and $\beta > 0$.

(1999).[21] They formulate a simple dynamic model of network formation in which, at every point in time, a new node arrives and forms new links with existing nodes. The probability that the new node connects to an existing node is proportional to the number of links the existing node has. This is referred to as *preferential attachment*. The property of preferential attachment is critical for the derivation of scale-free or power-law degree distributions.

The preferential attachment model is very close in spirit to the dynamic model discussed in section 8.2. Consider the following slight modification of the dynamics: suppose individual players move one after the other and there is some decay $\delta \in (0, 1)$. Suppose that every player is allowed to form one link. Then it is optimal for each individual to connect with the most linked player, with probability 1. This process leads to a star network. The preferential attachment model requires the probability of linking with a node to be increasing in the number of current links of this node; this together with an expanding number of players generates richer degree distributions, such as the scale-free distributions.

The research on network formation in computer science has been driven by questions arising out of the growing Internet and the World Wide Web. A distinctive feature of the Internet is that it is a network in which the links have been formed by service providers who are (in many instances) private firms. So it is reasonable to suppose that the links are formed by firms to maximize their individual (provider) profits. This raises the question, how closely will the resulting network resemble an efficient network? The ratio of the aggregate utility from the (worst) equilibrium network to the aggregate utility in the efficient network is termed the "*price of anarchy*." Interest has centered on deriving bounds on this price of anarchy (see, for example, Fabrikant et al. 2003; Anshelevich et al. 2004).

In the basic model links are assumed to be costly but proximity between nodes is valued. In network g the total costs to individual i are

$$C_i(g) = \sum_{j \in N} \hat{d}(i, j; g) + \eta_i^d(g)c. \tag{8.10}$$

The objective of a player is to minimize these costs. Social costs are simply the sum of individual costs. This model is clearly very similar to the two-way model with decay which was studied in section 8.3.1.

In this formulation, the distance between players who do not have a connecting path is infinite; this immediately implies that, for any finite cost c of forming links, an equilibrium network is always connected. Indeed, it is easy to see that if $c < 1$, then a Nash network is complete, while if $c > 1$, then a star is a Nash network. Similarly, it is quite easy to see that if $c < 2$, then the socially optimal network is

---

[21] Scale-free degree distributions have been the motivation behind a number of theoretical models over the years. For a pioneering theoretical model, see Simon (1955).

complete, while if $c > 2$ and finite, then the socially optimal network is a star. The equilibrium network attains the optimal costs for $c < 1$. However, for $c \in (1, 2)$, the optimal network is complete while any Nash network has a diameter of 2. Since $c < 2$ it can be checked that the star maximizes social costs in the class of networks with diameter of at most 2. The price of anarchy is then

$$
\begin{aligned}
\frac{C(g^s)}{C(g^c)} &= \frac{(n-1)(c-2+2n)}{n(n-1)((c-2)/2+2)} \\
&= \frac{4}{2+c} - \frac{4-2c}{n(2+c)} \\
&< \frac{4}{2+c} < \frac{4}{3}.
\end{aligned}
\tag{8.11}
$$

The star is an equilibrium for $c > 2$ but there also exist other equilibria and Fabrikant et al. (2003) show that the price of anarchy is $O(\sqrt{c})$.[22]

If $c > 2$ and finite, then the star is efficient as well as an equilibrium. This observation has motivated an alternative approach to the study of the tension between individual incentives and social requirement, which is termed the *price of stability*.

The price of stability approach was proposed by Anshelevich et al. (2004) and focuses on the best equilibrium, rather than under the worst equilibrium. Simple computations reveal that, in the context of the link formation model above, there are no costs of stability if $c < 1$ or if $c > 2$, while there are costs of stability when $c \in (1, 2)$. In recent years, an extensive literature has explored the price of anarchy and stability in different contexts; for a survey of this work, see Roughgarden (2005).

To summarize, the models in statistical physics as well as in computer science are very similar in spirit to the two-way flow model studied in sections 8.2 and 8.3.1. However, the questions addressed in the different subjects have been distinct and so the research has been, to a large extent, complementary. In statistical physics the emphasis has been on developing a simple mechanical linking process which yields real-world-like networks. The computer science literature has strived to develop bounds for the best and worst case equilibria, and has been less interested in characterizing the architecture of equilibrium networks. In the economic approach, by contrast, the emphasis has been on characterizing the networks that arise out of individually optimal and strategic linking activity and asking how the networks that arise compare with socially optimal networks.

---

[22] In other words, as c gets large, the price of anarchy divided by $\sqrt{c}$ is bounded above by a constant number.

8.6   Concluding Remarks

This chapter studied the implications of strategic link formation by individuals when links can be formed unilaterally. The payoffs in the game of network formation were kept relatively general. A number of insights into the architecture, the payoff distribution, and the efficiency of the equilibrium networks were obtained.

The first general finding was that strategic link formation leads to networks with simple architectures such as the star or interlinked stars. These networks exhibit low average degree, a very unequal degree distribution, and small average distances. Second, in many instances these simple network architectures are also efficient. The third finding is that equilibrium networks sustain very unequal payoff distributions; the case where the central player earned very large payoffs compared with the peripheral players was especially prominent.

The sharp predictions of the model have led to a number of experimental studies of network formation and to a comparison of the equilibrium predictions with empirical patterns in actual networks. This experimental work suggests that players are sensitive to the inequality entailed in a star, and that stars arise only if efficiency pressures in favor of such a structure are significant. Empirical work shows that unequal degree distributions, small average degrees, and small average distance are important features of real-world networks. The star network exhibits these features and this suggests that the theoretical predictions are consistent with empirical findings.

We conclude with two remarks. The first is based on a comparison of the theoretical predictions with the empirical work: the idea that payoffs are increasing in the number of people accessed and decreasing in the number of direct connections captures something which is central to the formation of networks in a variety of environments. The second remark concerns interesting open questions: the model we have studied in this chapter is very simple and this holds out the hope that a number of forces that are important in actual network formation, such as competition among players, congestion pressures, and incomplete information about the network and players attributes, can be incorporated on a case-by-case basis into the analysis.

8.7   Appendix

8.7.1   A Simple Model of Link Formation

Denote the set of nonnegative integers by $\mathbb{Z}_+$. Let $\phi : \mathbb{Z}_+^2 \to \mathcal{R}$ be such that $\phi(x, y)$ is strictly increasing in x and strictly decreasing in y. Recall that a player i's payoff function $\Pi_i : \mathcal{G} \to \mathcal{R}$ is $\Pi_i(g) = \phi(\hat{n}_i(g), \eta_i^d(g))$.

Theorem 8.6. *Suppose that the payoffs are given by (8.1) and that they satisfy assumption 8.1. Then a Nash network is either minimally connected or empty.*

Proof. Minimality of the equilibrium network follows from the fact that, if there is a cycle in a network, then there exists a player who can delete a link and still access all players. Thus a network with a cycle cannot be an equilibrium.

Let g be a nonempty Nash network and suppose that it is not connected. Then there exists a component C in g with $|C| = x \geq 2$. Suppose, without loss of generality, that $i \in C$ and $\eta_i^d(g) \geq 1$. Then it follows that $\phi(x, 1) \geq \phi(x, \eta_i^d(g)) = \phi(\hat{n}_i(g), \eta_i^d(g)) = \Pi_i(g)$. Since g is a Nash network, it follows that $\Pi_i(g) \geq \Pi_i(g_{-i}) = \phi(\hat{n}_i(g_{-i}), 0) \geq \phi(1, 0)$, where g_{-i} is the network g without any of the links formed by player i. Thus $\phi(x, 1) \geq \phi(1, 0)$. Since g is not connected, there exists a player $j \notin C$.

First consider the case that j constitutes a singleton component. From the assumption that payoffs are strictly increasing in the first argument, it follows that

$$\phi(x + 1, 1) > \phi(x, 1) \geq \phi(1, 0) = \Pi_j(g);$$

this violates the hypothesis that player j is choosing a best response. Suppose next that player $j \in C'$, where $|C'| = w \geq 2$. Without loss of generality, let $w \leq x$ and also suppose that $\eta_j^d(g) \geq 1$. Now if player j deletes all her links and instead forms a link with player i, then her payoffs are $\phi(x + 1, 1) > \phi(w, 1) \geq \Pi_j(g)$, where the first inequality again exploits the assumption that payoffs are strictly increasing in first argument and the hypothesis that $w \leq x$, while the second inequality follows from the assumption that payoffs are declining in number of links formed. This violates the hypothesis that j is playing a best response. Putting together the two cases for $j \notin C$ yields the conclusion that if g is nonempty, then it must be connected. $\square$

Theorem 8.7. *Suppose that the payoffs are given by (8.1) and that they satisfy assumption 8.1. Then a strict Nash network is either a center-sponsored star or the empty network. The center-sponsored star is strict Nash if and only if $\phi(n, n - 1) > \phi(x + 1, x)$ for all $x \in \{0, 1, 2, \ldots, n - 2\}$. The empty network is strict Nash if and only if $\phi(1, 0) > \phi(x + 1, x)$ for all $x \in \{1, 2, \ldots, n - 1\}$.*

Proof. Suppose g is a nonempty strict Nash network. Then there is a pair of players i and j such that $g_{ij} = 1$. It is next shown that $\hat{g}_{j,k} = 0$ for all $k \neq i$. If this were not true, then player i could delete her link with j and instead form a link with k and retain the same payoffs. This would contradict the hypothesis that g is a strict Nash network. Thus any player with whom player i is linked cannot have links with any other player. Since g is connected, this also implies that player i must be accessing everyone with a direct link. If $g_{l,i} = 1$, then the above argument implies that player l can switch links and retain the same payoffs.

This contradicts the strict Nash requirement. Thus g must be a center-sponsored star.

If $\phi(n, n - 1) > \phi(x + 1, x)$ for all $x \in \{0, 1, 2, \ldots, n - 2\}$, then it follows that a center-sponsored star is a strict equilibrium. On the other hand, suppose that there is some $x \in \{0, 1, 2, \ldots, n - 2\}$ such that $\phi(x + 1, x) \geqslant \phi(n, n - 1)$. Then the central player in a center-sponsored star g can delete all but x links and do at least as well, so that g cannot be a strict Nash network. Similar arguments apply in the case of the empty network. $\square$

Theorem 8.8. *Suppose that the payoffs are given by (8.1) and that they satisfy assumption 8.1. Let g be some initial network. If $\phi(x + 1, y + 1) > (<) \phi(x, y)$ for all $y \in \{0, 1, \ldots, n - 2\}$ and $x \in \{y + 1, y + 2, \ldots, n - 1\}$, then the dynamic process converges to the center-sponsored star (empty network) in finite time, with probability 1.*

The broad strategy of the proof is to show that there is a positive probability of transition from any initial network to a strict Nash network in finitely many steps. This argument together with the fact that the dynamic process is a finite-state Markov chain is sufficient to complete the proof. The first step in the proof is the following lemma.

Lemma 8.1. *Starting from any network g, the dynamic process converges with positive probability to a minimally connected network or to an empty network.*

Proof. First, we show that there is a positive probability of convergence to a minimal network. Start with any network g and let players move one by one until all players have moved. The resulting network g' must be minimal. Suppose not and there is a cycle, i.e., $g'_{i_1 i_2} = g'_{i_2 i_3} = \cdots = g'_{i_q i_1} = 1$, with $q \geqslant 3$. Let $S \subset \{i_1, i_2, \ldots, i_q\}$ be the subset of players who form at least one link in the cycle. Clearly, this set is nonempty. Let $i_s \in S$ be the player who moves last and assume without loss of generality that $g'_{i_s, i_{s-1}} = 1$. Let g'' be the network prior to player i_s's move. By definition of i_s it follows that

$$\hat{g}''_{i_1, i_2} = \cdots = \hat{g}''_{i_{s-2}, i_{s-1}} = 1. \tag{8.12}$$

Consider player i_s's response to g''. There are two possibilities: either $g''_{i_{s+1} i_s} = 1$ or $g''_{i_{s+1} i_s} = 0$. In the former case, clearly the link $g_{i_s i_{s-1}}$ is redundant and cannot be optimal. In the latter case, a cycle requires that player i_s forms a link with both i_{s+1} and with i_{s-1}; this is again clearly not optimal as one of the links is redundant. Hence no cycle exists in g'.

So let us fix some minimal network g and let C be the largest component in g. If $|C| = n$ or $|C| = 1$, then the proof is complete. So consider the case $|C| = x$, where $1 < x < n$. Define $T = N \backslash C$.

(i) Consider first the case where the unique best response of every player in T is to form no links: let all players in T move simultaneously, with all players in C exhibiting inertia. Call the resulting network g^1. Clearly, g^1 has one nonsingleton component C and $|T|$ singleton components. Now consider a singleton player j. If it is j's unique best response to form zero links, then it must be the case that $\phi(x + u, u) < \phi(1, 0)$ for all $u \in \{1, 2, 3, \ldots, |T|\}$. Now consider a player $i \in C$; the highest payoff she can earn from $u \geq 1$ links is $\phi(x + u, u)$; but from the hypothesis about the best response of player $j \in T$ it follows that $\phi(x + u, u) \leq \phi(1, 0)$; so to delete all links is a best response. If all players in C who have links are allowed to move simultaneously, the empty network is reached. If on the other hand there are singleton players who wish to form links, allow them to move one at a time and clearly the process arrives at a connected network, which is minimal.

(ii) Suppose on the other hand, that there is some player $j \in T$ such that every best response involves forming one or more links. Allow such a player to move. In the resulting network g', the largest component C' is larger than and includes C. Moreover, all components are minimal. Repeated application of steps (i) and (ii) leads to a connected or an empty network. □

Proof of theorem 8.8. Start with the case $\phi(x + 1, y + 1) > \phi(x, y)$ for all $y \in \{0, 1, \ldots, n - 2\}$ and $x \in \{y + 1, y + 2, \ldots, n - 1\}$. Note that from theorem 8.2 for this class of payoff functions the center-sponsored star is the unique strict equilibrium. Suppose we are at the empty network. Pick a single player to move and her best response is to form links with all players. This yields a center-sponsored star, which is a strict equilibrium.

Next consider the case where the network g is minimally connected. Define $\hat{\eta}_x(g) = |\{j \in N \mid \hat{g}_{j,x} = 1\}|$ as the number of players who are in the "undirected" neighborhood of player x in network g. Let player n be such that $\hat{\eta}_n(g) \geq \hat{\eta}_j(g)$, $\forall j \in N$. Since g is connected it follows that $\hat{\eta}_n(g) \geq 2$. Moreover, since g is minimal there is a unique (undirected) path between player n and every other player. Say that player i is outward pointing vis-à-vis n if i sponsors the link $\hat{g}_{i,i_q} = 1$ that lies on the path from i to n. Similarly, say that i is inward pointing vis-à-vis n if $g_{n,i} = 1$ in the case where there is a direct link or $g_{i_q i} = 1$, where i_q lies on the path from i to n. If player i is outward pointing vis-à-vis n and $d(i, n; g) \geq 2$, then a variant of the switching argument implies that player i can deviate by deleting his current link with i_q and instead forming a link with player n. Repeat this step with every outward-pointing player k such that $\hat{d}(k, n; g) \geq 2$. Denote the resulting network by g^1. Note that this network is minimally connected and in this network if a player l is such that $\hat{d}(l, n; g^1) \geq 2$, then player l must be inward pointing.

Now consider a player k such that $\hat{d}(k, n; g^1) \geq 3$. It follows from the previous step that there exist at least two players j_1 and j_2 such that $g_{j_1 j_2} = g_{j_2, k} = 1$.

Now a variant of the switching argument implies that player j_1 can delete her link with player j_2 and instead form the link with player k. This leaves her payoffs unchanged. This switch, however, has the implication of making player j_2 an outward-pointing player with respect to player n. The above argument with regard to agglomeration of outward players can now be used to show that player j_2 has a weakly profitable deviation, in which case she deletes her link with k and instead forms a link with n. Repeat this process with all players k such that $\hat{d}(k, n; g^1) \geqslant 3$. The resulting network g^2 at the end of this process is minimally connected and $\hat{d}(k, n; g^2) \leqslant 2$ for all $k \neq n$, and also any player who is distance 2 from n must be inward pointing vis-à-vis n.

Now in a connected directed network, g, define player k to be an end-player if $\hat{\eta}_k(g) = 1$. Suppose that $\hat{g}_{i,n} = 1$. There are four possible configurations for a player i linked with player n in g^2: (i) $g^2_{i,n} = 1$ and i has no other links; (ii) $g^2_{n,i} = 1$ and i has no other links; (iii) $g^2_{i,n} = 1$ and $g^2_{ij} = 1$ for all end-players $j \in E_i$, where E_i is the set of players who are distance 2 from n in $\hat{g}^2$ and have a link with player i; and (iv) $g^2_{n,i} = 1$ and $g^2_{ij} = 1$ for all end-players $j \in E_i$. Note that case (iv) can be reduced to case (iii) by applying the switching argument with regard to inward-pointing players developed above.

Consider i who is in case (iii). Since $\hat{\eta}_n(g^2) \geqslant 2$ there is a player $k \neq i$ such that $\hat{d}(k, n; g^2) = 1$. Suppose that $g^2_{k,n} = 1$. Let players i and k both choose best responses simultaneously. It is easy to see that player i has a best response in which she deletes her link with player n and instead forms a link with player k, and retains all her other links as in network g^2. Similarly, player k has a best response in which she deletes her link with n and instead forms a link with player i, while retaining all her other links as in g^2. This strategy choice is a miscoordination, resulting in players i and k disconnecting from n. Now have player n move and it is a best response for her to form a link with some $j \in E_i$. Label this new network g^3. Given g^3, have players i and k move again. It is now a best response for player i to delete her link with player k and with player j and instead form a link with player n. Similarly, it is a best response for player k to delete her link with player i and retain any other links she had in network g^3. Next have player n move and it is a best response for her to link with k. Denote the resulting network as g^4. It follows that g^4 is minimally connected, and that the number of direct connections of player n has strictly increased as the process moved from g^2 to g^4. Similar arguments apply to combinations of cases (i), (ii), and (iii) and imply that the number of direct connections of player n strictly increases until a star is reached. If the star is center-sponsored, the process has converged; if not, then miscoordination arguments can be applied to show convergence to a center-sponsored star.

The case $\phi(x + 1, y + 1) < \phi(x, y)$ for all $y \in \{0, 1, \ldots, n - 2\}$ and $x \in \{y + 1, y + 2, \ldots, n - 1\}$ can be proved by using variants of the above arguments; details are omitted. $\square$

Theorem 8.9. *Suppose that the payoffs are given by (8.1) and that they satisfy assumption 8.1. Any efficient network is minimal. If $\phi(x+1, y+1) \geqslant \phi(x, y)$ for all $y \in \{0, 1, \ldots, n-2\}$ and $x \in \{y+1, y+2, \ldots, n-1\}$, then an efficient network is connected.*

Proof. Minimality follows from the lack of decay. The rest of the result follows directly from the conditions on payoffs. ☐

8.7.2 The Linear Model with Decay

Recall that in the model with decay, the payoffs to player i in network g are

$$\Pi_i(g) = 1 + \sum_{j \in \mathcal{N}_i(g)} \delta^{\hat{d}(i,j;g)} - \eta_i^d(g)c. \tag{8.13}$$

Recall that aggregate welfare in network g is $W(g) = \sum_{i \in N} \Pi_i(g)$.

Theorem 8.10. *Suppose payoffs are given by (8.13). The unique efficient network is*

  (i) *the complete network if $0 < c < 2[\delta - \delta^2]$,*

  (ii) *the star network if $2[\delta - \delta^2] < c < 2\delta + (n-2)\delta^2$, and*

  (iii) *the empty network if $2\delta + (n-2)\delta^2 < c$.*

Proof. The joint marginal gains to players i and j from forming a direct link are bounded below by $2[\delta - \delta^2]$. If $c < 2[\delta - \delta^2]$, then it follows that forming a link is welfare enhancing. Thus for this range of costs, a complete network is the unique efficient network.

Next fix a component C_1 in g, with $|C_1| = m$. Focus on the case $m \geqslant 3$. Let $k \geqslant m - 1$ be the number of links in the component. Then it follows that the welfare in C_1 is bounded above by $m + k(2\delta - c) + [m(m-1) - 2k]\delta^2$. If the component is a star, then the welfare is $(m-1)[2\delta - c + (m-2)\delta^2] + m$. Under the hypothesis that $2(\delta - \delta^2) < c$ the former can never exceed the latter, and the two are exactly equal for $k = m - 1$. It can be checked that the star is the only network with m players and $m - 1$ links in which every pair of players is at distance of 2 or less. Hence, any other network with $m - 1$ links must have at least one pair of players who are at a distance of 3 or more. This immediately implies that the welfare in any other network with $k = m - 1$ links is strictly less than the welfare from the star. This implies that in an efficient network a component must be a star.

Next consider a network where two components have m and m' players respectively. Clearly, a component in an efficient network must have nonnegative welfare. It then follows by direct computation that a single component with $m + m'$ players has greater welfare than two distinct components which have the star structure. This implies that a single star maximizes social welfare in the class of all nonempty networks. The social welfare in a star is

$$n + (n-1)2\delta + [n(n-1)/2 - (n-1)]2\delta^2 - (n-1)c.$$

This exceeds the social welfare in the empty network if $2\delta + (n-2)\delta^2 > c$. This completes the proof.   □

8.7.3 Heterogeneity and Decay

Consider a setting with two groups. The payoffs to player i in group $l = 1, 2$ can be rewritten as follows:

$$\Pi_i(g) = 1 + \sum_{j \in \mathcal{N}_i(g)} \delta^{\hat{d}(i,j;g)} - \eta_i^{d,l} c_L - \eta_i^{d,k} c_H, \qquad (8.14)$$

where $l, k = 1, 2$ and $l \neq k$.

Proposition 8.3. *Suppose (8.14) holds, $n_l = \bar{n}$ for $l = 1, 2$, and that decay is small (δ close to 1).*

  (1) *Suppose $c_L \in (0, 1)$. Then*

      (1a) *if $c_H \in (c_L, \bar{n})$, any interlinked group-stars network is a strict equilib-
rium;*

      (1b) *if $c_H > \bar{n}$, any unconnected group-stars network is a strict equilibrium.*

  (2) *Suppose $c_L \in (1, \bar{n})$. Then*

      (2a) *if $c_H \in (c_L, \bar{n})$, the interlinked periphery-sponsored group-stars net-
work and the empty network are the only strict equilibria;*

      (2b) *if $c_H > \bar{n}$, then in an equilibrium each group is either a periphery-
sponsored star or empty.*

  (3) *If $c_L > \bar{n}$, the empty network is the unique strict equilibrium.*

Proof. The proof of parts (1) and (3) is straightforward and omitted. Consider part (2). First observe that as δ is close to 1 an equilibrium network is minimal. Second, observe that if $g_{ij} = 1$ for some $i \in N_l$, $j \in N_l \setminus \{i\}$, then group N_l is connected. Suppose not; then the payoff to a player $i' \in N_l \setminus \{i, j\}$ from sponsoring a link with player i is strictly higher than the payoff obtained by player i. Third, it is immediate that the empty network is always a strict equilibrium if $c_L > 1$. In what follows we focus on nonempty strict equilibrium networks, g. There are two possibilities.

(i) There are no links across groups, i.e., $g_{ij} = 0$, $\forall i \in N_x$, $j \in N_y$, $x \neq y$. The second observation above implies that in an equilibrium either a group of players is connected or there exist no links between players of the group. Next note that since there are no links across groups the problem for each group is analogous to the homogeneous case studied in section 8.3.1. Then it follows that if a group is connected then it forms a periphery-sponsored star. Hence, g is either an unconnected periphery-sponsored star network or a one-group periphery-sponsored star network. It is clear that such networks are strict equilibria only if $c_H > \bar{n}$.

(ii) There are links across groups, i.e., $g_{ij} = 1$ for some $i \in N_x$, $j \in N_y$, $x \neq y$. It is now easy to see that g must be connected. The following is now established. If $c_L \in (1, \bar{n})$, then there exists a $\tilde{\delta} < 1$ such that for any $\delta \in [\tilde{\delta}, 1)$ if $g_{ij} = 1$ for some $i \in N_l$ and $j \in N_{l'}$, $l \neq l'$, then $g_{j',j} = 1$ for any $j' \in N_{l'}$.

First, note that since $c_L > 1$ any end-player $\hat{j}$ (say) who is accessed by player i via $g_{ij} = 1$ sponsors her link; let $g_{\hat{j},y_1} = 1$. (Note that since $c_H > 1$ there exists at least one such end-player distinct from j.)

Second, it is shown that i only accesses players in $N_{l'}$ via the link $g_{ij} = 1$. Suppose not; then there exists a player $i' \in N_l$ accessed by i via the link $g_{ij} = 1$. Let $g' = g - g_{ij} + g_{i,i'}$, it is easy to see that $\mathcal{N}_i(g) = \mathcal{N}_i(g')$. Thus,

$$\Pi_i(g) - \Pi_i(g') = \sum_{j \in \mathcal{N}_i(g)} [\delta^{\hat{d}(i,j;g)} - \delta^{\hat{d}(i,j;g')}] - (c_H - c_L) < 0 \quad \text{as } \delta \to 1.$$

This contradicts Nash.

Third, it is shown that i accesses every player in $N_{l'}$ via $g_{ij} = 1$. Suppose not; then since g is connected, there exists some players in $N_{l'}$ accessed by i via some player $k \neq j$. Suppose, without loss of generality, that among such players j' is the player closest to player i and assume j' accesses i via the link $\bar{g}_{j',i'} = 1$. By construction $i' \in N_l$; the previous argument implies that $g_{i',j'} = 1$ and that any player accessed by i' via the link $g_{i',j'} = 1$ belongs to $N_{l'}$. Select one of the end-players, say j_1, whom player i' accesses via the link $g_{i',j'} = 1$.[23] Since $c_L > 1$, player j_1 sponsors her link, via a link say $g_{j_1,y_2} = 1$. Using a variant of the switching argument it is now easy to see that either $\hat{j}$ or j_1 strictly gains by deviating. This contradicts the hypothesis that the network constitutes a Nash equilibrium.

Fourth, note that, since group $N_{l'}$ is entirely internally linked, the arguments from section 8.3.1 on decay can be used to conclude that $N_{l'}$ forms a periphery-sponsored group-star. Finally, it is easy to see that player j must be the center of the periphery-sponsored star; for otherwise player i strictly gains by switching from j to the central player of group $N_{l'}$.

---

[23] There exists such an end-player since $c_H > c_L > 1$

Finally, note also that group N_l is entirely internally linked and therefore forms a periphery-sponsored star. Thus, if g is a strict equilibrium, it is an interlinked periphery-sponsored group-stars network.   □

8.7.4 The One-Way Flow Model

Recall, that in the one-way flow model $n_i(g) = |\mathcal{N}_i(g)| + 1$ and a player i's payoff function $\Pi_i : \mathcal{G} \to \mathcal{R}$ is $\Pi_i(g) = \phi(n_i(g), \eta_i^d(g))$.

Theorem 8.11. *Let the payoffs be given by (8.8) and suppose that they satisfy assumption 8.2. Then a strict Nash network is either a cycle with all players or the empty network.*

(a) *If $\phi(x + 1, x) > \phi(1, 0)$ for some $x \in \{1, \ldots, n - 1\}$, then the cycle is the unique strict Nash.*

(b) *If $\phi(x + 1, x) < \phi(1, 0)$ for all $x \in \{1, 2, \ldots, n - 1\}$ and $\phi(n, 1) > \phi(1, 0)$, then the empty network and the cycle are both strict Nash.*

(c) *If $\phi(x + 1, x) < \phi(1, 0)$ holds for all $x \in \{1, 2, \ldots, n - 1\}$ and $\phi(n, 1) < \phi(1, 0)$, then the empty network is the unique strict Nash.*

Proof. The first step in the proof is to show that a Nash network is either empty or minimally connected. The focus is on the case $\phi(n, 1) > \phi(1, 0)$; the proof for the case $\phi(n, 1) \leq \phi(1, 0)$ is straightforward and omitted.

Suppose g is a nonempty Nash network. Choose a player $i \in \arg\max_{j \in N} n_j(g)$. Since g is nonempty, $x_i = n_i(g) \geq 2$ and $y_i = \eta_i^d(g) \geq 1$. Furthermore, since g is Nash, $\Pi_i(g) = \phi(x_i, y_i) \geq \phi(1, 0)$. It is shown that $x_i = n$. Suppose instead that $x_i < n$. Then there exists $j \notin \mathcal{N}_i(g)$. Clearly, $i \notin \mathcal{N}_j(g)$, for otherwise player j would access (strictly) more players than player i. Suppose $y_j = 0$: in this case player j can strictly increase her payoffs by forming a link with i because $\phi(x_i + 1, 1) > \phi(x_i, 1) \geq \phi(x_i, y_i) \geq \phi(1, 0)$. Hence $y_j \geq 1$. Now a variant of the same argument can be used to show that player j can strictly increase her payoffs by deleting all her current links and instead form a direct link with player i. This contradicts the hypothesis of Nash equilibrium. It also implies that $j \in \mathcal{N}_i(g)$ and since j was arbitrary this, in turn, means that $x_i = n$ in a Nash network.

Let i be a player with $x_i = n$ as above. A player j is critical to player i if $n_i(g_{-j}) < n_i(g)$. Let E be the set of noncritical players for player i in network g. If $j \in \arg\max_{i' \in N} d(i, j; g)$, then j is noncritical, so that E is clearly nonempty. Next it is shown that if $j \in E$ then $n_j(g) = n$. Suppose this is not true. If $\eta_j^d(g) = 0$, then from the earlier argument above there is a deviation for player j that increases her payoff strictly. Thus $\eta_j^d(g) \geq 1$. If $x_j = n_j(g) < n$, then player j can delete all her links and instead form a single link with player i. The argument in the previous step can be used to show that she benefits strictly from such a deviation. Thus g is not a Nash network. This contradiction implies that $n_j(g) = n$ for all $j \in E$.

The next step in the proof of connectedness establishes that, for every $j_1 \notin E \cup \{i\}$, there exists $j \in E$ such that $j \in N_{j_1}(g)$. Since j_1 is critical there exists $j_2 \in N_{j_1}(g)$ such that every path from j_2 to i involves j_1. Hence $d(i, j_2; g) > d(i, j_1; g)$. If $j_2 \in E$, then the claim is proved; otherwise, by a similar argument, there exists a player $j_3 \in N_{j_2}(g)$ such that $d(i, j_3; g) > d(i, j_2; g)$. Since i accesses every player and n is finite, repeating the above argument no more than $n - 2$ times will yield a player $j \in E$ such that $j \in N_{j_1}(g)$. Since $n_j(g) = n$ from above, it now follows that $n_{j_1}(g) = n$ as well. Hence g is connected. If g is Nash but not minimal, then some player can delete a link and the network would still remain connected. This means the player can strictly increase her payoffs by deleting a link, contradicting the definition of Nash equilibrium. We have therefore shown that a nonempty network is minimally connected.

The second part of the proof shows that the cycle with all players is the unique nonempty strict equilibrium network. Let $g \in \mathcal{G}$ be a nonempty strict Nash network. It is shown that for every player k there is one and only one player i such that $g_{ik} = 1$. First note that since g is nonempty and an equilibrium it must be minimally connected. So there is some player i such that $g_{ik} = 1$. Suppose there is another player $j \neq i$ such that $g_{j,k} = 1$. Since g is minimal it follows that $g_{ij} = 0$. Now consider a strategy g_i' for player i in which she deletes the link with k and instead forms a link with j and define $g' = \{g_{-i}, g_i'\}$. Then $\eta_i^d(g) = \eta_i^d(g')$. Furthermore, since $k \in N_j^d(g) = N_j^d(g')$, clearly $n_i(g') \geq n_i(g)$. Hence i earns weakly higher payoffs from this new strategy, g_i', which contradicts the hypothesis that g is a strict Nash network. As each player has exactly one player forming a link with her, and the network is connected, it follows that the network must be a cycle which contains all players. Parts (a)–(c) now follow by direct verification. $\qquad\square$

9

Two-Sided Link Formation

9.1 Introduction

In many social and economic contexts the creation of a link between two individuals requires that both agree to the link; familiar examples of this include friendships, coauthorships in research papers, collaboration between firms, ties between buyers and sellers, and free trade agreements between nations. The possibility of individuals deliberately forming links and shaping the network to their own ends gives rise to the following three classical questions. What is the architecture of the resulting networks? Are these networks socially efficient? What are the distributional properties of the networks that arise? The aim of this chapter is to show how a strategic approach to network formation helps us in addressing these questions in a setting with two-sided link formation.

The basic concepts required in the analysis of network formation with two-sided links were introduced in chapter 7. There are a number of different contexts in which this approach has been applied and these applications have in turn given rise to an extensive literature in recent years. This chapter presents detailed analysis of network formation in four specific contexts to illustrate the nature of arguments that have been developed in this area.[1] The four applications I consider are social connections, structural holes and intermediary advantages, coauthorship, and international free trade agreement networks. These applications yield a number of insights into the architecture of actual networks; they also highlight two general features of networks: the first is the tension between individually rational networks and the efficient networks, while the second is the prospect of sharp inequality in number of connections (as well as in payoffs) across individuals.

The tension between individual incentives and social objectives has been a classical theme in economics, and naturally raises the question, are there ways in which the incentives in the network formation process can be altered which would resolve this conflict and lead individuals to form efficient networks? This chapter addresses this question by discussing different types of remedies—both centralized and decentralized—for the resolution of this tension.

---

[1] Chapter 10 will take up another application: networks of collaboration among firms.

The discussion on network formation in specific contexts illustrates the existence of sharp inequalities in the number of connections across individuals. These findings raise two general questions: what are the forces that lead to such inequality and what are the payoff implications of such inequalities? The discussion in this chapter will consider the role of different types of externality in generating degree inequality and then assess the relation between degree inequality and payoff inequality.

The rest of the chapter is organized as follows. Section 9.2 provides a detailed analysis of network formation in four specific contexts: social connections, intermediary advantages and the creation of structural holes, coauthorship, and free trade agreements among countries. Section 9.3 examines the tension between individual incentives and efficiency, while section 9.4 studies economic pressures leading to inequality in degrees and payoffs. Section 9.5 concludes. The proofs of all the results are presented in an appendix to the chapter.

9.2 Network Formation: Four Applications

This section explores network formation in different contexts. These applications have been chosen to illustrate three points. First, they illustrate the wide range of social and economic contexts in which strategic network formation arises. Second, they highlight the rich structure of externalities that can be captured by models of network formation. Third, the analysis shows how an application of game theoretic solution concepts yields sharp predictions on network architectures, payoff distributions, and welfare.[2]

9.2.1 The Connections Model

It is generally agreed that social connections give individuals access to informational and influence advantages while forming links is costly as it takes time and effort and may also involve material resources. The connections model due to Jackson and Wolinsky (1996) captures these ideas in a natural way. The presentation here will focus on stability, efficiency, and payoff distributions in the basic model.[3]

Recall from chapter 7 that, in the connections model, the payoffs to player i in network g are

$$\Pi_i(g) = 1 + \sum_{j \in \mathcal{N}_i(g)} \delta^{d(i,j;g)} - \eta_i(g)c. \qquad (9.1)$$

---

[2] For a detailed discussion of the different solution concepts, see chapter 7.

[3] In recent years the connections model has been extended in a number of directions. Some of these extensions are very close in spirit to the extensions of the one-sided link formation model, discussed in chapter 8 above, so they will not be covered here. For a more detailed discussion of this work, see the survey by Jackson (2005).

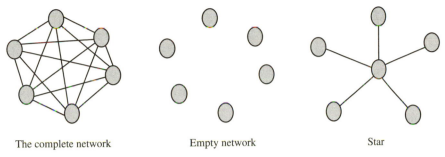

The complete network   Empty network   Star

Figure 9.1. Connections model: pairwise stable networks.

The following result, due to Jackson and Wolinsky (1996), offers a partial characterization of pairwise stable networks.

Proposition 9.1. *Suppose payoffs are given by (9.1). A pairwise stable network has at most one nonsingleton component. For $c < \delta - \delta^2$, the unique pairwise stable network is the complete network g^c. For $\delta - \delta^2 < c < \delta$, a star is a pairwise stable network. For $\delta < c$, the empty network is pairwise stable and any pairwise stable network which is nonempty is such that each player has at least two links.*

Figure 9.1 illustrates some equilibrium networks. This result shows that stars—embodying small average degree, an unequal degree distribution, and short average distances—arise in this model.

The following result, due to Jackson and Wolinsky (1996), offers a complete characterization of the architecture of efficient networks.

Theorem 9.1. *Suppose payoffs are given by (9.1). The unique efficient network in the connections model is*

(i) *the complete network if $c < \delta - \delta^2$,*

(ii) *the star if $\delta - \delta^2 < c < \delta + [(n-2)/2]\delta^2$, and*

(iii) *the empty network if $c > \delta + [(n-2)/2]\delta^2$.*

The considerations underlying this efficiency result are very similar to those presented in the context of efficient networks in the one-sided links model. The star is the only minimal network in which every pair of players is at a distance of 2 or less, and the star also minimizes the number of links needed to have a path between every pair of players since it is minimally connected. In a context with decay it is then not surprising that the star is efficient so long as costs for linking are not too small or too large.

The analysis of the two-sided link formation model shows that properties like centrality and short distances, embodied in a star, are robust features of pairwise stable networks, and that they also maximize welfare. There are three remarks worth making here. First, in the star network the center actually earns a lower payoff than the peripheral players. This pattern of inequality is closely related to the fact that the star is only pairwise stable for low costs of forming links. The second remark is that it is difficult to provide a full characterization of stable networks. The third point is about the differences between the results in the one-sided and the two-sided link formation models. Recall that, in the one-sided link formation model, periphery-sponsored stars arise for a very wide range of parameter values, and in such networks the central player earns a higher payoff than the peripheral player. This is in contrast to the findings of the connections model. These differences are clearly related to the assumptions on sharing of costs and benefits. The next section illustrates this point by introducing intermediation advantages in the connections model.

9.2.2 Intermediation Advantages and Structural Holes

In some important contexts—for example, trading opportunities, novel ideas for research—individuals can hope to gain advantages by bridging gaps in the network between others. For instance, if trade between two individuals i and j requires personal connections—due to trust considerations in a world with high contract enforcement costs[4]—then a person k who knows both i and j can act as an intermediary. This role potentially creates the possibility for person k to earn some share of the surplus created by the transaction between i and j. The precise share of the surplus that person k will actually earn depends of course on the nature of alternative channels of trade between i and j, in other words, on the competition between the different players who wish to be intermediaries. The potential gains from bridging different parts of a network play a prominent role in the early work of Granovetter (1973) and are central to the notion of *structural holes* developed by Burt (1994). In recent years, a number of empirical studies have shown that individuals or organizations who bridge "structural holes" in networks gain significant payoff advantages.[5] Given these significant payoffs effects, it seems natural that an individual will make investments in connections so as to become structurally important, while other individuals will likewise form connections to circumvent such attempts. Are special structural positions and the corresponding large payoff differences sustainable when individual entities form connections strategically? This section studies the implications of these

---

[4] For a recent model on the implications of contract enforcement problems, see Dixit (2003).

[5] See Burt (1994) and Mehra, Kilduff, and Brass (2001) for work on the influence of structural positions on promotions and performance evaluation, Podolny and Baron (1997) for work on network positions and mobility, and Ahuja (2000) for work on the influence of a firm's position in inter-organizational networks on its innovativeness and overall performance. For instance, the work on promotions and performance evaluation argues that the differences in structural location of individuals, in particular, whether they bridge structural holes in the social network, explains a significant part of the variation in promotion timing of otherwise similar people.

strategic considerations by introducing intermediation advantages in the connections model discussed in section 9.2.1. The presentation here follows the model developed in Goyal and Vega-Redondo (forthcoming).[6]

Suppose that players are traders who can exchange goods and that this exchange creates a surplus of 1. Networks are relevant because this exchange can be carried out only if these traders know each other personally or if there is a path of personal connections which indirectly link the two traders. We now discuss how the potential surpluses are allocated between the different traders. In the case where traders know each other they each get one-half of the surplus. If they are linked indirectly, then the allocation of the surplus depends on the competition between the intermediary agents. One way to proceed is to think of each "path" of intermediaries between these two players as providing a service: the service of intermediation. It is then reasonable to suppose as a first step that any two paths between two players j and k fully compete away all the possible intermediation surplus. This is in the spirit of Bertrand competition between paths. This idea leads to the notion of essential players: player i is *essential* for j and k if i lies on *every* path that joins j and k in the network.[7]

A strategy profile $s = (s_1, s_2, \ldots, s_n)$ is the set of announcements of intended links by all players. In the two-sided link setting this profile induces an undirected network $g(s)$.[8] Also recall that $\mathcal{N}_i(g)$ is the set of other players whom player i accesses in network g. For any $j \in \mathcal{N}_i(g)$, define $E(i, j; g)$ as the set of players who are essential to connect i and j in network g and let $e(i, j; g) = |E(i, j; g)|$. Then, the (net) payoffs to player i in network g are

$$\Pi_i(g) = \sum_{j \in \mathcal{N}_i(g)} \frac{1}{e(i, j; g) + 2} + \sum_{j,k \in N} \frac{I_{\{i \in E(j,k; g)\}}}{e(j, k; g) + 2} - \eta_i(g)c, \qquad (9.2)$$

where $I_{\{i \in E(j,k)\}} \in \{0, 1\}$ stands for the indicator function specifying whether i is essential for j and k, $\eta_i(g) \equiv |\{j \in N : g_{ij} = 1\}|$ refers to the number of players with whom player i has a link, and $c > 0$ is the cost per link.[9] In this model an additional link formed by player i can have positive as well as negative effects on the payoffs to others. For instance, the formation of an additional link between two peripheral players in a star network reduces the payoff to the center

---

[6] Similar ideas have been explored in two other recent papers (Galeotti and Melendez 2004; Buskens and van den Rijt 2005). Galeotti and Melendez (2004) assume that agents are involved in an infinitely repeated prisoner's dilemma that determines how linking costs are shared. Buskens and van den Rijt (2005) study a network formation game in which the payoff function is based on Burt's (1994) "constraint" measure.

[7] For example, the number of essential players between any pair of players in a cycle network is zero, while in a star every pair of peripheral players has a single and common essential player, namely the center of the star.

[8] See chapter 7 for a discussion of the details of this formulation.

[9] If intermediary rents are zero, then payoff (9.2) becomes $|\mathcal{N}_i(g)|/2 - \eta_i(g)c$; this is a variant of the payoffs in the connections model, in which $\delta = 1$ and joint returns to access are normalized to 1.

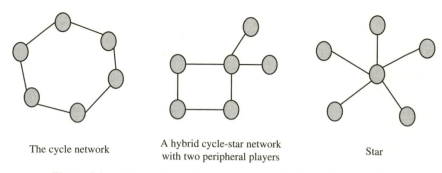

| The cycle network | A hybrid cycle-star network with two peripheral players | Star |

Figure 9.2.   Intermediary advantages: some pairwise stable networks.

of the star, while the formation of a link between a peripheral player and an isolated player increases the payoff to the central player.

We start the analysis of the model with an exploration of pairwise stable networks. It is easily seen that the star, the cycle network containing all players, and hybrid cycle-stars[10] are all pairwise stable. In the star the center earns a payoff of $(n-1)[\frac{1}{2} + \frac{1}{6}(n-2) - c]$ and has no incentive to delete a single link so long as $c < \frac{1}{2} + \frac{1}{3}(n-2)$. Two peripheral players have no incentive to form a link between them if $c > \frac{1}{6}$, while no peripheral player has an incentive to delete a link if $c < \frac{1}{2} + \frac{1}{3}(n-2)$. Thus a star is pairwise stable so long as $\frac{1}{6} < c < \frac{1}{2} + \frac{1}{3}(n-2)$. In a cycle, every player gets a payoff of $\frac{1}{2}(n-1) - 2c$. An additional link is clearly not attractive since it does not create any extra surplus while it increases costs. Deleting one link is not attractive for an individual player as it makes a neighboring player essential for all transactions, which lowers individual payoffs by at least $\frac{1}{6}(n-2)$. This clearly exceeds the cost c for large enough n. Similar arguments can be used to show that hybrid cycle-star networks are pairwise stable (for some range of costs). Figure 9.2 illustrates some (nonempty) pairwise stable networks.

These arguments show that no player has an incentive to add or delete a link in a range of networks going from the star to the cycle. This leaves open the possibility that two players may want to deviate by adding and deleting links in a coordinated way. To see how this may work, consider the cycle network containing all players. Consider two players that are far apart in the cycle and establish a direct link. By simultaneously breaking one link each, they can produce a line and become central in it. In a line, they must pay intermediation costs to a number of others, but on the other hand they both occupy prominent centrality positions in the line network. Computations in the appendix to this chapter show that the gains from

---

[10] A hybrid-cycle star network is a network in which there are two sets of players; one set of players constitutes a cycle, and a second set has one link for each player and this link is with a single player who is located in the cycle. The cycle has x players and the remaining $y = n - x$ players are directly linked to a single player in the cycle.

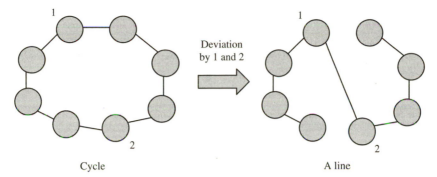

Figure 9.3. Bilateral deviations from cycle.

being central dominate and so it is strictly profitable to deviate and thereby destroy the cycle. This argument is illustrated in figure 9.3.

The above incentive pressures lead to a consideration of strict bilateral equilibrium. Bilateral equilibrium was defined in chapter 7; a bilateral equilibrium is strict if it is a bilateral equilibrium and is moreover immune to deviations (unilateral or bilateral) that alter the network but leave the payoffs to players unaltered.[11] The appendix provides a formal definition of strict bilateral equilibrium.

The following result, due to Goyal and Vega-Redondo (forthcoming), provides a partial characterization of strict bilateral equilibrium (SBE) networks for large societies.

Theorem 9.2. *Suppose payoffs are given by (9.2) and that n is large. If $c < \frac{1}{6}$, then there does not exist any SBE network. If $\frac{1}{6} < c < \frac{1}{2}$, then the unique SBE network is the star, while if $\frac{1}{2} < c < \frac{1}{2} + \frac{1}{6}(n-2)$, then the star and the empty network are the only SBE networks. If $c > \frac{1}{2} + \frac{1}{6}(n-2)$, then the empty network is the unique SBE network.*

Figure 9.4 illustrates the SBE networks.

There are four arguments in the proof. The first argument exploits access and intermediation advantages to show that an equilibrium network is either connected or empty. The second argument demonstrates agglomeration pressures: a minimal network with long paths cannot be sustained. This is because players located at the periphery of the network benefit from connecting to a central player in order to save on intermediation costs (shortening path lengths) while a central player is ready to incur the cost of an additional link because such a link reduces the number of players with whom she has to share intermediation rents. This deviation is illustrated in figure 9.5.

---

[11] One motivation for the study of a strict equilibrium concept is dynamic: a gradual adjustment process that allows pairs of players to move among different best responses will only come to rest at strict bilateral equilibrium networks.

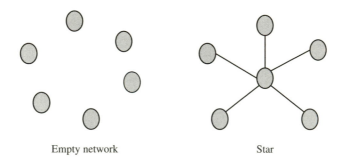

Empty network   Star

Figure 9.4.   Intermediary advantages: strict bilateral equilibrium networks.

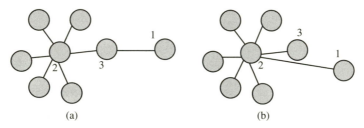

(a)   (b)

Figure 9.5.   Incentives in minimal networks: (a) minimal network with
two essential players; (b) players 1 and 2 deviate yielding a star.

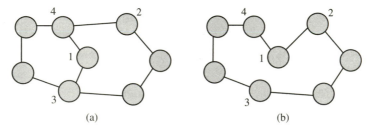

(a)   (b)

Figure 9.6.   Incentives in networks with two cycles: (a) cycles with
common players; (b) players 1 and 2 deviate and retain old payoffs.

The third argument builds on the above example of bilateral deviations to show
that a cycle or a hybrid cycle-star network is not sustainable (see figure 9.3 for an
illustration of this deviation). The fourth argument rules out networks with two
or more cycles. It is here that the requirement of strictness is invoked. Figure 9.6
illustrates how players 1 and 2 are indifferent between the network with two
cycles and a network in which there is only one cycle.

The above result covers large societies and assumes that $c > \frac{1}{6}$. Goyal and
Vega-Redondo (forthcoming) show that in small societies also strategic pressures
will create the potential for structural holes and there will be players who will
earn large intermediation payoffs by spanning them. When $c < \frac{1}{6}$, the star is
not a bilateral equilibrium, since peripheral players have a strict incentive to link

up. For large societies, the above arguments show that no other network is a strict bilateral equilibrium. Thus if $c < \frac{1}{6}$, then there exists no strict bilateral equilibrium network in large societies.

Efficient networks.   Observe that from a social point of view there is no gain in adding links in a connected network, while there is a cost to adding links since $c > 0$. So efficient networks must be minimal or empty. Moreover, due to positive externalities generated by individual linking activity, it is easy to see that networks with distinct (nontrivial) components cannot be efficient. It is possible to check that the aggregate net payoff in a minimal connected network is $\frac{1}{2}n(n-1) - 2c(n-1)$ while the payoff in the empty network is 0, so it follows that a connected network is efficient if and only if $c \leqslant \frac{1}{4}n$. Clearly, the star is a minimally connected network and is therefore efficient for large n. From theorem 9.2 it then follows that for a given cost of linking c, an efficient network can be sustained in equilibrium, provided that n is large.

In the star network the central player earns $(n-1)[\frac{1}{2} + \frac{1}{6}(n-2) - c]$ while each of the peripheral players earns $[\frac{1}{2} + \frac{1}{3}(n-2) - c]$. Thus the payoff difference between the central player and the peripheral player is large (with the central player earning more). Moreover, the ratio of the two payoffs is unbounded as n gets large.

The idea of locational advantages in networks has a long and distinguished history in sociology (see, for example, Burt 1994; Granovetter 1973). Seen from the perspective of economics, this work naturally motivates the question, can location advantages and large payoff differences be sustained among otherwise identical individuals? The above model shows that the strategic struggle for these advantages leads to a star architecture, where a single player is essential for connecting every other pair of players, and that such a network is robust with respect to individual and bilateral attempts to alter the structure. This result may be interpreted as a formalization of the idea in the sociological literature that structural holes open the potential for large benefits to those individuals who succeed in bridging them.

We now place the model of intermediary advantages in perspective, by discussing, first, the relation between this model and the connections model, and, second, the role of the payoff function. Proposition 9.1, in the connections model, shows that a star network can be sustained only over a small range of parameter values, and that the central player who is bridging the structural holes actually earns a lower payoff than the peripheral players. By contrast, in the present model, the star is sustainable for practically the entire range of parameters and the central player earns a much higher payoff than the peripheral players. This difference highlights the role of intermediation advantages in shaping equilibrium architectures, the corresponding payoff distribution, as well as in attaining efficient networks.

Next consider the role of the payoff function. Two aspects of the payoffs are worth noting. First, the absence of decay in flow of value across the network, and, second, the formulation of competition among intermediaries. The analysis shows that star networks arise in the absence of decay, and standard considerations suggest that agglomeration pressures will only get reinforced with decay, making the star more likely. With regard to competition between intermediaries, the formulation is in the spirit of Bertrand behavior among alternative paths between players. In some settings, it is arguable that players will have to commit to using one of the shortest paths, and that players along the shortest path will then be able to extract some surplus, in proportion to the number of shortest paths which are competing. This is more in line with the idea of Cournot competition in a market. The payoff function will be affected and this in turn will have a bearing on some of the arguments that were developed above. A general analysis of alternative forms of competition among intermediaries appears to be an open problem.

9.2.3 Coauthorship

Intellectual collaboration takes different forms ranging from informal discussions on subjects of common interest all the way to coauthorship. The empirical properties of coauthorship networks have been extensively studied in recent years and this work has highlighted a number of striking properties of such networks. In this section we present a strategic model of coauthorship and compare its predictions with the observed empirical patterns. This model is taken from Jackson and Wolinsky (1996).

Consider a group of researchers who each have a fixed amount of time available which they can allocate across a set of projects that are jointly carried out with others. Starting a new project allows access to the skills of a new partner and this is attractive, but a new project also takes time away from existing projects, which reduces their worth. Moreover, less time availability on existing projects also lowers the worth of the projects for existing partners, and therefore an additional individual project creates negative externalities for others.

Recall that $N_i(g)$ refers to the set of neighbors of player i in network g and $\eta_i(g) = |N_i(g)|$. The payoffs to player i in network g are

$$\Pi_i(g) = \sum_{j \in N_i(g)} \left[\frac{1}{\eta_i(g)} + \frac{1}{\eta_j(g)} + \frac{1}{\eta_i(g)\eta_j(g)} \right]$$

$$= 1 + \left(1 + \frac{1}{\eta_i(g)} \right) \sum_{j \in N_i(g)} \frac{1}{\eta_j(g)} \tag{9.3}$$

if $\eta_i(g) > 0$, and $\Pi_i(g) = 0$ if $\eta_i(g) = 0$. This payoff function assumes that a researcher allocates an equal amount of time across projects, and that for each project the productivity depends on the time spent on the project $1/\eta_i(g) +$

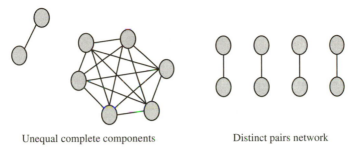

Unequal complete components   Distinct pairs network

Figure 9.7. Coauthor model: pairwise stable and efficient networks.

$1/\eta_j(g)$ and on some synergy in the production process captured by the interactive term $1/(\eta_i(g)\eta_j(g))$.

To get some intuition for the effects at work, it is useful to consider a network constituted of distinct pairs of players. In such a network each player gets a payoff of 3. What are the effects of starting a new project with a new coauthor? A player with two links will earn $[\frac{1}{2} + 1 + \frac{1}{2}]$ from the existing project, and she will earn $[\frac{1}{2} + \frac{1}{2} + \frac{1}{4}]$ from the new project (which will be carried out with someone who already has an existing project). Thus players have an incentive to start up new projects. Notice, however, that if all players carried out an additional project, then the payoffs for each player would be $\frac{5}{2}$, which is smaller than 3, their payoff in the original network.

The following result, due to Jackson and Wolinsky (1996), builds on this basic intuition and provides a (partial) characterization of stable and efficient networks.

Proposition 9.2. *Suppose payoffs are given by (9.3) and that n is an even number. An efficient network consists of n/2 separate pairs. Any pairwise stable network can be partitioned into complete components of unequal size. In particular, if m is the size of a component and m' is the size of the next larger component, then $m' > m^2$.*

The efficiency result derives from the observation that forming additional links creates significant negative externalities on existing coauthorship relations. The structure of pairwise stable networks arises from the curvature of the payoff function. The formation of an additional link means the launching of an additional project and this generates positive benefits; however, the creation of a link also means that resources are diverted away from existing projects, and this reduces their productivity, which is a cost of forming an additional link. The payoff function (9.3) has two implications for pairwise stable networks: (i) if $\eta_i(g) = \eta_j(g)$ then $g_{ij} = 1$ and (ii) if player i has links with player k, then she is willing to form a link with any player who has (weakly) fewer links than k. These two facts put together yield the complete and unequal components architecture of stable networks. Figure 9.7 illustrates efficient and pairwise stable networks.

There are two aspects of the result worth noting. The first aspect is the impact of negative externalities: when i forms a link with j, she reduces the time she puts in each of the current projects, which negatively affects the productivity of each of these other projects. This decline in productivity affects i but also affects each of her current partners. However, player i only takes into account the negative effect on her own utility and ignores the effect on her current partners. Thus the private costs of additional links are smaller than the social costs. The over-connectedness of pairwise stable networks is a consequence of this negative externality.

The second point concerns the architecture of pairwise stable networks: from the observation that $m' > m^2$, it follows that pairwise stable networks exhibit significant degree inequality.

How does the prediction of pairwise stable networks compare with the structures of actual coauthor networks? In recent years, a lot of empirical research has been done on the architecture of coauthor networks in a number of subjects; see, for example, Goyal, van der Leij, and Moraga (2006) for the coauthor network of economists and Newman (2001) for coauthor networks in physics, biology, and medicine. This work has helped identify a number of key empirical regularities in large real-world networks. Table 9.1 summarizes information on some key features of these networks: the degree distribution, average distance in the network, and the clustering coefficient.[12] These statistics highlight the following features.

Average degree. The average number of connections is very small relative to the total number of nodes. For instance, in the economics coauthor network, over 80 000 authors published in economics journals, but the average number of coauthors was less than 2. Similarly, in biology, while there were over one and a half million active nodes, the average degree was only 15.5.

Average distance. The average distance between nodes is very low. For instance, in the economics coauthor network, the largest group of interconnected economists—the giant component—consists of 33 000 authors and the average degree is around 3. However, the average distance is only 9.47.

Unequal degree distribution. The key to reconciling the small number of connections and small average distance is the striking inequality in the degree distribution. For instance, in the economics coauthor network, the average degree in the whole network was 1.67, while the average degree of the 100 most linked authors was over 25.[13]

Clustering. Clustering levels are very high compared with what may be expected if the probability of link formation was uniformly random. In the economics coauthor network the clustering coefficient was 0.157. If links were randomly drawn then the clustering coefficient should be roughly equal to the ratio of

---

[12] See chapter 2 for definitions of these network measures.
[13] These numbers are taken from Goyal, van der Leij, and Moraga (2004).

Table 9.1. Data on coauthor networks.

Period	Physics	Biology	Economics
Total nodes	52 909	1 520 521	81 217
Giant component as percentage	0.85	0.92	0.417
Average degree	9.3	15.5	1.7
Clustering coefficient	0.45	0.09	0.16
Average distance	6.2	4.9	9.47
Diameter	20	24	29

The data in this table are taken from Goyal, van der Leij, and Moraga (2004) and Newman (2001, 2004). The data for physics and biology are for the period 1995–1999, while the date for economics is for the period 1990–1999.

average degree divided by the number of nodes, i.e., $1.67/81\,217 \approx 0.000\,02$. The observed clustering is over 7000 times this number! Similarly high levels of clustering are also observed in the other coauthor networks.

A comparison of pairwise stable networks in the coauthor model with the empirical networks suggests that this model yields rather different architectures from those observed in the data. The average degree and the clustering in pairwise stable networks appear to be much higher than what is observed in the empirical networks. These points relate closely to an important difference which concerns the correlation in degrees across partners in the pairwise stable networks. There is perfect correlation in degrees of partners, while in the empirical networks there appears to be a significant difference between the degrees of partners (especially between the "central" players and their partners). These points are perhaps best explained by discussing the local network of a specific node in the economics coauthors network. Figure 9.8 presents the local network of a prominent economist, Joseph E. Stiglitz.

This network looks very much like an interconnected star with an implicit hierarchical structure. Mr. Stiglitz works with a number of economists who do not seem to coauthor with each other: thus, clustering around a hub node is very low. Moreover, the coauthors of the coauthors of Mr. Stiglitz typically do not work with each other or with Mr. Stiglitz. Indeed the average degree within the network is very low (relative to the number of nodes in the component). The prominence of the hub nodes is widespread in such networks. Goyal, van der Leij, and Moraga (2006) show that these "star"-like nodes are located in different parts of the network and that they are critical to integrating the network and thereby reducing the average distance in the network. The prominence of hubs has a number of important implications: they shape the level of degree inequality and are key to an understanding of the low average distances in these networks (in spite of the very low average degree).

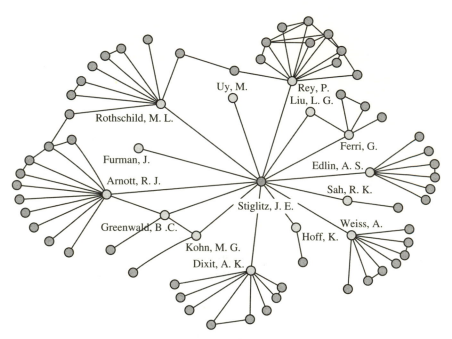

Figure 9.8.   Local network of Joseph E. Stiglitz.

To summarize, the coauthor network captures an essential feature of collaborative work—the potential negative externalities on coauthors as a person forms
additional links—but it seems to overlook some other powerful economic pressures that are active in coauthorship networks. This suggests the need for a richer
model which captures such pressures. One such pressure is informational externality; it seems natural that well-connected individuals in coauthorship networks
will have privileged access to new ideas in different subjects and this will make
them potentially more attractive collaborators.[14]

9.2.4   Free Trade Agreements

In recent years there has been a sharp increase in regional trade agreements among
countries; a significant majority of them are bilateral and involve a commitment
to mutual free trade.[15] These trade agreements are referred to as *free trade agreements* and their wide prevalence has led to a study of the incentives of countries to
undertake these agreements and the effects such agreements have on the welfare
of third countries. An important question is whether these local trade agreements

---

[14] Recall that these informational externalities play a central role in the link formation model in chapter 8, as well as in the connections model in section 9.2.1; those models predict the emergence of star
networks.

[15] For a discussion of different forms of regional trade agreements and their prevalence, see Crawford
and Fiorentino (2005).

facilitate or hinder the emergence of global free trade. This section presents a model of network formation—in which trade agreements are the links between nodes—to explore these questions. The presentation here is based on Goyal and Joshi (2006a).[16]

Suppose there are n countries each of which have a single firm that can sell in its own market as well as in foreign markets. National governments can affect the competitiveness of firms by choosing different levels of import tariffs. Moreover, these governments can also sign free trade agreements with other governments which facilitate trade. To keep things simple, suppose that, at the start, tariffs are prohibitive. However, any two countries can form free trade agreements which remove all tariffs between them and allow the firms in the two countries to compete freely (by choosing quantities).

Let $N_i(g)$ be the set of countries with whom country i signs a free trade agreement. Under our assumptions, only firms from these countries can compete in country i's market. Let the output of firm j in country i be denoted by Q_i^j. The total output in country i is $Q_i = \sum_{j \in N_i(g)} Q_i^j + Q_i^i$. In each country $i \in N$ there is an identical inverse linear demand $P_i = \alpha - Q_i$, $\alpha > 0$. All firms have a constant and identical marginal cost of production, $\gamma > 0$. Assume that $\alpha > \gamma$. Let the initial pre-agreement import tariff in each country be $T > \alpha$. Countries can form agreements which lower the tariff to 0.

Given a network g, it follows that the number of active firms in market i is $\eta_i(g) + 1$. If firm i is active in market j, then its output is

$$Q_j^i = \frac{\alpha - \gamma}{\eta_j(g) + 2}.$$

Equipped with this notation, we can now write the welfare of country i in network g as

$$\Pi_i(g) = \frac{1}{2}\left[\frac{(\alpha - \gamma)(\eta_i(g) + 1)}{\eta_i(g) + 2}\right]^2 + \sum_{j \in N_i(g) \cup \{i\}}\left[\frac{\alpha - \gamma}{\eta_j(g) + 2}\right]^2. \tag{9.4}$$

The following result, due to Goyal and Joshi (2006a), provides a complete characterization of pairwise stable and efficient free trade networks.

Proposition 9.3. *Suppose payoffs are given by (9.4). A pairwise stable network is either a complete network or consists of two components: one completely connected group of $n - 1$ countries and a single isolated country. The complete network is the only efficient network.*

Figure 9.9 illustrates pairwise stable networks. In the above setting, bilateral trade agreements lower trade tariffs to zero. Thus the result demonstrates that

---

[16] Furusawa and Konishi (2002) develop a closely related model of bilateral free trade agreements with a continuum of differentiated goods. Belleflamme and Bloch (2004) extend the model presented here to study collusion among local monopolists.

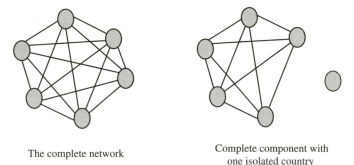

The complete network   Complete component with
one isolated country

Figure 9.9.   Free trade agreements: pairwise stable networks.

bilateralism can be viewed as a building block for the creation of global free trade. What are the incentive pressures which rule out all networks apart from the complete (and an almost complete) network?

There are three direct effects at work when a pair of countries sign a trade agreement which lowers import tariffs. First, the domestic firm is faced with greater competition from a foreign firm, which lowers its profits from the home market. Second, the domestic firm gets greater access to the foreign market, which increases profits from foreign market sales. Third, domestic consumers benefit from greater competition, in terms of lower prices. In addition, there is an interesting indirect effect of a bilateral free trade agreement: it makes the markets of the countries signing the agreement less valuable to other active firms in the market. This is termed *concession diversion* by Ethier (1998). Thus a bilateral free trade agreement generates a negative externality on current partners of the two countries signing the agreement.

Individual incentives to form links are reflected in the marginal payoffs to country i:

$$\Pi_i(g + g_{ij}) - \Pi_i(g) = \frac{1}{2}\left[\frac{(\alpha - \gamma)(\eta_i(g) + 2)}{\eta_i(g) + 3}\right]^2 - \frac{1}{2}\left[\frac{(\alpha - \gamma)\eta_i(g) + 1}{\eta_i(g) + 2}\right]^2$$

$$+ \left[\frac{\alpha - \gamma}{\eta_i(g) + 3}\right]^2 - \left[\frac{\alpha - \gamma}{\eta_i(g) + 2}\right]^2 + \left[\frac{\alpha - \gamma}{\eta_j(g) + 3}\right]^2.$$
$$(9.5)$$

It is easily checked that $\Pi_i(g + g_{ij}) \geqslant \Pi_i(g)$ if

$$2[\eta_i(g) + 1]^2 - 5 + \frac{2(\eta_i(g) + 3)^2(\eta_i(g) + 2)^2}{(\eta_j(g) + 3)^2} \geqslant 0. \qquad (9.6)$$

This inequality holds if $\eta_i(g) \geqslant 1$, i.e., if there are two or more active firms in the market i. This shows that once a country has signed a free trade agreement, it has incentives to sign further such agreements and this pressure leads to the complete network. The above computations also indicate how an almost complete network can arise: an isolated country which signs a free trade agreement with a highly connected country gains relatively little from having access to a competitive market, while its firm loses a significant share of its profits in the domestic market. If n is large enough, then the isolated country will prefer to remain in autarchy.

In this model, aggregate welfare is the sum of the welfare of all countries. An increase in free trade agreements lowers the profits of firms but raises consumers' surplus. Standard economic arguments suggest that the rise in consumers' surplus dominates the fall in firms' profits, and so world welfare is maximized under global free trade, i.e., the complete network. Thus the efficient network is also pairwise stable.

Proposition 9.3 makes a sharp prediction with regard to pairwise stable networks and this motivates a comparison with the empirical structure of free trade networks. Two features of the empirical network are worth noting. The first feature is cliques; regional agreements such as the North Atlantic Free Trade Agreement (NAFTA), involving Canada, Mexico, and the United States, create fully interconnected groups of countries. The second feature is the existence of nonexclusive relations: Mexico has free trade agreements with Costa Rica and Bolivia, while its partners in NAFTA do not have such agreements and moreover Bolivia and Costa Rica do not have a mutual free trade agreement either.

This comparison motivates a closer examination of the assumptions underlying the above analysis. For instance, the model assumes that governments maximize a welfare function which assigns equal weight to consumer surplus and producers profits. The other assumption is one of symmetry: clearly countries differ in size and competitiveness of markets and the efficiency of their firms. Similarly, countries have different transportation costs vis-à-vis each other, which are determined to some extent at least by geographic location. These issues have been examined in Goyal and Joshi (2006a), Furusawa and Konishi (2002), and Zissimos (2005). In particular, Furusawa and Konishi (2002) show how countries with very different levels of efficiency may want to avoid free trade agreements, leading to the creation of trading blocks. Zissimos (2005) uses models of strategic trade policy to explain why neighboring countries with lower (mutual) transportation costs are more likely to sign free trade agreements or treaties. This helps explain why these trading blocks are likely to be regional in the first place. Ethier (1998) and Goyal and Joshi (2006a) discuss the role of political economy considerations in shaping free trade agreements.

9.3 Stability and Efficiency

One of the central themes in the economic analysis of network formation has been the relationship between efficient and strategically stable networks. The discussion in the previous section suggests that the relation between efficiency and stability is complicated. In some instances—such as the connections model with small costs of linking, the model of intermediary advantages and structural holes, and the free trade networks—efficient networks are also stable. However, in other cases—such as the connections model with moderate costs of linking and the coauthor model—efficient networks are not stable. These examples reflect the rich externality effects that arise in network formation models. From a theoretical point of view, this motivates the question, is it possible to allocate the returns to networking activity in ways which align the social and private returns? The presentation here draws on Jackson and Wolinsky (1996) and Jackson (2005).

To get a sense of the issues involved, it is useful to start with a simple egalitarian allocation rule: in every network, each player gets an equal share of the total value generated by the network. Faced with this allocation rule it is clear that individual incentives are aligned with social incentives and every efficient network will be pairwise stable.[17] This discussion suggests that if there exists a designer who has complete power to redistribute the value generated in a network, then there is no conflict between the requirements of efficiency and individual incentives. In many (if not most) economic and social contexts, however, there are limitations to the power of the central designer, and it is therefore useful to ask if a similar congruence between social and private incentives can be obtained when the power of the designer is constrained in reasonable ways.

The following discussion will show that if the designer is constrained to allocations which are component balanced (the sum total of allocations within a component do not exceed the value generated by a component), then there will be games in which efficient networks are not pairwise stable. The formal statement of this result requires some additional terminology.

Recall that a network formation game has a set of players $N = \{1, 2, \ldots, n\}$, where $n \geq 3$. Let $V : \mathcal{G} \to \mathcal{R}$ be a value function which defines the aggregate value generated by any network g, and let $\mathcal{V}$ be the set of all value functions. Let $Y : G \times \mathcal{V} \to \mathcal{R}^n$ be an allocation function which specifies, for every value function, the payoff accruing to each player, in any network $g \in \mathcal{G}$. The value depends only on the architecture of the network and not on who occupies which position. To formalize this idea let $P : N \to N$ be a permutation of players in the network formation game. We define V^P as $V^P(g^P) = V(g)$. In many economic applications it is natural to suppose that the value generated by a component depends only on the component itself, in other words there are no externalities across components.[18] Let $\mathcal{C}(g) = \{C_1, C_2, \ldots, C_m\}$ denote a partition of the network g into components. We now define the property of component additivity.

---

[17] Clearly, under this allocation rule, an efficient network will also satisfy stronger stability requirements.

[18] Note that the four models of network formation discussed in section 9.2 all satisfy this property.

Definition 9.1. A value function is component additive if

$$V(g) = \sum_{C_k \in \mathcal{C}(g)} v(C_k),$$

where $v(C_k)$ is the value generated by component C_k.[19]

We will assume that a singleton component has value 0. The interest now turns to reasonable allocation rules. The first two requirements are anonymity and balance.

Definition 9.2. The allocation rule is anonymous if $Y_{P(i)}(g^P, V^P) = Y_i(g, V)$ for any permutation P.

Anonymity requires that, for a fixed network architecture, the allocation rule does not depend on the identity of the players occupying the different nodes. The next requirement on allocation rules deals with the ways in which value can be distributed across components. In settings where the value function satisfies additivity, it seems reasonable to require that the allocation rule does not redistribute resources across components.

Definition 9.3. The allocation rule is component balanced if $\sum_{i \in C_k} Y_i(g, v) = v(C_k)$, $C_k \in \mathcal{C}(g)$, for every g and component additive V.

Equipped with this terminology the following result on the conflict between efficiency and private incentives, due to Jackson and Wolinsky (1996), can now be stated.

Theorem 9.3. *If $n \geq 3$, then there is no allocation rule Y which is anonymous and component balanced such that for every value function V an efficient network is pairwise stable.*[20]

The proof of this result shows that there exists a value function for which there exists no allocation rule satisfying the required properties which can support an efficient network. Suppose that $n = 3$ and that the value function V is as follows: $V(g^c) = 1$, $V(g^e) = 0$, $V(g) = 1$ for networks g with one link, and $V(g) = 1 + \epsilon$ for networks g with two links. The efficient network has two links. It can be checked that the value function is component additive and anonymous and there is a unique efficient network. Anonymity and component balance imply that each player in g^c gets $\frac{1}{3}$, and the linked players in a network with one link get $\frac{1}{2}$ each and the isolated player gets 0. Pairwise stability of efficient network therefore requires that in the two-link network for the player with two links j it must be the case that $Y_j(g_{ij} + g_{jk}, V) \geq \frac{1}{2}$. This, together with component

---

[19] The definition here allows for singleton components, and is therefore slightly more general compared with the original formulation in Jackson and Wolinsky (1996).

[20] Clearly, the same result holds if we require stronger stability requirements such as pairwise equilibrium or bilateral equilibrium.

balance and anonymity, implies that the two players with one link each can earn at most $\frac{1}{4} + \frac{1}{2}\epsilon$. However, $\frac{1}{4} + \frac{1}{2}\epsilon < \frac{1}{3}$ for small ϵ, and so the two peripheral players have a strict incentive to form a link and deviate to the complete network, g^c. This completes the argument.

Theorem 9.3 has inspired an extensive literature which studies different ways in which efficiency can be attained in network formation models. It is useful to view this work as following two broad approaches. The first approach may be roughly termed as the "central designer" model. In this approach, there is a designer who chooses an allocation function; here interest has centered on the scope of specific allocation rules. The second approach allows for players to bargain or make transfers and form links and so the allocation rule may be seen as arising endogenously along with the network.

To get a flavor of the first approach,[21] consider an allocation rule which is a natural variant of the egalitarian allocation rule discussed above. Consider a component additive value function V and let the allocation function be defined to be $\bar{Y}_i(g, V) = v(C)/n(C)$ for a player i in component C, in network g. This allocation rule allocates an equal share of the value generated by a component to its members.[22] Is there an interesting class of value functions for which this allocation rule will support an efficient network? The analysis of this issue requires some additional notation. A link g_{ij} is critical in network g if its deletion leads to a strict increase in the number of components; in other words, $|\mathcal{C}(g - g_{ij})| > |\mathcal{C}(g)|$. The pair (g, V) satisfies critical link monotonicity if, for any critical link in g and its associated components C, C', and C'', $v(C) \geqslant v(C') + v(C'')$ implies that $v(C)/|C| \geqslant \max[v(C')/|C'|, v(C'')/|C''|]$, where $|\hat{C}|$ refers to the number of players in a component $\hat{C}$. Equipped with this terminology, it is possible to state the following result, due to Jackson and Wolinsky (1996).

Theorem 9.4. *Consider a component additive V and let g be an efficient network. Then g is pairwise stable under allocation rule $\bar{Y}$ if and only if (g, v) satisfies critical link monotonicity.*

Theorems 9.3 and 9.4 show how allocation rules have a profound impact on the prospects of attaining efficiency. This raises the question, what types of allocation rules are plausible? The issue of a plausible allocation rule can be addressed in an axiomatic way. This approach has a long and distinguished tradition; notable contributions include the early work of Shapley (1953) and the more recent extension of this work to the context of networks by Myerson (1977).[23] Another possibility

---

[21] The discussion here will be brief; for an extended discussion of this literature see the survey papers by Jackson (2005, 2006).

[22] Observe that a pairwise stable network always exists under this allocation rule. Construct a set of components where at each stage the new component is chosen so as to maximize the average payoff $v(C)/n(C)$ among the set of all players still left.

[23] See Jackson (2005) and van den Nouweland (2005) for a survey of this work.

is to derive the allocation rule endogenously from bargaining among the players. This naturally ties in with the second approach to resolving the conflict between efficiency and stability mentioned above and we turn to that now.

In this second approach, players have two types of decision to make: they choose their links and they also make demands on potential partners (or on everyone) conditional on their links being accepted. In this setting, a network is strategically stable if there exist link proposals and demands or transfers which constitute, roughly speaking, an equilibrium. To get a flavor of the issues and the results that have been obtained, it is useful to discuss two specific models.

The first model is due to Currarini and Morelli (2000).[24] In this model, players move one at a time and each player makes a set of link proposals as well as payoff demands conditional on acceptance of the links. The link proposals and demands are observed by all players and this is therefore a game of perfect information. After everyone has moved the network is formed and the demands of different players implemented. Link proposals are only accepted if the corresponding demands are feasible (they can be implemented given the aggregate value of the network thereby created).

The main result they obtain exploits a restriction on value functions: size monotonicity. A value function satisfies the size monotonicity property if $V(g) > V(g - g_{ij})$ for every critical link g_{ij} in g and for every network g.[25] Currarini and Morelli (2000) show that *if the value function satisfies size monotonicity, then every (sub-game perfect) equilibrium of the demand and link formation game leads to an efficient network.*[26] The intuition underlying this result is as follows: at every stage, given the existing link proposals and the demands from previous players, a player proposes links and makes demands that reflect her marginal contribution to the creation of an efficient network. The game has a prespecified ending and so early movers will generally have an advantage as they make take-it-or-leave-it offers to subsequent players.[27]

A comparison of theorem 9.3 with the Currarini and Morelli (2000) result suggests that bargaining between players potentially allows greater flexibility in shaping private incentives compared with allocation rules set by a central designer. This is an important insight. While their model involves bargaining among players, it is worth noting that individual demands are centralized in the sense that they

---

[24] Also see Slikker and van den Nouweland (2001) for a model where allocation rules arise endogenously.

[25] This is a fairly general class of value functions; in particular, note that the example used in theorem 9.3 satisfies size monotonicity.

[26] Mutuswami and Winter (2002) study a closely related model in which players' benefits are increasing in the size of the network and players sequentially announce their contributions to the creation of the network. They find that sub-game perfect equilibria of this subscription mechanism game yield efficient outcomes.

[27] See Dutta, Ghosal, and Ray (2005) for a dynamic model of network formation with no prespecified ending.

are not directed to specific links or specific individuals. From a practical point of view, therefore, it is not clear how such demands can be implemented. Indeed, the discussion in chapter 7 (as well as the examples in the previous section) suggest that decentralization and local exchange are critical features of networks. This concern motivates the study of a more genuinely decentralized framework for the formation of a network.

We start with a consideration of bilateral transfers. The first attempts to model bilateral transfers were in the context of specific examples; Jackson and Wolinsky (1996) consider their role in obtaining efficiency in the connections model, while Goyal and Joshi (2003) study their role in generating asymmetries in collaboration networks among firms. Bloch and Jackson (2007) develop a general framework to study the role of bilateral transfers in supporting efficient networks and the exposition below draws on their paper.

Suppose that the function $U : \mathcal{G} \to \mathcal{R}^n$ defines the (gross) payoff to every player for every network $g \in \mathcal{G}$. There are a number of different ways in which transfers can be modeled. It is useful to start with the simplest case: a player i announces a set of transfers $t^i = \{t_{i1}^i, \ldots, t_{ii-1}^i, t_{ii+1}^i, \ldots, t_{in}^i\} \in \mathcal{R}^{n-1}$, with t_{ij}^i being the transfer from player i to player j on link g_{ij}. Suppose that a link g_{ij} is formed if and only if $t_{ij}^i + t_{ji}^j \geq 0$. Formally, given a strategy profile $t = (t^1, t^2, \ldots, t^n)$, the network that forms is defined as $g(t) = \{g_{ij} = 1 \mid t_{ij}^i + t_{ji}^j \geq 0\}$. The payoffs net of transfers are then defined as follows:

$$\Pi_i(g(t)) = u_i(g(t)) - \sum_{j:g_{ij}=1} [t_{ij}^i - t_{ji}^j], \qquad (9.7)$$

where $u_i(g(t))$ refers to the payoff from the network per se and the second term is the sum of net transfers from player i to player j on the different links that form after the announcements. Implicit in this formulation is the assumption that offers of transfers on links that are not formed do not cost anything.[28] This game has a straightforward interpretation: every player announces a set of transfers, with a positive transfer being an offer of resources to set up the link and a negative transfer being the demand of a subsidy required to acquiesce in the formation of the link. The set of players, their strategies, and the payoff functions constitute a normal form game, which can be solved by using a refinement of Nash equilibrium which takes into account pairwise incentives.

More general transfer schemes can be easily accommodated within this framework. A player can offer to make transfers for each of the possible links, and the transfer strategy is then $t^i \in \mathcal{R}^{n(n-1)/2}$, with $t_{l,k}^i$ being the transfer proposed by player i for an arbitrary link g_{lk}. This formulation allows for transfers which are indirect, i.e., player 1 may make transfers for a link between players 2 and 3.

---

[28] This corresponds to the assumption in the network formation game (see examples in previous section) where announcements of links, if they are not reciprocated, do not entail any costs.

However, these transfers are still unconditional, in the sense that the transfer $t^i_{l,k}$ is independent of the structure of the network at large. In principle transfers can be made contingent on the nature of the realized graph.

Bloch and Jackson (2007) derive a number of results on the types of games in which transfers can sustain efficient networks. These results show how varying the extent of coverage (going from direct to indirect transfers) and the level of conditionality (having transfers in a link depend on realization of other links) allows for efficient networks to be sustained in a progressively broader class of games.

9.4 Unequal Degrees and Payoffs

One of the most prominent features of empirical networks is their unequal degree distribution. The average degree in these networks is typically small (relative to the total number of nodes) but a few nodes have a very large degree. Chapters 2 and 8 discussed this feature and it was also discussed in section 9.2.3.[29] The empirical findings on inequality in degrees raise two important questions: what are the economic circumstances which give rise to unequal degree distributions as against an equal degree distribution, and what are the implications of such degree distributions for payoff distribution? The analysis of the connections model and structural holes suggests that inequality in both degree distribution and payoffs obtains in equilibrium. However, in the free trade agreements the outcome is (more or less) symmetric. Do these differences in equilibrium networks reflect a difference in the incentives in these contexts? This section will argue that positive and negative externalities generated by links play an important role in shaping inequality in networks. The exposition here is based on Goyal and Joshi (2006b).

Externality effects take on a variety of forms in network contexts. This richness is one of the great strengths of the networks approach but it also makes general results difficult to obtain. The presentation here will focus on a class of games where an individual's payoffs depend on the number of own links and the aggregate number of links of all other players. These games will be referred to as *playing-the-field* games.

We consider n-player games of link announcement. The strategy of a player is denoted by s_i and the strategy profile is denoted by $s = (s_1, s_2, \ldots, s_n)$. A strategy profile s induces an undirected network $g(s)$. Let $L(g)$ be the total number of degrees in network g. It is useful to define g_{-i} as the network obtained by deleting player i and all his links from the network g and $L(g_{-i}) = \sum_{j \neq i} \eta_j(g_{-i})$ as the total number of degrees in g_{-i}. Given a strategy profile $s = (s_1, s_2, \ldots, s_n)$, the

---

[29] Unequal degrees are also a prominent feature of interfirm collaboration networks; see chapter 10 for a discussion of such networks.

payoffs to a player i are

$$\Pi_i(g(s_i, s_{-i})) = \Phi(\eta_i(g), L(g_{-i})) - c\eta_i(g), \tag{9.8}$$

where $c > 0$ is the constant cost of forming a link.

Broadly speaking, two types of externality effect arise in this context: an externality across links of the same player and externality effects across links of different players. The analysis will focus on the case where these externality effects are either positive or negative. This motivates the following definitions.

Definition 9.4. The payoffs to player i are convex (concave) in own links if, for every $y \geq 0$, the marginal returns $\Phi(x + 1, y) - \Phi(x, y)$ are strictly increasing (decreasing) in x for $x \geq 0$.

The next definition captures externality effects across players.

Definition 9.5. The payoffs to player i satisfy the strategic substitutes property if, for $y' > y \geq 0$, $\Phi(x + 1, y') - \Phi(x, y') < \Phi(x + 1, y) - \Phi(x, y)$, for every $x \geq 0$, while they satisfy the strategic complements property if, for $y' > y \geq 0$, $\Phi(x + 1, y') - \Phi(x, y') > \Phi(x + 1, y) - \Phi(x, y)$ for every $x \geq 0$.

The following two examples illustrate the scope of these games.

Example 9.1 (collaboration among oligopolistic firms). This model is taken from Goyal and Joshi (2003). Consider a homogeneous product Cournot oligopoly consisting of n *ex ante* identical firms which face a linear inverse demand: $p = \alpha - \sum_{i \in N} q_i, \alpha > 0$. The firms initially have zero fixed costs and identical costs of production. Bilateral collaborations lower marginal costs, $C_i(g) = \gamma_0 - \gamma \eta_i(g)$, $i \in N$, where γ_0 is a positive parameter representing a firm's marginal cost if it has no links. Given any network g, the Cournot equilibrium output can be written as[30]

$$q_i(g) = \frac{(\alpha - \gamma_0) + n\gamma\eta_i(g) - \gamma L(g_{-i})}{n + 1}, \quad i \in N. \tag{9.9}$$

The payoffs to a firm i in network g are

$$\Pi_i(g) = \frac{[(\alpha - \gamma_0) + n\gamma\eta_i(g) - \gamma L(g_{-i})]^2}{(n + 1)^2} - c\eta_i(g). \tag{9.10}$$

It can be verified that the payoffs to every player satisfy convexity in own links and the strategic substitutes property.   △

Example 9.2 (cooperation in a patent race). This example is taken from Goyal and Joshi (2006b) and represents a simple variation on the classical patent race model (see, for example, Dasgupta and Stiglitz 1980). Consider n firms who

---

[30] In order to ensure that each firm produces a strictly positive quantity in equilibrium, we will assume that $(\alpha - \gamma_0) - (n - 1)(n - 2)\gamma > 0$. See chapter 3 for an example where the details of the derivation of Cournot equilibrium quantities and profits are presented.

are racing to innovate a new product. The firm which wins the race is awarded a patent of value 1; the loser earns 0. All firms use the same discount rate ρ. Suppose that firms are endowed with one unit of research capability. Firms can speed their research by sharing their research capability. Let $\tau(\eta_i(g))$ denote the random time at which firm i innovates in network g. We assume that τ has an exponential distribution:

$$\Pr\{\tau(\eta_i(g)) \leqslant t\} = 1 - e^{-\eta_i(g)t}. \tag{9.11}$$

Thus as firm i establishes more links it increases the probability of innovating successfully before time t. In addition to this technological uncertainty, there is also market uncertainty: any of the rival $n-1$ firms may successfully innovate before firm i. Assuming that the distribution of the time of innovation is independent across the firms, the expected payoff to a firm i in network g is

$$\Pi_i(g) = \int_0^\infty e^{-\rho t} \eta_i(g) e^{-tL(g)} \, dt - c\eta_i(g) = \frac{\eta_i(g)}{\rho + L(g)} - c\eta_i(g), \tag{9.12}$$

where $L(g) = \sum_{j=1}^n \eta_j(g)$. It can be checked that payoffs are concave in own links and that they satisfy the strategic substitutes property. $\triangle$

The first result, due to Goyal and Joshi (2006b), provides a characterization of pairwise equilibrium networks if individual payoffs are convex in own links.[31]

Proposition 9.4. *Suppose the payoffs to players are given by (9.8) and they satisfy convexity in own links. A pairwise equilibrium network is either empty, complete, or has the dominant group architecture.*[32]

In a game with five players there are 34 distinct network architectures (see, for example, Harary 1969). However, only five architectures, which can be parametrized in terms of the size of the dominant group, can arise in pairwise equilibrium networks. Figure 9.10 presents these architectures.

The following transitivity property is central to the proof: in a pairwise equilibrium network g, if players i and j have any links, then they must also be linked with each other. Since g is a pairwise equilibrium, the marginal return from the last link for both i and j must exceed the costs. It now follows from convexity in own links that the marginal returns of linking with each other are strictly greater while the marginal costs are constant. Hence both players have a strict incentive to link with each other. This transitivity property immediately implies that every component in a pairwise equilibrium network must be complete. It also implies that there can be at most one nonsingleton component in a pairwise equilibrium

---

[31] See chapter 7 for a definition of pairwise equilibrium networks.

[32] There exists a pairwise equilibrium network if payoffs satisfy either the strategic complements property or the strategic substitutes property; for details on the proof of existence, see Goyal and Joshi (2006b).

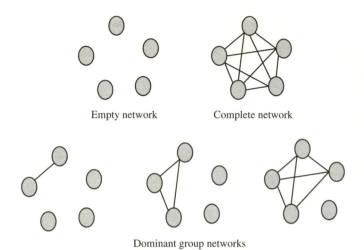

Empty network   Complete network

Dominant group networks

Figure 9.10.   Pairwise equilibrium networks under convexity in own links.

network. Thus there are only three candidates for pairwise equilibrium networks: the empty network, the complete network, and the dominant group network.

The networks in figure 9.10 exhibit very different levels of inequality in degrees, and this raises the question, what determines the relative likelihood of different networks? It turns out that the answer to this question is related to the nature of the externality effects across links of players. If the payoffs exhibit strategic complementarity, then players will be encouraged to form links as others form links and so the empty network or the complete network is always a pairwise equilibrium network. On the other hand, if payoffs satisfy the strategic substitutes property, then, for a range of link formation costs, only dominant groups of intermediate size, which exhibit considerable degree inequality, arise in a pairwise equilibrium network.[33]

The next result, due to Goyal and Joshi (2006b), takes up the case where payoffs are concave in own links.

Proposition 9.5. *Suppose payoffs to players are given by (9.8), and they satisfy concavity in own links and the strategic complementarity property. A regular pairwise equilibrium network always exists. In an irregular pairwise equilibrium network all nonmaximal degree players are mutually linked.*[34]

Figures 9.11 and 9.12 illustrate some pairwise equilibrium networks. To get some intuition for the result it is useful to sketch the argument underlying the first statement. Start from the empty network. If it is a pairwise equilibrium network, the statement follows. If it is not, then construct an "improvement path"

---

[33] Recall that example 9.1 satisfies convexity in own links and the strategic substitutes property. Chapter 10, on networks among firms, discusses this example in detail.

[34] For regular networks of all degrees to exist, we need to assume that n is even valued.

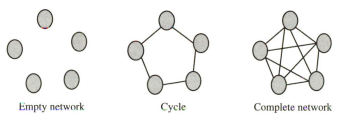

| Empty network | Cycle | Complete network |

Figure 9.11. Regular pairwise equilibrium networks:
concavity in own links and strategic complements.

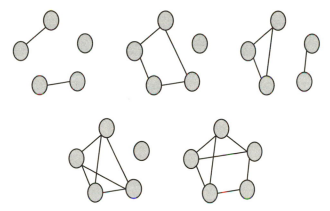

Figure 9.12. Irregular pairwise equilibrium networks:
concavity in own links and strategic complements.

of networks where links are formed by distinct pairs of players which strictly
increase payoffs for the concerned players.[35] From strategic complementarity it
follows that along such an improvement path every player strictly increases utility
when others form links. This implies that the improvement path will proceed to
a regular network with a higher degree. Either this higher degree network is a
pairwise equilibrium network or pairs of players have an incentive to form an
additional link. In the latter case, repeat the above argument and the existence
of regular pairwise equilibrium networks follows from the fact that the set of
networks is finite.

Next consider an irregular network g. Suppose that $x \in N_m(g)$ and $y, z \in$
$N_k(g)$, with $k < m$, and suppose that $g_{yz} = 0$.[36]

If g is a pairwise equilibrium, then

$$\Phi(\eta_x(g), L(g_{-x})) - \Phi(\eta_x(g) - 1, L(g_{-x})) \geq c.$$

---

[35] For a definition of improving paths, see chapter 7.
[36] Recall, from chapter 2, that $N_x(g)$ is the set of players who have x links in network g.

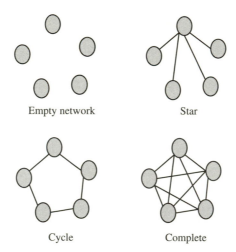

Figure 9.13. Pairwise equilibrium networks:
concavity in own links and strategic substitutes.

However, the marginal returns to player y from forming a link with player z are

$$\Phi(\eta_y(g) + 1, L(g_{-y})) - \Phi(\eta_y(g), L(g_{-y}))$$
$$> \Phi(\eta_x(g), L(g_{-x})) - \Phi(\eta_x(g) - 1, L(g_{-x})) \geq c. \qquad (9.13)$$

This is true because $\eta_y(g) \leq \eta_x(g) - 1$ and $L(g_{-x}) < L(g_{-y})$ and payoffs are concave in own links and exhibit strategic complementarity. Thus players y and z have a strict incentive to form a link with each other. Since y and z were arbitrary, every pair of nonmaximally connected players will be mutually linked.

More generally, the above argument suggests that every irregular pairwise equilibrium network is vulnerable to entry of new players, since a nonmaximally connected player in the existing network has an incentive to form links with the newcomer. By contrast, in any (incomplete) regular pairwise equilibrium network no player has such an incentive. Thus concavity in own links and strategic complementarity will generally lead to regular networks.

The discussion now turns to the case where payoffs are concave in own links but satisfy strategic substitutability. The following result, due to Goyal and Joshi (2006b), provides a partial characterization of pairwise equilibrium networks for this case.

Proposition 9.6. *Suppose payoffs to players are given by (9.8), and they satisfy concavity in own links and the strategic substitutes property. Regular networks and the star can be sustained in pairwise equilibrium.*

Figure 9.13 illustrates some of the networks that arise under this structure of externalities.

The above results bring out the central role of externalities across the links of players: if own links and the links of others are strategic complements, then regular networks arise naturally, while if links are strategic substitutes, then an unequal degree distribution is more likely to arise in a pairwise equilibrium network.

Our interest now turns to the payoff implications of degree inequality. General results on the relationship between degree and payoffs are not available, so we discuss some special cases. Consider the case when payoffs are increasing and convex in own links and satisfy the strategic substitutes property. Suppose, in addition, that the payoff function $\Phi(k, l)$ is strictly decreasing in l. From proposition 9.4 it follows that a pairwise equilibrium network (with unequal degrees) has the dominant group architecture. The payoff to a player in a dominant group with $0 < k < n - 1$ players, $\Phi(k - 1, (k - 1)(k - 2)) - (k - 1)c \geqslant \Phi(0, (k-1)(k-2))$, the payoff from deleting all links. Since $\Phi(k, l)$ is decreasing in l, it follows that the payoff to the isolated player in the pairwise equilibrium network $\Phi(0, k(k - 1)) < \Phi(0, (k - 1)(k - 2))$ and so the players with connections earn higher payoffs than the isolated players.

Next consider the case when payoffs are increasing and concave in own links and satisfy the strategic substitutes property. Suppose again that individual payoffs are falling in links of others. From proposition 9.6 we know that a star is a pairwise equilibrium network. It is easy to see that pairwise stability, along with properties of payoffs $\phi(\cdot, \cdot)$, implies that $\Phi(n - 1, 0) - (n - 1)c \geqslant \Phi(0, 0) > \Phi(0, 2(n - 2))$. The central player, with $n - 1$ links, therefore earns a higher payoff than the peripheral players, who have one link each.

The approach developed in this section can also be applied to games where externality effects are local: the payoffs to player i depend only on her own links and the links of her partners. The free trade agreements game, discussed in section 9.2.4, is an example of such a game. The convexity and concavity of payoffs in own links and the strategic substitutes and complements properties, defined above, have natural analogues in this setting. For an analysis of such games, see Goyal and Joshi (2006b).

9.5 Concluding Remarks

This chapter provides an overview of games of network formation in which link formation is two-sided. This is a very active field of research, both in terms of theoretical developments and in terms of applications, and the chapter has focused on three key issues. What are the network architectures that arise when individuals form links in a strategic way? Are the networks that arise out of strategic linking activity efficient? And what are the economic circumstances which give rise to networks that exhibit significant inequality in degrees and payoffs?

The chapter started with a detailed discussion of four applications. The aim here was to show how the nature of externalities created by individual links shapes the architecture of resulting networks. The analysis of the models highlighted the point that the strategic approach leads to sharp predictions. Moreover, the predicted networks have simple architectures. In particular, structures like the star, the complete network, and networks consisting of complete components and isolated players were shown to be stable, and the intuition underlying their emergence was explained. In some cases, these structures appear to be consistent with empirically observed networks; star-like structures are observed in social networks as well as in trading contexts and so it seems that the connections model and the model of intermediary advantages and structural holes capture some basic forces at work. However, in other applications, such as coauthorship, the network formation model captures an essential economic trade off—the capacity constraints faced by researchers—but generates predictions which differ significantly from empirically observed coauthor networks. This suggests the need for richer models which incorporate additional economic forces.

The second theme of the chapter was the relation between stable networks and efficiency. In some applications, such as intermediary advantages and free trade agreements, there is a close overlap between stability and efficiency. However, in other contexts, such as the connections model and coauthorships, there is a sharp conflict between individual incentives and efficiency. This led to a discussion of mechanisms, centralized as well as decentralized, which could resolve the conflict. In the centralized approach there is a "planner" who can design the allocation among players. To make this approach interesting, the allocation rules are subject to some normative constraints, such as fairness, budget balance, and anonymity. Alternatively, players can allocate the surplus generated by the networks via bargaining among themselves. If the bargaining is with regard to the set of all players, then it may also be viewed as a type of centralized allocation mechanism. Alternatively, the bargaining could be at the pairwise level, and then it is more natural to think of the allocation rule as being decentralized. The discussion showed that the success of mechanisms in bringing individual incentives in line with efficiency depends on the type of externalities that are present.

The third major theme of the chapter has been inequality. Inequality in the degree distribution appears to be a critical feature of many empirical networks; this degree inequality also arises in some of the applications that were studied, such as the connections model and the model of intermediary advantages and structural holes. These observations motivated a study of the circumstances, i.e., the types of externality, that are conducive to the emergence of degree inequality and payoff inequality. The results in this chapter bring out the idea that if own links and the links of others are strategic complements, then regular networks with identical payoffs for different players arise naturally, while if links are strategic substitutes, then an unequal degree and payoff distribution is more likely to arise. While these results are promising, the discussion also suggests that our understanding of the forces that give rise to inequality is quite poor and further work is needed on this subject.

As in the case of one-sided links, most of the work on two-sided link formation has looked at one–zero links. The study of weighted links remains an open area. The discussion of decentralized allocation rules, derived endogenously, naturally suggests the role of prices. A closer integration of network formation with classical models of price formation and general equilibrium seems to be a promising avenue for further work. The discussion on unequal degrees and payoffs shows some ways in which the origins and implications of unequal degree distribution can be studied. Unequal degree distributions seem to be ubiquitous and a better understanding of their economic origins is needed.

9.6 Appendix

9.6.1 Connections Model

The proof of proposition 9.1 follows from simple computations, while the proof of theorem 9.1 is analogous to the proof of the corresponding theorem in the one-sided links model in chapter 8, and is therefore omitted.

9.6.2 Intermediation Advantages and Structural Holes

The (net) payoffs to player i in network g are

$$\Pi_i(g) = \sum_{j \in \mathcal{N}_i(g)} \frac{1}{e(i,j;g)+2} + \sum_{j,k \in N} \frac{I_{\{i \in E(j,k;g)\}}}{e(j,k;g)+2} - \eta_i(g)c. \quad (9.14)$$

This section uses the concept of strict bilateral equilibrium.

Definition 9.6. A network g can be supported in a *strict bilateral equilibrium* (SBE) if the following conditions hold.

(i) There exists a strategy profile s^* which supports g as a bilateral equilibrium.

(ii) For any $i \in N$ and every $s_i \in S_i$ such that $g(s_i, s_{-i}^*) \neq g(s^*)$, $\Pi_i(g(s^*)) > \Pi_i(g(s_i, s_{-i}^*))$.

(iii) For any pair of players $i, j \in N$ and for every strategy pair (s_i, s_j) with $g(s_i, s_j, s_{-i-j}^*) \neq g(s^*)$,

$$\Pi_i(g(s_i, s_j, s_{-i-j}^*)) \geq \Pi_i(g(s_i^*, s_j^*, s_{-i-j}^*))$$
$$\Rightarrow \quad \Pi_j(g(s_i, s_j, s_{-i-j}^*)) < \Pi_j(g(s_i^*, s_j^*, s_{-i-j}^*)). \quad (9.15)$$

Theorem 9.5. *Suppose payoffs are given by (9.14) and that n is large. If $c < \frac{1}{6}$, then there does not exist any SBE network. If $\frac{1}{6} < c < \frac{1}{2}$, then the unique SBE network is the star, while if $\frac{1}{2} < c < \frac{1}{2} + \frac{1}{6}(n - 2)$, then the star and the empty network are the only SBE networks. If $c > \frac{1}{2} + \frac{1}{6}(n - 2)$, then the empty network is the unique SBE network.*

The argument underlying nonexistence for $c < \frac{1}{6}$ has already been given in the text. We focus on the other cases. The proof of the theorem rests on a number of lemmas, which are now stated and proved independently.

Lemma 9.1. *A bilateral equilibrium (BE) network is either empty or connected.*

Proof. This lemma makes use of two claims.

Claim 1. Consider any network g. If $g_{ij} = 1$ and the link is critical, then the net payoffs to players i and j from the link are equal.

By hypothesis g_{ij} is critical, and so it follows that i and j lie in different components in the network $g - g_{ij}$. Let C_i and C_j be the components that contain i and j, respectively. The marginal payoff of the link g_{ij} for player i is

$$M_i(g_{ij}; g) = \frac{1}{2} + \sum_{k \in C_j \setminus \{j\}} \frac{1}{e(i, k; g) + 2}$$

$$+ \sum_{l \in C_i \setminus \{i\}} \sum_{k \in C_j \setminus \{j\}} \frac{1}{e(l, k; g) + 2} + \sum_{l \in C_i \setminus \{i\}} \frac{1}{e(l, j; g) + 2} - c,$$

where the first two terms refer to access benefits while the third and fourth terms refer to essentialness benefits. Similarly, the marginal payoffs to player j from link g_{ij} can be written as

$$M_j(g_{ij}; g) = \frac{1}{2} + \sum_{l \in C_i \setminus \{i\}} \frac{1}{e(j, l; g) + 2}$$

$$+ \sum_{l \in C_i \setminus \{i\}} \sum_{k \in C_j \setminus \{j\}} \frac{1}{e(l, k; g) + 2} + \sum_{k \in C_j \setminus \{j\}} \frac{1}{e(i, k; g) + 2} - c.$$

It then follows that $M_i(g_{ij}; g) = M_j(g_{ij}; g)$.

Claim 2. In a network g, a component with $m \geq 2$ players has at least two nonessential players.

First, note that from any arbitrary connected network one can reach a line network by a series of steps that involve only two operations: (i) removal of links; (ii) reconnection of existing links to extremal players (i.e., players with only one link). It is easy to see that any such operation will (weakly) increase the number of essential players and decreases the number of nonessential players. Since in the line network only the two end-point players are nonessential, it follows that any component must have at least two nonessential players.

The proof of lemma 9.1 can now be presented. Let g be a nonempty BE network, and suppose it is not connected. Let $\hat{C}$ be the largest component in g, which must therefore contain at least two players. Next we show that there is a player $j \notin \hat{C}$ who can establish a mutually profitable link with some player in $\hat{C}$. For simplicity, consider the extreme (and least favorable) case where j constitutes a singleton component.

From claim 2, $\hat{C}$ has a nonessential player $i \in \hat{C}$. Two possibilities need to be considered. The first is that $\eta_i(g) = 1$ and $g_{il} = 1$. Then, it is clear that, since i and l both find it profitable to keep their link, player l would find it optimal to create a link with j if given the opportunity, and so would player j. This contradicts that the hypothesis that g is a BE network.

The second possibility is that $\eta_i(g) \geq 2$ for every nonessential player. Define $\mathcal{N}_i^m(g) = |\{j \in \hat{C} : e(i, j; g) = m\}|$ to be the players whom i accesses via m essential players and let $\eta_i^m(g) = |\mathcal{N}_i^m(g)|$. The payoffs to player i are

$$\frac{\eta_i^0(g)}{2} + \frac{\eta_i^1(g)}{3} + \frac{\eta_i^2(g)}{4} + \cdots + \frac{\eta_i^r(g)}{r+2} - \eta_i(g)c \qquad (9.16)$$

for some $r \leq n - 2$. Since g is a BE network, it then follows that

$$\frac{1}{\eta_i(g)} \left[\frac{\eta_i^0(g)}{2} + \frac{\eta_i^1(g)}{3} + \frac{\eta_i^2(g)}{4} + \cdots + \frac{\eta_i^r(g)}{r+2} \right] \geq c. \qquad (9.17)$$

Recall that j is a singleton component. Then the *marginal returns* to j from link g_{ij} are

$$\frac{\eta_j^0(g + g_{ij})}{2} + \frac{\eta_j^1(g + g_{ij})}{3} + \frac{\eta_i^2(g + g_{ij})}{4} + \cdots + \frac{\eta_i^r(g + g_{ij})}{r+2} - c. \qquad (9.18)$$

Note now that for every $k \in \hat{C} \backslash \{i\}$, $e(j, k; g + g_{ij}) = e(i, k; g) + 1$. Thus $\eta_j^m(g + g_{ij}) = \eta_i^{m-1}(g)$ for every $m \geq 1$ and $\eta_j^0(g + g_{ij}) = 1$. Using these facts the marginal returns of player j from the link with i can be written as

$$\frac{1}{2} + \frac{\eta_i^0(g)}{3} + \frac{\eta_i^1(g)}{4} + \cdots + \frac{\eta_i^r(g)}{r+3} - c. \qquad (9.19)$$

Now we can argue that

$$\frac{1}{2} + \frac{\eta_i^0(g)}{3} + \frac{\eta_i^1(g)}{4} + \cdots + \frac{\eta_i^r(g)}{r+3}$$

$$> \frac{1}{2} \left[\frac{\eta_i^0(g)}{2} + \frac{\eta_i^1(g)}{3} + \frac{\eta_i^2(g)}{4} + \cdots + \frac{\eta_i^r(g)}{r+2} \right]$$

$$\geq \frac{1}{\eta_i(g)} \left[\frac{\eta_i^0(g)}{2} + \frac{\eta_i^1(g)}{3} + \frac{\eta_i^2(g)}{4} + \cdots + \frac{\eta_i^r(g)}{r+2} \right]$$

$$\geq c.$$

The first inequality is immediate, $\eta_i(g) \geq 2$ can be used in deriving the second inequality, and the final inequality follows from 9.17. Apply claim 1 to conclude that player i also has a strict incentive to form a link with j, given that all existing links are retained. But note that, given that link g_{ij} is formed, player i has no incentive to delete any of his erstwhile links since (roughly speaking) the marginal returns from each of these links have actually increased. Thus players i and j have a strict incentive to form an additional link. These arguments extend directly to cover the case where j belongs to a nonsingleton component. Thus g is not a BE network, a contradiction that completes the proof. $\square$

Lemma 9.2. *The star is the only minimal network which can be sustained in a BE for large n.*

Proof. Consider a g that is minimally connected but not a star. Then, there are two players, say i and j, such that $\eta_i(g) = \eta_j(g) = 1$ and $e(i, j; g) \geq 2$. Then, it readily follows that for at least one of them, i say, the following holds: there is a player x with $e(i, x; g) = 1$ (thus, x is two links away from i in g) and the set of players for whom x is essential in connecting i has a cardinality that is at least $(n-4)/2$, i.e., $|\{k \in N : x \in E(i, k, g)\}| \geq (n-4)/2$.

It is shown that such a network g cannot be a BE. First note that, given the linking cost c, the number of essential players that can be supported in equilibrium between any two players has some (finite) upper bound $\hat{e}(c)$, independent of n. Consider then the possibility that i and x were to form a link. The gross marginal gains, $\Delta \Pi_i$ and $\Delta \Pi_x$, induced by that change for i and x (if all other links were to remain in place) is bounded below as follows:

$$\min\{\Delta \Pi_i, \Delta \Pi_x\} \geq \frac{(n-4)/2}{\hat{e}(c) - 1} - \frac{(n-4)/2}{\hat{e}(c)} = \frac{n-4}{2\hat{e}(c)(\hat{e}(c) - 1)}. \tag{9.20}$$

This expression is larger than c if n is large enough, which implies that both i and x benefit from a deviation that creates a link between them and keeps all other links. $\square$

Lemma 9.3. *There can be at most one cycle in an SBE network.*

Proof. Suppose g is a nonempty SBE network and there are two or more cycles in it. Since g is connected it follows that there are two possibilities: (i) cycles have players in common and (ii) the cycles have no players in common.

(i) Cycles have players in common. Let $\chi_1 = (i_1, i_2, \ldots, i_n)$ be an ordering of the players in one cycle, and let $\chi_2 = (j_1, j_2, \ldots, j_m)$ be an ordering in the other cycle. The ordering reflects the links, neighboring players in the cycle in g are represented as adjacent players in the ordering. If there is a single common player i_1 in two cycles, then it is easy to see that the partners of, say, $i_1, i_2 \in \chi_1$ and $j_2 \in \chi_2$, have a strict incentive to delete their links with i_1 and instead form a link with each other. Consider next the case in which two or more players are common. Let $(i_{x_1}, i_{x_2}, \ldots, i_{x_k})$ be the players in common. We focus on the case where $k \geq 3$; the case of $k = 2$ is simple and omitted. There exist players i_y, j_z such that $i_y \in \chi_1$ but $i_y \notin \chi_2$, and $j_z \in \chi_2$ but $j_z \notin \chi_1$: and $g_{i_y, i_{x_1}} = g_{i_{x_1}, j_z} = g_{i_{x_1}, i_{x_2}} = \cdots = g_{i_{x_{k-1}}, i_{x_k}} = 1$. Note also that like player i_{x_1}, i_{x_k} must again have links with players who belong to one of χ_1 and χ_2 only. It then follows that $i_{x_{k-1}}$ and j_z have a (weak) incentive to delete their current link with i_{x_k} and i_{x_1}, respectively, and instead form a link with each other. It then follows that g cannot be sustained in a strict bilateral equilibrium.[37]

(ii) Cycles have no common players. Since g is a nonempty SBE network, by hypothesis, it follows from lemma 9.1 that it is connected and so there exists a path between the two cycles χ_1 and χ_2. Let $(i_1, i_2, \ldots, i_k)$ be players on this path with $i_1 \in \chi_1$ while $i_k \in \chi_2$. Suppose $g_{i_1, i_x} = 1$ and $g_{i_k, j_y} = 1$, where $i_x \in \chi_1$ and $j_y \in \chi_2$. Now it is easy to use a variant of the earlier argument for case (i) above to show that players i_x and j_y have a strict incentive to delete their link with i_1 and i_k and instead form a link with each other. The proof is complete. $\square$

Lemma 9.4. *A cycle containing all players cannot be sustained in a BE for $n \geq 4$.*[38]

Proof. Suppose g is a cycle and consider two players i and j who are furthest apart in terms of geodesic distance in the cycle. Now consider the deviation in which each of the players deletes one link and they form a link with each other in such a way that they create a line. Assume, for simplicity, that n is even, so that there are $(n - 2)/2$ players to one side of player i and $(n - 2)/2$ players to the other side of player j in the line created. We show that players i and j can strictly increase their payoff with this coordinated deviation.

The argument proceeds in two steps. The first step is to show that individual payoffs are strictly increasing for players closer to the center of the line. Number the players on a line as $1, 2, \ldots, n$. The access returns to player l are

$$\frac{1}{l} + \frac{1}{l-1} + \cdots + \frac{1}{2} + \frac{1}{2} + \cdots + \frac{1}{n-l+1}, \tag{9.21}$$

while the access returns to player $l + 1$ are

$$\frac{1}{l+1} + \frac{1}{l} + \cdots + \frac{1}{2} + \frac{1}{2} + \cdots + \frac{1}{n-l}. \tag{9.22}$$

It now follows that the access returns for player $l + 1$ are larger than access returns for player l if $l < n/2$.

---

[37] This is the only point in the proof of theorem 9.5 where the requirement of strictness is used. Note that even here strictness can be dispensed with if three-player deviations are considered, since in the above deviation player i_{x_k} benefits strictly as she has to support one fewer link.

[38] For $n = 3$ a complete network (which is also a cycle) can be sustained in equilibrium if $c < \frac{1}{6}$.

The essentialness payoff to player l can be written as follows:

$$\sum_{i=1}^{l-1}\sum_{j=l+2}^{n}\frac{1}{e(i,j;g)+2}+\sum_{i=1}^{l-1}\frac{1}{e(i,l+1;g)+2}. \tag{9.23}$$

Similarly, the essentialness payoffs to player $l+1$ can be written as

$$\sum_{i=1}^{l-1}\sum_{j=l+2}^{n}\frac{1}{e(i,j;g)+2}+\sum_{j=l+2}^{n}\frac{1}{e(l,j;g)+2}. \tag{9.24}$$

The first part of the essentialness payoffs to the two players is equal, while the second part of the payoffs is greater for player $l+1$ if $l < n/2$.

Let g^{cycle} and g^{line} denote the cycle and line network prevailing before the deviation and after it, respectively (with i and j at the center of the line). Note that the aggregate (gross) payoffs obtained in both cases are the same. The above argument implies that i and j enjoy a greater share of total gross value in the line than the other players. This implies that players i and j earn a higher gross payoff in the line. Since their linking cost is the same in both cases (i.e., $2c$), it follows that they obtain higher net payoffs as well, which completes the proof.   □

A hybrid star-cycle network contains a cycle with x players while the remaining $y = n - x$ players are directly linked to a single player in the cycle.

Lemma 9.5. *A BE network with a cycle has the hybrid star-cycle architecture for large enough n.*

Proof. We first show that, for $c > \frac{1}{6}$, there is an $x(c)$ such that $x \leqslant x(c)$ in a BE. Given lemma 9.4, clearly $y \geqslant 1$. Suppose $g_{ij} = 1$ for some $i \in X$ and $j \in Y$, where X and Y denote the players in the cycle and the set of players outside the cycle, respectively. Clearly, player $k \in X$, with $g_{ik} = 1$, strictly prefers to switch link from i to j. This reduces the essentialness payoffs she has to pay out to i and keeps her costs constant. On the other hand, j benefits from such an adjustment if $(x - 1)/6 > c$. So given c, in order for the cycle to be stable, $x \leqslant x(c) \equiv 6c + 1$.

Next, arguments from lemma 9.2 can be used to show that there is at most one player $i \in X$ who has links with players outside the cycle. Similarly, a variation of the argument of lemma 9.2 can be used to establish that, for any two nodes in Y, u, and v, the number of essential players $e(u, v; g) \leqslant 1$. This still leaves open the possibility that there is a path with two or more players leading away from $i \in X$, with the following feature: there is a central node i_c that is not part of the cycle (but has a link to a node in the cycle). But, in that case, the node i_c and any of the neighbors of i in the cycle k (say) strictly profit from establishing a direct link, for large enough n.   □

Lemma 9.6. *The star is the unique hybrid star-cycle BE for large n.*

Proof. We first observe that $x \geqslant 4$ in a BE network if $c > \frac{1}{6}$. As argued in lemma 9.5, $x \leqslant x(c)$ for a function $x(c)$ which is independent of n. Thus, fixing some c, consider the class of hybrid networks g in which $x \leqslant x(c)$. Let $i \in X$ be the player at the center of the star and suppose that $j, k \in X$, with $g_{ij} = g_{ik} = 1$. Next it is shown that j and k have a strict incentive to form a link if the number of peripheral players $y \geqslant n - x(c)$ is sufficiently large. The payoffs to players j and k in the hybrid network g are

$$\Pi_j(g) = \Pi_k(g) = \frac{y}{3} + \frac{x-1}{2} - 2c. \tag{9.25}$$

Now consider a deviation by players j and k in which player k deletes his link with player i and player j deletes his link with player m in the cycle and instead players j and k form a link with each other. The resulting network is a minimal network g' in which there are y "peripheral" players linked to i, and a line starting with player i which consists of x players. The payoffs to player j in g' are

$$\Pi_j(g') = \frac{y}{3} + \frac{1}{2} + \sum_{k=2}^{x-1} \frac{1}{k} + y \sum_{k=4}^{x+1} \frac{1}{k} + \sum_{k=3}^{x} \frac{1}{k} - 2c. \tag{9.26}$$

These payoffs are bounded below by

$$\frac{y}{3} + y\frac{x-2}{x+1} - 2c = M. \tag{9.27}$$

Next note that $M > y/3 + (x-1)/2 - 2c$ if

$$y > \frac{x-1}{2}\frac{x+1}{x-2}. \tag{9.28}$$

Since $x \geqslant 4$, the right-hand side is increasing in x and bounded above by $[x(c) - 1][x(c) + 1]/2[x(c) - 2]$. The final step is to note that $y = n - x \geqslant n - x(c)$ and so (9.28) applies for sufficiently large n. Thus player j has a strict incentive to switch links to player k for large n. Consider next the incentives of player k. The payoffs to player k in g' are

$$\Pi_k(g') = \frac{y}{4} + \frac{1}{3} + \frac{1}{2} + \sum_{k=2}^{x-2} \frac{1}{k} + y \sum_{k=5}^{x+1} \frac{1}{k} + \sum_{k=4}^{x} \frac{1}{k} - 2c. \tag{9.29}$$

These payoffs are bounded below by

$$\frac{y}{4} + y\frac{x-3}{x+1} - 2c = M'. \tag{9.30}$$

Note that $M' > y/3 + (x-1)/2 - 2c$ if

$$y > \frac{6(x-1)(x+1)}{11x - 37}. \tag{9.31}$$

Since $x \geqslant 4$, the right-hand side is positive and increasing in x and so is bounded above by $6[x(c) - 1][x(c) + 1]/[11x(c) - 37]$. Note that $y = n - x \geqslant n - x(c)$ is larger than this term for sufficiently large n. Thus player k has a strict incentive to switch links to player j for sufficiently large n.

The proof of the theorem follows by combining lemmas 9.1–9.6.   □

9.6.3 Coauthorship

The payoffs to player i in network g are

$$
\Pi_i(g) = \sum_{j \in N_i(g)} \left[\frac{1}{\eta_i(g)} + \frac{1}{\eta_j(g)} + \frac{1}{\eta_i(g)\eta_j(g)} \right]
$$

$$
= 1 + \left(1 + \frac{1}{\eta_i(g)} \right) \sum_{j \in N_i(g)} \frac{1}{\eta_j(g)} \tag{9.32}
$$

for $\eta_i(g) > 0$, while $\Pi_i(g) = 0$ for $\eta_i(g) = 0$. The following result is due to Jackson and Wolinsky (1996).

Proposition 9.7. *Suppose payoffs are given by (9.32) and that n is an even number. An efficient network consists of $n/2$ separate pairs. Any pairwise stable network can be partitioned into complete components of unequal size. In particular, if m is the size of a component and m' is the size of the next larger component, then $m' > m^2$.*

Proof. First consider efficiency. Note that, for any network g, the total payoffs

$$
\sum_{i \in N} \Pi_i(g) = \sum_{i:\eta_i(g) > 0} \sum_{j \in N_i(g)} \left[\frac{1}{\eta_i(g)} + \frac{1}{\eta_j(g)} + \frac{1}{\eta_i(g)\eta_j(g)} \right]. \tag{9.33}
$$

So it follows that

$$
\sum_{i \in N} \Pi_i(g) \leqslant 2n + \sum_{i:\eta_i(g) > 0} \sum_{j \in N_i(g)} \frac{1}{\eta_i(g)\eta_j(g)}, \quad \forall g \in \mathcal{G}. \tag{9.34}
$$

Note that equality only holds if $\eta_i(g) > 0$ for all players $i \in N$. Next note that

$$
\sum_{i:\eta_i(g) > 0} \sum_{j \in N_i(g)} \frac{1}{\eta_i(g)\eta_j(g)} \leqslant n \tag{9.35}
$$

with equality holding only if $\eta_i(g) = 1$ for all $i \in N$. The argument is completed by noting that a network with $n/2$ pairs exactly attains aggregate payoffs $3n$.

Next consider pairwise stable networks. Suppose that in network g two players i and j are not linked. Player i will strictly want to link with player j only if $\Pi_i(g + g_{ij}) > \Pi_i(g)$, i.e.,

$$
\frac{1}{\eta_j(g) + 1} \left(1 + \frac{1}{\eta_i(g) + 1} \right) > \left[\frac{1}{\eta_i(g)} - \frac{1}{\eta_i(g) + 1} \right] \sum_{k:k \neq j, g_{ik} = 1} \frac{1}{\eta_k(g)},
$$

$$
\tag{9.36}
$$

which simplifies to

$$\frac{\eta_i(g) + 2}{\eta_j(g) + 1} > \frac{1}{\eta_i(g)} \sum_{k:k \neq j, g_{ik}=1} \frac{1}{\eta_k(g)}. \qquad (9.37)$$

This inequality can be used to establish two properties of a pairwise stable network g.

(i) If $\eta_i(g) = \eta_j(g)$, then $g_{ij} = 1$. Note that if $\eta_j(g) \leq \eta_i(g)$, then $(\eta_i(g) + 2)/(\eta_j(g) + 1) > 1$. On the other hand,

$$\frac{1}{\eta_i(g)} \sum_{k:k \neq j, g_{ik}=1} \frac{1}{\eta_k(g)} \leq 1,$$

since it is the average of $\eta_i(g)$ fractions. Therefore, if $\eta_i(g) = \eta_j(g)$, then i and j would strictly like to form a link.

(ii) If $\eta_h(g) \leq \max\{\eta_k(g) \mid k \in N_i(g)\}$, then i wants to link with h. Let j be the maximally connected partner of i in g. First consider the case $\eta_i(g) \geq \eta_j(g) - 1$. Clearly, then $(\eta_i(g) + 2)/(\eta_h(g) + 1) \geq \eta_i(g) + 2/(\eta_j(g) + 1) \geq 1$. If the inequality is strict, then it follows from (9.37) that player i has a strict incentive to link with h. If there is an equality, then $\eta_h(g) \geq 2$, which implies that $\eta_j(g) \geq 2$. However, this implies that the right-hand side of (9.37) is strictly less than 1. Second consider the case $\eta_i(g) < \eta_j(g) - 1$. Then $(\eta_i(g) + 1)/\eta_j(g) < (\eta_i(g) + 2)/(\eta_j(g) + 1) < (\eta_i(g) + 2)/(\eta_h(g) + 1)$. Since $g_{ij} = 1$, it follows from (9.37) that

$$\frac{\eta_i(g) + 1}{\eta_j(g)} \geq \frac{1}{\eta_i(g) - 1} \sum_{k:k \neq j, g_{ik}=1} \frac{1}{\eta_k(g)}. \qquad (9.38)$$

Moreover,

$$\frac{1}{\eta_i(g) - 1} \sum_{k:k \neq j, g_{ik}=1} \frac{1}{\eta_k(g)} \geq \frac{1}{\eta_i(g)} \sum_{k:g_{ik}=1} \frac{1}{\eta_k(g)} \qquad (9.39)$$

due to the fact that the extra term on the right-hand side, $1/\eta_j(g)$, is smaller than (or equal to) all terms in the sum. Thus

$$\frac{\eta_i(g) + 2}{\eta_h(g) + 1} > \frac{1}{\eta_i(g)} \sum_{k:k \neq j, g_{ik}=1} \frac{1}{\eta_k(g)} \qquad (9.40)$$

and the claim is proved.

Now observe that claims (i) and (ii) together imply that if g is pairwise stable, then all players with maximal links must be connected to each other and to no one else. The mutual connection feature follows from claim (i), while the exclusivity feature follows from claim (ii): to see this suppose a maximally connected player

i is linked to player j who is not maximally connected. Since $\eta_i(g) > \eta_j(g)$ it follows that there is a player k such that $g_{ik} = 1$ but $g_{jk} = 0$. However, since $\eta_j(g) < \eta_i(g)$ and $\eta_k(g) \leq \eta_i(g)$ it follows from claim (ii) that players j and k have a strict incentive to form a link, contradicting the claim that g is pairwise stable. Similar considerations can be used to show that players with maximal number minus 1 links will only connect to each other and no one else. Observe that this implies that the players with a certain number of links must constitute a complete component.

Finally, consider the relative size of the different components. Observe from claim 1 that players in a larger component want to link with players in smaller components. For a player i in a smaller component not to want to link with player j in a larger component it must be the case that $(\eta_i(g)+2)/(\eta_j(g)+1) \leq 1/\eta_i(g)$ (where the right-hand side follows from noting that all members of i's component have exactly $\eta_i(g)$ links). It then follows that $\eta_j(g)+1 \geq \eta_i(g)(\eta_i(g)+2)$, which yields the required inequality. (Observe that $\eta_i(g) \geq 1$ in any pairwise stable network, since there cannot be an isolated player in a pairwise stable network, given the assumption that $\Pi_i(g) = 0$ if $\eta_i(g) = 0$.) $\square$

9.6.4 Free Trade Agreement Networks

We write the welfare of country i in network g as

$$\Pi_i(g) = \frac{1}{2}\left[\frac{(\alpha - \gamma)(\eta_i(g) + 1)}{\eta_i(g) + 2}\right]^2 + \sum_{j \in N_i(g)\cup\{i\}}\left[\frac{\alpha - \gamma}{\eta_j(g) + 2}\right]^2. \qquad (9.41)$$

Proposition 9.8. *Suppose payoffs are given by (9.41). A pairwise stable network is either a complete network or consists of two components, one completely connected group of $n - 1$ countries and a single isolated country. The complete network is the only efficient network.*

Proof. Consider a network g in which $g_{ij} = 0$. Note that a free trade agreement (FTA) between i and j leaves all other markets unaffected and raises the number of active firms in markets of countries i and j by one each. Therefore,

$$\Pi_i(g + g_{ij}) - \Pi_i(g)$$
$$= \frac{1}{2}\left[\frac{(\alpha - \gamma)(\eta_i(g) + 2)}{\eta_i(g) + 3}\right]^2 - \frac{1}{2}\left[\frac{(\alpha - \gamma)(\eta_i(g) + 1)}{\eta_i(g) + 2}\right]^2$$
$$+ \left[\frac{\alpha - \gamma}{\eta_i(g) + 3}\right]^2 - \left[\frac{\alpha - \gamma}{\eta_i(g) + 2}\right]^2 + \left[\frac{\alpha - \gamma}{\eta_j(g) + 3}\right]^2. \qquad (9.42)$$

Rearranging the above expression tells us that $\Pi_i(g + g_{ij}) \geq \Pi_i(g)$ if and only if

$$2[\eta_i(g) + 1]^2 - 5 + \frac{2(\eta_i(g) + 3)^2(\eta_i(g) + 2)^2}{(\eta_j(g) + 3)^2} \geq 0. \qquad (9.43)$$

It is easily seen that this inequality is satisfied if $\eta_i(g) \geq 1$, i.e., if there are two or more active firms in the market. Thus, if country i is involved in one or more FTAs, then it has an incentive to forge an additional FTA with j. This implies that, in any network g, if i and j have one or more bilateral trade agreements, then pairwise stability requires that they have an agreement with each other as well. This means that any component in a stable trading network must be complete. Further, in any pairwise stable network, there can be at most one nonsingleton component. Thus, if there are two or more components in a stable network, then all but one of them will be singletons.

We next show that two countries in autarky have an incentive to form a trade agreement. Suppose that a network g is such that i and j are in singleton components. Then, the welfare of these countries is identical and is

$$\Pi_i(g) = \frac{1}{2}\left[\frac{(\alpha - \gamma)}{2}\right]^2 + \left[\frac{(\alpha - \gamma)}{2}\right]^2. \tag{9.44}$$

If i and j establish an FTA, then the welfare of i (and j, by symmetry) is

$$\Pi_i(g + g_{ij}) = \frac{1}{2}\left[\frac{2(\alpha - \gamma)}{3}\right]^2 + 2\left[\frac{(\alpha - \gamma)}{3}\right]^2. \tag{9.45}$$

It is easily verified that $\Pi_i(g + g_{ij}) > \Pi_i(g)$. Thus two singleton components are not sustainable in a stable trading network.

This leaves only candidates for pairwise stable FTA networks: the complete network and the network with a complete component with $n - 1$ countries and an isolated country.

Consider next the set of efficient networks. World welfare is

$$W(g) = \sum_{i \in N} \Pi_i(g).$$

Using (9.41) this can be expanded and written as

$$W(g) = \sum_{i \in N} \frac{1}{2}\left[\frac{(\alpha - \gamma)(\eta_i(g) + 1)}{\eta_i(g) + 2}\right]^2 + \sum_{i \in N} \sum_{j \in N_i(g) \cup \{i\}} \left[\frac{\alpha - \gamma}{\eta_j(g) + 2}\right]^2. \tag{9.46}$$

World welfare is thus the sum of the consumer surplus in each country plus the producer surplus of every firm in the world. It is convenient to express the latter term a little differently in terms of the sum of producer surpluses generated in each of the different markets. Thus world welfare is

$$W(g) = \sum_{i \in N} \frac{1}{2}\left[\frac{(\alpha - \gamma)(\eta_i(g) + 1)}{\eta_i(g) + 2}\right]^2 + \sum_{i \in N} [\eta_i(g) + 1]\left[\frac{\alpha - \gamma}{\eta_i(g) + 2}\right]^2. \tag{9.47}$$

In the complete network, the welfare of every country is the same and is

$$\frac{1}{2}\left[\frac{(\alpha - \gamma)n}{n + 1}\right]^2 + n\left[\frac{\alpha - \gamma}{n + 1}\right]^2. \tag{9.48}$$

By comparison, in an arbitrary network g, the welfare generated in country i is

$$\Pi_i(g) = \frac{1}{2}\left[\frac{(\alpha - \gamma)(\eta_i(g) + 1)}{\eta_i(g) + 2}\right]^2 + [\eta_i(g) + 1]\left[\frac{\alpha - \gamma}{\eta_i(g) + 2}\right]^2. \qquad (9.49)$$

It is easily seen that (9.48) is larger than (9.49) for every i, so long as $\eta_i(g) < n-1$. Since the network g was arbitrary, the proof follows. □

9.6.5 Stability and Efficiency

Theorem 9.6. *If $n \geq 3$, then there is no allocation rule Y which is anonymous and component balanced such that for every value function V an efficient network is pairwise stable.*

Proof. The proof is by example. Suppose $n = 3$ and consider the following component additive and anonymous V: $V(g^c) = 1$, $V(g^e) = 0$, $V(g) = 1$ for networks g with one link, and $V(g) = 1 + \epsilon$ for networks g with two links. The efficient network has two links. Anonymity and component balance of the allocation function Y imply that each player in the complete network gets $\frac{1}{3}$, and that the linked players in a network with one link get $\frac{1}{2}$ each while the isolated player gets 0. Pairwise stability of an efficient network $g_{ij} + g_{jk}$ requires that $Y_j(g_{ij} + g_{jk}, V) \geq \frac{1}{2}$, since $Y_j(g_{ij}, V) = \frac{1}{2}$. This together with component balance and anonymity implies that each of the two single link players in a two-link network, $g_{ij} + g_{jk}$ can earn at most $\frac{1}{4} + \frac{1}{2}\epsilon$. However, $\frac{1}{4} + \frac{1}{2}\epsilon < \frac{1}{3}$ for small ϵ, and so the two peripheral players have a strict incentive to form a link and deviate to the complete network, g^c. □

Recall the definition of critical link monotonicity. A link g_{ij} is critical in network g if its deletion leads to a strict increase in the number of components. The pair (g, V) satisfies critical link monotonicity if, for any critical link in g and its associated components C, C_1, and C_2, it is true that $v(C) \geq v(C_1) + v(C_2)$ implies that $v(C)/|C| \geq \max[v(C_1)/|C_1|, v(C_2)/|C_2|]$.

Theorem 9.7. *Consider a component additive V and let g be an efficient network. Then g is pairwise stable under allocation rule $\bar{Y}$ if and only if (g, V) satisfies critical link monotonicity.*

Proof. Suppose that g is efficient given V, and is also pairwise stable given $\bar{Y}$. Since g is efficient for any critical link and associated components C, C_1, and C_2, $v(C) \geq v(C_1) + v(C_2)$. Pairwise stability implies that for any critical link $g_{ij} = 1$, it must be the case that players i and j both gain from the link. Given the allocation function $\bar{Y}$ this implies that $Y_i(g) = v(C)/|C| \geq v(C_1)/|C_1|$ and that $Y_j(g) = v(C)/|C| \geq v(C_2)/|C_2|$. The "only if" part follows.

Consider next the "if" part. Suppose g is efficient under V and the critical link monotonicity condition is satisfied. Adding or deleting a noncritical link will not increase the value generated by a (nonsingleton) component. Since g is efficient and V is component additive, the value of this component is already maximal. So such a change cannot lead to a gain to any player in the component under $\bar{Y}$.

Next consider the addition or deletion of a critical link. Deleting a critical link does not lead to benefits for a player since efficiency and component additivity imply that $v(C) \geqslant v(C_1) + v(C_2)$, and, from the critical link monotonicity property, this implies that $v(C)/|C| \geqslant \max[v(C_1)/|C_1|, v(C_2)/|C_2|]$. By efficiency and component additivity, adding a critical link implies that $v(C) \leqslant v(C_1) + V(C_2)$ (where C_1 and C_2 are existing components and C is the new resulting component). Suppose that g is not pairwise stable; then one of the players i or j must gain strictly from the added link. Without loss of generality, say, $v(C)/|C| > v(C_1)/|C_1|$ and that $v(C)/|C| \geqslant v(C_2)/|C_2|$. Then it follows that $[v(C)/|C|] \times [|C_1|/|C|] > [v(C_1)/|C_1|] \times [|C_1|/|C|]$ and that $[v(C)/|C|] \times [|C_2|/|C|] \geqslant [v(C_2)/|C_2|] \times [|C_2|/|C|]$. Adding these two inequalities yields $v(C) > v(C_1) + v(C_2)$, which contradicts the efficiency of g. $\qquad\square$

9.6.6 Unequal Degrees and Payoffs

Recall that in a playing-the-field game the payoffs to a player i are

$$\Pi_i(g(s_i, s_{-i})) = \Phi(\eta_i(g), L(g_{-i})) - c\eta_i(g). \qquad (9.50)$$

Proposition 9.9. *Suppose the payoffs to each player are given by (9.50) and satisfy convexity in own links. A pairwise equilibrium network is empty, complete, or has the dominant group architecture.*

Proof. Convexity in own links has the following implication: *for any two players* $i, j \in N$ *if* $\eta_i(g), \eta_j(g) \geqslant 1$, *then* $g_{ij} = 1$. Suppose not and let $g_{ij} = 0$. By the definition of pairwise equilibrium:

$$\left.\begin{array}{l} \Pi_i(g) - \Pi_i(g - g_{ik}) = \Phi(\eta_i(g), L(g_{-i})) - \Phi(\eta_i(g) - 1, L(g_{-i})) \geqslant c, \\[4pt] \Pi_j(g) - \Pi_j(g - g_{jl}) = \Phi(\eta_j(g), L(g_{-j})) - \Phi(\eta_j(g) - 1, L(g_{-j})) \geqslant c. \end{array}\right\} \tag{9.51}$$

Since each player's marginal payoffs are strictly increasing in own links it is true that, for player i,

$$\begin{aligned} \Phi(\eta_i(g) + 1, L(g_{-i})) &- \Phi(\eta_i(g), L(g_{-i})) \\ &> \Phi(\eta_i(g), L(g_{-i})) - \Phi(\eta_i(g) - 1, L(g_{-i})) \\ &\geqslant c. \end{aligned} \tag{9.52}$$

Similarly, for player j,

$$\begin{aligned} \Phi(\eta_j(g) + 1, L(g_{-j})) &- \Phi(\eta_j(g), L(g_{-j})) \\ &> \Phi(\eta_j(g), L(g_{-j})) - \Phi(\eta_j(g) - 1, L(g_{-j})) \\ &\geqslant c. \end{aligned} \tag{9.53}$$

This implies that players i and j have a strict incentive to form a link and, therefore, g is not a pairwise equilibrium. This transitivity property implies that any component must be complete and that there can be at most one nonsingleton component in a pairwise equilibrium network.   □

Proposition 9.10. *Suppose payoffs are given by (9.50) and satisfy concavity in own links and the strategic complements property. A regular pairwise equilibrium network always exists. In an irregular pairwise network all nonmaximal degree players are mutually linked.*

Proof. Consider a regular network of degree k, g^k, $0 \leqslant k \leqslant n-1$. For any given cost $c > 0$ of forming links, there are two possibilities.

(i) $\Phi(k, k(n-2)) - \Phi(k-1, k(n-2)) \leqslant c, \forall k \in \{1, 2, \ldots, n-1\}$. In this case the empty network is a pairwise equilibrium network.

(ii) $\Phi(k', k'(n-2)) - \Phi(k'-1, k'(n-2)) > c$ for some $k' \in \{1, 2, \ldots, n-1\}$. No player in $g^{k'}$ has an incentive to delete the last link. Now consider the incentives of players to form links. If there is no improving path from this network, then $g^{k'}$ is a pairwise equilibrium network and the argument is complete. If not then a pair of players has an incentive to form a link. Since strategic complements holds it follows that every other pair of players also has an incentive to form links. The argument proceeds by getting distinct players at each stage to form links in a manner so that no player has more than $k' + 1$ links. Thus there exists an improvement path until $g^{k'+1}$. If $\Phi(k'+2, (k'+1)(n-2)) - \Phi(k'+1, (k'+1)(n-2)) < c$, then the degree $k' + 1$ regular network is a pairwise equilibrium network and the argument is done. Otherwise, proceed further by adding links; since there are only a finite number of degrees possible, the improvement path has to converge. The limit network is a regular pairwise equilibrium network.

Finally, consider irregular networks. We show that in any pairwise equilibrium network g if $i, j \notin N_m(g)$, the set of maximally linked players, then $g_{ij} = 1$. Take some player $k \in N_m(g)$. It follows from the hypothesis of pairwise equilibrium that $\Phi(\eta_k(g), L(g_{-k})) - \Phi(\eta_k(g) - 1, L(g_{-k})) \geqslant c$. Suppose $i, j \notin N_m(g)$, and $g_{ij} = 0$. Since $\eta_i(g) < \eta_k(g)$, it follows that $L(g_{-i}) > L(g_{-k})$. Hence, it follows that

$$\Phi(\eta_i(g) + 1, L(g_{-i})) - \Phi(\eta_i(g), L(g_{-i}))$$
$$> \Phi(\eta_i(g) + 1, L(g_{-k})) - \Phi(\eta_i(g), L(g_{-k}))$$
$$\geqslant \Phi(\eta_k(g), L(g_{-k})) - \Phi(\eta_k(g) - 1, L(g_{-k}))$$
$$\geqslant c. \tag{9.54}$$

The first inequality follows from strategic complements, while the second inequality follows from noting that $\eta_k(g) > \eta_i(g)$ and applying concavity in own links. The final inequality follows from the hypothesis that g is a pairwise equilibrium network. Similar reasoning establishes that $\Phi(\eta_j(g) + 1, L(g_{-j})) - \Phi(\eta_j(g), L(g_{-j})) > c$. Hence, i and j have a strict incentive to form a link, contradicting our hypothesis that g is a pairwise equilibrium network.   □

Proposition 9.11. *Suppose payoffs to every player are given by (9.50) and satisfy concavity in own links and the strategic substitutes property. If*

$$\Phi(k+1, k(n-2)) - \Phi(k, k(n-2)) < c < \Phi(k, k(n-2)) - \Phi(k-1, k(n-2))$$

for some $k \in \{1, 2, 3, \ldots, n-2\}$, then a regular pairwise equilibrium network with degree k exists. If

$$\Phi(2, 2(n-2)) - \Phi(1, 2(n-2))$$
$$< c < \min\{\Phi(n-1, 0) - \Phi(n-2, 0), \Phi(1, 2(n-2)) - \Phi(0, 2(n-2))\},$$

then a star network is a pairwise equilibrium.

Proof. Consider a regular network with degree k. The marginal (gross) payoff from a link is $\Phi(k+1, k(n-2)) - \Phi(k, k(n-2))$. This expression is decreasing in k under concavity in own links. Therefore, there are three possible cases.

(i) $\Phi(1, 0) - \Phi(0, 0) < c$. The empty network is a pairwise equilibrium network in this case.

(ii) $\Phi(k+1, k(n-2)) - \Phi(k, k(n-2)) < c < \Phi(k, k(n-2)) - \Phi(k-1, k(n-2))$ for $k \in \{1, 2, 3, \ldots, n-2\}$. Proceed "upward" from a degree $k-1$ regular network by forming links between distinct pairs of players in sequence such that no player has more than k links along the way. If $\Phi(k, k(n-2)) - \Phi(k-1, k(n-2)) > c$, then proceed until the regular network with degree k is formed, which is a pairwise equilibrium network under (ii).

(iii) $c < \Phi(n-1, (n-2)(n-2)) - \Phi(n-2, (n-2)(n-2))$. In this case, repeat the argument of case (ii). If $\Phi(n-1, (n-1)(n-2)) - \Phi(n-2, (n-1)(n-2)) < c$, then no regular pairwise equilibrium network exists, while if $\Phi(n-1, (n-1)(n-2)) - \Phi(n-2, (n-1)(n-2)) > c$, then the complete network is pairwise equilibrium.

The inequalities in the last statement of proposition 9.11 can be verified directly.   □

10

Research Collaboration among Firms

10.1 Introduction

Research collaboration among firms takes a variety of forms, such as joint ventures, technology sharing, cross licensing, and joint R&D. In recent years, joint R&D has become especially prominent.[1] Moreover, a general feature of research collaboration is that firms enter into different projects with nonoverlapping sets of partners. Thus it is natural to represent collaboration relations as a network. Empirical work shows that the networks of collaboration links exhibit several striking features: the average degree is relatively small (compared with the total number of firms), the degrees are unequally distributed, the architectures resemble a core–periphery network, and the average distance between firms is relatively small.[2]

These empirical findings motivate an enquiry into the economic origins and the implications of interfirm research collaboration networks. In particular, we will examine the following three questions.

(i) Why do firms enter into extensive and nonexclusive relations?

(ii) What are the sources of the core–periphery network structure?

(iii) What are the effects of interfirm ties on firm profits and market outcomes?

A simple model of network formation is developed by using the following ideas. Firms compete in a market, and having lower costs is advantageous, as it leads to larger market share and profits. Collaboration between firms is a way to share knowledge and skills and this lowers costs of production. Thus a collaboration between two firms makes them relatively more competitive vis-à-vis other firms.[3]

---

[1] For a survey of these developments, see Hagedoorn (2002). These empirical trends are discussed in section 10.5. In this chapter the focus will be on research ties between firms. Firms also form ties with each other with a view to trading production inputs and intermediate goods. The analysis of buyer–seller networks raises a number of conceptual questions and is an important subject of ongoing research; for a pioneering theoretical study of such networks, see Kranton and Minehart (2000, 2001).

[2] See figure 10.6 for an illustration of the network of collaboration among firms in the pharmaceutical and the biotechnology sectors. These network features are discussed in section 10.5.

[3] This idea is also echoed in the literature on business strategy. Harrigan (1988), Porter and Fuller (1986), and Contractor and Lorange (1988) discuss the role of alliances as an aspect of a competitive strategy. For a popular introduction to this subject, see Brandenberger and Nalebuff (1996).

On the other hand, collaboration with other firms involves resources and is costly. So a firm compares the costs and returns from collaboration when deciding on how many links to form. At the heart of the analysis is the issue of how a collaboration link between two firms alters the incentives of other firms to form collaboration links.

These externalities arise from the disadvantages that a firm suffers in competing with firms which have lower costs. The economic effects of cost differentials depend on the nature of market competition. Thus an important point we want to bring out is the two-way flow of influence between markets and networks: the nature of market competition shapes the incentives for collaboration. However, the pattern of collaboration among firms determines the cost structure in an industry and this in turn shapes the nature of market competition.

The presentation in this chapter uses the classical Cournot model of quantity competition as a way to formalize market competition. The key insight here is that the marginal returns from an additional link to a firm are increasing in its own links and they are decreasing in the links of other firms. In a context where the cost of a new link is either constant or only increasing slowly it then follows that an equilibrium network has the dominant group architecture: there is a group of fully linked firms and the rest of the firms are isolated.[4] We also show that firms with more degrees have a higher market share and earn higher profits than isolated firms.

We then examine the structure of the network more closely. A dominant group network is quite different from the core–periphery structures observed in empirical work. This motivates a closer examination of the incentives to form collaboration links. It was noted above that marginal returns to new links are increasing in the number of own links and decreasing in links of others. This suggests the following possibility: a network may be sustained by transfers from highly linked firms to poorly linked firms. This idea is explored by using a network formation model where transfers between firms are allowed.

The main finding is that transfers facilitate the emergence of the star network and variations on the star network such as interlinked stars. Figure 10.4 illustrates these networks. These networks are indeed sustained by the transfers from highly connected core firms to poorly connected peripheral firms. Moreover, these transfers allow the core firms to make larger profits than the peripheral firms.

These findings are obtained in a theoretical framework where firms know the structure of the network as well as the value of linking with other firms, and there is no problem in eliciting efforts from partner firms in a collaboration. These are strong assumptions, as, in actual practice, incomplete information and the attendant incentives problems are likely to be important factors. These considerations

---

[4] For a formal definition of such a network architecture, see chapter 2. Figure 10.1 illustrates such networks.

lead to a discussion of the types of contracts which may be appropriate[5] as well as the role of the existing network of links as a conduit for valuable information.[6]

The economic study of collaboration among firms has a distinguished history. This work starts from the premise that the research activity of a firm has technological spillovers on other firms. Since an individual firm does not take these spillovers into account, it will underestimate the social value of its own research and this could lead to an under-investment in research by firms. The literature has explored the role of cooperative research between firms as a way of internalizing these spillovers and thereby resolving this incentive problem; influential contributions in this line of work include d'Aspremont and Jacquemin (1988), Katz (1986), Kamien, Muller, and Zang (1992), Leahy and Neary (1997), and Suzumura (1992). Initially, the literature examined two "group" situations: either firms were on their own or all firms formed a single group for joint research. More recently, the formation of the group itself has been the object of study. This line of work uses a coalition framework to study formation of collaboration groups.[7] In this framework, a firm can be a member of only one group at a time. A distinctive element of the network formation approach is that firms can enter into several collaboration projects which involve different firms.[8] The coalition approach and the network approach lead to different predictions concerning collaboration relations as well as market outcomes. These differences are discussed in detail in section 10.4.2.

The rest of this chapter is organized as follows. Section 10.2 examines the reasons underlying the prevalence of extensive and nonexclusive links. Section 10.3 develops a formal model in which firms strategically choose collaboration links, with a view to examining the interplay between incentives for forming links and market competition. Section 10.4 discusses related themes in sociology, organization theory, business strategy, and economics. Section 10.5 presents a summary of empirical patterns in research collaboration among firms, while section 10.6 concludes. The proofs of all the results are presented in the appendix to the chapter.

10.2 Why Extensive and Nonexclusive Links?

A general feature of research collaboration networks is that firms have different projects with nonoverlapping set of partners. "Extensive" refers to the number of distinct collaboration arrangements, while "nonexclusive" refers to the idea that research collaboration ties between firms i and j do not preclude a tie between

---

[5] The issue of appropriate contracts is part of the study of corporate governance, and will be discussed in section 10.4.1.

[6] The role of social embeddedness of firms is taken up in section 10.4.

[7] For a survey of the literature on coalition formation, see Bloch (1997).

[8] For a general discussion on the relationship between coalitions and networks, see chapters 1 and 7.

firms j and k. The following examples from the automobile sector illustrate this pattern.

- Daimler-Chrysler AG has independently obtained a series of patents in the area of gear change transmissions for motor vehicles and, at the same time, has been engaged in collaborative research with BMW Group and Volkswagen AG on processes and systems aimed at reducing the emissions of internal combustion engines. The Toyota Motor Co. has patented a series of inventions developed in-house in the area of carburetors while it has been collaborating with the Daihatsu Motor Co. Ltd. in intake manifolds for multi-cylinder internal combustion engines, and with Aisin-Warner in the area of four-wheel-drive transmissions.

This section examines the reasons underlying this pattern of collaboration links.

Firms produce services and products which involve the use of different technologies and bodies of knowledge. The complexity of technology means that an individual firm is at the frontier of some but not all the aspects of its business. Research collaboration can be seen as a mechanism for firms to pool distinct skills and technology advantages. For firms producing goods that involve many different technologies, such as automobiles, there are many areas in which they can form potentially profitable collaboration partnerships. A similar argument applies to large diversified firms which produce a range of different products. The pressures to form collaboration links are greater in industries where new technologies have emerged; this is reflected in the large number of alliances between biotechnology and pharmaceutical firms that are discussed in section 10.5.

The drive to pool distinct skills to create value is influenced by a number of considerations. An important consideration is market competition among firms. Forming collaborative alliances alters the relative competitive positions of firms: for instance, if collaboration reduces the costs of production, then partnering firms may gain competitive advantage relative to the rest of the firms. Moreover, collaboration among firms i and j may have effects on the returns from partnering for other firms. Once a certain number of firms have formed collaboration links, it is possible that the returns to other firms from forming collaboration links may not cover the costs of forming such links. These considerations suggest that there is a natural and probably critical relationship between market competition and research collaboration among firms. The model in section 10.3 explores this relationship.

Three constraints on diversified research collaboration appear to be important. First, firms will have only incomplete information about the capabilities of other firms, which means that the potential gains from collaboration are uncertain. The uncertainties about capabilities of other firms may be mitigated by previous experience with these firms. More generally, information about a firm can be informally obtained from its former partners. Thus a firm can acquire important information about skills and capabilities of other firms through reliable indirect sources of knowledge, such as common partners. This means that the location of a firm in a collaboration network at a point in time may influence costs and (hence potential) benefits of collaboration compared with doing independent in-house research. This line of reasoning has been an important theme in the business strategy and organization theory literature and will be discussed in section 10.4.1.

A second consideration is the possibility of free riding. A collaboration partnership involves efforts by different firms which are privately costly. The returns to individual effort are shared among the partners and so private returns may be less than collective returns; this creates incentives for under-provision of effort. These incentive problems can be addressed to some extent by contractual agreements. However, the measurement of R&D efforts and outcomes is in many cases difficult and there remains significant scope for free riding. Repeated collaboration between firms is one possible mechanism for inducing higher effort.[9] In the present context, these considerations suggest that a firm may choose to continue partnering with its existing collaborators even if these firms are not the ideal partners for specific projects, as this increases the likelihood of "good" behavior from current partners in on-going projects. The role of repeated collaboration has been empirically explored in the strategy literature as well as in the sociology literature and will be discussed in section 10.4.1.

A third consideration is the potential spillover from one project to other projects of the firms: a collaboration between firms i and j may benefit firm j in a number of other projects, some of which are in-house while others may be in collaboration with other firms. These benefits may, in turn, give firm j, and its collaborating partners, competitive advantage vis-à-vis firm i. The possibility that the efforts of firm i may be used by other firms in ways that are detrimental to its own interests will reinforce the free-riding pressures mentioned in connection with the second consideration above, and may even discourage the firm from doing collaborative research altogether. In principle, these spillovers can be subject to specific contractual arrangements between firms i and j. However, in practice it is difficult to control and contract on such spillovers. See Baker, Gibbons, and Murphy (2004) for a discussion on corporate governance issues arising from spillover considerations.

10.3 Collaboration among Competing Firms

This section presents a model in which firms form collaboration links with other firms, with a view to improving their competitive position in the market.[10] A

---

[9] The prospect of future gains from joint projects acts as a carrot and may induce firms to exert high effort in the current collaboration project.

[10] This model was summarized as example 9.1. The presentation here develops the details of cost reduction via linking and is self-contained.

link between two firms lowers the costs of production of both the collaborating firms (but has no effect on the costs of other firms). Each collaboration link requires a fixed investment. A profile of collaboration links therefore induces a corresponding profile of costs for different firms in the industry. Given these costs, firms compete in a market by choosing quantities. The interest here is in understanding how market competition shapes the incentives of firms to form collaboration alliances and how these alliances in turn determine the competitive position of firms and therefore shape the market outcome. The presentation here is based on Goyal and Joshi (2003).[11]

There are two stages. In stage 1, n firms play a game of two-sided link formation. Every firm announces a set of firms $s_i = (s_{i1}, s_{i2}, \ldots, s_{in})$ with which it wishes to form links. The collection of links formed by the announcements defines an (undirected) network $g(s)$. Let $N_i(g)$ be the collaboration partners of firm i in network g, and define $\eta_i(g) = |N_i(g)|$.

We now elaborate on the nature of research collaboration. The basic idea is that collaboration links lower the costs of production. There are $K > n$ components in the product that firms produce and we will assume that all firms use the same k components. Let the cost for firm i of component k be given by $c_{i,k}$. The marginal cost of production for firm i is $c_i = \sum_{k=1}^{K} c_{i,k}$. The component-wise costs $c_{i,l}$ take on a value of c^H or c^L, with $c^H > c^L$. Assume that for each firm i there is one and only one $\hat{k}$ such that $c_{i,\hat{k}} = c^L$. Moreover, suppose that $c_{j,\hat{k}} = c^H$ for all other firms, $j \neq i$. Then it follows that if two firms form a collaboration link, they can both reduce their costs by $c^H - c^L$. Define $\gamma = c^H - c^L$. This is probably the simplest model of firms which have different capabilities but are *ex ante* similar in costs of production.

A network g therefore induces a marginal cost profile for the n firms, $c(g) = (c_1(g), c_2(g), \ldots, c_n(g))$. From the above discussion it follows that the marginal cost of firm i is a linear and declining function of the number of collaboration links with other firms:

$$c_i(g) = \gamma_0 - \gamma \eta_i(g), \quad i \in N, \tag{10.1}$$

where $\gamma_0 > 0$ is a positive parameter representing a firm's marginal cost when it has no links and $\gamma > 0$ is the cost reduction from a link. Thus in this formulation the cost reduction in each link is exogenously fixed.[12]

---

[11] In recent years, the theory of network formation among firms has been an active field of study and a number of themes have been studied. See Deroian (2006) for a study of spillovers across firms in interfirm networks, Billand and Bravard (2002) for a model in which firms can unilaterally form links, and Song and Vannetelbosch (2005) for a study of public policy interventions in shaping network formation.

[12] See chapter 3 for a model in which firms choose effort levels as a function of the network of alliances. In the present section, we have taken the cost reduction to be exogenous as the focus is on the network formation aspects of the process.

In stage 2, firms compete in the market by choosing quantities.[13] Suppose that firms face an inverse linear demand $P = \alpha - Q$, where P is the price and Q the total output produced by all the firms. Define $L(g_{-i}) = \sum_{j \in N} \eta_j(g) - 2\eta_i(g)$. For a network g, the Cournot equilibrium output of firm i can be written as[14]

$$q_i(g) = \frac{(\alpha - \gamma_0) + (n-1)\gamma\eta_i(g) - \gamma L(g_{-i})}{n+1}, \quad i \in N. \tag{10.2}$$

It can be checked that the Cournot profits for firm i in network g are $q_i^2(g)$.

Assume that every link involves a fixed cost $c > 0$. We can now write the net payoffs to firm i in network g as follows:

$$\Pi_i(g) = \left[\frac{(\alpha - \gamma_0) + (n-1)\gamma\eta_i(g) - \gamma L(g_{-i})}{n+1} \right]^2 - \eta_i(g)c. \tag{10.3}$$

We will analyze the architecture of pairwise equilibrium networks and payoff distributions.[15]

10.3.1 Strategic Alliances and Market Dominance

The incentives to form collaboration links are intimately related to the desire of firms to improve their competitive position in the market. We start with an observation about the effects of a collaboration link between firms i and j on the profits of other firms. From (10.3) it follows that a firm's quantity and therefore its profits are declining in the links of other firms. We turn next to the effects of other firms' collaboration links on a firm's marginal returns from an additional link. Given a network g, the marginal (gross) returns from an additional link g_{ij} are

$$\frac{(n-1)\gamma}{(n+1)^2}[\lambda(n) + 2(n-1)\gamma\eta_i(g) - 2\gamma L(g_{-i})], \tag{10.4}$$

where $\lambda(n) = 2(\alpha - \gamma_0) + (n-1)\gamma$. It is now easy to verify that the marginal (gross) returns from an additional link are increasing in the number of own links $\eta_i(g)$ and decreasing in the number of links of other firms $L(g_{-i})$. Recall that the total costs of links are linearly increasing in the number of links. Putting together these observations we can conclude that the game of collaboration links is a playing-the-field game in which payoffs satisfy convexity in own links and the strategic substitutes property (between own links and links of other firms). We can therefore apply proposition 9.4 and obtain the following result.

---

[13] The analysis of strategic collaboration formation when firms compete in prices can be carried out by using similar arguments. See Goyal and Joshi (2003) for an analysis of such a model. For an analysis of network formation among firms which are producing differentiated goods, see Deroian (2004).

[14] In order to ensure that each firm produces a strictly positive quantity in equilibrium, assume that $(\alpha - \gamma_0) - (n-1)(n-2)\gamma > 0$. See chapter 3 for computations which lead to equilibrium quantities in a model of Cournot competition.

[15] See chapter 7 for a definition of pairwise equilibrium networks.

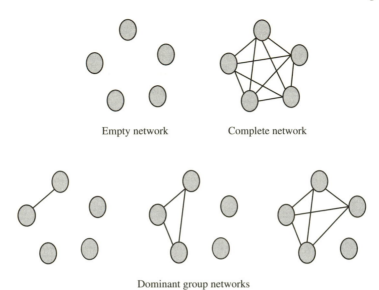

Empty network   Complete network

Dominant group networks

Figure 10.1.   Pairwise equilibrium networks $n = 6$.

Proposition 10.1. *Suppose that payoffs are given by (10.3). A pairwise equilibrium network is either empty, the dominant group network, or the complete network.*

Figure 10.1 illustrates the network architectures that can arise in pairwise equilibrium.

We now examine how the size of the nonsingleton component in the dominant group network varies with the cost of forming links. Let g^k refer to a dominant group network in which the dominant group has k firms. The size of the dominant group is determined by the incentive constraints of the different firms. A firm in the dominant group should not have an incentive to delete any subset of its links. Given that payoffs are increasing and convex in own links, it is sufficient to check whether a firm has an incentive to delete all its links. Simple computations with equation (10.3) show that this incentive constraint implies that

$$Y(k) \equiv \frac{(n-1)\gamma}{(n+1)^2}[2(\alpha - \gamma_0) + (k-1)(n+3-2k)\gamma] \geqslant c. \qquad (10.5)$$

An examination of (10.5) reveals an interesting property of payoffs: the average returns from links are nonmonotonic with respect to the size of the dominant group. They are initially increasing, until some critical size k^*, and declining thereafter. From the hypothesis of pairwise equilibrium it follows that firms in the dominant group do not wish to delete links. It then follows from the increasing returns in own links' property that each firm in the dominant group would like to form links with isolated firms. So for the dominant group network to be stable

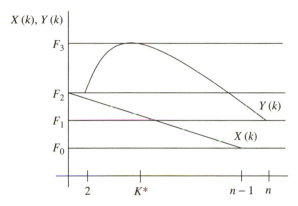

Figure 10.2. Incentives of firms.

an isolated firm should have a strict incentive *not* to form such a link. This yields the following incentive constraint for isolated firms:

$$X(k) \equiv \frac{(n-1)\gamma}{(n+1)^2}[2(\alpha - \gamma_0) + (n-1)\gamma - 2k(k-1)\gamma] < c. \qquad (10.6)$$

An inspection of (10.6) reveals that the marginal returns to the isolated firm are declining in the size of the dominant group. Hence as the costs of forming links become larger, smaller dominant groups are sufficient to deter the isolated firms from forming a link. Figure 10.2 illustrates the incentives of firms in the dominant group and the isolated firms, as a function of the size of the dominant group, respectively. In this figure the terms F_0, F_1, F_2, and F_3 are defined as follows:

$$F_0 = \frac{(n-1)\gamma}{(n+1)^2}[2(\alpha - \gamma_0) + (n-1)(3-2n)\gamma],$$

$$F_1 = \frac{(n-1)\gamma}{(n+1)^2}[2(\alpha - \gamma_0) + (n-1)(3-n)\gamma],$$

$$F_2 = \frac{(n-1)\gamma}{(n+1)^2}[2(\alpha - \gamma_0) + (n-1)\gamma],$$

$$F_3 = Y(k^*).$$

Observe that, at low costs of forming links, the incentive constraint of an isolated firm is binding. However, since the marginal payoff to an isolated firm from an additional link is declining in the size of the dominant group, as the costs of links increase, smaller dominant groups are sufficient to discourage an isolated firm from forming a link. At first glance this suggests that larger costs of links will sustain a wider range of dominant group sizes. The actual situation is, however, more complicated. The principal complication is that, beyond a certain cost level, the incentive constraint for a firm in the dominant group is binding. We have

Size of dominant group

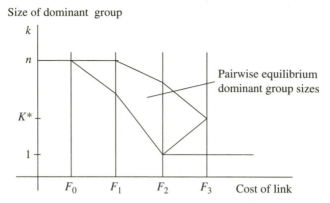

Figure 10.3.   Dominant group size and costs of links.

already noted that the returns from links to a dominant group firm are increasing in group size until some critical value k^* and then they are declining in group size. This implies that at high cost levels, small and large dominant groups are not sustainable and only medium sized groups are sustainable. These observations are summarized in figure 10.3.

A number of remarks are worth making at this point. First, for a range of parameters ($F_2 < c < F_3$), middle size dominant groups are the *only* ones which can be sustained in pairwise equilibrium networks. This means that collaboration links can create interesting asymmetries between *ex ante* identical firms. Moreover, note that such asymmetries are especially prominent when costs of forming links are high.

Second, consider the distribution of quantities and profits in a dominant group network. It follows from the difference in links and the cost reduction function (10.1) that firms in the dominant group have a lower cost of production. From (10.2) we can infer that these firms also have a larger market share. Next we examine the profits of firms. While the market profits of better linked firms are higher, their costs of linking are also higher, and so the ranking of profits across firms with different degrees needs to be examined more closely. From the hypothesis of pairwise equilibrium, it follows that the payoff to a firm in a dominant group is (weakly) larger than the payoff that it would earn after deletion of all its links. We have noted above that (gross) payoffs to a firm are decreasing in the links of other firms. It therefore follows that the payoffs to the isolated firm in the pairwise equilibrium dominant group network are strictly smaller than the payoffs that a firm which is in the dominant group can earn upon deletion of all its links. Thus every firm in the dominant group earns strictly higher payoffs than the isolated firms.

The results in this section show how firms can use collaboration links as a strategy to create market dominance and increase profits.

10.3.2 Stars and Core–Periphery Structures

The results in the previous section tell us that an unequal distribution of links arises in pairwise equilibrium networks. But the architecture of these networks differs from the empirically observed networks in one critical aspect: empirical networks have a core set of firms which have links with a large number of firms who are relatively poorly linked. This difference motivates a closer examination of the process of link formation.

Recall that, in the model of collaboration developed, the marginal returns to a firm from an additional link are increasing in own links and declining in the links of others. This suggests that when a high degree firm forms a link with a low degree firm, it earns a higher marginal payoff than the low degree firm. Thus a high degree firm may have an incentive to offer transfers to a low degree firm to encourage link formation. This consideration motivates an analysis of the network formation when firms are allowed to make transfers.

Let $t^i = \{t^i_{i1}, \ldots, t^i_{in}\} \in \mathcal{R}^n$, with t^i_{ij} being the transfer from firm i to firm j on link g_{ij}. We will assume that $t^i_{ij} \geq 0$ for all $i, j \in N$ and that $t^i_i = 0$ for all $i \in N$. Once transfers are allowed a link is attractive for firms i and j so long as the joint marginal returns exceed the total costs of the link. The following definition of stability builds on the idea of pairwise equilibrium and incorporates this idea.

Definition 10.1. A network g is stable against transfers if

(i) for all $g_{ij} = 1$, $[\Pi_i(g) - \Pi_i(g - g_{ij})] + [\Pi_j(g) - \Pi_j(g - g_{ij})] > 2c$;

(ii) for all $g_{ij} = 0$, $[\Pi_i(g + g_{ij}) - \Pi_i(g)] + [\Pi_j(g + g_{ij}) - \Pi_j(g)] < 2c$;

(iii) there exist transfers $t^i \in R^n$, $i = 1, 2, \ldots, n$, such that

$$\Pi_i(g) - \eta_i(g)c - \sum_{j \in N_i(g)} (t^i_{ij} - t^j_{ji}) \geq \Pi_i(g_{-i}). \qquad (10.7)$$

The property of increasing marginal returns in own links continues to obtain in this setting. This in turn implies that there can be at most one nonsingleton component in a stable network. Another implication of payoffs (10.3) is the following property of networks which are stable against transfers.

Property 1. Consider a network g which is stable against transfers. If a firm i has a link with firm j, then it must also have a link with every firm k which has as many links as j in the network $g - g_{ij}$.[16]

On the one hand, marginal returns of firm i from a link with firm k are higher than from the link with firm j (due to the property of increasing marginal returns in own links). On the other hand, the marginal returns to firm k from a link with

---

[16] This property is developed in lemma 10.1 in the appendix and a proof is also provided.

i are potentially lower than the marginal returns that firm j gets from the link with firm i (due to the property of decreasing marginal returns in others' links). The above property tells us that the former positive effect dominates the latter negative effect.

In particular, this property implies that no regular network of degree k with $0 < k < n - 1$ can be stable against transfers. Thus the empty network and the complete network are the only regular networks which can be stable against transfers.

We next examine irregular networks. The following result focuses on the conditions under which a star network is stable against transfers.

Proposition 10.2. *Let* $n \geq 4$. *Suppose that payoffs are given by (10.3). Then there exist* F_H *and* F_L, *where* $0 < F_L < F_H$, *such that the star network is stable against transfers if and only if the cost of forming a link* $c \in (F_L, F_H)$.

Transfers are critical to the emergence of a star network. If the marginal returns of a peripheral firm from the link with the central firm are positive, then it follows, from the property of increasing returns in own links, that the peripheral firm would also want to form links with all the other peripheral firms. Thus a star is *only* stable in a situation where the links in the star are not individually profitable for the peripheral firms. In other words, all the links between the central firm and the peripheral firm are sustained by transfers from the central firm!

However, in spite of this subsidy, the central firm earns a higher payoff than the peripheral firms. To see why this is true note first that, since the star is stable with respect to transfers, condition (iii) in the definition of stability is satisfied, and so the payoff to the central firm in the star is (weakly) higher than the payoff it can earn in the empty network. Second, we note that the construction in the proof of the proposition relies on the central firm making the peripheral firm indifferent between a link and being isolated. So in the star network the peripheral firm earns a payoff equal to the payoff it would make if it were to remain isolated and face a "star" network with $n - 2$ peripheral firms. Third, note that the central firm can earn a higher payoff in the empty network compared with what the peripheral firm earns when it is isolated. This is because the payoffs to a firm are declining in the links of other firms: the peripheral firm faces $2(n-2)$ links of other firms in a star network, while the central firm faces zero links of other firms in the empty network. Putting together these observations, we obtain the ranking of payoffs which was claimed above.

Are there other networks architectures that can arise in the presence of transfers? A characterization of networks which are stable with respect to transfers is not available. However, the stability properties of connected networks are well understood, and the discussion here will focus on them.

Recall, from chapter 2, that $\{N_1, \ldots, N_{x_m}\}$ is a partition of firms into sets with distinct degrees. A generalized interlinked star network has a partition with two

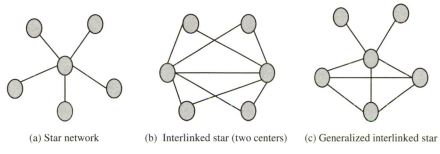

(a) Star network   (b) Interlinked star (two centers)   (c) Generalized interlinked star

Figure 10.4. Interlinked stars $n = 6$.

or more sets, $\{N_{x_1}, N_{x_2}, \ldots, N_{x_m}\}$, such that $|N_{x_m}| = x_1 < x_2 < \cdots < x_m = n - 1$ and, for every $j \in N_{x_1}$, $g_{j,k} = 1$ if and only if $k \in N_{n-1}$. The following result is due to Goyal and Joshi (2003).

Proposition 10.3. *Suppose that payoffs satisfy (10.3). Let g be a connected network which is stable against transfers. Then g is either complete or has a generalized interlinked star architecture. Moreover, in the latter case, if $\eta_i(g) \neq \eta_j(g)$, then $|\eta_i(g) - \eta_j(g)| \geq 2$.*

Figure 10.4 presents some interlinked star networks which are stable against transfers. The intuition underlying the interlinked star structure is as follows. Consider an irregular connected network g which is stable against transfers. Suppose that firm $i \in N_{x_1}$. Since the network is connected it follows that $\eta_i(g) \geq 1$. Let us first see why i does not form a link with some $j \notin N_{x_m}$. If this were the case, then from property 1, stated earlier in this section, it follows that firm j would have a link with all firms in the network. However, this would imply that firm $j \in N_{x_m}$, a contradiction with the initial hypothesis. Since $\eta_i(g) \geq 1$, it must be the case that there is some firm $k \in N_{x_m}$ such that $g_{ik} = 1$. But then from property 1 it follows that $\eta_k(g) = n - 1$ and so $x_m = n - 1$. Clearly, every firm in N_{n-1} is linked to all firms in N_{x_1}. The last statement in the proposition also follows from property 1.

10.3.3 Firm Heterogeneity

The discussion of the model so far has assumed that firms are *ex ante* identical. The interest has been in showing how even in such a symmetric setting strategic formation of collaboration ties can generate significant inequality in connections as well as payoffs and also yield very specific structures of collaboration. In practice, firms exhibit significant heterogeneities. This section elaborates on some implications of firm heterogeneity.[17]

---

[17] For a related discussion on the role of player heterogeneity in games of one-sided link formation, see chapter 8.

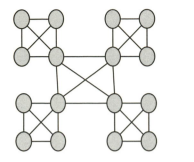   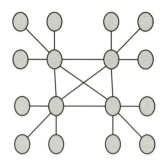

(a) Interlinked clusters (no transfers)   (b) Core–periphery (with transfers)

Figure 10.5.   Networks with linking cost heterogeneity.

First, consider differences in the initial costs of production. In the context of the model discussed above such differences are analogous to differences in the number of links and so the arguments developed above carry over in a straightforward manner.

Second, consider differences in the costs of forming links across firms. An inspection of the payoff function (10.3) suggests that linking activity is sensitive to the costs of linking. If costs are sufficiently low for a link between two firms i and j, then they will form a link, while if they are sufficiently high, then the firms will not form a link. In other words, any observed network of collaboration can be rationalized in terms of underlying heterogeneities in the costs of forming links. This possibility motivates an exploration of specific forms of cost heterogeneity.

A natural way to model such differences is to suppose that firms can be divided into groups, and the costs of linking are lower between members of the same group. The groups may be defined in terms of cultural, legal, or geographical proximity.[18] We will not present a formal analysis of such a model here but restrict ourselves to a general discussion of some possibilities only.

In such a setting variants of the dominant groups architecture and interlinked stars arise in equilibrium. Figure 10.5 illustrates these structures. Figure 10.5(a) considers the case without transfers. The members of each group form links since the costs of forming links are small. However, only highly linked firms want to form links across groups, since the costs of cross-group links are high. The result is a highly clustered network with few inter-group links. Figure 10.5(b) reflects networks in a setting with transfers and significant costs of forming links for both within-group and across-group ties. Here a single firm from each group connects with all other firms in the group as well as with one firm from each of the other groups. The costs of within-group links are high enough that this firm subsidizes the links within its own group, and the other members of the group do not have an incentive to form a link among themselves. Moreover, firms from outside a group

---

[18] This form of heterogeneity is analogous to the insider–outsider model discussed in chapter 8.

do not want to subsidize links with peripheral groups within this group, due to the high costs of forming cross-group links. There are no subsidies in cross-group ties between the central firms. The result is a simple core–periphery network.

Finally, returns may be firm specific: links with some firms may be more productive. The arguments in the previous section suggest that pressures towards the creation of core–periphery structures would be accentuated, as more productive firms can more easily subsidize link formation with other firms.

10.4 Related Themes

Research collaboration among firms is a widespread economic activity with potentially important implications for the performance of firms and the functioning of the economy at large. It is therefore not surprising that it has been extensively studied in sociology, organization theory, business strategy, as well as in economics. This section briefly discusses some of the themes that have been explored.

10.4.1 Social Embeddedness and Collaboration Links

The discussion so far has focused on the strategic role of collaborations in shaping market dominance. In this discussion the implicit assumption was that there is no informational asymmetry between firms, about skills and expertise or about the level of research effort that different partners put in.

In practice, a firm is more likely to know about the knowledge and skills of other firms with which it has collaborated in the past. Similarly, individual firms are likely to have significant private knowledge about own efforts and skills: this private knowledge is likely to create the familiar incentive problems relating to moral hazard and adverse selection. In the context of R&D, formal contracts will typically not be able to address these problems fully.[19] This suggests that firms may prefer repeated collaboration with existing collaboration partners or with firms about which they can get reliable information via existing and past common partners. In other words, the network structure of past collaborations may well play an important role in shaping the performance of existing collaborations as well as the pattern of new collaborations.

These considerations constitute key elements of the influential work of Granovetter (1985) on the social embeddedness of economic activity.[20] Broadly

---

[19] For a general discussion on the role of contracts in the theory of the firm, see Hart (1995) and Williamson (1985).

[20] For some recent theoretical work in sociology, see, for example, Buskens and Raub (2002), Raub and Weesie (1990), and Weesie and Raub (2000). The role of social embeddedness in shaping business networks has also been exploded in Kali (1999) and Kranton (1996). For a general discussion of the conceptual issues, see Noteboom (1999).

speaking, three questions have been explored in this research. What types of firm enter into collaborative agreements and with whom? How does the existing pattern of collaboration links relate to the governance structure of a new collaboration partnership—is there a formal contract or are loose research sharing agreements used? The third question relates to the effects of network position of firms on their performance: how is the network position of the partners related to performance of a collaboration link? Empirical work on the third question has faced measurement problems: it is often difficult to clearly distinguish the resource input into specific projects and similarly it is difficult to assess the effects of particular projects on firm performance. The discussion here will therefore focus on the first two questions.

Let us start with the first question. Empirical research suggests that the history of past collaboration, as well as the identity of the new partners, plays an important role in determining the likelihood of a firm entering a new collaboration. In particular, firms that have had more past alliances, and were more centrally located in the old network of collaborations, are more likely to enter into new collaboration ventures (Kogut, Sham, and Walker 1992; Gulati 1995b; Powell, Koput, and Smith-Doerr 1996).[21] Empirical work also suggests that two firms with a past history of mutual collaboration are more likely to have further collaborative projects in the future. Similarly, presently unconnected firms are more likely to enter into a collaborative project if they are relatively closer to each other in the existing network of collaboration relations.

The second question is related to the general issue of the governance of network forms of organization. The traditional approach has been to distinguish markets from hierarchies (which are reflected in firms). Organizational theorists have explored the implications of multiple interfirm links for the organization and the governance of a firm (see, for example, Gulati 1998; Nohria and Eccles 1992; Powell 1990; Podolny and Page 1998). Empirical work has examined the nature of contracts and governance structures which define collaboration links between firms. This work suggests that collaboration agreements become less formal if partners are embedded in social networks of previous collaboration links (Gulati 1995a). This is suggestive of the growth of trust via participation of firms in a social network of collaborative links.

The gradual building of trust in bilateral links has also been studied in economic theory (see, for example, Ghosh and Ray 1996). However, in these models an individual only takes part in one interaction at any point in time, and if this relationship breaks down, then there is no information flow across different partnerships. By contrast, in the above setting, information flow—both about skills and about actions—across firms is a key element of the process. The formal

---

[21] For a study of the effects of an existing network of relations on the formation of new links in the context of scientific coauthorship, see Fafchamps, Goyal, and van der Leij (2006).

study of evolving network relations in a context characterized by informational asymmetries appears to be an open problem.[22]

10.4.2 Coalitions of Collaborating Firms

Traditionally, the formation of research collaboration groups among firms has been studied within a framework of coalitions. Recall that in a coalition model a firm can be a member of only one group at a time. Bloch (1995) studies formation of collaboration coalitions among Cournot competitors under the assumption that the costs of forming links (given by c in the model in section 10.3) is zero. He finds that there is a unique outcome: in this outcome there are two groups of unequal size with the firms in the larger group comprising (roughly) three-quarters of all firms while the smaller group contains the remaining quarter of firms.[23] How does this result compare with what we find by using a network formation approach?

The biggest difference is that structures like the star and interlinked star are stable in the network formation model but they are not permitted in a coalitions framework. Moreover, empirical networks exhibit such architectures as well.

Structures like the star are, however, supported by transfers and only arise when the costs of forming links are substantial. However, in the coalition model studied in Bloch (1995) the costs of forming links are assumed to be zero. So we now examine more closely the network formation model with zero costs of forming links. An inspection of figures 10.2 and 10.3 suggests that if $c = 0$, then the unique pairwise equilibrium network is the complete network. Thus the predictions of the two approaches are quite different even in the case with zero costs of collaboration. The reason for this difference is as follows. Consider firm i which belongs to a complete component g, with $k \geqslant 2$ firms. It follows from (10.3) that starting at any network g a pair of unlinked firms is strictly better off by forming a link. So the complete network is the only possible outcome in a network formation game if costs of forming links are zero. By contrast, in a coalitions model, firm i can form a link with j if and only if all other $k - 1$ firms in the same coalition as i agree to do likewise. However, in this case, it follows from (10.1) that each of the $k \neq i$ firms in the coalition lowers costs of production by γ and firm j lowers costs by $k\gamma$. It then follows from (10.2) that if $k > (n + 1)/2$, then firm i will not want to expand the coalition of size k by bringing in a new member.

The above discussion brings out the different types of incentive considerations that arise in the two approaches. This discussion also gives us some idea about

---

[22] For a model of repeated games on fixed networks with exchange of information among players, see Haag and Lagunoff (2006). This model was briefly discussed in chapter 4. For a recent attempt at studying network formation and exchange of information in accompanying games, see Vega-Redondo (2006).

[23] For an analysis of coalition formation under different rules of coalition formation, also see Yi (1997, 1998).

the attractiveness of the two approaches in different circumstances. In a context where spillovers across projects are clear and significant and the relative costs of coordinating with different—existing and prospective—partners are relatively small the coalition approach appears to be more appropriate. On the other hand, in a technologically dynamic environment, where the spillovers across projects are less clear and the costs of coordinating with different partners are relatively large, a bilateral link formation approach appears to be more appropriate.

10.5   Empirical Patterns

The empirical properties of collaboration networks have been extensively studied in recent years. The aim of this section is to provide a brief summary of some of the findings with regard to two issues. We will first discuss the different types of research collaborations that firms undertake and indicate their relative popularity. We will then discuss some features of the architecture of the network of interfirm collaboration.

It is important to keep in mind that research collaboration among firms takes on a variety of forms. Perhaps the most prominent ones are joint ventures and joint R&D contracts.

Joint ventures and research corporations. This reflects the setting up of a "distinct" new firm which is based in equity investments put together by two or more firms. In this arrangement, profits and losses are usually shared according to equity investments.

Joint R&D and technology exchange. These are agreements which regulate technology sharing and transfer between two or more firms. They generally cover cross-licensing and mutual second-sourcing arrangements. Joint R&D refers to agreements such as research pacts which establish joint undertaking of research projects with shared resources and in some cases also common product development.

In a recent paper, Hagedoorn (2002) provides a survey of empirical work on research collaboration among firms. This survey covers a period of almost forty years starting in the 1960s and is a very useful source of information on overall trends. The first finding is that there has been a significant increase in the number of such collaboration agreements between firms since the 1960s. This number rose sharply in the early 1980s and, after a small fall at the end of the decade, rose sharply in the 1990s and has remained high in recent years. The second finding is that the relative importance of joint ventures in this activity has gone down dramatically in this period. In the early years, most collaboration took the form of joint ventures, while in recent years almost 90% of the collaborations take the form of joint R&D and technology sharing agreements. The third finding pertains to the sectoral pattern of R&D partnerships. Over the years, the share of industries such as pharmaceuticals, information technology, aerospace, and defense has increased at the expense of other industries such as instrumentation and medical equipment, consumer electronics, and chemicals. In the 1970s, the latter group of industries accounted for over 50% of the total number of collaborations. By the late 1990s, their share had come down sharply while the share of the former group of industries increased to over 80%. In particular, the information technology sector accounted for over 50% and the pharmaceutical industry accounted for about 30% of all R&D collaborations in the 1990s.

We turn next to the cross-sectional distribution of collaborations. A number of studies have examined the structure of interfirm collaboration networks in different industries. These networks exhibit some common features: an unequal degree distribution across firms, a core–periphery structure, and short average distances. We present data on two industries—pharmaceuticals and biotechnology—to bring out these features of the network. The exposition here is based on Baker, Gibbons, and Murphy (2004).[24]

The data set has information on 12 451 publicly disclosed contracts between pharmaceutical and biotechnology firms. The period of coverage is 1973–2001. Tables 10.1 and 10.2 summarize these data. These tables suggest a number of observations about the architecture of collaborations among biotechnology and pharmaceutical firms.[25]

Small average degree. There were 12 451 contracts covered, and the number of firms involved is 4231. The number of firms per contract was typically not very large, and so we may infer that the average degree was fairly low as well. Indeed, about half of the firms appear to have only one link each.

Unequal degrees. The 24 most linked firms, comprising less than 1% of all firms involved, were involved in 32% of all the contracts. The 12 most linked pharmaceutical firms each had over 150 contracts in this period; putting together this observation with the earlier point about one-half of all firms (roughly 2160) having only one link each leads us to infer that the degree distribution was very unequal. Table 10.1 presents related data for other biotechnology and pharmaceutical firms.

Core–periphery structure. The 12 most linked pharmaceutical and the 12 most linked biotechnology firms had a dense network of linkages among themselves. For instance, each of these 24 firms had a link to at least 15 of the remaining 23 others. However, these highly linked firms also had a very large number of

---

[24] They base their work on a database put together by Recombinant Capital (which is a specialist on biotechnology alliances).

[25] The discussion here focuses on the pharmaceutical and biotechnology sectors. Similar patterns obtain in other industries; for an interesting study of the patterns of collaboration, see Delapierre and Mytelka (1998).

Table 10.1. The 12 most linked pharmaceutical firms, 1973–2001.

Top 12 Pharma. firms	Contracts	Links	Pharma. links (%)	Biotech. links (%)	Links in top 24
1. GlaxoSK	373	248	11.7	58.5	20
2. Pharmacia	370	271	12.2	44.1	21
3. Pfizer	287	194	14.4	57.7	19
4. Novartis	230	167	16.2	54.5	18
5. Elan	228	156	22.2	38.6	14
6. Hoffman-La Roche	224	164	11.7	62.0	17
7. Johnson (JNJ)	212	170	16.5	37.6	16
8. Abbott (ABT)	201	174	13.3	49.7	14
9. American (AHP)	175	124	21.0	56.5	19
10. Lilly (Lly)	164	132	13.6	62.9	16
11. Merck	164	118	16.1	58.5	16
12. Bristol-Myers (BMY)	150	128	10.9	57.8	15

Tables 10.1 and 10.2 are taken from Baker, Gibbons, and Murphy (2004); these data were extracted from the Recombinant Capital Database of alliances in the pharmaceutical and biotechnology industry, which is based on 12 451 publicly disclosed contracts and agreements over the period 1973–2001. The alliances reported exclude those with entities that ultimately became wholly owned subsidiaries of the companies in the table. Contracts are assigned to the surviving parent regardless of whether the parent was involved in the original arrangement.

In the tables, note that "Pharma. links" refers to number of partners in the pharmaceutical industry, while "Links in top 24" refers to the number of collaboration partners in the set of the 12 most linked pharmaceutical and the 12 most linked biotechnology firms. Finally, note that the number of contracts is larger than the number of links because a firm sometimes had multiple contracts with the same firm.

links with other firms: the data suggest that they had links with over 1300 partners outside this set. This suggests that the collaboration network had a core–periphery structure. Figure 2.10 is reproduced here as figure 10.6 to illustrate this point.[26]

Short average distance. The top linked pharmaceutical firms were also linked to 1308 firms outside the top 24 linked firms. These partner firm in turn had over 11 000 links with over 2000 other firms. This means that about 3400 firms (which is over 80% of all firms in these industries) were within two links of the core group of the 24 most linked firms. Thus a peripheral firm was almost always within "two phone calls" of the core group of firms, which in turn were within two phone calls of most other peripheral firms. Thus the average distance between firms in the collaboration network was around 4, which is rather small in view of the average degree and the total number of firms.

---

[26] In this figure, the 24 most linked pharmaceutical and biotechnology firms form the core hub firms, and the nodes in the outer ring are intermediate hubs. The core hub firms and the intermediate hub firms have a large number of links with nonhub firms which have been omitted, for simplicity.

Table 10.2. The 12 most linked biotechnology firms, 1973–2001.

Top 12 Pharma. firms	Contracts	Links	Pharma. links (%)	Biotech. links (%)	Links in top 24
1. Appera	224	183	13.7	38.3	15
2. Chiron	172	136	20.0	31.1	12
3. Genentech	124	92	14.1	54.3	14
4. Genzyme	122	92	14.7	32.4	6
5. Shira	119	85	24.7	36.5	12
6. Incyte	107	90	25.8	42.7	17
7. Celltech	106	89	25.8	37.1	15
8. Affymetrix	81	69	26.1	30.4	10
9. Medarex	88	73	16.4	41.1	10
10. Medimure	86	67	22.4	25.4	10
11. Vertex	79	63	25.8	32.3	12
12. Amgen	78	66	21.2	42.4	12

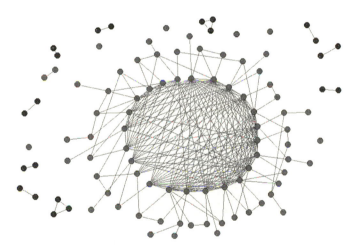

Figure 10.6. Research collaboration: pharmaceutical and biotechnology firms.

10.6 Concluding Remarks

Empirical work suggests that research collaboration between firms is common and that it has increased significantly in the last two decades. This empirical work has also highlighted certain structural features of collaborative activity. Typically, collaboration links are bilateral and are embedded within a broader network of similar links with other firms. Moreover, the network of links exhibits three distinct features: considerable inequality in the number of links across firms, a core–periphery structure, and short average distances between firms. This chapter examined the origins and the implications of these empirical patterns.

We took the view that the network of collaboration arises out of deliberate decisions of firms with regard to the formation of collaboration links. The incentives
of firms to form links are influenced by the competitive pressures but the formation of links in turn shapes the nature of market competition. This two-way flow
of influence between networks and markets was an important object of study.

The chapter studied a simple model of strategic network formation in which
firms form links to lower costs of production and then competed in a market by
choosing quantities. In this classical setting, it was shown that link formation by
ex ante identical firms leads to networks with an unequal degree distribution. The
unequal degrees matter from an economic point of view: firms with higher degree
have a larger share of the market and also make higher profits.

An important part of the analysis was the identification of externalities that
link formation generates. We showed that in this model total as well as marginal
returns of a firm are increasing in own links but are decreasing in the links of
others. This suggests that firms with more links may want to subsidize link creation
with poorly linked firms and this led us to explore the implications of transfers
among firms. We found that transfers facilitate the emergence of the star network
and core–periphery type structures. These results provide a theoretical account of
how firms can use collaboration links as a strategy to create market dominance.
They also provide insights into the origins of network architectures, such as the
core–periphery structure and the star network, which are empirically observed.

This analysis was carried out in a context where firms have full information
about each other's capabilities and there were no significant issues concerning
free riding in the sharing of knowledge or the carrying out of research work.
Clearly, these are important concerns, and the second part of the chapter was
devoted to them.

Here the interest was in understanding the role of social embeddedness—the
network of existing links—in shaping the formation and evolution of collaboration links over time. The incompleteness of information about capabilities of
prospective partners as well as the potential for free riding and shirking in research
collaborations suggests that the history of past collaboration and informal communication with common partners are likely to play an important role in determining
collaboration patterns. This general idea has motivated a rich and important body
of empirical work. However, the formulation of a theoretical framework in which
link formation is a dynamic process and information about skills and behavior of
firms flows through the network of links appears to be an open problem.

10.7   Appendix

The results and the proofs in this section are taken from Goyal and Joshi (2003).
It follows from the discussion in section 10.3 that the (net) payoffs to a firm i in

network g are

$$\Pi_i(g) = \left[\frac{(\alpha - \gamma_0) + (n-1)\gamma\eta_i(g) - \gamma L(g_{-i})}{n+1}\right]^2 - \eta_i(g)c. \qquad (10.8)$$

Proposition 10.4. *Suppose that payoffs are given by (10.8). A pairwise equilibrium network is either empty, the dominant group network, or the complete network.*

Proof. It follows from the discussion in the chapter that this is a playing-the-field game and the payoffs (10.8) satisfy convexity in own links. The result then follows as a corollary of proposition 9.4. □

Proposition 10.5. *Let $n \geq 4$. Suppose that payoffs are given by (10.8). Then there exist F_H and F_L, where $0 < F_L < F_H$, such that the star network is stable against transfers if and only if $c \in (F_L, F_H)$.*

Proof. Suppose that g^s is a star network; denote the central firm by n and typical peripheral firms by i and j. If firm n deletes all its links, we then get the empty network g^e. If firm i or firm n deletes the link between them, we then get the network $g^s - g_{n,i}$. The requirement that firm n and firm i wish to maintain their link may be written as

$$[\Pi_n(g^s) - \Pi_n(g^s - g_{n,i})] + [\Pi_i(g^s) - \Pi_i(g^s - g_{n,i})] > 2c. \qquad (10.9)$$

The requirement that firms i and j do not have an incentive to form a link may be written as follows:

$$[\Pi_i(g^s + g_{ij}) - \Pi_i(g^s)] + [\Pi_j(g^s + g_{ij}) - \Pi_j(g^s)] < 2c. \qquad (10.10)$$

The requirement that there exists a set of transfers such that firms have no incentives to isolate themselves by deleting all their links is written as follows. There exist transfers t^i for $i = 1, 2, \ldots, n$ such that

$$\left.\begin{array}{l}
\Pi_n(g^s) - (n-1)c - \displaystyle\sum_{j \in N_n(g)} (t^n_{nj} - t^j_{jn}) \geq \Pi_n(g^e), \\[1em]
\Pi_i(g^s) - c - (t^i_{in} - t^n_{ni}) \geq \Pi_i(g^s - g_{n,i}), \quad \forall i \in N \setminus \{n\}.
\end{array}\right\}$$

We note that the gross profits for firms under different networks can be written as follows:

$$\left.\begin{array}{l}
\Pi_n(g^s) = \dfrac{[\alpha - \gamma_0 + (n-1)^2\gamma]^2}{(n+1)^2}, \\[1em]
\Pi_n(g^e) = \dfrac{[\alpha - \gamma_0]^2}{(n+1)^2},
\end{array}\right\} \qquad (10.12)$$

$$\Pi_n(g^s - g_{n,i}) = \frac{[\alpha - \gamma_0 + (n-2)(n-1)\gamma]^2}{(n+1)^2}, \qquad (10.13)$$

$$\Pi_i(g^s) = \frac{[\alpha - \gamma_0 + (3 - n)\gamma]^2}{(n + 1)^2},$$

$$\Pi_i(g^s - g_{n,i}) = \frac{[\alpha - \gamma_0 - 2(n - 2)\gamma]^2}{(n + 1)^2},$$

$$(10.14)$$

$$\Pi_i(g^s + g_{ij}) = \frac{[\alpha - \gamma_0 + 2\gamma]^2}{(n + 1)^2}. \tag{10.15}$$

We now substitute the above payoff terms in the incentive conditions (10.9)–(10.11). After substitution and rearrangement, we can rewrite (10.9) as follows:

$$\frac{\gamma(n - 1)[4(\alpha - \gamma_0) + (n - 1)\gamma(2n - 3) - \gamma(3n - 7)]}{(n + 1)^2} > 2c. \tag{10.16}$$

Similarly, (10.10) can be rewritten as follows:

$$\frac{2\gamma(n - 1)[2(\alpha - \gamma_0) + \gamma(2 - n + 3)]}{(n + 1)^2} < 2c. \tag{10.17}$$

Define

$$F' = \frac{\gamma(n - 1)[4(\alpha - \gamma_0) + (n - 1)\gamma(2n - 3) - \gamma(3n - 7)]}{2(n + 1)^2}, \tag{10.18}$$

$$F_L = \frac{2\gamma(n - 1)[2(\alpha - \gamma_0) + \gamma(2 - n + 3)]}{2(n + 1)^2}. \tag{10.19}$$

Conditions (10.9) and (10.10) are satisfied if and only if the fixed costs are such that $F_L < c < F'$. It is easily verified that $F_L < F'$ if $n > 3$.

Finally, we construct the set of transfers. Recall that we only require that there exists a set of transfers which makes firms want to retain their links in g^s rather than delete all their links. Note that for the star to be stable it must be the case that the peripheral firms do not have an incentive to form a link with each other. Given the symmetry in their situation, it follows that their marginal payoffs from the additional link are the same. This requirement taken along with increasing returns implies that if the star is to be stable, then it must be the case that each of the peripheral firms also does not have an incentive to form a link with the central firm. Thus transfers have to be made by the central firm to each of the peripheral firms. The minimum value of this transfer is

$$t_{ni}^n = \Pi_i(g^s - g_{n,i}) - \Pi_i(g^s) + c. \tag{10.20}$$

Given (10.14) we can rewrite this minimum transfer as

$$t_{ni}^n = c - \frac{(n - 1)\gamma[2(\alpha - \gamma_0) - \gamma(3n - 7)]}{(n + 1)^2}. \tag{10.21}$$

We wish to show that the central firm has an incentive to make such transfers to each of the peripheral firms rather than delete all links. This incentive is satisfied if and only if

$$\Pi_n(g^s) - (n - 1)(c + t_{ni}^n) \geq \Pi_n(g^e). \tag{10.22}$$

After some rearrangement this requirement can be expressed as

$$\frac{(n-1)\gamma[4(\alpha-\gamma_0)+(n-1)^2\gamma-\gamma(3n-7)]}{(n+1)^2} \geqslant 2c. \tag{10.23}$$

Define

$$F'' = \frac{(n-1)\gamma[4(\alpha-\gamma_0)+(n-1)^2\gamma-\gamma(3n-7)]}{2(n+1)^2}. \tag{10.24}$$

It can be checked that $F'' > F_L$ for all $n > 3$. Define $F_H = \min\{F', F''\}$. The proof now follows. $\qquad\square$

The following lemma shows that property 1 holds in our model.

Lemma 10.1. *If a firm i has a link with firm j in network g which is stable against transfers, then it must also have a link with every firm k which has as many links as j in the network $g - g_{ij}$.*

Proof. Since g is stable with respect to transfers, i and j should have no incentive to sever their link. It is convenient to define $\Delta\Pi_i(g-g_{ij}) \equiv \Pi_i(g)-\Pi_i(g-g_{ij})$:

$$\Delta\Pi_i(g-g_{ij}) + \Delta\Pi_j(g-g_{ij}) > 2c. \tag{10.25}$$

Let $T_i(g-g_{ij}) \equiv (\alpha-\gamma_0)+n\gamma\eta_i(g-g_{ij})-\gamma\sum_{l\neq i}\eta_l(g-g_{ij})$. Using (10.8) the above inequality can be rewritten as

$$\frac{(n-1)\gamma}{(n+1)^2}[T_i(g-g_{ij})+T_j(g-g_{ij})+(n-1)\gamma] > 2c. \tag{10.26}$$

Now consider $k \neq i, j$ such that $\eta_k(g-g_{ij}) \geqslant \eta_j(g-g_{ij})$ but $g_{ik}=0$. Consider the network $g+g_{ik}$ and now define $\Delta\Pi_i(g) \equiv \Pi_i(g+g_{ik})-\Pi_i(g)$ and $\Delta\Pi_k(g) \equiv \Pi_k(g+g_{ik})-\Pi_k(g)$. Then

$$\Delta\Pi_i(g) + \Delta\Pi_k(g) = \frac{2(n-1)\gamma}{(n+1)^2}[T_i(g)+T_k(g)+(n-1)\gamma]. \tag{10.27}$$

Note that

$$\left.\begin{array}{l} \eta_l(g) = \eta_l(g-g_{ij})+1, \quad l=i,j, \\ \eta_k(g) = \eta_k(g-g_{ij}) \geqslant \eta_j(g-g_{ij}), \\ \eta_l(g) = \eta_l(g-g_{ij}), \quad l\neq i,j,k. \end{array}\right\} \tag{10.28}$$

Therefore, $T_i(g) = T_i(g-g_{ij}) + (n-1)\gamma$ and $T_k(g) \geqslant T_j(g-g_{ij}) - 2\gamma$. Substituting in (10.27) and recalling (10.26) it follows that

$$\Delta\Pi_i(g) + \Delta\Pi_k(g)$$

$$= \frac{2(n-1)\gamma}{(n+1)^2}[T_i(g-g_{ij})+(n-1)\gamma+T_j(g-g_{ij})-2\gamma+(n-1)\gamma]$$

$$= \Delta\Pi_i(g-g_{ij})+\Delta\Pi_j(g-g_{ij})+\frac{2(n-1)(n-3)\gamma^2}{(n+1)^2}$$

$$> 2c. \tag{10.29}$$

Therefore, i and k find it strictly profitable to form a link. This contradicts the stability of g against transfers. $\qquad\qquad\qquad\qquad\qquad\qquad\qquad\qquad\qquad\qquad\qquad\square$

Proposition 10.6. *Suppose that payoffs satisfy (10.8). Let g be a connected network which is stable against transfers. Then g is either complete or has the generalized interlinked star architecture. Moreover, in the latter case, if $\eta_i(g) \neq \eta_j(g)$, then $|\eta_i(g) - \eta_j(g)| \geqslant 2$.*

Proof. We first note that from property 1 it follows that the only regular connected network which can be stable against transfers is the complete network. We next consider an irregular network g and let $\{x_1, x_2, \ldots, x_m\}$ be a degree partition of the firms. Since g is connected, it must be the case that, for any $i \in \mathcal{N}_{x_1}(g)$, $\eta_i(g) \geqslant 1$. We next show that $g_{ij} = 0$ if $j \notin \mathcal{N}_{x_m}(g)$. Suppose not; then it follows from property 1 that firm j is linked to all firms. This implies that $j \in \mathcal{N}_{x_m}(g)$, which contradicts the original hypothesis that $j \notin \mathcal{N}_{x_m}(g)$. This proves that there is some firm in $\mathcal{N}_{x_m}(g)$ which has links with firms in $\mathcal{N}_{x_1}(g)$. It then follows from property 1 that this firm has links with all firms in $\mathcal{N}_{x_1}(g)$ and another application of property 1 tells us that this firm therefore has links with all firms in the network, i.e., $\eta_k(g) = n - 1$, and so $x_m = n - 1$. We have therefore proved that a firm $i \in \mathcal{N}_{x_1}(g)$ is linked with a firm j if and only if $j \in \mathcal{N}_{n-1}$; thus $\eta_i(g) = \mathcal{N}_{n-1}$ for $i \in \mathcal{N}_{x_1}(g)$. It is possible that there are intermediate elements between $x_1 = |\mathcal{N}_{n-1}|$ and $n - 1$, and therefore g has a generalized interlinked star structure.

Next consider the difference in degrees. Suppose g is connected and asymmetric. It then follows that g induces a partition with at least two elements. The claim is proved if we show that $\eta_i(g) - \eta_j(g) \geqslant 2$ for any pair $i \in N_{x_{l+1}}(g)$ and $j \in \mathcal{N}_{x_l}(g)$ with $1 \leqslant l \leqslant m - 1$. Suppose $\eta_i(g) - \eta_j(g) = 1$. Then there exists some firm $k \neq i, j$ such that $g_{ik} = 1$ but $g_{jk} = 0$. However, note that $\eta_i(g - g_{ik}) = \eta_j(g - g_{ik}) = \eta_j(g)$. Hence, from property 1 it follows that k will have link with j, and so g is not stable against transfers, a contradiction. $\quad\square$

References

Ahuja, G. 2000. Collaboration networks, structural holes, and innovation: a longitudinal study. *Administrative Science Quarterly* 45:425–55.

Aiello, W., F. Chung, and L. Lu. 2000. A random graph model for power law graphs. In *Proceedings 32nd ACM Symposium on Theoretical Computation*, pp. 171–80.

Akerlof, G. 1970. The market for lemons: quality uncertainty and the market mechanism. *Quarterly Journal of Economics* 84:488–500.

Albert, R., and L. A. Barabasi. 2002. Statistical mechanics of complex networks. *Review of Modern Physics* 74:47–97.

Aliprantis, C., and K. Border. 1999. *Infinite Dimensional Analysis.* Springer.

Allen, B. 1982. Some stochastic processes of interdependent demand and technological diffusion of an innovation exhibiting externalities among adopters. *International Economic Review* 23:595–607.

Anderlini, L., and A. Ianni. 1996. Path dependence and learning from neighbors. *Games and Economic Behavior* 13:141–77.

Anshelevich, E., A. Dasgupta, J. Kleinberg, E. Tardos, T. Wexler, and T. Roughgarden. 2004. The price of stability for network design with fair allocation. *Proceedings 45th IEEE Symposium on Foundations of Computer Science*, pp. 295–304.

Aumann, R. J. 1959. Acceptable points in general cooperative *n*-person games. In *Contributions to the Theory of Games IV* (ed. A. W. Tucker and R. D. Luce), pp. 287–324. Princeton University Press.

Aumann, R., and R. Myerson. 1988. Endogenous formation of links between players and coalitions: an application to the Shapley value. In *The Shapley Value* (ed. A. Roth), pp. 175–91. Cambridge University Press.

Axelrod, R. 1997. *The Complexity of Cooperation: Agent-Based Models of Competition and Collaboration.* Princeton University Press.

Bacharach, M. 2006. *Beyond Individual Choice: Teams and Frames in Game Theory* (ed. N. Gold and R. Sugden). Princeton University Press.

Bailey, N. T. 1975. *The Mathematical Theory of Infectious Diseases and Its Applications.* New York: Hafner Press.

Baker, G., R. Gibbons, and K. J. Murphy. 2004. Strategic alliances: bridges between "islands of conscious power." Mimeo, MIT.

Bala, V. 1997. Notes on network formation. Mimeo, McGill University.

Bala, V., and S. Goyal. 1998. Learning from neighbours. *Review of Economic Studies* 65:595–621.

——. 2000a. A non-cooperative model of network formation. *Econometrica* 68:1181–230.

——. 2000b. A strategic analysis of network reliability. *Review of Economic Design* 5:205–29.

——. 2001. Conformism and diversity under social learning. *Economic Theory* 17:101–20.

Ball, M. O., C. J. Colburn, and J. Provan. 1995. Network reliability. In *Handbooks in Operations Research and Management Science* (ed. M. O. Ball et al.). Elsevier Science.

Ballester, C., A. Calvó-Armengol, and Y. Zenou. 2006. Who's who in networks. Wanted: the key player. *Econometrica* 74:1403–17.

Bandiera, O., I. Barankay, and I. Rasul. 2006. Social connections and incentives in the work place: evidence from personnel data. Mimeo, University College London.

Banerjee, A. 1992. A simple model of herd behavior. *Quarterly Journal of Economics* 107:797–817.

Banerjee, A., and K. Munshi. 2004. How efficiently is capital allocated? Evidence from the knitted garment industry in Tirupur. *Review of Economic Studies* 71:19–42.

Barabasi, A.-L. 2002. *Linked*. Boston, MA: Perseus Books.

Barabasi, A.-L., and R. Albert. 1999. Emergence of scaling in random networks. *Science* 286:509–12.

Baron, R., J. Durieu, H. Haller, and P. Solal. 2002. A note on control costs and potential functions for strategic games. *Journal of Evolutionary Economics* 12:563–75.

Basu, K., and J. Weibull. 2002. Punctuality: a cultural trait as equilibrium. MIT Department of Economics Working Paper 02-26.

Bearman, P. S., J. Moody, and K. Stovel. 2004. Chains of affection: the structure of adolescent romantic and sexual networks. *American Journal of Sociology* 110:44–91.

Belleflamme, P., and F. Bloch. 2004. Market sharing agreements and collusive networks. *International Economic Review* 45:387–411.

Bergin, J., and B. Lipman. 1996. Evolution of state dependent mutations. *Econometrica* 64:943–56.

Bernheim, D., B. Peleg, and M. Whinston. 1987. Coalition proof Nash equilibria. I. Concepts. *Journal of Economic Theory* 42:1–12.

Berninghaus, J., K.-M. Ehrhart, and C. Keser. 2002. Conventions and local interaction structures: experimental evidence. *Games and Economic Behavior* 39:177–205.

Berry, D. A., and B. Fristedt. 1985. *Bandit Problems: Sequential Allocation of Experiments.* New York: Chapman and Hall.

Bertrand, M., E. Luttmer, and S. Mullainathan. 2000. Network effects and welfare cultures. *Quarterly Journal of Economics* 115:1019–55.

Besen, S. M., and J. Farrell. 1994. Choosing how to compete: strategies and tactics in standardization. *Journal of Economic Perspectives* 8(2):117–131.

Bian, Y., and S. Ang. 1997. Guanxi networks and job mobility in China and Singapore. *Social Forces* 75:981–1005.

Bikhchandani, S., D. Hirshliefer, and I. Welch. 1992. A theory of fads, fashion, custom, and cultural change as informational cascades. *Journal of Political Economy* 100:992–1023.

Billand, P., and C. Bravard. 2002. Non-cooperative networks in oligopolies. Mimeo, University of Jean Monnet, Saint-Etienne.

Billingsley, P. 1985. *Probability and Measure*. Wiley.

Blau, D., and P. K. Robins. 1990. Job search outcomes for the unemployed and the employed. *Journal of Political Economy* 98:637–55.

Bloch, F. 1995. Endogenous structures of association in oligopolies. *Rand Journal of Economics* 26:537–56.

———. 1997. Non-cooperative models of network formation in games with spillovers. In *New Directions in the Economic Theory of the Environment* (ed. C. Carraro and D. Siniscalo). Cambridge University Press.

Bloch, F., and B. Dutta. 2005. Communication networks with endogenous link strength. Mimeo, Marseille and Warwick.

Bloch, F., and M. O. Jackson. 2007. The formation of networks with transfers among players. *Journal of Economic Theory* 133:83–110.

Blume, L. 1993. The statistical mechanics of strategic interaction. *Games and Economic Behavior* 4:387–424.

Bollobás, B. 1980. A probabilistic proof of an asymptotic formula for the number of labelled regular graphs. *European Journal of Combinatorics* 1:311–16.

——. 1998. *Modern Graph Theory.* Springer.

Bolton, P., and C. Harris. 1999. Strategic experimentation. *Econometrica* 67:349–74.

Bonacich, P. 1972. Factoring and weighting approaches to status scores and clique identification. *Journal of Mathematical Sociology* 2:113–20.

Bondonio, D. 1998. Predictors of accuracy in perceiving informal social networks. *Social Networks* 20:301–30.

Borgatti, S. P., and S. L. Feld. 1994. How to test the strength of weak ties theory. *Connections* 17:45–46.

Boorman, S. 1975. A combinatorial optimization model of transmission of job information through contact networks. *Bell Journal of Economics* 6:216–49.

Bramoullé, Y. 2007. Anti-coordination and social interactions. *Games and Economic Behavior* 58:30–49.

Bramoullé, Y., H. Djebbari, and B. Fortin. 2006. Identification of peer effects through social networks. Mimeo, University Of Laval.

Bramoullé, Y., and G. Saint-Paul. 2004. Social networks and labor market transitions. Mimeo, Toulouse and Laval.

Bramoullé, Y., and R. Kranton. Forthcoming. Local public goods in networks. *Journal of Economic Theory.*

Brandenberger, A., and B. Nalebuff. 1996. *Co-opetition.* Doubleday.

Brenzinger, M. 1998. *Endangered Languages in Africa.* Berlin: Rudiger Koppe.

Bridges, W., and W. Villemez. 1986. Informal hiring and income in the labor market. *American Sociological Review* 51:574–82.

Broder, A., R. Kumar, M. Farzin, P. Raghavan, S. Rajagopalan, R. Stata, A. Tomkins, and J. Weiner. 2000. Graph structure in the Web. *Computer Networks* 33:309–20.

Brueckner, J. 2003. Friendship networks. Mimeo, University Of Illinois.

Buhai, S., and M. van der Leij. 2006. A social network analysis of occupational segregation. Tinbergen Institute Discussion Paper 06-016/1.

Burdett, K., and K. Judd. 1983. Equilibrium price dispersion. *Econometrica* 51:955–70.

Burt, R. S. 1994. *The Social Structure of Competition.* Harvard University Press.

Buskens, V. 1996. The social structure of trust. *Social Networks* 20:265–89.

Buskens, V., and W. Raub. 2002. Embedded trust: control and learning. *Advances in Group Processes* 19:167–202.

Buskens, V., and A. van den Rijt. 2005. Dynamic networks if everyone strives for structural holes. ISCORE Paper 227, Utrecht.

Callander, S., and C. Plott. 2005. Principles of network development and evolution: an experimental study. *Journal of Public Economics* 89:1469–95.

Calvó-Armengol, A., and R. Ilkilic. 2004. Pairwise-stability and Nash equilibria in network formation. Mimeo, Pompeu Fabra University.

Calvó-Armengol, A., and M. O. Jackson. 2004. The effects of social networks on employment and inequality. *American Economic Review* 94:426–54.

Calvó-Armengol, A., and M. O. Jackson. 2007. Networks in labor markets: wage dynamics and inequality. *Journal of Economic Theory* 132:27–46.

Calvó-Armengol, A., E. Patacchini, and Y. Zenou. 2006. Peer effects and social networks in education. Mimeo, University Autonoma de Barcelona.

Calvó-Armengol, A., T. Verdier, and Y. Zenou. 2007. Strong and weak ties in employment and crime. *Journal of Public Economics* 91:203–33.

Camerer, C. F. 2003. *Behavioral Game Theory: Experiments in Strategic Interaction.* The Roundtable Series in Behavioral Economics. Princeton University Press.

Casciaro, T. 1998. Seeing things clearly: social structure, personality, and accuracy in social network perception. *Social Networks* 20:331–51.

Case, A., and L. Katz. 1991. The company you keep: the effects of family and neighborhood on disadvantaged youths. NBER Working Paper 3705.

Cassar, A. Forthcoming. Coordination and cooperation in local, random and small world networks: experimental evidence. *Games and Economic Behavior.*

Cassella, A., and N. Hanaki. 2006. Transmitting information: network vs. signalling. Mimeo, Columbia University.

——. Forthcoming. Information channels in labor markets. On the resilience of referral hiring. *Journal of Economic Behavior and Organization.*

Castells, M. 1999. *The Information Age: Economy, Society and Culture*, volumes I–III. Oxford: Blackwell.

Chatterjee, K., and S. Xu. 2004. Technology diffusion by learning from neighbors. *Advances in Applied Probability* 36:355–76.

Chwe, M. S.-Y. 2000. Communication and coordination in social networks. *Review of Economic Studies* 65:1–16.

Coleman, J. 1988. Social capital in the creation of human capital. *American Journal of Sociology* 94:95–120.

——. 1994. *The Foundations of Social Theory.* Harvard University Press.

Coleman, J. S., E. Katz, and H. Mentzel. 1966. *Medical Innovation: Diffusion of a Medical Drug among Doctors.* Indianapolis, MN: Bobbs-Merrill.

Conley, T., and G. Topa. 2002. Socio-economic distance and spatial patterns in unemployment. *Journal of Applied Econometrics* 17:303–27.

Conley, T. G., and C. R. Udry. 2005. Learning about a new technology: pineapple in Ghana. Mimeo, Yale University.

Corcoran, M., L. Datcher, and G. Duncan. 1980. Information and influence networks in labor markets. In *Five Thousand American Families: Patterns of Economic Progress*, volume 7 (ed. G. Duncan and J. Morgan). Ann Arbor, MI: Institute for Social Research.

Contractor, F., and P. Lorange. 1988. *Cooperative Strategies in International Business*, pp. 169–86. Lexington, MA: Lexington Books.

Cornes, R., and T. Sandler. 1996. *The Theory of Externalities, Public Goods, and Club Goods*, 2nd edn. Cambridge University Press.

Crawford, J.-A., and R. V. Fiorentino. 2005. The changing landscape of regional trade agreements. WTO Discussion Paper 8, Geneva.

Currarini, S., and M. Morelli. 2000. Network formation with sequential demands. *Review of Economic Design* 5:229–49.

Dasgupta, P., and I. Serageldin. 1999. *Social Capital: A Multifaceted Perspective.* Washington, DC: World Bank Publications.

Dasgupta, P., and J. Stiglitz. 1980. Uncertainty, industrial structure and the speed of R&D. *Bell Journal of Economics* 11:1–28.

d'Aspremont, C., and A. Jacquemin. 1988. Cooperative and non-cooperative R&D in duopoly with spill-overs. *American Economic Review* 78:1133–37.

Davis, G. F., M. Yoo, and W. Baker. 2001. The small world of the American corporate elite, 1982–2001. *Strategic Organization* 1:301–26.

Debreu, G. 1959. *Theory of Value: An Axiomatic Analysis of Economic Equilibrium.* Yale University, NH: Cowles Foundation.

Debreu, G., and I. N. Herstein. 1953. Non-negative square matrices. *Econometrica* 21:597–607.

DeGroot, M. 1970. *Optimal Statistical Decisions.* New York: McGraw-Hill.

Delapierre, M., and L. Mytelka. 1998. Blurring boundaries: new inter-firm relationships and the emergence of networked, knowledge-based oligopolies. In *The Changing Boundaries of the Firm* (ed. M. G. Colombo). London: Routledge Press.

De Marzo, P. M., D. Vayanos, and J. Zwiebel. 2003. Persuasion bias, social influence, and unidimensional opinions. *Quarterly Journal of Economics* 118:909–68.

Demange, G., and M. Wooders. 2005. *Group Formation in Economics: Networks, Clubs and Coalitions.* Cambridge University Press.

Dercon, S. 2004. *Insurance against Poverty.* Oxford University Press.

Deroian, F. 2004. A note on cost-reducing alliances in vertically differentiated oligopoly. *Economics Bulletin* 12:1–6.

———. 2006. Dissemination of spillovers in cost reducing alliances. Mimeo, University of Marseille.

Deroian, F., and F. Gannon. 2005. Quality improving alliances in differentiated oligopoly. *International Journal of Industrial Organization* 24:629–37.

Dixit, A. 2003. Trade expansion and contract enforcement. *Journal of Political Economy* 111:1293–317.

Doreian, P., and F. Stokman. 2001. Evolution of social networks (special volume). *Journal of Mathematical Sociology* 25.

Dorogovtsev, S. N., and J. F. F. Mendes. 2002. *Evolution of Networks.* Oxford University Press.

Duflo, E., and E. Saez. 2003. The role of information and social interactions in retirement plan decisions: evidence from a randomized experiment. *Quarterly Journal of Economics* 118:815–42.

Dutta, B., S. Ghosal, and D. Ray. 2005. Farsighted network formation. *Journal of Economic Theory* 122:143–64.

Dutta, B., and M. O. Jackson (eds). 2003. *Models of the Strategic Formation of Networks and Groups.* Springer.

Dutta, B., and S. Mutuswami. 1997. Stable networks. *Journal of Economic Theory* 76:322–44.

Dutta, B., A. van den Nouweland, and S. Tijs. 1998. Link formation in cooperative situations. *International Journal of Game Theory* 27:245–56.

Easley, D., and N. Kiefer. 1988. Controlling a stochastic process with unknown parameters. *Econometrica* 56:1045–64.

Economides, N., and C. Himmelberg. 1995. Critical mass and network size with application to the U.S. FAX market. Mimeo, NYU.

Elias, N. 1978. *The Civilizing Process,* Volume 1: *The History of Manners.* Oxford: Basil Blackwell.

Ellison, G. 1993. Learning, local interaction, and coordination. *Econometrica* 61:1047–71.

——. 1994. Cooperation in the prisoner's dilemma with anonymous random matching. *Review of Economic Studies* 61:567–88.

Ellison, G., and D. Fudenberg. 1993. Rules of thumb for social learning. *Journal of Political Economy* 101:612–44.

——. 1995. Word-of-mouth communication and social learning. *Quarterly Journal of Economics* 109:93–125.

Erdős, P., and A. Rényi. 1960. On the evolution of random graphs. *Publication of Mathematical Institute of Hungarian Academy of Sciences* 5:17–61.

Esary, J. D., F. Proschan, and D. W. Walkup. 1967. Association of random variables, with applications. *Annals of Mathematical Statistics* 38:1466–74.

Eshel, I., and L. L. Cavalli-Sforza. 1982. Assortment of encounters and evolution of cooperativeness. *Proceedings of the National Academy of Sciences* 79:1331–35.

Eshel, I., L. Samuelson, and A. Shaked. 1998. Altruists, egoists, and hooligans in a local interaction model. *American Economic Review* 88:157–79.

Ethier, W. 1998. Regionalism in a multilateral world. *Journal of Political Economy* 106:1214–45.

Fabrikant, A., A. Luthra, E. Maneva, C. Papadimitriou, and S. Shenker. 2003. On a network formation game. *Proceedings of 22nd Annual Symposium on Principles of Distributed Computing* 2003:347–51.

Fafchamps, M. 2003. *Rural Poverty, Risk, and Development*. New York: Elgar Publishing.

——. 2004. *Market Institutions and Sub-Saharan Africa: Theory and Evidence*. Cambridge, MA: MIT Press.

Fafchamps, M., S. Goyal, and M. van der Leij. 2006. Matching and network effects. Mimeo, University of Cambridge and University of Oxford.

Falk, A., and M. Kosfeld. 2005. It's all about connections: evidence on network formation. Mimeo, University of Zurich.

Fehr, E., and K. Schmidt. 2003. Theories of fairness and reciprocity—evidence and economic applications. In *Advances in Economics and Econometrics, Eighth World Congress of the Econometric Society*, volume 1 (ed. M. Dewatripont et al.). Cambridge University Press.

Feick, L. F., and L. P. Price. 1987. The market maven: a diffuser of marketplace information. *Journal of Marketing* 51:83–97.

Feri, F. 2005. Stochastic stability in networks with decay. Mimeo, University of Venice.

Fevre, R. 1989. Informal practices, flexible firms and private labor markets. *Sociology* 23(1):91–108.

Freeman, L. 1979. Centrality in social networks: conceptual clarification. *Social Networks* 1:215–39.

Freidlin, M. and A. Wentzel. 1984. *Random Perturbations of Dynamical Systems*, 2nd edn. Springer.

Friedkin, N. 1980. A test of the structural features of Granovetter's "strength of weak ties" theory. *Social Network* 2:411–22.

Fudenberg, D., and J. Tirole. 1991. *Game Theory*. Cambridge, MA: MIT Press.

Furusawa, T., and H. Konishi. 2002. Free trade networks. Mimeo, Boston College.

Gale, D., and S. Kariv. 2003. Bayesian learning in social networks. *Games and Economic Behavior* 45:329–46.

Gladwell, M. 2000. *The Tipping Point*. New York: Little, Brown and Company.

Galeotti, A. 2005. Consumer networks and search equilibria. Tinbergen Institute Discussion Paper 2004-75.

———. 2006. One-way flow networks: the role of heterogeneity. *Economic Theory* 29:163–79.

Galeotti, A., S. Goyal, M. O. Jackson, F. Vega-Redondo, and L. Yariv. 2006. Network games. Mimeo, Essex University.

Galeotti, A., S. Goyal, and J. Kamphorst. 2006. Network formation with heterogeneous players. *Games and Economic Behavior* 54:353–72.

Galeotti, A., and M. Melendez. 2004. Exploitation and cooperation in networks. Tinbergen Institute Discussion Paper 04-076/1.

Ghosh, P., and D. Ray. 1996. Cooperation in community interaction without information flows. *Review of Economic Studies* 63:491–519.

Gilles, R., S. Chakrabarti, and S. Sarangi. 2005. Social network formation with consent: Nash equilibrium and pairwise refinements. Mimeo, Virginia Technical University, Blacksburg.

Gilles, R., and S. Sarangi. 2004. Social network formation with consent. CentER Discussion Paper 2004-70.

Glaeser, E., B. Sacerdote, and J. Scheinkman. 1996. Crime and social interactions. *Quarterly Journal of Economics* 111:507–48.

Glaeser, E., and J. Scheinkman. 2002. Non-market interactions. In *Advances in Economics and Econometrics: Theory and Applications, Eight World Congress* (ed. M. Dewatripont, L. Hansen and S. Turnovsky). Cambridge University Press.

Goeree, J., A. Riedl, and A. Ule. 2005. In search of stars: network formation among heterogeneous agents. Mimeo, University of Amsterdam and Caltech.

Goyal, S. 1993. Sustainable communication networks. Tinbergen Institute Discussion Paper, TI 93-250.

———. 1996. Interaction structure and social change. *Journal of Institutional and Theoretical Economics* 152:472–95.

———. 2005a. Learning in networks. In *Group Formation in Economics* (ed. G. Demange and M. Wooders). Cambridge University Press.

———. 2005b. Strong and weak links. *Journal of European Economic Association* 3:608–16.

Goyal, S., and M. Janssen. 1997. Non-exclusive conventions and social coordination (with Maarten Janssen). *Journal of Economic Theory* 77:34–57.

Goyal, S., and S. Joshi. 2003. Networks of collaboration in oligopoly. *Games and Economic Behavior* 43:57–85.

———. 2006a. Bilateralism and free trade. *International Economic Review* 47:749–78.

———. 2006b. Unequal connections. *International Journal of Game Theory* 34:319–49.

Goyal, S., A. Konovalov, and J. L. Moraga. 2003. Hybrid R&D. Tinbergen Institute Discussion Paper 2003-41.

Goyal, S., M. van der Leij, and J. L. Moraga. 2004. Economics: an emerging small world? Tinbergen Institute Discussion Paper 04-001/1.

———. 2006. Economics: emerging small world. *Journal of Political Economy* 114:403–12.

Goyal, S., and J. L. Moraga. 2001. R&D networks. *Rand Journal of Economics* 32:686–707.

Goyal, S., and F. Vega-Redondo. Forthcoming. Structural holes in social networks. *Journal of Economic Theory*.

Granovetter, M. 1973. The strength of weak ties. *American Journal of Sociology* 78:1360–80.

———. 1978. Threshold models of collective behavior. *American Journal of Sociology* 83:1420–43.

Granovetter, M. 1985. Economic action and social structure: the problem of embeddedness. *American Journal of Sociology* 3:481–510.

———. 1994a. *Getting a Job: A Study of Contacts and Careers*. Evanston, IL: Northwestern University Press.

———. 1994b. Business groups. In *Handbook of Economic Sociology* (ed. N. Smelser and R. Swedberg). Princeton University Press.

Griliches, Z. 1957. Hybrid corn: an exploration in the economics of technological change. *Econometrica* 25:501–22.

Gulati, R. 1995a. Does familiarity breed trust? The implications of repeated ties for contractual choice in alliances. *Academy of Management Journal* 38:85–112.

———. 1995b. Social structure and alliance formation pattern: a longitudinal analysis. *Administrative Science Quarterly* 40:619–52.

———. 1998. Networks and alliances. *Strategic Management Journal* 19:293–317.

Gulati, R., N. Nohria, and A. Zaheer. 2000. Strategic networks. *Strategic Management Journal* 21:203–15.

Haag, M., and R. Lagunoff. 2006. Social norms, local interaction, and neighborhood planning. *International Economic Review* 47:265–96.

Hagedoorn, J. 2002. Inter-firm R&D partnerships: an overview of major trends and patterns since 1960. *Research Policy* 31:477–92.

Harary, F. 1969. *Graph Theory*. Cambridge, MA: Perseus Books.

Harrigan, K. R. 1988. Joint ventures and competitive strategy. *Strategic Management Journal* 9:141–58.

Harris, C. C. 1987. Redundancy and social transition. In *Redundancy and Recession in South Wales* (ed. C. C. Harris, P. Brown, R. Fevre, G. G. Leaver, R. M. Lee, and L. D. Morris). Oxford: Basil Blackwell.

Harsanyi, J. 1969. Games with incomplete information played by "Bayesian" players. *Management Science* 14:1967–68.

Harsanyi, J., and R. Selten. 1988. *A General Theory of Equilibrium Selection in Games*. Cambridge, MA: MIT Press.

Hart, O. 1995. *Firms, Contracts and Financial Structure*. Oxford University Press.

Heckman, J., and G. Borjas. 1980. Does unemployment cause future employment? Definitions, questions and answers for a continuous time model of heterogeneity and state dependence. *Economica* 47:247–83.

Hojman, D., and A. Szeidl. 2006. Core and periphery in endogenous networks. Mimeo, Department of Economics, Harvard University.

Holzer, H. J. 1987. Hiring procedures in the firms: their economic determinants and outcomes. NBER Research Working Paper 2185.

———. 1988. Search method use by unemployed youth. *Journal of Labor Economics* 6:1–20.

Ianni, A. 2001. Correlated equilibria in population games. *Mathematical Social Sciences* 42:271–94.

Jackson, M. O. 2005. A survey of models of network formation. In *Group Formation in Economics: Networks, Clubs and Coalitions* (ed. G. Demange and M. Wooders). Cambridge University Press.

———. 2006. The economics of social networks. In *Proceedings of the 9th World Congress of the Econometric Society* (ed. R. Blundell, W. Newey, and T. Persson). Cambridge University Press.

Jackson, M. O., and B. Rogers. 2005. The economics of small worlds. *Journal of European Economic Association (Papers and Proceedings)* 3:617–27.

Jackson, M. O., and A. van den Nouweland. 2005. Strongly stable networks. *Games and Economic Behavior* 51:420–44.

Jackson, M. O., and A. Watts. 2001. The existence of pair-wise stable networks. *Seoul Journal of Economics* 14:299–321.

——. 2002. On the formation of interaction networks in social coordination games. *Games and Economic Behavior* 41:265–91.

Jackson, M. O., and A. Wolinsky. 1996. A strategic model of economic and social networks. *Journal of Economic Theory* 71(1):44–74.

Johnson, C., and R. P. Gilles. 2000. Spatial social networks. *Review of Economic Design* 5:273–99.

Kali, R. 1999. Endogenous business networks. Mimeo, School of Business, ITAM, Mexico.

Kamien, M. I., E. Muller, and I. Zang. 1992. Research joint ventures and R&D cartels. *American Economic Review* 82:1293–306.

Kandori, M. 1992. Social norms and community enforcement. *Review of Economic Studies* 59:63–80.

Kandori, M., G. Mailath, and R. Rob. 1993. Learning, mutation and long run equilibria in games. *Econometrica* 61:29–56.

Katz, M. 1986. An analysis of cooperative R&D. *Rand Journal of Economics* 17:527–43.

Katz, M., and C. Shapiro. 1994. Systems competition and network effects. *Journal of Economic Perspectives* 8(2):93–115.

Kempe, D., J. Kleinberg, and E. Tardos. 2003. Maximizing the spread of influence in a social network. *Proceedings of the 9th ACM SIGKDD Conference* 2003:137–46.

Kirman, A. 1997. The economy as an evolving network. *Journal of Evolutionary Economics* 7:339–53.

Kirman, A., and J.-B. Zimmermann. 2001. *Economics with Heterogeneous Interacting Agents*. Lecture Notes in Economics and Mathematical Systems. Springer.

Kochen, M. (ed.). 1989. *The Small World*. Norwood, NJ: Ablex.

Kogut, B., W. Sham, and G. Walker. 1992. The make-or-buy cooperate decision in the context of an industry network. In *Networks and Organizations* (ed. N. Nohria and R. Eccles). Cambridge, MA: Harvard Business School Press.

Kosfeld, M. 2004. Economic networks in the laboratory: a survey. *Review of Network Economics* 3:20–42.

Kotler, P., and G. Armstrong. 2004. *Principles of Marketing*, 10th edn. New York: Prentice Hall.

Kranton, R. 1996. Reciprocal exchange: a self-sustaining system. *American Economic Review* 86:830–51.

Kreps, D. 1988. *Notes on the Theory of Choice*. Boulder, CO: Westview Press.

Kumbasar, E., A. K. Romney, and W. Batchelder. 1994. Systematic biases in social perception. *American Journal of Sociology* 100:477–505.

Leahy, T., and J. P. Neary. 1997. Public policy towards R&D in oligopolistic industries. *American Economic Review* 87:642–62.

Lee, I. H., A. Szeidl, and A. Valentinyi. 2003. Contagion and state dependent mutations. *Berkeley Electronic Press Journals, Advances in Theoretical Economics* 3:24–52.

Lee, I. H., and A. Valentinyi. 2000. Noisy contagion without mutation. *Review of Economic Studies* 67:17–47.

Liggett, T. 1985. *Interacting Particle Systems*. Springer.

Lewis, D. 1969. *Convention: A Philosophical Study*. Harvard University Press.

Liljeros, F., C. R. Edling, L. A. Amaral, H. E. Stanley, and Y. Aberg. 2001. The web of human social contacts. *Nature* 411:907–8.

Lin, N. 1990. Social resources and social mobility: a structural theory of status attainment. In *Social Mobility and Social Structure* (ed. R. Breiger). Cambridge University Press.

Mailath, L., and Samuelson, L. 2006. *Repeated Games and Reputations: Long-Run Relationships*. Oxford University Press.

Mailath, G., L. Samuelson, and A. Shaked. 1997. Correlated equilibria and local interaction. *Economic Theory* 9:551–68.

Marsden, P. V. 1988. Homogeneity in confiding relations. *Social Networks* 10:57–76.

Marsden, P. V., and K. Campbell. 1990. Recruitment and selection processes: the organizational side of job searches. In *Social Mobility and Social Structure* (ed. R. L. Breiger), pp. 59–79. Cambridge University Press.

Marsden, P. V., and J. Hurlbert. 1988. Social resources and mobility outcomes: a replication and extension. *Social Forces* 66:1038–59.

Maskin, E. 2006. Bargaining, coalitions and externalities. Mimeo, Institute of Advanced Studies, Princeton.

McBride, M. 2006a. Position specific information in social networks: are you connected? Mimeo, University of California, Irvine.

——. 2006b. Imperfect monitoring in communication networks. *Journal of Economic Theory* 126:97–119.

Mehra, A., M. Kilduff, and D. Brass. 2001. The social networks of high and low self-monitors: implications for workplace performance. *Administrative Science Quarterly* 46:121–46.

Milgram, S. 1967. The small world problem. *Psychology Today* 2:60–67.

Mills, C. W. 1956. *The Power Elite*. Oxford University Press.

——. 1976. *The Sociological Imagination*. Oxford University Press.

Mobius, M. 2006. Lecture notes on networks. Mimeo, Department of Economics, Harvard University.

Mobius, M., D. Quoc-Anh, and T. S. Rosenblat. 2004. Social capital in social networks. Mimeo, Harvard University.

Mobius, M., and A. Szeidl. 2006. Trust and cooperation in social networks. Mimeo, Harvard University and University of California, Berkeley.

Montgomery, J. 1991. Social networks and labor-market outcomes: toward an economic analysis. *American Economic Review* 81:1408–18.

——. 1992. Job search and network composition: implications of the strength of weak ties hypothesis. *American Sociological Review* 57:586–96.

Moody, J. 2004. The structure of a social science collaboration network: disciplinary cohesion from 1963 to 1999. *American Sociological Review* 69:213–38.

Morris, S. 2000. Contagion. *Review of Economic Studies* 67:57–78.

Mortenson, D. 2003. *Wage Dispersion: Why Are Similar Workers Paid Differently?* Cambridge, MA: MIT Press.

Munshi, K. 2004. Social learning in a heterogeneous population. *Journal of Development Economics* 73:185–213.

Mutuswami, S., and E. Winter. 2002. Subscription mechanisms for network formation. *Journal of Economic Theory* 106:242–64.

My, K. B., M. Willinger, and A. Ziegelmeyer. 1999. Global versus local interaction in coordination games: an experimental investigation. Mimeo, University Louis Pasteur, Strasbourg.

Myers, C. A., and G. P. Schultz. 1951. *The Dynamics of a Labor Market*. New York: Prentice-Hall.

Myerson, R. 1977. Graphs and cooperation in graphs. *Mathematics of Operations Research* 2:225–29.

——. 1991. *Game Theory: Analysis of Conflict*. Harvard University Press.

Newberry, D. 2002. *Privatization, Restructuring, and Regulation of Network Utilities*. Cambridge, MA: MIT Press.

Newman, M. E. J. 2001. The structure of scientific collaboration networks. *Proceedings of the National Academy of Sciences USA* 98:404–9.

——. 2003. The structure and function of complex networks. *SIAM Review* 45:167–256.

——. 2004. Analysis of weighted networks. *Physical Review* E 70:056131.

Newman, M. E. J., and Girvan, M. 2004. Finding and evaluating community structure in networks. *Physical Review* E 69:026113.

Nohria, N., and R. Eccles. 1992. *Networks and Organizations: Structure, Form and Action*. Boston, MA: Harvard Business School Press.

Noteboom, B. 1999. *Inter-Firm Alliances: Analysis and Design*. London and New York: Routledge.

Nowak, M., and R. May. 1992. Evolutionary games and spatial chaos. *Nature* 359:826–29.

Nowak, M., and K. Sigmund. 2005. Evolution of indirect reciprocity. *Nature* 437:1291–97.

Page, F., M. Wooders, and S. Kamat. 2005. Networks and farsighted stability. *Journal of Economic Theory* 120:257–61.

Pantz, K., and A. Zeigelmeyer. 2003. An experimental study of network formation. Mimeo, Max Planck Institute.

Pastor-Satorras, R., and A. Vespignani. 2001. Epidemic spreading in scale free networks. *Physical Review Letters* 86:3200–3.

——. 2002. Immunization of complex network. *Physical Review* E 65:036104:1–8.

Pellizzari, M. 2004. Do friends and relatives really help in getting a good job? CEPR Discussion Paper 623.

Podolny, J., and K. Page. 1998. Network forms of organization. *Annual Review of Sociology* 24:57–76.

Podolny, J. N., and J. M. Baron. 1997. Resources and relationships: social networks and mobility in the workplace. *American Sociological Review* 62:673–93.

Porter, M., and M. B. Fuller. 1986. Coalitions and global strategy. In *Competition in Global Industries* (ed. M. Porter), pp. 315–44. Boston, MA: Harvard Business School Press.

Powell, W. W. 1990. Neither market nor hierarchy: network forms of organization. *Research in Organizational Behavior* 12:295–336.

Powell, W. W., K. Koput, and L. Smith-Doerr. 1996. Inter-organizational collaboration and the locus of innovation: networks of learning in biotechnology. *Administrative Science Quarterly* 41:116–45.

Raub, W., and J. Weesie. 1990. Reputation and efficiency in social interactions: an example of network effects. *American Journal of Sociology* 96:626–54.

Rauch, J., and A. Casella. 2001. *Networks and Markets*. New York: Russell Sage Foundation.

Ray, D., and R. Vohra. 1997. Equilibrium binding agreements. *Journal of Economic Theory* 73:30–78.

Rees, A. 1966. Information networks in labor markets. *American Economic Review* 56:559–66.

Rees, A., and G. P. Schultz. 1970. *Workers in an Urban Labor Market*. University of Chicago Press.

Robson, A., and F. Vega-Redondo. 1996. Efficient equilibrium selection in evolutionary games with random matching. *Journal of Economic Theory* 70:65–92.

Rogers, B. 2005. A strategic theory of network status. Mimeo, Caltech.

Rogers, E. 2003. *Diffusion of Innovations*. New York: Free Press.

Rogers, E., and D. L. Kincaid. 1981. *Communication Networks: Toward a New Paradigm for Research*. New York: Free Press.

Rogerson, R., R. Shimer, and R. Wright. 2005. Search-theoretic models of the labor market: a survey. *Journal of Economic Literature* 43:959–88.

Rothschild, M. 1974. A two-armed bandit theory of market pricing. *Journal of Economic Theory* 9:185–202.

Roughgarden, T. 2005. *Selfish Routing and the Price of Anarchy*. Cambridge, MA: MIT Press.

Ryan, B., and N. Gross. 1943. The diffusion of hybrid seed corn in two Iowa communities. *Rural Sociology* 8:15–24.

Sah, R. 1991. Social osmosis and patterns of crime. *Journal of Political Economy* 99:1272–95.

Saloner, G. 1985. The old boys' network as a screening mechanism. *Journal of Labor Economics* 3:255–67.

Schelling, T. 1960. *The Strategy of Conflict*. New York: Norton.

———. 1975. *Micromotives and Macrobehavior*. New York: Norton.

Sen, A. 1997. *On Economic Inequality*. Oxford: Clarendon Press.

Shapley, L. 1953. A value for *n*-person games. In *Contributions to the Theory of Games* (ed. H. W. Kuhn and A. W. Tucker), pp. 307–17. Princeton University Press.

Shy, O. 2001. *The Economics of Network Industries*. Cambridge University Press.

Skyrms, B., and R. Pemantle. 2000. A dynamic model of social network formation. *Proceedings of the National Academy of Sciences* 97:9340–46.

Slikker, M., and A. van den Nouweland. 2001a. A one-stage model of link formation and payoff division. *Games and Economic Behavior* 34:153–75.

———. 2001b. *Social and Economic Networks in Cooperative Game Theory*. Boston, MA: Kluwer.

Smelser, N., and R. Swedberg. 1994. *The Handbook of Economic Sociology*. Princeton University Press.

Song, H., and V. Vannetelbosch. 2005. International R&D collaboration networks. CORE Discussion Paper 2005/40.

Spagnolo, G. 1999. Social relations and cooperation in organizations. *Journal of Economic Behavior and Organization* 36:1–26.

Sugden, R. 2004. *The Economics of Rights, Co-operation and Welfare*, 2nd edn. Palgrave Macmillan.

Suzumura, K. 1992. Cooperative and non-cooperative R&D in oligopoly with spillovers. *American Economic Review* 82:1307–20.

Szekli, R. 1995. *Stochastic Ordering and Dependence in Applied Probability*. Springer.

Taylor, R. 1979. *Medicine out of Control: The Anatomy of a Malignant Technology*. Melbourne: Sun Books.

Tieman, A., H. Houba, and G. van der Laan. 2000. On the level of cooperative behavior in a local interaction model. *Journal of Economics* 71:1–30.

Topa, G. 2001. Social interactions, local spillovers and unemployment. *Review of Economic Studies* 68:261–95.

Ullman, J. C. 1966. Employee referrals: prime tool for recruiting workers. *Personnel* 43:30–35.

Ullman-Margalit, E. 1977. *The Emergence of Norms.* Oxford: Clarendon Press.

van Damme, E. 1991. *Stability and Perfection of Nash Equilibrium,* 2nd edn. Springer.

van Damme, E., and J. Weibull. 2002. Evolution in games with endogenous mistake probabilities. *Journal of Economic Theory* 106:298–315.

van den Nouweland, A. 2005. Models of network formation, in cooperative games. In *Group Formation in Economics: Networks, Clubs, and Coalitions* (ed. G. Demange and M. Wooders). Cambridge University Press.

van der Leij, M., and S. Goyal. 2005. Strong ties in a small world. Mimeo, Erasmus and Essex.

Vega-Redondo, F. 2006. Building up social capital in a changing world. *Journal of Economic Dynamics and Control* 30:2305–38.

——. 2007. *Complex Social Networks.* Econometric Society Monographs. Cambridge University Press.

Wasserman, S., and K. Faust. 1994. *Social Network Analysis: Methods and Applications.* Cambridge University Press.

Watanabe, S. 1987. *Job-Searching: A Comparative Study of Male Employment Relations in the United States and Japan.* PhD thesis, University of California, Los Angeles.

Watkins, S. 1991. *Provinces into Nations: Demographic Integration in Western Europe, 1870–1960.* Princeton University Press.

Watts, D. 1999. *Small Worlds: The Dynamics of Networks between Order and Randomness.* Princeton University Press.

Watts, D., and S. Strogatz. 1998. Collective dynamics of "small world" networks. *Nature* 393:440–42.

Weesie, J., and Raub, W. 2000. *The Management of Durable Relations.* Amsterdam: Thela-Thesis.

Williamson, O. 1985. *The Economic Institutions of Capitalism: Firms, Markets, Relational Contracting.* New York: Free Press.

Wynne-Edwards, V. 1986. *Evolution through Group Selection.* Oxford: Blackwell.

Yi, S. 1997. Stable coalition structures with externalities. *Games and Economic Behavior* 20:201–37.

——. 1998. Endogenous formation of joint ventures with efficiency gains. *Rand Journal of Economics* 29:610–31.

Young, P. 1993. The evolution of conventions. *Econometrica* 61:57–84.

——. 1998. *Individual Strategy and Social Structure.* Princeton University Press.

——. 2005. Diffusion of innovations in social networks. In *Economy as a Complex Evolving System,* Volume III (ed. L. E. Blume and S. N. Durlauf). Oxford University Press.

Zissimos, B. 2005. Why are free trade agreements regional? Mimeo, University of Vanderbilt.

Index